ABOUT THE A

Angela Goode has been a long-time rura
in Adelaide, as well as for *The Weekly Times*, Melbourne and a commentator for the ABC's South Australian *Country Hour*.

She misguidedly began paying compliments in 1988 to working dogs as possibly the only employees that never went on strike and inadvertently unleashed wagging tails of agreement around the nation. The result was *Great Working Dog Stories* (1990), *More Great Working Dog Stories* (1992), and *Working Dogs, Stories from All Round Australia* (1993), books she compiled, edited and wrote along with dog owners far and wide. Other ABC Books have been *Great Working Horse Stories* (1995, 2002) and *For Love of the Land* (2000).

Angela lives on a cattle farm near Naracoorte, South Australia and still occasionally argues with Basil the kelpie about the best way of doing things.

Mike Hayes contributed several stories to *Great Australian Working Dog Stories*. Some of his most popular stories during 20 years of writing about the Prickle Farm for the ABC were about dogs.

Mike died on 12 February 2003, aged 58.

Great Australian
WORKING
DOG
STORIES

Angela Goode & Mike Hayes

ABC
Books

The ABC 'Wave' device is a trademark of the
Australian Broadcasting Corporation and is used
under licence by HarperCollins*Publishers* Australia.

This compilation was first published as *The Complete Book of Working Dog Stories*
in 1998. The compilation was a one-volume collection of three previous books:
Great Working Dog Stories (1990); *More Great Working Dog Stories* (1992); and
Working Dogs (1993)
Published as *Great Australian Working Dog Stories* in 2009
This edition first published in 2009 by ABC Books for
the Australian Broadcasting Corporation.
Reprinted by HarperCollins*Publishers* Australia Pty Limited
ABN 36 009 913 517
harpercollins.com.au

HarperCollins*Publishers*
Level 13, 201 Elizabeth Street, Sydney NSW 2000, Australia
31 View Road, Glenfield, Auckland 0627, New Zealand
A 53, Sector 57, Noida, UP, India
77–85 Fulham Palace Road, London, W6 8JB, United Kingdom
2 Bloor Street East, 20th floor, Toronto, Ontario M4W 1A8, Canada
10 East 53rd Street, New York NY 10022, USA

ISBN 978 0 7333 2482 6

Cover design by Josh Durham, Design By Committee
Illustrations in *Great Working Dog Stories* by Angela Goode
Illustrations in *More Great Working Dog Stories* by Helen Semmler
Photographs in *Working Dogs* by Angela Goode
Typeset in 12/15pt Granjon by Midland Typesetters, Australia
Printed and bound in China by RR Donnelley

10 9 8   13 14

CONTENTS

FOREWORD

The brilliant idea in the late 80s that Australia's working dogs deserved praise has gone far too far. On farms around the nation, there's every chance that kelpies and collies are getting ideas above their station. Don't, whatever you do, read any of these glowing stories to any dog in your employ—not if you want them to keep being the uncomplaining workaholics we have become reliant on.

It all started innocently enough. During a time of fierce hardship on the land, it seemed sensible that those who toil through drought and debt should be celebrated. After all, these workers don't go on strike, they're tough and accommodating, resourceful and eager to please. We were thinking two-legged. Somehow dogs, they of the comforting licks and happy grins, ended up getting the accolades. Fair enough—they do make the sun shine when things are at their darkest: a pity they can't make it rain.

At farm kitchen tables all around the nation, stories were written, 2000 of them, by ABC Country Hour listeners exploring every aspect of working dogs' contribution to farm life and the economy. About 330 of those stories appear in this book, an amalgam of three individual volumes.

With their battle scars and cocky attitude, these dogs clearly are not bred for beauty or manners, just brains, intuition and athleticism. They can be rude, barking abuse at other dogs on passing utes in main streets of local towns. They'll piss on tyres, curl their lips and raise their hackles. I've witnessed one astute dog lifting its leg on the trousers of a visiting bank manager.

Tough they may be, but they adapt distressingly quickly to the soft life. Instead of running all day behind a horse, they now sit up front on the ag-bike, cruise around in the back of utes, ride on bales of hay, and snooze in the dog boxes of livestock trucks. Who do they think they are pretending they are essential adornments to every farm vehicle with their eyes blown to slits and their pink tongues trailing behind?

Sure, they may be all lean concentration in the paddock, with their rumps in the air, creeping forward on their elbows watching for break-aways, controlling mobs with finesse and grace. But that's what they get fed to do, with luxuries thrown in like a 44-gallon drum lined with old carpet.

We acknowledge these workers are reliable and good value. They never hit the grog, don't want holidays or pay rises, rarely take a sickie and only occasionally answer back. An enterprise bargain is an extra bone. Workers' comp is a holey blanket. The super payout is a chair in the sun on the back verandah.

A good dog is treasured—and when no-one's looking, we'll hold his head in our hands and let him know. These days, with the human farm workforce trimmed by the need for off-farm jobs and a general lack of labour, dogs are earning their keep more than ever in paddocks and yards. Perhaps they could learn to check fences and drive tractors. They might also like to not get pregnant at shearing time, and refrain from perfuming themselves with eau de manure.

Since the first book of working dog stories appeared in 1990, Casterton in Victoria has turned over the annual Queen's Birthday weekend to a celebration of the kelpie. A world record price of $7,400 was set in 2008 at its working dog auction. A bronze statue of a kelpie commemorating the breed's foundation bitch, named Kelpie, is in the main street. She was born nearby in about 1870 by George Robertson and was swapped as a pup by Jack Gleeson for his horse. The kelpie breed took off when Gleeson's Kelpie, by then living near Ardlethan in New South Wales, was introduced to famous sire, Moss. Their genes infect most good working kelpies—and Casterton and Ardlethan, which also has a kelpie statue, enjoy arguing over which is the true home of the breed.

These tributes to our working dogs reveal plenty about Australian character and farm life. Cheeky, irreverent, loyal, unpretentious, with larrikin energy and hunger for hard work—our working dogs deserve every bit of the praise they get in these exceptional stories. But please keep that to yourself.

Angela Goode
2008

Great
WORKING
DOG
STORIES

PART 1
COCKCROW

It all begins with a pup (though Minus prefers kittens)
and then the training—or trouble—starts. It seems
some are born to it, some come good eventually (even
at ten!) and others—well . . .

BORN AT THE DRAFTING GATES

Ian Jackson, Tirlta Station, Broken Hill

The September shearing was approaching at Rowena Station and Spike, the two-tan kelpie bitch, sits by my side in the shed awaiting the arrival of the sheep from the outstation. Yard and shed work is her specialty. She doesn't like paddock work.

It was with horror that I realised that at this, the busiest time of the year, just as the annual harvest of the fleeces was about to commence, I was about to lose my right hand 'man' Spike's belly swelled in tandem with the increase in her work load. Shearing progressed steadily, but I knew that at any time she would have to give up her job to deliver her pups.

I couldn't understand how she could always be at my side when there was yard work to be done. I knew she was a totally dedicated working dog, but I was nevertheless surprised, considering the advanced state of her pregnancy. One Wednesday, she was really struggling to help us draft 2000 sheep. I had to rescue her several times from the top of the yard fences where she had been caught in limbo. Her love of sheep meant that she wouldn't leave the shed, even at night. I felt abandoned when I drove the 12 miles home without her, but she wouldn't come.

On Thursday morning, I went mustering to bring in 500 ewes for the afternoon run. I was by myself and as I was pushing the sheep up into the drafting race, Spike rushed up, bounding over the fences, smiling and happy, obviously trying to tell me she had delivered the pups.

She had delivered them right at the foot of the drafting gates where I usually stand. They were minute, fresh pups, the whole seven of them. I relocated them at the beginning of the race, so they could still feel involved.

I drafted the ewes with Spike's help before she returned to the pups and I had to leave for Tirlta Station.

That evening, my brother, who had come up from South Australia to help during shearing, much needed when the best dog is out of action, asked me if I had seen the new pups. I said I had seen her seven little beauties and that she had helped me draft the ewes. My brother said she had also helped him draft sheep, but that she now had ten pups.

It seems that she had produced another three after helping me a few hours earlier.

Four weeks later, she suffered a severe case of milk fever and nearly died. Too much hard work as well as the caring of her pups was to blame. We organised an emergency flight to Broken Hill where she was treated by the local vet on the airport lawns. He saved her life.

A few days later, she was back in the yards and shed. All pups are healthy and strong. One of the male pups looks like being a champion—like his mother.

THE GOANNA
Barry Smith, Cowell

It was late December, about 1940, when my uncle, his workman and my cousin who was about ten years old, headed out in the truck to load bags of wheat. My cousin, being a real farm boy, had with him a young sheepdog about six months old.

As soon as they arrived in the paddock, the boy and the pup started exploring. Within a very short time, my uncle heard the pup start a continual yap as young dogs do when chasing something they are not able to catch.

Upon casting his eye around, my uncle (who was loading the bags from the ground) spotted the pup chasing a goanna about three to four feet long. The sight of the goanna up on all four legs speeding through the stubble with the yapping pup right behind was, at the least, very enter-taining—until the goanna decided to head for safety. There being no trees in sight, my uncle represented the only chance for the goanna to climb to safety from the pup.

All of a sudden, uncle saw the large goanna speeding straight towards him. Panic set in and he turned and fled.

After a few quick paces out into the paddock and a glance over his shoulder, he saw a rapidly gaining, frightened goanna. A second glance, and with presence of mind, uncle jumped into the air with legs wide apart. The speeding goanna zoomed through. Uncle landed and, with a great sigh of relief, watched as the speeding goanna ran off.

After only a few yards, though, it did a wheelie and sped back to an astonished uncle who took to his heels for the truck. With a quick glance, he calculated he was not going to make it. So he did a second jump, and the goanna sped through towards the truck, wheeled around and came back again.

By this time, on a hot day, uncle was becoming alarmed and exhausted. As the goanna came back for try number three, uncle made sure he did not run as fast and end up too far from the truck. With a calculated third jump and evasion as soon as the frightened reptile shot through, uncle spun around and headed for the truck.

As his build was somewhat short and stocky, the height of the truck tray appeared enormous. Uncle hit it with a thud and managed to roll on just as the speeding goanna and pup shot through.

A very red-faced, exhausted, and slightly irritated farmer turned upon his workman (who by this stage was rolling around on the tray splitting his sides with laughter) and roared, 'Why didn't you call that . . . pup off?'

Eventually he managed to squeeze out—'I couldn't'.

MINUS PLUS FOUR
Lorna Schwarz, Ceduna

Our dog, Minus, was born with her left leg missing. There was just a stump where her leg should have been.

She was one of a litter of six and predictably the poor little pup with the stump won the hearts of the children. We thought she should have been put down.

Minus thrived and, despite her handicap, could almost keep up to the other dogs. In the paddock and the yards, she was just as competent and able.

We were terribly surprised one day to discover that Minus had adopted four small kittens. They were actually suckling from her, and getting milk, despite the fact that Minus had never had pups.

These kittens, whose mother had either abandoned them or died, grew and were constant companions to Minus. They followed her everywhere, constantly.

One day, a neighbour found Minus and her family out on our main road about four kilometres from home—just out walking!

They were an extraordinary sight.

Minus was well-known by all the folk around here, so they were brought home.

RUNNING BACKWARDS
Kath Alcock, Naracoorte

Digger was my dog. By this I mean that he stayed by me, whereas other dogs which I handled and 'broke in' clung to the boss.

He was an odd-looking dog, large heavy body and rather spindly legs, mostly black, with white under the neck and on his toe tips. His mother was a border collie, moderately long-haired, and I suspect his sire was a short-haired border collie whose ancestry, I was told by the neighbouring owner, included a very intelligent Scotch collie. This, I believe, is where Digger's odd body shape came from.

At about four months, he obediently came when whistled and sat when ordered to, but as for showing any inclination to work sheep, he was just a wood-head!

We had a small flock of very quiet stud sheep, and Digger commenced his training on these. I believe that sheepdogs should always be trained whilst the owner is on foot. Then he should graduate to a horse and lastly, to a vehicle.

At the start, he was only interested in scooping up the droppings of the very new lambs. But I persisted until one day he suddenly realised what he was on this earth for, and went ahead in leaps and bounds. As he progressed, he did a lot of thinking for himself, but wasn't headstrong at all.

One time, I drove the car down the paddock with Digger racing enthusiastically ahead, until we came to the point of rounding up the sheep. When we had them in one mob, I got back into the car and we moved off in the right direction.

There always will be those cunning and wily ewes which break off at a tangent and rapidly lead the rest of the mob away. This is just what happened. There was a lot of confusion with ewes and lambs veering off in two directions, and a few keeping to the correct path. So I got out of the vehicle and rounded them up again and instructed Digger to 'wing' each side back and forth, which he quickly learned. We got to the gate and then to the sheepyards with no further trouble. Drafting sheep with Digger was a breeze and whenever I gave him praise, he smiled with his eyes and wagged his tail. He truly loved the learning process.

He was an eager learner and had only to be shown a new order the one time. He even learned to shut the houseyard gate which I opened and deliberately left that way as I passed through. Dig got behind the gate and put both front paws on the mesh and gave it a vigorous shove until it crashed into position.

He knew not to come into the houseyard until invited and would lie with his nose in line with the fence if the gate happened to be open and there were no chooks around.

If I was working in the orchard, and he was off the chain, he would sneak between the shed and the garden fence, hop over a low part and, trying to make himself small, would creep up to me.

'What are you doing here?' I'd say, and those loving eyes would just about melt a rock.

One day we were out walking in the pine plantation. It was late spring and a fairly warm day. Suddenly, from the corner of my eye, I noticed Digger prop in his stride and saw, about a metre in front of him, a big brown snake. Its head was upraised. I think this was more in warning, than a sign it was about to strike.

'No Dig!' I yelled. I can still picture that tableau—the snake and dog, rigidly eyeing each other. Digger was on three backward slanting legs and one forepaw was up and bent at the knee. At the fear in my shout, he 'ran' backwards for several paces! I had never seen any dog do that before. The snake slid under a heap of pine slash in fluid motion.

WEE TROUBLES

Sue Hood, Naracoorte

Gus wasn't the best-looking pup, but we were told he had plenty of potential. He was always a little too frisky with the children and the wonder dog was never that wonderful with the sheep. We loved him though—that is, until he developed this disgusting habit of urinating on people whenever they patted him on the back.

We were horrified, but soon got wise to his insulting behaviour and would shun him on opening the back door. No-one ever tied him up at night, just in case he let fly. He was always left to the master of the house.

It happened that my husband had to go away for the night. So, for convenience, I tied Gus to an old post in the garden.

During the night, a storm blew up. Gus, on his post, started whining and barking. I tried to shut it out by putting my head under the pillow, but the noise got worse.

Eventually, in nightie, parka and rubber boots, I went out into the storm. The dog's chain was wound around the post very tightly and he was choking. I proceeded to untangle him when, inadvertently, I touched his back. Over he rolled and urinated all over me.

He is now dead, and I miss him not a bit.

THE PUPPY IN THE DUST

Rachel Biven, Beaumont

Around twelve years ago, my son Peter went to Esperance in Western Australia. After working at odd jobs on various farms, he obtained a 3000 acre block which he and his Danish wife, Kirsten, were developing.

Peter and Kirsten had leased some grain-cleaning works to help them finance the work on the block.

It was a busy time for them as huge loads of grain would arrive in road trains to be cleaned and pickled. My husband and I were visiting them to give them a hand. My husband helped maintain the noisy 'Heath

Robinson' machinery. I helped sew up bags of grain while Kirsten flipped them from the trolley onto a pile.

One day, Peter found a little black puppy amongst the dust and dirty, empty bags. Above the noisy machinery, he roared 'Get this thing out of here.'

Kirsten and I felt motherly, and between jobs we managed to pet it and feed it.

The day ended, and Peter said firmly, 'We don't want any more animals to feed.' They already had three stray cats and his working dog, Ben. The pathetic-looking pup was left in the shed and ignored in the hope that a truck driver who may have left it behind would reclaim it.

Next morning, the puppy was still there. But suddenly there was a drama as it was noticed that Ben was looking very sick. Peter recognised the signs of poisoning and immediately dropped everything and rushed the dog to the vet. He was too late to save him, despite drips and injections.

Gradually, the puppy soothed our sad hearts. Ben had been a great friend and worker.

The little pup sensed she must win Peter's affection. She sat watching him with her big, black eyes, trying to charm the man of the house. She licked him and watched his every move. She sat at his feet, with her little white, dainty paws crossed.

Instead of continually trying to give her away to everyone who came to the shed, Peter finally gave her a name—Molly.

Harvest time came out on the block, 130 kilometres out into the bush. The convoy of caravans, tractors, harvesters, a water tank and the utility, with Molly firmly sitting on the loaded back, finally got away.

Molly was happy at the block, darting around barking at birds and lizards. When she killed a brown snake in the bush shower, she was suddenly a heroine. Her efforts at sheep work were, nevertheless, scorned after the well-trained Ben. No-one, of course, expected her to be any good. She was just a whippet-border collie cross.

Molly, however, gradually wormed her way firmly into her family's hearts. She danced on her hind legs and popped balloons with her teeth at Christmas. She grovelled at Peter's feet, she smiled and made people laugh and finally, they even let her sleep on their bed when winter came.

Shearing time came around and we were all trying to push sheep into the yards. Pete was still without a working dog. Suddenly, Molly came bouncing into the yards. She yapped, nipped the heels of the ewes, and leapt onto their backs. Expertly, she pushed those sheep into the yards and we were able to pen up without any trouble. She learnt to pull a ration sheep down, and eventually became everything a working dog should be.

She was petted and loved, minded the children and still 'made eyes' at Peter.

She had pups every year and everyone wanted them.

Rabbits were bad one year so the Council spread 1080 poison. Molly got a dose and was terribly ill. After three days at the veterinary hospital on drips she returned to carry on her duties.

Some years later, we returned to see Peter and Kirsten's new baby. There was Molly, sitting beside the bassinet with her white paws crossed, watching and keeping alert. When the baby cried, she would run off and tug at Kirsten's jeans. Then, when she heard the utility, she would leap on to the tray, yapping and wanting to help with the sheep—pleased to leave her women's work behind.

The neighbour at the farm next door often went spotlighting for rabbits and foxes. One night, Molly must have been out chasing rabbits herself, and she returned next morning bleeding and hurt. We found that a bullet had gone right through her collar and neck and passed out the other side. Apart from the hole and wound, she was uninjured.

She was an extraordinary, versatile dog and she had an amazing capacity for survival.

A CAR FULL OF GOATS

Mrs Noel Greatz, Renmark

After a heavy rain, my husband decided to drive out to the far corner of the property to check the catchment of water in the dams.

As usual in the bush, when Dad went in the car, Mum, kids and an assortment of dogs went too. Our mode of transport was an elderly Holden sedan minus the boot-lid—removed so we could stand in the back while spotlighting.

On this particular day, we had only one 'worthy' sheepdog, a border collie named Trixie, as well as a small Heinz housedog and a six-month-old red kelpie, Tip.

About four miles from home, we came upon a small mob of eight wild goats on a grassy plain. Being a bit sceptical about the red kelpie ever making a good sheepdog, I suggested to my husband that we put the dogs around the goats to test Tip's mustering ability.

Away they went, including the housedog, chasing the mob of goats away from us. Suddenly all our scoffing stopped as the mob changed direction and headed straight for our car. Soon the goats were milling around us as we stood by the car bursting with laughter. Then one very pregnant nanny jumped into the back seat and refused to move. The rest took refuge in the boot of the car. We couldn't believe our eyes, and regret not having a camera.

The dogs were racing in circles around the vehicle screaming about how clever they were. But our big problem was how to get rid of them out of the car. All seven goats lay down and refused to budge. Yelling with excitement, the children suggested Dad drive off at full speed (20 mph in soft ground) and then perhaps the goats would jump out with fright. They didn't. They clung on for dear life. After about a mile of wheelies, we had to stop and physically lift every damned goat out, including the fat nanny who was sitting with the children on the back seat. Tip grew up to be an excellent sheepdog.

CITY SLICKER
C. Bryce, Yankalilla

As a boy, I spent most of my spare time wandering the different places in the bush where we lived. I walked the hills of the Barossa, explored the wide flat country of Keith and trekked through the sandhills near Robe. Always by my side was my mate, Skeet.

His mother was a stray who was caught killing sheep. She was about to be shot when it was noticed she was heavily pregnant. We let her have the pups and Skeet was the one we kept. He wasn't very handsome, but

I didn't care. He made up for his lack of looks by learning everything I taught him. He would sit until I told him to move, sometimes for half an hour. He would bark, fetch balls, jump, come, go and I think he even tried to speak. Anyway, we were great mates. Sometimes when it was very cold, I'd even sneak him inside and let him sleep on my bed. Mum never found out because he had learned to tiptoe silently.

Eventually, I went off to ag. college. Dad had died so Mum moved to the city. She looked after him for me and he gave her company and barked at strangers.

When I finished my three-year course, I went off to be a jackeroo in the station country down south. They were running 20,000 merinos and I was one of twelve jackeroos. Every bloke had to have a dog, and some of the big shots had two. We were heavily into proving our manhood and a couple of dogs in the back of the ute was better than one.

Every morning, we would all assemble by the quarters to get our day's jobs from the boss. Actually, most of the time, we couldn't even hear him because if you can imagine twelve blokes all with at least one dog and the boss with his dog—our morning briefings were usually just one big dogfight.

The boss's dog was the worst. I mean, his dog seemed to know he was the top dog, so to speak. He would go around picking on all the other dogs, just giving them a nip or a push in a sneaky, thuggish sort of way. We couldn't do anything much about it because, well, we were just the underlings. When one of our dogs did snarl in retaliation, though, the boss's kelpie would hurl himself at him and fight until the other was a bloody mess. He was a dirty fighter.

The boss would pretend he didn't even notice. He would just drone on as though nothing was happening—even though the rolling, screaming bodies might have been right at his feet. I think he liked seeing other blokes' dogs beaten up. And you didn't dare try to rescue your dog either, because that would mean you thought yours was a bit of a sis or something. All you could do was to kick the boss's dog when the boss wasn't looking, or chuck rocks at him out in the paddock. I did that once and he yelped and limped for ages. The boss thought he had been kicked by a cow.

Anyway, with Mum widowed and not much money to go around among the eight of us, I couldn't think of getting a fancy sheepdog for myself. Skeet was all I had. Besides, I loved the old bugger. He had never seen sheep close-up because we only had cattle or crops on our places. But he had a bit of working dog in him, and better than that, he was a bloody good fighter. I knew that if anyone laughed at his funny-shaped body or tatty ears, I could set him on his dog. There's no greater crime in the bush than criticising a bloke's dog. You can say his wife's ugly but you can't laugh at his dog. People have been shot for that.

So, I rolled up with my old mate sitting beside me in my ute. He would have been offended if I had put him in the back. He peered down his scarred old nose at all the mutts that came out from under the jackeroos' quarters to bark at us, and when he alighted, he regally peed on the wheel of my ute, surveyed the milling throng and trotted stiffly, with his head in the air and his hackles bristling slightly, with me to my room. He slept on my bed and accepted his change of address without any fuss.

At the briefing next morning, Skeet sat beside me, surveying the morning dogfights with disdain. When the boss's thug walked up to check him out, Skeet's old lips curled, his hackles rose and he let out a fearsome, gravelly growl. The thug froze, and retreated. I patted the ugly old bugger's head, but he probably didn't know he'd done anything special.

For a few months, I didn't get much sheep work. The blokes with proven dogs got most of the yard work and mustering, and although Skeet was doing all right with the cattle and enjoyed following my horse all day, no-one had much time for him.

I did get my turn eventually. Now I don't know if old Skeet had been watching what the top dogs had been doing, but he worked in the yards like he'd been doing it all his life. Look, he was basically a city dog. He knew about roads and traffic and chasing cats, but here he was leaping rails, speaking up, backing sheep, forcing and staying back just like the best of them. I felt my chest was bursting with pride. And although the old fellow was ten when he worked his first sheep, he never let up even if it was stinking hot or pelting with rain.

Later on, he moved with me to Western Australia and if I hadn't had such a good dog, I wouldn't have got the good jobs I did. In time, old Skeet sired Louie with the cooperation of some station hussy . . . and this dog of even less breeding surpassed even his great old dad as a worker. Which all goes to show that pedigrees haven't got a lot to do with talent.

TAKE A DOG

Jill Dobbs, Port Augusta

The working dogs in my life are, to a man, male chauvinist pigs.

My husband owns three sheepdogs—one old, one not so old and one quite young. They are fawningly devoted to him, and except for the odd inexplicable occasion, they do most things he requires of them in most situations.

They are devoted to me too—and so they should be. In each case it was me who was left with the eight-week-old, sleepy bundle of fur at the end of its first day here. Admiration time over, the boss would yawn and stretch and say, in his lordly way, 'I'm for bed. You'll fix him up, won't you?'

In each case it was me who converted a carton into a snug puppy nest with an old boss-smelling pullover. It was me who crept out in the cold night in response to the whimpers of the occupant. It was me who dispensed comforting saucers of milk and me who mopped up afterwards.

It was me who attended to wormings, vaccinations, diet and pest control. As the dogs grew older, it was me who nursed them through ailments and injuries ranging in severity from bee-stung nose to fractured pelvis. To this day, it is me who feeds and waters them and ties them up at sundown, and when the boss is away, or engaged in dogless work, it is me who lets them off for exercise.

They reward me with effusive displays of affection, to which I respond with enthusiasm, but will they work for me? Never.

'If you'll just load the last of those rams in the ute and take them to the ewes,' says the boss, poised to do something else, 'I'll leave a dog to help you get them up the ramp.'

Does A Dog do anything of the sort? Not he! When asked, cajoled, ordered, and finally yelled at, he simply remains at my side, tail slightly wagging and eyes fixed on my face.

'What's she on about?' his expression plainly says. 'She only ever calls me to come and be fed, or chained, or dosed or fussed over, and here I am, obediently at her side, waiting for any one of those things to happen. Surely, she can't be expecting me to do anything about these sheep. That's work for the boss and me—not her and me.'

13

Eventually, A Dog tires of looking at my face and it goes and lies in the shade of the ramp while I struggle on alone, manhandling every unwilling ram up the ramp and into the stock crate.

Another time, with another dog, I go off on the horse to muster a small holding paddock, during shearing.

'If the sheep are at the back of the paddock,' says the boss, 'bring them home along the fence. It will be slightly longer, but easier than bringing them over the hill. It'll be a breeze if you take A Dog.'

It is. I follow his instructions and arrive home with three sheep.

Shortly after, A Dog turns up with the remaining five hundred, having wilfully ignored me from the first sheep sighting, and brought them home over the hill.

'Take A Dog,' advises the boss when I tell him I can see that a small relation here on holiday is having trouble putting sheep through a gate on his own.

I duly take A Dog, up on the bike behind me, and speed to the scene. Almost at the gate, the bike splutters and dies, I dismount and between us, small helper on lethargic pony and me on foot, succeed in putting the sheep through the gate—without, of course, any help from A Dog. He is still sitting on the bike, gazing fixedly back to where he last saw the boss.

I wonder if things would change if I selected female pups instead of male.

GIVE HIM TIME
Angela Goode

Farmers are pretty pragmatic about their dogs. If they work, they'll live. And the honour of these most uncomplaining of jackeroos will be defended hotly.

The good dogs, the workers, are chauffered around all day in battle-scarred utes. They'll stand high on bales of hay, or smugly on the backs of a load of sheep.

A dog that won't work is useless. It doesn't matter that it's all happiness and joy, a wriggling, fawning body and darting, caressing tongue. A dog that doesn't work gets shot. Normally.

There is no point getting sentimental about them. No-one else wants them. One of the most impossible things to do in the country is give away a dog that won't work. But it is here that this tale of tough-minded practicality falters, for this is a story about one of those useless non-workers—a freeloader earmarked for an overdose of lead—who somehow survived.

Sam was a beguiling puppy, like most of them are. But what made him especially appealing was his breeding. His mother and father were out-and-out champions. They lived to work and did everything with pride and a sense of achievement. Sheep and cattle men queued to obtain pups of the duo, and those pups, through heat or sleet, went on to win widespread acclaim.

When Sam was born there was no question that he, too, would not follow in the footsteps of his hard-working clan. He was handed over to his new owner with the words: 'Give him time. He'll be a late developer. This line takes a while to mature.'

Prophetic words. Thirteen years later he still hadn't developed. In fact, in his whole easy-going life he did not do a day's work.

Oh, he liked riding in the back of the ute all right, and he was really expert at hanging on to the pillion seat of the motorbike as the boss mustered the cows. But ask him actually to get down among the action, to tail the mob down the road, help in the yards, retrieve a breakaway, and he'd walk off, deaf to all protestations and pleadings. Insult him, and he'd sulk for days.

How Sam escaped going the way of other useless dogs, no-one quite knows. About a dozen times the rifle was loaded, but perhaps it was those words 'give him time' that kept coming back. The boss would again empty the chamber and put the gun back in the rack saying, 'He could come good yet. They said he was a late developer.'

But late developer or not, Sam was an embarrassment. No farmer worth his salt keeps a useless dog. If any visitors were around, Sam would be kept locked in his kennel . . . couldn't let anyone else see how he peeled himself away from the rest of the workers to sniff around rabbit holes, gaze at the corellas or snooze under the tea-trees.

Again and again, the boss tried to trigger Sam's instinct for work. Year after year, he tried. He begged, he cajoled, threatened and cursed. He was seen as a challenge to be conquered, a wayward to be tamed, a delinquent who just needed understanding. And so the old boy became a bit of a joke who had to see out his idle days in peace.

Once the jokes had started, it was too late. Who could kill a bloke who made us all laugh?

'He could come good yet,' the boss would say to gales of laughter about his grey-muzzled, arthritic old mate. 'It's not too late.'

Well, time did catch up with old Sam. Last week he died, his paws untarnished by toil and his record for laziness intact.

Perhaps it was all those champion genes that were to blame. Instead of workaholism, they produced a bloke with an analytical mind, a fellow who had too many brains for mere physical labour. He certainly had more fun than any other dog on the place. We've buried him down by the cattle yards, under his favourite tree—from where he used to watch all the other dogs earn their keep.

But you were lucky, Sam. We'll never be conned by the likes of you again.

PART 2
HUNTERS, LEADERS AND LONERS

A DIP IN THE DAM

Bruce Mills, Tumby Bay

Karla was given to me by a stud breeder friend in New South Wales and she arrived on the Indian Pacific train at Port Augusta.

My daughter and I picked her up: a pathetic-looking blue and tan pot-bellied kelpie pup, terribly smelly and covered in her own excrement. We washed her down under a tap near the platform. Her big eyes looked up at us all the while and the little tail wagged. After all that humans had put her through, she still called us friends.

Karla grew into a large kelpie, but was no world-beater in good looks—she had a blue-grey coarse-haired coat and one ear that never managed to stand erect—but as a clever worker, and in intelligence, she had few equals.

It seemed that whenever I left the station, my wife would get a call to say that there were sheep on the road, on the railway line, or somewhere else where they shouldn't be. Although we had at least six working dogs, Karla was always the one for that job. After showing her the rogue sheep, my wife would then drive the ute to the point where she wanted Karla to take them. Karla would then do the rest, no matter how difficult the task.

I remember one day when my brother was visiting and we went to a dam to check for stragglers. There were sheep near the dam so I sent Karla around them. Then I noticed some more sheep disappearing over a hill in the opposite direction. I said to my brother, 'Help Karla yard these sheep, while I go after the others.'

Not knowing the property, he noticed a gate into the dam enclosure and opened it. He tried to direct Karla and the sheep to it, but Karla completely disregarded his directions and took the sheep straight to the yards, penned them, and sat down in the gateway. My brother followed behind and on shutting the gate turned around to pat Karla, but she was on her way to help the boss—knowing I couldn't manage without her.

Another time, when the neighbour's yearling cattle were found on one of our dams, Karla again demonstrated her intelligence and persistence. Four cattle were on the dam and we had three kelpies with us.

The dogs were very excited as they hadn't seen cattle before. I sent them around the beasts and surprisingly they held them, first with eye,

18

and then moved in aggressively with some nose bite. We decided to yard them in the sheepyards overnight.

Returning next day with the owners of the cattle and a large horse float and high portable gates, we intended loading the cattle there to save ourselves a long drive. Before we got organised, however, the yearlings jumped out of the yards. The dogs yarded three, but one went into the dam to escape the dogs. Karla immediately dived into the water and swam to the animal's head to try to turn it. The beast lunged up out of the water and came down on Karla. She came out coughing and sneezing.

I sent her straight back into the water and this time she swam up behind the beast and up its side to its ear which she barked into and bit. This turned the beast around. Then she dropped back and scratched at its tail with her swimming forelegs. Then she swam up the other side to redirect it, repeating the snapping at the ear and returning to the tail until she brought the animal into the shallows where we threw a rope over it and wrestled it into the horse float.

In hindsight, it would have been better to have driven the cattle home, but then we would never have witnessed the capabilities of this dog. Sadly, a few years later, we had to put this great canine friend down as she was suffering from cancer.

THE WONDER DOG
Mike Hayes

*As I write, a chook is cackling like billyo over near the sheep yards, where a
rude scar of freshly dug red earth mars the promising green of the new spring
growth. It's Wal's grave, its site selected because, of all the places in the home
paddock, it was there he'd have most liked to be—where he could doze in the
sun, with the shearing plant buzzing soothingly in the background, safe in the
knowledge that eventually he'd be whistled up to help put the mob back up the
top paddock. I suspect that Wal wasn't really much chop as sheepdogs go. His
achievements were rarely the sort of thing you'd boast about in the pub. But
he was mine.*

The news wasn't particularly heartening. Milly Duckwalk looked quite
worried when she broke it to us. She was the wife of the new hobby
farmer bloke with those huge flaming horses, the one who'd bought the
fibro place on a couple of acres at the top end of the village.

'I thought I'd best tell you. Bill Potter just shot your pup's dad for
killing lambs.'

Bill Potter's property was the largest of those immediately adjoining
the village. Bill had seen the whole district change. The huge holdings,
selected by pioneers like his ancestor, had gradually been split up into
smaller blocks, most recently being snapped up by hobby farmers testing
the water in their quest for a better lifestyle outside the urban dullness
they were used to. With them came their naivety regarding the ways of
the bush, their trendy ideas and their ratbag dogs.

Bill was a rare bird. He'd paid enough attention to the changes affect-
ing the district to remain reasonably tolerant of the newcomers—both
the two-and four-legged variety. Unlike others, more bitter, long-time
local cockies, he was unlikely to go blasting away with his trusty twelve-
gauge at a strange canine trespassing on his rolling acreage, unless there
was a bloody good reason. And in the Duckwalks' case, it certainly
wasn't merely a minor incursion by someone's footloose chihuahua,
nipping through the Ringlock to gnaw on some tasty morsel of fresh
cow-pat. No, the offender was Raglan, the Duckwalks' hulking great
Alsation-Doberman-Pit Bull-Rotweiller cross. Apparently he'd been

regularly raiding Potter's lambing paddocks, slaughtering the odd lamb or twenty, before carting the tastiest ones off to sample at his leisure.

'It didn't help that Raglan was actually eating one of the poor little things on the front doormat when Potter came around to see if we knew anything about his movements,' continued Milly dolefully.

Oh Dear! In fact—Double Oh Dear! You see, lying on our front verandah, gnawing diligently on an old gumboot in a manner probably not unlike dear-departed Raglan's lamb-chewing style, was a pot-bellied little black pup, about eight weeks old.

We'd called him Wally-Wally the Wonder Dog. Not only was he destined to be a partner in our burgeoning black wool empire, but he was also rumoured to be the son and heir of poor old Raglan. Not that anyone could actually prove it, mind you. Wally and about eight other slippery little devils had made a somewhat unwelcome appearance into the world at the nearby home of Claude Butcher, the village vet. Despite his vast knowledge of animal health, Butcher hadn't foreseen the lack of discrimination exhibited by Laverne, his promiscuous Kelpie-Collie cross bitch. When she came on heat, she'd attracted so many suitors, nobody could swear blind who'd sired the brood. It may well have been Wilfred, the postmistress's corgi, or even McHaughey, the big red setter from across the river, but Raglan's sheer size and determination to get his own way had to make him the main contender for the dirty deed. It didn't help the blame-layers that none of the pups resembled anyone but their Mum. That's often the way with sheepdogs, eh?

Whatever Wally's background, there was bugger-all we could do about it now. In the light of Milly's revelations, were we harbouring a monster? We couldn't really parcel him up and send him back to Claude, demanding our money back. The cunning bugger had let us have him free. In fact, he'd turned up at a barbecue at our place, with each of his own abundant offspring carrying a couple of wriggling, adorable puppies and, without even mentioning they were available for adoption, managed to get rid of the lot in the time it took him to eat a sausage sandwich and drink most of our beer.

The Child Bride, who was really the one who allowed herself to be conned into accepting Wal, hated herself in the morning. But by then, I too had been sucked in, realising that Wal could well be the live-in musterer we'd always wanted. In the past, we'd done our rounding-up by press-ganging crowds of useless humans (most of them softened up first by vast quantities of strong drink). We only had about twenty sheep in those days but, in order to get them to do anything, we usually had to do it on a one-to-one basis—one human musterer for each dusky ewe. Despite his questionable genes, little Wal represented some sort of light at the end of the mustering tunnel.

Wally had a pretty conventional upbringing, I suppose. There's nothing much you can do with a sheepdog pup until he's old enough to count to ten and recite the alphabet. Accordingly, his heritage was gradually revealed to him (but not the Raglan part).

He got to know sheep fairly early in the piece. We had, living temporarily in the backyard, two animals that more or less fit that description. Charlie Pride was an elderly, grotesquely Eat Suffolk-Border Leicester cross with an appetite for anything that didn't move (and one or two things that did, especially young chicks and ducklings). Then there was Bunny, an equally grotesque black Border Leicester ram with an appetite for ewes of any age and bugger-all else.

Wal's major problem with Charlie was the latter's habit of breaking down any barriers to get at a decent feed of dog pellets. The adolescent pup was no match for the Galloping Gourmand and had to be fed indoors to avoid starving to death. Bunny the ram was a different problem again. At the back of what passed for his mind was a notion that the skinny, little black dog might indeed be a skinny black ewe. Wally wisely kept well out of his way—which didn't augur well for future confrontations in the paddock.

Wal's first encounter with the sheep as a mob augured even less well. He took one look at the ewes defiantly gathered in a defensive circle in the village street—into which they'd found their unwelcome way after ripping the essentials out of yet another of our valuable antique fences—and fled home. But I persevered.

Training a working sheepdog isn't something you can learn from a book. If you go to the so-called experts, it's even harder. Some tie the trainee pup to a regular worker in the hope they'll stop struggling against each other and finally work out how to do the job together. It might work on Sesame Street, but from what I'd seen of the practice, all it taught the pup was how to gradually enjoy slow strangulation while totally stuffing up the technique of a perfectly good adult working dog (No letters, please!).

Most other theories tended to have a boarding school ring to them, involving beating, starving and abusing the students, and lots of cold showers. I took the gentler road—a combination of patience, practice and generally letting the dog do what he liked. The fact that it didn't always work is incidental.

Several times a week, we'd go together to a paddock at the fringe of the village and try to re-route our wethers through the fence joining us with the village common, hose them back up our paddock and tuck them neatly into what was once an old pigsty. Crikey, that was a long winter. Wal got the general hang of it all right, but he had an unfortunate habit of always putting the sheep between himself and the boss (me!). 'He won't git behind,' many a more-experienced dog handler kept reminding me. They weren't wrong, Narelle!

In desperation I decided to meet Wal halfway. I worked out a whole technique of mustering where Wal more or less did what he wanted to with the sheep while I compensated for his inability to 'Git behind.' As he moved the mob towards me, I'd back towards the yard. If we actually got them to the gate, we'd improvise as best we could. Those were heart-warming days of frustration and anger, and invariably ended up with the wethers splitting into individual escape parties and thundering back up to the farthest end of the common. However, Wal did manage to prove that if he couldn't quite handle a mob, he *could* pick out a single sheep and conquer it.

In later years this single talent proved invaluable when selecting a killer out of the mob, isolating a fly-struck individual or taming some cranky ewe who'd hidden a lamb somewhere and had no intention of going anywhere with the rest of the flock. But that was later. The job immediately at hand was to get those wethers into the pigsty. We worked hard at it and eventually everything clicked.

On one particularly blustery, freezing, sleety winter's day, Wal actually dipped in behind the mob, held them while they decided whether or not to make a break for it and coaxed them into the tumbled-down shed at the far end of the sty . . . it didn't matter that they kept going through the ant-eaten slab wall of the rickety structure and completed their usual triumphant return to the common. We'd completed a muster. Wal and I had become a team. That's when I first experienced that warm inner glow which always followed a session with Wal.

Of all the many things I've tried in life, nothing's quite produced the satisfaction of working with a sheepdog. I once tried explaining it to the Child Bride, but she wouldn't have a bar of it.

'He smells and he barks all the time,' was all she'd say about that poor unwanted waif she'd naively accepted all those years ago.

Wal responded to her prejudice with total indifference. Above anything else, Wally was a one-man dog. I'm almost certain I was that one man. We'd both get the shits whenever an outsider joined us in the paddock. Even the best-meaning people have this funny, elitist attitude towards someone else's working dogs. They bellow nonsensical orders and when the poor old Holler Log quite rightly ignores them, he's written off as 'bloody useless.'

But it's always that useless dog that completes the task at hand. If Wal wasn't exactly Rin Tin Tin, it was hardly his fault. Despite any criticism that could be levelled at him by the pedantic and finicky, he lived up to his side of our partnership agreement as best he could. He was Boris Karloff to my Baron Frankenstein. So stuff 'em.

Nothing anyone could say could lessen that feeling of satisfaction, working with Wal. His successes were my successes. The failures? Well, any stupid bastard and his mongrel could have pulled *them* off. Besides, many of the cockies who raised a quizzical eyebrow at Wal's little quirks were the sort of blokes who couldn't get anything done with less than a horde of 37 or so dogs, anyway. At least whatever Wal and I achieved— no matter how long it took—the success was due to just the two of us.

Thankfully, the spectre of his alleged father's homicidal tendencies being inherited never came to anything. In all our years together, Wal never bared a single fang at a single lamb. The nearest he came to it was when a sheep bit him. Charlie Pride, mistaking him for a giant black duckling, actually sank his shrivelled gums into Wal's haunch.

The only inkling we ever received that Wal's genetic soup might contain one or two little oddments that weren't normally found in sheepdogs came a couple of years later, when a local looney, Gumboots Farquhar, eyed him outside the post office and declared Wal 'the finest flamin' fighting dog I ever did see.' Gumboots was known to see quite a few things not normally discernible to the (sober) human eye, so at first I didn't pay a lot of attention. Then, out of the blue, he whistled up his own mutt, a hulking blue heeler called Fluffy, and ordered 'Sic him.' Poor old Wal, who was attempting to suck the last morsels out of a particularly inviting disembowelled possum in the middle of the road, looked up to find Fluffy descending upon him like an express train. He didn't have time to run and he didn't want to. Thinking Fluffy wanted a share of his gourmet's delight, he stood his ground. Seconds later, Fluffy was heading back up the road, mewing like a kitten. There was a side of Wal I hadn't seen before.

It happened again, years later, after Wal and I had helped a neighbour hose his rams back into their paddock. Wal was trotting happily back home when the neighbour's bull-terrier suddenly roared out of the back of his ute. The bull gripped Wal firmly by the throat. Apart from a yelp of surprise, Wal didn't bat an eyelid. He walked quietly over to a big red gum fence post and with the bull snarling and spitting but refusing to relinquish its hold, belted the savage little bastard a few hundred times against the sturdy strainer.

The surprised bull-terrier, possibly motivated by the very real fear of severe major fractures, suddenly gave in and fled. After that, other dogs tended to leave Wal alone. Bigger than the average sheepdog, he was more than able to take care of himself. But he never sought a fight and he never showed any savagery to sheep. It was more typical of him that, after the run-in with the bull-terrier, he hid in his kennel for three days, shaking like a leaf.

Oh, there were one or two little idiosyncracies I suspect neither Raglan nor My Good Self could really accept the blame for—one being Wal's habit of deciding he'd had enough and knocking off in the middle of intensely delicate negotiations with the mob. It usually occurred just when we'd almost succeeded in threading them through a particularly uncooperative gate. On such occasions, he'd slink off under the ute, where I had no chance of reaching him. There he'd lie, panting pathetically and regarding me balefully with his big yellow eyes, clearly telling me exactly where I could shove today's feeling of ecstatic satisfaction.

His worst habit was his uncontrollable urge to move his bowels over the interior of vehicles. God knows why he did it. When we were solvent enough to afford to register our old ute, it wasn't so bad, because Wal would get his rocks off (or out) all over the tray, but during the poor times, after the bloke at the local motor registry became hysterical with laughter at our request for a pink slip and we were forced to use the family car to travel between properties, Wal's defilement of the upholstery wasn't all that amusing. It happened without fail, usually along the stretch of road near the old lightning-shattered apple gum, exactly halfway between the home-spread at Tussock Flat and the outstation at Blacksnake. If we were really lucky, he'd also bring up the contents of his stomach not long afterwards. I knew how he felt.

The result of those indiscretions was the firm refusal by the rest of the family to join us on our excursions. Wal and I made the best of it by assuring ourselves that we didn't need anyone else on our team, anyway. Here we were, windows down in a feeble attempt to clear the air, hurtling through the silent bush, our ears (in my case, hair) streaming in the breeze . . . two footloose adventurers living life to the full. Our second property at that lonely spot called Blacksnake, on the Lachlan River, became our personal domain. We'd share the thrill of the chase, the honest toil of the day's crutching and the happy brotherhood of the bush. We'd drive slowly home afterwards in a welter of comradeship, bone weariness, that indefinable feeling of satisfaction—and slowly drying dog shit. Then, out of the blue, it ended.

Wal had been fine when I fed him in the morning. He was still a bit shagged-out from the previous afternoon's mustering, but he slurped up his meaty bites with his usual gusto and settled down in the shade of his kennel. We came out later to do something or other with the chooks. The first inkling that something was wrong was the total lack of hysterical barking which usually heralded the presence of any of us around the yard. When I first noticed the silence, I imagined Wal had got off his chain. 'Bloody hell!'

In Wal's youth, every escape was a bit of a worry. We always feared the worst and that he'd loped off to terrorise a neighbour's flock, but in recent years, all Wal did was head straight for the defunct ute, now rotting quietly on flat tyres at the back of the machinery shed. He loved the battered old relic, remembering when it served as our valiant charger whenever we sallied forth to do battle with the woolly hordes at Black-snake. It became his first port of call whenever he was freed from his chain. He was always optimistic about the possibility of it becoming suddenly resurrected to whisk us off for a day's satisfying yakka.

But this time Wal wasn't off the chain. This time there wasn't the slightest chance of a day's satisfying yakka. Wal lay in the shade of his doghouse, strangely still. He'd been dead an hour or so. There was no sign of what had stopped his noble heart. To all appearances, it had just given up the ghost like Wal did whenever he figured he'd done enough work out in the paddock. It had just knocked up in mid-muster. The silence became darker and deeper.

Like I said, we selected a possie at the head of the sheepyards to lay him down. It's still strange without him. Even the Child Bride admits it. Every time we hear a bark, we look up to see if it's Wal warning us of visitors, or an escape attempt by the goats, or another dog in the yard, or a bird flying overhead. Wal enjoyed issuing regular news bulletins and had a special, identifiable bark for every eventuality. But, of course, these days it's not Wal at the newsdesk—just someone else's noisy bloody mutt bellowing for no apparent reason.

After the last winter's rains, the grass is growing back over the bare circle he'd inscribed around his kennel with his chain. His feed bowl's almost sunk into the ground. Even the cats have started taking for granted the fact that they can share his favourite sunny spot and loll contentedly on the warm iron roof of his old home. They've probably already forgotten about his indignant charges if they ever got too close to his food bowl. But I won't forget him. There'll always be a warm remnant of that deep satisfaction that only someone who's worked with a sheepdog enjoys.

The void left by Wal couldn't remain completely unfilled. A week before writing this, someone advertised for sale, in the local rag, a litter of sheepdog pups. God knows why I chose him, but I came home with a bleary-eyed little bundle, mostly white with a black smudge over one eye and that indefinable something that attracts a bloke to a dog. I suppose I could wax poetic about the streak of independence he showed compared to the other pups, or the way his ears cocked up when he noticed a mob of sheep in an adjoining paddock . . . but that'd only be wanking. I picked him because I liked him. That's a pretty good start to rekindling that magic I acquired from Wal. He will never be another Wal, but his name's Max and when he's old enough, he'll go out and carve his own niche in that mystic world only he and I can share.

GO, PLUTO!

Bill Sleep, Peterborough

Pluto came into my life as a foundling in 1972. One of the girls on the school bus which I drove at the time came to me and said, 'Would you like a puppy? I found him wandering on the railway line. I want to keep him but Mum says no. 'He's got big feet and will grow too big to keep in the town. Get rid of him.'

Mum proved to be right. He grew, not tall, but very strong and nuggetty; not savage, but aggressive, and he'd never knock back a fight no matter how tired. And he'd never give up until he came out on top.

He didn't receive any expert training but would always 'sit', 'come back', 'speak up' and so on when asked. The words 'Go, Pluto' would send him flat strap around the nearest mob of sheep, to bring them back to me equally as fast—and never mind any poor sheep that could not keep up. He'd get them next time and enjoy that just as much as the last trip. It was all in the game.

In August 1981 we were shearing, as we usually do at that time of the year. In the late afternoon, we had turned out about 400 ewe hoggets into our 1200-acre hills paddock as it was fairly cold with a south-west wind blowing. The hills had some shelter, being thick with low tussock bush and slate rocks standing out from the ground. There were also some gullies. However, around 8 pm the wind became a storm with intermittent showers and a threat of hail and possibly snow. Despite the shelter, the ewes were in danger of freezing and had to be brought to the shed.

I took Pluto and the ute and set off around the road to the north-east corner of the paddock and sure enough, there they were, just beginning to huddle up in the corner where there was no shelter—a recipe for disaster!

Abandoning the ute, Pluto and I set off to drive the ewes the two and a half kilometres back to the shed, straight into the gale, up over the hills. There were occasional showers and only starlight between the showers as the clouds raced by. There was no moon.

We got about halfway when two of the ewes started to knock up and needed my urging to keep them going while the rest strung out into the darkness ahead. After an exceptionally strong wind gust and shower,

I suddenly realised that the mob had turned and disappeared back the way they had come and I was left with two sheep.

Knowing Pluto's habit of 'flat out and bring what comes' I was reluctant to send him back. However, I knew that if I left the two I had, they would die for sure. But then, if I did not get the rest, with the wind chill the way it was, they could all die. So it was 'Go, Pluto' and hope he brought at least some. The rest would have to take their chance.

I kept going with my two sheep for quite some time. Then, out of the darkness behind me, came the leaders of the mob, not flat out, but just trotting along with Pluto behind, working gently back and forth. Eventually we put them into the shed.

In another ute, we then went back to the far corner of the paddock for a quick look with the headlights. There were no sheep to be seen, so at about 1 am, I got to bed.

Next morning, with the weather clearer, we counted the sheep out of the shed. All were present. Pluto had brought them all!

ON HER OWN
Mary Noll, Wilmington

Years ago, my Dad had a farm at Murray Town and one also at Fullerville.

Dad owned a black kelpie dog, Jip, who at his command would take a mob of sheep to the Fullerville property completely unaided. The distance between farms was about four and a half miles. Dad would arrange for someone at Fullerville to open the gate. Jip would drive the sheep the distance, put them in the paddock and drive them to water. She would then wait at the open gate until Dad came and picked her up.

Jip did this job many times while Dad went on with other farm work.

At other times, Jip would take Dad's lunch in a basket, out to him in the paddock, along with any messages we wanted to give to him.

She was a much loved, beautiful dog.

THE GOAL SNEAK

M. Pearce, Arno Bay

Tiger was a dog with a terrific personality, and he left unforgettable memories of many humorous and outstanding incidents.

He was an Alsation-staghound cross, dark brindle in colour, but with a generally gentle nature. He seemed to understand conversation which he interpreted quite quickly. For instance, if we were driving along the track in the old Chev, and the boys said, 'Let's give Tiger a race,' he would be off like a flash.

His main job was to kill kangaroos and foxes, but he also helped provide us with meat.

When we needed a rooster, we only had to show Tiger which one and he would follow it, then pounce on it and hold it, a paw on each wing until we arrived to collect it. Never did he harm the bird.

There was an old man kangaroo living on adjoining land which was mainly covered with scrub. He was so large and had injured so many dogs who had attacked him, that he had acquired the title of 'The Legend'. Due to his senior years, no doubt, he would fight rather than run.

The boys were riding their horses through the area and hoping they wouldn't meet The Legend because they weren't big enough or old enough to help the dogs if there was a confrontation. But sure enough, much to their dismay, there he was, large as ever, looking taller than seven feet and as wide across the rump as a Clydesdale horse. The boys decided to go quietly so as not to disturb him, but apparently his hearing was good.

When The Legend saw the dogs, he turned around and came towards them, intending as usual to demoralise the enemy. However, when Tiger, who had not previously been among the hunters, saw what was happening, he retreated a few yards to gain momentum, took a flying leap, and grabbed the offender by the throat. The weight and surprise of the attack overbalanced The Legend and gave Tiger supremacy.

After a struggle, Tiger was successful in killing The Legend.

Foxes in the area were always a menace. They killed poultry and lambs. Tiger, however, killed many foxes. Rabbits also had to be caught for feed for the dogs, and again Tiger was busy. As Tiger aged, he decided the easiest way to get them was to trot along the edge of the shelter scrub and snap them up in his jaws. The sheepdogs would chase the rabbits and Tiger would intercept them close to the scrub. Rarely did he ever miss. He was referred to as a goal sneak for his efforts.

SUGAR RAY HARRY
Milton Green, Bute

This happened in January 1985 when Dad and I, with our three dogs, decided to make our routine check of the sheep.

Our best dog is called Sugar Ray Harry and he is black. He got this name because of his unequalled fighting ability against the neighbour's dogs. We call him Harry for short.

The other two dogs with us were Cola, and Ricky, who was only young and learning the ropes.

We went around the sheep, which were in a fairly large paddock, and started heading home. We hadn't gone far when we noticed a fox which had been startled by the ute. It was running away hell for leather.

Since it was a big paddock, we thought we'd give him a run for his money. I stopped the dogs from jumping off while Dad tried to head him off and run him out of steam a bit. After a while, Harry got sick of this and decided it was time for action. So all three dogs jumped off and went after the fox.

The fox was fully grown and although he had run some distance, was still pulling away from the dogs. We headed him off a couple of times which tired him out a bit more, and also gave the dogs a chance to catch up.

Being cunning, the fox got through a fence and kept on running parallel to it. At this stage, Harry was about twenty yards behind, with the other dogs a bit further back again. We raced up past the fox with the fence between us, and the fox baulked and cut through the fence back into the same paddock.

By this time, the fox and the three dogs were getting pretty tired. Although they had caught up to him and had had a couple of snaps at him, he still led them by ten yards. The fox then ran into a dam with the dogs close behind. We were waiting for the fox to reappear out the other side, but he didn't.

We drove over to the dam and, to our amazement, there was the fox swimming in the middle of the dam with the three dogs circling around the edge barking furiously. It was a small dam which contained in its centre about three feet of water. It was about twenty feet across.

Harry hated foxes. He'd seen what they did to young lambs. He jumped into the dam and swam to the fox, lunging at it to grab it by the throat. Due to the forces of gravity, both fox and dog sank to the bottom with the only sign above water being Harry's black tail waving vigorously. Seconds ticked by and then Harry rose to the surface, gasping for air. Not long after, the fox did the same. Harry again lunged at the fox and again both sank to the bottom.

This happened over and over again with the fox coming up considerably more slowly every time. Cola and Ricky, meanwhile, were circling the water's edge giving much needed vocal support while Dad and I rolled around the bank with laughter.

Eventually Harry, having conquered his foe, swam out to the bank and crawled out of the water for a victory shake. The fox eventually surfaced and also swam to the bank where what little life left in him was finished with the back of a shovel.

This is an incident I shall never forget. Harry's courage, fighting ability and determination were highly praised.

Now, Harry is eight years old and semi-retired. He has a dislocated shoulder and a bit of a prostate problem.

PART 3
WORTH ANY
TWO MEN

And then there are the smart ones, the ones who know
what to do without being told, who can count and find
their way home, who know what's what and
can do the job better than the boss!

THE ABATTOIRS DOG

Angela Goode

The local stock agent, Alan, lit up when we got talking about good dogs.

'In my forty years of working at saleyards, I reckon I've seen none better than old Whisky,' he said. 'He was the most intelligent dog I've ever worked with. I got him when I started work at fifteen and any task you set him, he would do.'

Alan and his brother Ross were drovers at the Gepps Cross saleyards on the outskirts of Adelaide. They needed good, strong, sensible dogs because the days often started before dawn and didn't end until after dark. They would spend each Tuesday unloading and yarding up animals in readiness for the next day's market. Then, after the sheep were sold, they had to move mobs to holding paddocks where they awaited slaughter, or straight to the abattoirs. Often, there would be mobs of lambs to walk to the irrigated pasture at the government sewage farm two and a half miles down a busy main road from the saleyards.

It was doing this job that Whisky made his name. Being newly-weaned and inexperienced at being mustered, lambs tend to scatter in all directions. To help keep them together, a bloke on a horse would go in front, and dogs and others on horseback would walk behind. These mobs would number between 1000 and 3000 lambs, and it took a bit of skill to get them over intersections without losing any.

Whisky accompanied Alan on one of these trips and, the following week, put himself at the front of the mob. No-one had instructed him. It was simply what Whisky chose to do. For six years, mobs of nervous lambs were led down Regency Road to the farm by this lone dog, and back again for slaughter, with never a one lost.

Alan says Whisky's style was relaxed and his manner casual. He used to lope along sniffing at posts, but if ever any lambs were going too quickly, he would authoritatively push them back into the mob. For some reason this shaggy black, white and tan kelpie cross was a born leader. If ever he had taken the wrong road, or lost concentration, there could have been sheep scattered far and wide.

An open drain carrying raw sewage ran through the farm and from time to time, lambs would fall in. Whisky had no fear of filth, so in he would dive, swim around the lambs and push them to the bank so someone could pull them out.

'It was lucky that Whisky didn't mind swimming in sewage, because none of us would have dived in after those lambs,' Alan says. Whisky learned the skills of a yard dog by being tied up near the end of the drafting race in the saleyards. From there, he watched the other dogs working. When he was let off in the afternoon of his first day there, he immediately threw himself into the job of drafting and penning up as professionally as any other dog in the yards.

Alan said he never needed any training, and seemed to know what any of Alan's commands meant—remembering that he had to pick, out of the noise and bustle, the words of his own particular master which competed with the whistles and calls of at least six other men to about fifteen dogs.

Every working day, Whisky would ride to the saleyards on the back of Alan's horse. The horse was nearly sixteen hands, but Whisky would leap onto its back and lie down just behind the saddle for the half-hour trot and canter to Gepps Cross from Woodville Gardens where Alan and Ross lived. On odd occasions, the horse lurched, causing Whisky to dig in his nails to keep his position. This would rather annoy the horse, which would buck. It must have been quite a sight, but the dog never fell off.

If ever Alan had to leave the dog at home for any reason on a Tuesday or Wednesday, there'd be hell to pay. Whisky would scream, bark and howl well into the morning—something he would never do on other days when he was left on the chain.

'Although there was absolutely no change to my routine, whatever the day, there is no doubt that he knew when it was sheep day,' said Alan. 'I am sure he knew the days of the week.'

COUNT TO TEN
Greg Twelftree, Minlaton

In the early 1960s we were given a puppy from a local farmer and named him Smith, after that farmer, Jim Smith.

The puppy turned out to be a very faithful, hard-working dog and this is a true incident.

We had yarded cross-bred lambs to send to market and our stock agent was helping us. We ran the lambs up the loading ramp into the truck. We realised six more lambs could be fitted in to complete the load.

My father called Smith and said, 'Smith, we need six more.' With that, Smith ran down, cut six lambs from the mob and ran them up the ramp into the truck.

The stock agent, dumbfounded, asked, 'Good Lord, can that dog count?'

Dad replied, 'He's all right until he gets to ten. After that, he makes a hell of a mess of it!'

I'LL HAVE THIRTY-TWO
Wally Karger, Vale Park

A dog worth mentioning was a red kelpie owned by our neighbour on the River Murray. He wasn't a brilliant dog but useful in the yard. When dipping sheep after shearing, Toby excelled.

Jack, our neighbour, stipulated that twenty-eight sheep in the shower dip was the required number, but Toby always insisted on thirty-two.

How he knew we couldn't guess, but on counting the sheep out after dipping, we found he'd sent in thirty-two, no more, no less, every time.

No-one prompted him to send in that number, as he always ran over their backs, jumped down and drove them in by himself. Yet thirty-two was always the number.

EXACTLY EIGHT
Wally Karger, Vale Park

I sold some sheep to a chap at Kersbrook and he brought along a double-deck semi-trailer.

I offered Lassie to help load them, but he said his dog would do the job. And she did.

After he put eight sheep in the small pen against the cabin and closed the gate, his almost-white border collie bitch loaded the bottom and top pens on her own with exactly eight sheep in every one.

A TOTAL WORKAHOLIC
Max Verco, Marcollat

Every now and again you get an outstanding dog, a champion. Well, Joker was one of those.

In the 1930s, I worked on a property in the Flinders Ranges. Central Mount Stuart was on this place. The country was very steep and the ranges were terribly craggy. The scenery was magnificent, but, oh, it was very hard country to work. You were constantly up and down rocky mountains, with lovely native pines on their slopes and creeks at their base.

Joker lived with me out on camp. It was only him and me. We became very close. He used to come inside the building but it was a pretty rough old place and only had dirt floors. There were no beds in it, so I cut some pine logs and nailed a few bags between them to save me camping on the floor. It was a little bit of luxury. In the really cold weather, old Joker used to sleep on my feet.

Now, when I was mustering in those ranges, I used to ride along on the top of the range. The idea was that I would chase the sheep off the top of the range down the steep slopes to the valleys on either side where it was easier travelling for the sheep and horses. About half way down one side of the craggy range, I'd place a man and his horse, and another horseman down at the base. The bloke half way down would pick up my sheep and push them down to the next bloke, who would collect them and drive them along the creekbeds to the end of the range. On the other side, I needed only Joker to do the work of these two men on their horses. I only had to show him the job once, and ever after that he knew that he was the bottom man. He had so many more brains than any other dog. If there were sheep halfway down, he would go up and get them and take them along. When we got to the end of the range, he'd have his mob, and the other two fellows would have theirs.

When I left there, I got a job on a station in New South Wales. I went round by boat from Adelaide, and when I went in to get my ticket round to Sydney, I told the people in the office that I had a very good sheepdog and that I wanted to take him with me on the boat. They told me to put him in the care of the butcher. I told them I was very fond of this dog, that he was a mighty dog, and to tell the butcher to really look after him, or we would have an argument at the end of the trip. By that he had to make sure the dog had food, water, a bed, and didn't fall overboard, or I would deal with him.

It only took three or four days to get around to Sydney. When I went to get old Joker from the butcher, he was like a bloated toad! This butcher, he looked after him all right. I reckon he used to sling him a shoulder two or three times a day. Old Joker could hardly walk. It was a hell of a shock for a dog used to getting only a few scraps out of my saddlebag when we were out for a week at a time in that tough country.

When I got up to the station, because he was so good, I was straight away dropped in to all the best droving jobs. If I hadn't had a top dog, I would have got jobs like cleaning out the sheep manure from under the shearing shed, doing a bit of fencing, all the odd jobs. It's much more fun out droving with your horse and dog.

Joker and I did a lot of droving. Once, in 1932, I was bringing a mob down from New South Wales to Hallett in South Australia. We were out on the road for about six weeks. Out in that back country, there were no fences. You just let the mob spread. I was the youngest on the team, so while the others had a feed, I got the job of riding slowly around the mob to keep them more or less together. I only had to do that for two or three days, and then I just gave old Joker a sign.

Every dinner time after that, he'd take over. I'd go into the camp with the men while we boiled our billy and had a bit of tucker. Joker would start one side and gradually work his way right around the mob, just easing a few in here or there that were heading out. Pretty well every day, it would take him almost twenty minutes to do the round. We used to time him! When he got opposite us he would look over at me and I'd just wave again, and he would start on his way back.

There wouldn't be many dogs you could teach to do this. Most would go around them if you sent them, but they'd push the sheep in on you, and have them milling all around the camp. Joker loved his job and was never happy unless he was working. He was a total workaholic.

Dogs are pampered today. My dog now rides on my motorbike, but in those days, they had to trot by your horse for two or three hours before you got out into the paddock. They were tough dogs.

In those days there was no refrigeration, and in that country, it was as hot as hell. We had to salt all our meat, and when you were out on camp, you had salt meat and damper and hot plum jam. You didn't eat much. You couldn't. It was hot. You'd toss a bit to the old dog, and that's about all he had—a bit of old salt meat.

He couldn't stop working. When we got some chooks, he didn't know what they were but being a good sheepdog he loved to round them up just because they moved. I used to scold him a bit. I'd say, 'Hey, you shouldn't be rounding up chooks'—and look, he knew. I'd creep along the side of the shed and he'd look around and see me looking, so off he'd go, as though he had no interest in a chook at all. He'd cock his leg on a tree or something and wander away as though it was the last thing on his mind. He was nearly human.

THE RABBIT TRAP
Errol Crossing, Berri

I had a grazing property at Tungkillo where I taught Towser to catch fly-blown sheep for me.

Being rough and stony country, I used to ride on horseback around my sheep. Towser would sniff out the blown sheep so I could treat them in the paddock.

I was doing this one day when Towser took off after a sheep. I called him back, knowing it wasn't fly-blown, as they had just been shorn.

He ignored my whistle and calling, knocked the sheep over and held it. I rode up to chastise him for not doing as he was told.

That sheep had a rabbit trap on its foot. He knew it had to be caught.

Towser lived to be eighteen years old.

HE FOUND HIS OWN MOB
Bruce Mills, Tumby Bay

Spike was quite a character. He had one glazed eye, obtained after a kick from a horse which he loved to tease. A good, hardy worker, he was always ready to go, and he was a great mate for a young fellow (as I was in those days.)

It was mustering time, and we were in thick mallee country, west of the Middleback Range. My mate and I set out from the homestead, on the east side of the range. We were on horseback and accompanied by Spike. Our destination was an old caravan which had been placed by a mustering paddock and dam a few days earlier. It had been equipped for a week's mustering.

About three and a half miles from our destination, we saw a mob of sheep camped on the edge of a clearing, with very thick scrub behind them. The sheep saw us and stood up. Knowing that the scrub was very thick and hard to gallop through, we decided to send Spike around the sheep.

Now Spike, in spite of his faults, had a very good cast. Away he went, and we waited for ages for him to move the sheep, but nothing happened. The sheep started to drift off into the scrub. We decided that Spike must have put up a kangaroo (his main fault!) and left the sheep. After much scrub bashing and many scratches we turned the sheep ourselves and, cursing the useless dog, we took them to camp.

We arrived there at sundown, and, after seeing to the horses' needs, set to getting something to eat for ourselves.

I was worried about my dog. I thought he must have been ripped open by an old scrubber kangaroo and was probably lying injured or dead out in the scrub somewhere. We were just about to climb into bed when we heard movements in the bushes outside. On investigating, we found the caravan ringed with sheep, held there by Spike.

No doubt in his original cast, he had found another mob of sheep further out and had followed us into camp with his own mob.

Spike had never been to this camp before and to get there had had to find and negotiate a narrow neck in the salt lake, a fact we checked out next morning. Needless to say Spike received much praise and a good feed, and I slept well.

BACK IN TOWN
Stella Tiller, Balaklava

We live in a small country town, in semi-retirement, so our tan kelpie, Toby, was kept on the farm where our son and his family live.

However, Toby went everywhere with my husband in his ute. The farm is about two miles as the crow flies, or about three by road, from our home.

At one stage, my husband had to go away for about three weeks. He took his ute and left Toby at the farm. He arrived back late one night and put the ute in the shed at the house in town. He left the shed door open.

Next morning, Toby was in the back of the ute waiting to go to work. He hadn't been to our place in town during those three weeks.

How did he know the ute was back? Could he smell it, or my husband, or both from that distance?

CHAUVINISM ON THE FARM
Muriel Freeman, Port Neill

Most farmers' wives will be able to relate to this incident which occurred about twenty-seven years ago. I still get a laugh when I think of it.

We had just taken over our farm which had very rundown fences and sheepyards. It had no gates and sheep-handling was very difficult.

The workforce was one husband with a very short straw as far as temper goes, one very young, untrained sheepdog, and me, a virtual new-comer to farming. We coped reasonably well, bringing the sheep home from the very farthest paddock, two miles, with one husband and one dog sitting in the ute and me droving the sheep along by foot. The dog was relegated to my seat after the first 100 yards as he was too fast, ran through the middle of the sheep, and had sheep lying down and scattering in all directions. He was a very smart dog.

On arriving at the yards and after many words of wisdom on how to yard the sheep, we eventually had them in the drafting and 'holding' yards. As there were no gates, the dog and I had to keep pushing the whole mob of 2000 up from behind, while keeping them away from the outer fences. We had reduced the mob down to a manageable number so I asked the boss if we could stop for a drink break.

'No,' he said, 'not until we finish.'

It was a long, hot, hard day's work. He had me at it from 8.30 am until three in the afternoon. The dog, however, was quite fresh.

A HERITAGE OF COUNTRY GENES
Angela Goode

When I left the city to marry the boss and live on a sheep and cattle station, one link with my city days did remain. That was my faithful and much loved Lucy. Originally a pup from an abandoned dogs' home, she was a border collie who for eleven years subjugated her rural instincts to live amongst asphalt and cement.

We had always spent a lot of time in the bush, when at weekends

I would saddle up my horse and ride through the back tracks of the Adelaide Hills. She would follow me for hours, checking out the smells and delights on the way.

During the week, she would be the ultimate city girl, bringing my morning paper to me, guarding the house during my absences at work, and going for runs before or after work with me. I would ride my bike and she would gallop along the footpath.

Actually, when I said that she would guard the house during the day, that's what I thought she was doing. It was only after some years that I discovered that as soon as I had left for work, she would thump open the gate, squeeze through and head for the shopping centre. There she would camp all day on the footpath outside the butcher shop and next to a bakery, being fed slices of sausage, buns and pies by the people who got to know her. (I had noticed that she had put on weight and had accused my elderly neighbour of throwing his scraps over the fence.) She would always be home waiting for me when I finished work.

I had always felt a bit guilty about having a sheepdog living in the city, even though I was giving her plenty of exercise. I felt bad about making her live in a place that clashed with her heritage of rural genes and away from the working life for which such dogs are bred.

After tiring of her shopping expeditions, Lucy tried another tack to make life in the city less boring. I was working at a radio station in the University of Adelaide and would ride my bicycle into the city each day. Lucy took it upon herself to find out where I went. She had never seen where I worked.

I was in a meeting about an hour after arriving one day when someone came in and said a very excited black and white dog was scratching at the front door. He opened the door and straight into the meeting room galloped my overjoyed companion. I felt a whole series of emotions at the same time—pride at her ability, anger at the danger of crossing city streets, shame that she was so lonely, delight that she was so devoted. She could only have followed the scent of my bicycle tracks on a route that took her through the heart of the city and six sets of traffic lights.

Once the game had started, I had no hope of keeping her at home. I chained her up, but she arrived with the clip hanging from her collar. I got a new chain and she arrived without the collar. I got a new collar and

43

she arrived dragging a section of chain. I tied her to the tank-stand and fully expected her to come dragging the tank.

A vote among staff members determined that she could go on the payroll as recreation officer, so until I left to travel to Western Australia she accompanied me every day legitimately, running along footpaths while I cycled.

In Western Australia, we stayed on my brother's farm and that was her first introduction to sheep. It was as if all those generations of working dog genes exploded at once. Her face lit up, her body tensed with excitement and, given the opportunity, she would work in paddock and yards until her sides were heaving. I left her with my brother when I journeyed north and he was most reluctant to part with her when I returned.

I went to Melbourne for university studies and Lucy went too. However, I was away from my house from early in the morning until late at night and she again found life too boring. She decided to register a complaint by wrecking the garden, chewing through the back door, destroying the screen on a window and munching through the curtains. I got the message and sent her back to Adelaide by train the next day. She grinned all the way down the platform, wheeled on a trolley in one of those wooden cages with iron bars.

I would drive home to Adelaide about once every three months and my parents said that every time, well before I reached their house, she would leap up, all alert and delighted, and bound to the front gate. When I pulled up in my old car, she would always be there wagging and squealing with joy. She had somehow memorised the pitch and thump of the engine. No other vehicle produced this reaction. She was never there on the day I left to return to Melbourne, always disappearing to avoid the farewell.

Actually, several times I nearly had to say farewell permanently to her. Once, when she had severe gastroenteritis, she decided to end it all. She dragged herself outside and lay in the blazing sun on a piece of corrugated iron. A good vet pulled her through but she had not been far from death by the time I found her.

Another time, she fell into a ground-level open water tank. She must have been swimming around for over an hour trying to get out. Her front paws were bloody stumps where she had desperately scratched at the walls. She was barely keeping herself afloat. Her eyes and nostrils were all that were out of the water. When I dragged her out, she lay, heaving—a sodden, half-drowned wreck—until she recovered enough to lick her gratitude.

When we went to live in the bush permanently, Lucy was in her element. She could do a bit of sheep work, although her enthusiasm was sometimes more than the boss could cope with.

She abandoned the domestic scene for entire days spent in the back of the ute doing important things like tagging calves, fixing gates and pulling windmills. My tasks couldn't compete with that lot and I did feel a bit rejected. But to see that dog shining with health and loving her new life was some compensation. She lost the middle-aged spread acquired from soft, city living.

When the boss wasn't winning her over with his glamorous jobs, Lucy and I would go for long walks. It was with her that I explored my new domain. Together we waded through the creek and together we hunted through sheds and pushed through the scrub. Her enthusiasm for life on the land was infectious. Although I had spent holidays in the bush before, and loved it, it was her boundless joy for each new day and its tasks that helped me assimilate into the ranks of seasoned country women.

As time went on, Lucy grew blind and deaf. She would track me around the farm by following the scent of my footsteps. Her hips were a bit rickety and she spent long hours sleeping in her basket.

One day, just as she used to disappear to avoid farewells when I returned to Melbourne, she walked off into the bush. She was seventeen and ready to die. We found her body after a few days and buried her at the bottom of the garden. We planted a West Australian flowering gum over her.

She was my last tangible tie with the city, the last visible remnant of my former life in the world beyond dirt roads and rolling paddocks.

She, with her heritage of country genes, helped me become one with the land.

ON AUTOMATIC
Bill Franklin, Cowell

Our border collie, Bob, was a great sheepdog, but this incident concerns the house cow.

Every day, Bob would go and fetch the cow for milking, whenever he heard the rattle of the milk bucket.

By the time one of us had walked from the house to the milking shed 300 metres away, Bob would have the cow waiting in the yard.

One morning, however, some months after we had sold the house cow, I had reason to use the old milk bucket.

I was amazed when, about half an hour later, Bob turned up with the jersey from the adjoining farm two kilometres away.

SIX MONTHS ACROSS THE GULF
Dick Mills, Kanmantoo

A few years prior to the First World War my grandfather, WG Mills, MHR, assisted his second son, Richard, to purchase a property near Elbow Hill, south of Cowell.

It fell to Alec, my father, to take across a flock of sheep from Millbrae to Cowell to stock the place. Alec was seventeen or eighteen years old at the time.

The sheep were driven by him on foot to Port Adelaide, then loaded aboard a lighter. The dog, called Shep, was of great assistance to Alec and travelled with him and the sheep to Cowell. Here the sheep were unloaded and Shep assisted to get them to the farm down along the coast.

One can just imagine the fond pat that Shep got when finally the paddock gate was shut. That pat was even fonder than Shep imagined it would be because he was to be left behind to assist Richard on the farm. After a few days' stay to acquaint himself with the country his brother had taken up, Alec returned by the next regular ship to Port Adelaide. He then travelled back to Millbrae at Kanmantoo.

Soon after Alec left the new farm, Shep disappeared. Alec knew nothing of this until eventually the news reached him via letter. Alec resigned himself to the loss of another good dog. This was not an uncommon occurrence and new dogs were constantly being bred and trained.

Time passed by after the letter. Winter came with green grass coming in the paddocks again, and the cry of new-born lambs was heard across the valley. Lamb-tailing passed, then shearing.

Then, one bright morning, Alec opened the back door and there was Shep, wagging his tail with great joy. There was a very fond reunion and the family at Millbrae was amazed to think that a dog could find its way across the gulf.

It had taken him six months to complete the journey.

SIXTY MILES HOME
Clare Lawrie, Naracoorte

During the war years, most of us had to be useful, either indoors or out-of-doors.

To help my brother at Waikerie, in the Riverland, with the mustering for shearing, I travelled with my sheepdog, Kim, by train from Copeville in the Murray Mallee. We had quite a few successful days getting the sheep together.

One evening, I forgot to tie Kim up. The next morning, he had gone. I rode all over the district trying to find him, with no luck.

Shearing ended and I went to Adelaide to meet my husband who was coming down on leave from the Darwin area.

A fortnight later, I had a phone call from my father at Copeville telling me that Kim had found his way home. He was very footsore and weary. Naturally, I was more than delighted to get the news. I have often wondered, though, how he did it. Copeville was over sixty miles from Waikerie.

Since Kim had travelled there in a dog box, he wouldn't have seen where he was going.

I'M SURE IT WOULD BE HELPFUL ...

David and Nancy Pearce, Maitland

King didn't need any training, nor did he have fancy casts. He could work out where the sheep had to go and so got on with the job. He seemed to like to have a human with him, but just for companionship.

We are crop farmers as well as graziers, so it was customary for King to travel out to paddocks being ploughed, reaped or whatever. He would go a couple of rounds behind the implements, checking all was well. Then he would rest at a suitable corner of the paddock until lunch, when he would expect a ride home.

One day, we were working in a paddock that had a few acres of scrub. About 400 ewes and lambs were grazing there. For some reason, King got left behind when we went home for lunch.

Perhaps that's what set his mind to tick over like this: 'My man usually invites me to ride home with him, but not today. I wonder if he's intending to draft those lambs off. He did mention it. I'm sure it would be helpful if I took the sheep home, while he's having lunch with his wife.

'He's even left the gate open, too. He doesn't usually do that unless he is moving sheep.'

So off he went and delivered, right to the back gate, the ewes and their lambs, who are often difficult to keep in one mob.

The amazing thing was that he did the job in less than an hour. It took us one and a half hours to return them to the paddock—with the help of two humans.

We still wonder how he managed to get the lambs and ewes past all the trees without losing any. Then he took them over the crossroads at the paddock gate where the mob could have gone in any of four directions. The last leg of the trip was along the busy main road, before he was able to turn up the driveway.

WE'RE MATES FOREVER

DA Treloar, Wiawera Station, Olary

I don't have a story as such, but I have a poem. I wrote it in the middle of our last drought while I was sitting in the truck waiting for the pump to fill my water tank. I was carting water for the house, for showers and toilet only. It was roughly a 14-mile round trip. All but one of our dams were dry and the wells and bores were forking and breaking down all the time.

I have been looking after the place for Dad, most of the time on my own, for the past two and a half years as he had to go to Yaramba Station when my brother left. So I was really flat out and felt at the end of my tether and didn't know where to turn. I had lost the use of over 45 square miles of our 90 square mile block due to bores and dams packing up on me.

My dogs, Red and Jed, were the only comfort I had. That is why I wrote this poem. It is actually what happened. I had been trying for months to get the squatters tank full, or even a foot in it, to no avail as the well kept forking.

One hot night I went over to check it only to see a trickle flowing in. I lay down on the top and thought, 'Oh, shit, what am I going to do?' I felt really lost. Then my two dogs Red and Jed ran up the side of the tank pillar and started to whine and lick me. They knew I was upset and I'm sure they were trying to cheer me up. They did. It got me going again, and it rained within another month.

They're both good working dogs and I love them both.

Now that I've explained the situation a bloke was in, maybe you'll understand what I meant to say in the poem.

There is no doubt that if you have a good dog and treat him kindly, he will understand your condition or feelings and worry about you when you're not so good. They're the best mates you can get, I reckon.

RED DOG

I sat there on the old stone tank,
Watching the salt water trickle in,
Worrying about the money we haven't got in the bin,
And this bloody drought,
That we could do without.
Listening to the old pump jack grinding away,
In its slow methodical way,
Whilst catching the blood red sunset of another stinking hot day.

Gazing occasionally to the west and east,
Hoping for one cloud at least.
There was not one in sight,
And the bloody wind refused to blow,
So the windmills stayed still,
And the stock tanks wouldn't fill.
The sheep were hanging around,
Waiting for that liquid gold to come out of the ground.
They were all dying for a drink,
And reckoned their lives were on the brink,
'Cause the troughs were as dry as the empty kitchen sink.

The bores were breaking down and the dams were nearly dry.
It was enough to make a grown man cry.
Then up on to the tank jumped my old mate Red,
Close by my little black kelpie Jed.
They both gave me a slobbery lick,
As if to say shit a brick.
We're mates forever,
So pick yourself up and we'll stick this drought out together.
So I sat up straight instead of half on my back,
Figuring they've got the right idea Jack!
And thinking as it got further into the night,
I'm not going to give in without a bloody fight.
Hoping all the time the good Lord up above would hear my cries,
Before everything withers up and dies.

A PARTICULARLY GOOD 'EYE'

Margaret Hancock, Bute

Toby was the greatest sheepdog this farm has ever seen. A black and white animal, Toby is remembered as a well-trained dog with a heap of natural ability and a particularly good 'eye'. He must have been some dog. At shearing time, his exploits are told and retold every year, especially if there is someone new in the shed.

During shearing the order to 'Go fetch the woolly ones' would send him off past the newly-shorns to the back paddock where the self-satisfied woollies grazed unsuspectingly. A quick skirt around the fence to check for strays and he would soon have the mob in a nice little bunch, edging them through the gate and up to the yards.

He was as reliable as the sunrise and worth any two working men. Like all farm dogs, he was a constant companion to his master, no matter what the job. It was on one of these non-sheep jobs that Toby became almost immortal—well, his memory did anyway.

The men were fencing and Toby watched everything intently. He scratched the dirt as he pretended to dig post holes, and he supervised the wire-straining strand by strand. He walked twice as many miles as the men—backwards and forwards. He chased birds and had some fun with a hare.

By sundown, Toby had had a full and satisfying day. The men packed their gear into the dray and rode home. Nobody noticed that Toby was missing until someone went to feed him. There was a scramble as the lanterns were lit and a couple of fellows went back to the day's work site. Was Toby hurt? Had he been run over by the dray? Perhaps he had got upwind of a neighbour's bitch.

Nothing so mundane would have caused Toby's story to be recalled so often.

When the men arrived back at the day's task, there was Toby—lying midway between two fence posts staring at the fence. The lanterns revealed the men had got the wires crossed.

Folk who recall this event insist that this was not a shaggy dog story.

PART 4
TIME OUT

We all need to stop work sometimes, whether it's to vote in town, go to a dog trial, or just because it's tucker-time. It seems some of us, though, take a break for no reason at all.

THE VERY LAST LAP
DH Turnbull, Cleve

As a young man, I spent many long hours driving a horse team to clear a scrub block.

My black and white border collie, Spotty, would come out in the morning behind the team and follow for the first round of the paddock. He would then spend the rest of the day sitting around the lunch box or sniffing out rabbits.

Then, with some uncanny sense of timing, he would follow the team for the very last lap of the paddock before knock-off time.

Only once did he make a mistake and have to do two laps.

THE YARD DOG FUNDRAISER
Angela Goode

We thought we'd run a yard dog competition at the local school fete. It was a good way, we reckoned, of getting the men along to what was traditionally a pretty tedious affair.

So the research was done and the experts gathered and showed us what to do. We set the course up in a paddock adjoining the school, alongside the side road. In one corner, we put a yard for all the sheep that would, in groups of ten, be pushed by the competing dogs to another yard. In this yard, there was a drafting race and a ramp leading to a truck. The dogs would have to help draft the sheep and then push a few up the ramp and then unload them again.

Nothing like this had been held in the district before, so interest in the event was running pretty high. Every bloke, of course, thinks his dog is the best; but all the pub talk and bragging in the world won't necessarily convince anyone else that this is so.

The idea of doing the sort of work that's done on the farm to test out the dogs in public made sense. On the day, eighteen, dogs and owners turned up to compete for the $100 prize. Winning was pretty important, so tension was high. There were a few brawls between ragged-eared mutts around the wheels of the utes, a fair bit of yelling by their owners and a huge crowd of spectators around the fences.

Most of the dogs, though, were experienced workers who had been around yards and sheds for years. They weren't much bothered by the people and noise. They loped around on the end of their chains, taking the scene in calmly through narrowed eyes, and marking out their territory on every ute wheel and fence post.

The young dogs, the ones that their bosses had high hopes for, were in a frenzy of delight. They were beside themselves with joy that all these people and children with ice-creams had gathered to entertain them. They would drag their red-faced owners from one child to another, getting pats and giving licks, and ignoring all calls for reason.

When the competition finally got underway, the dogs and owners assembled up one end of the ground, near the top yard. The judge stood in a tyre on the ground in the middle of the paddock so he could observe every movement of the competing dogs. Timekeepers and other officials went to their allocated spots.

The whistle blew and out came old Bluey. This efficient old dog only had eyes for his sheep and ears for his master. With head down and rump in the air, he coerced his jumpy wethers down through the race and dispatched them through the gates in a display that was slick, quick and looked boringly simple. What followed made Bluey's effort seem even more masterful. Out came Susie. She hadn't had a lot of experience, and she was terribly excited about being there at all.

She wriggled and squirmed at the end of her lead. She rolled and jumped on her boss's legs. The whistle blew. The sheep were let out and Susie's lead was unclipped. With great speed, she flew at the sheep and barked wildly. They scattered like sparks off a wheel, and then ran in blind terror.

Now the fence alongside the paddock was pretty good as far as some farm fences go. It wasn't made, however, to cope with the force of a mob of heavy sheep galloping full tilt. Susie, ignoring her furious master's commands, was having a great time. Her sheep hit the fence. Its slack wires parted and Susie's mob galloped to freedom down the road and towards the shopping centre.

This unanticipated entertainment was greatly enjoyed by the onlookers, some of whom raced down the road after the sheep. Susie was eliminated and her owner, trying to laugh off the humiliation, took himself to the bar.

The next contestant, a cool-headed brown kelpie, looked as though he'd be a bit dull after the sprightly Susie. He was giving a faultless display, but suddenly he lost concentration. His owner whistled, and whistled again. The kelpie—Mick was his name—put his nose on the ground and started following some scented trail through the grass.

Now the rules for the competition stated that no bad language could be used. Owners could help their dogs control the sheep, could speak and whistle as much as they liked, but they were not allowed to swear or lose their tempers. Mick's owner, a popular bloke who had been laying bets that Mick would finish in the first three places, was having a hell of a battle. He shouted, he roared, he hit the side of his leg with a stick—but Mick was entranced. The mirth of the crowd around the barriers made the poor man even more red-faced and furious.

Mick found the source of the aroma. It was a chop from the barbecue that someone had dropped. Mick grabbed it and lay down in the grass with it between his paws to deal with it. Striding up behind him, Mick's boss shoved the dog with his boot. But Mick wouldn't be moved. He finished his chop, got up, had a pee against a post, and then trotted back to the sheep to finish his test. The owner was furious and even more so when rumours circulated the ground that the chop had been put there by one of his rivals.

One by one, the dogs tackled the course. When another mob of sheep was driven through the fence—but this time, the fence leading into the schoolyard—the organisers realised there were easier ways to raise money. Having ten crazed wethers dashing through sweet and cake stalls, frightening the ponies giving rides, and hurtling through the plant stall doesn't do a lot for the reputations of the local dogs.

The day did end with three proficient, sensible dogs scoring the ribbons—but the dogs everyone remembered were the idiots, the enthusiasts and the disobedient.

The following year, no-one felt like staging another competition. We had a dunking pool instead.

THE TRAVELLING MUSICIAN

Fay Story, Tumby Bay

After a year working sheep at the farm where my son Tim worked, Bomber came to live with us. Tim had got a job in a town.

He was a black and white dog which Dad often threatened to shoot because he was always found sitting in the car's driver-seat. This habit of his was perhaps our first indication of Bomber's love of travel.

Not having sheep on our small farm, Bomber became a pig dog who was expert at finding the boar in each paddock of dry sows.

In the last term of our youngest son Keith's school life, Bomber started school. This began one day when the school bus was travelling homewards. The bus was rounding a corner when Keith saw him and asked the driver if he could pick him up.

Quite often after that, Bomber would be found waiting at the door of the bus when the final siren rang. He would walk into town just so he could get a bus ride home. The other pupils on the school bus loved Bomber and he loved the attention.

The feat of actually finding the right bus was in itself remarkable as there were five which delivered pupils in many different directions from Tumby Bay. On only one day did he make a mistake. A teacher found him sitting in the wrong bus and told Keith.

One day, Keith left school early to play the Last Post at a funeral. We arrived home just prior to the arrival of the school bus at the gate. Instead of going straight past, it drew to a halt. The door opened and out hopped Bomber. He turned around, wagged his tail to say 'thank you' to the driver and trotted home. He looked at us as if to say, 'Well, here I am. Where were you?'

Living only a few kilometres from the sea, we often go swimming. Bomber also loves the sea and on hot days sometimes goes off on his own, returning home in the evening tired and salt-encrusted.

One afternoon, our son was out in the boat fishing off a reef. He spotted a black head swimming towards him. It was Bomber, who was duly heaved over the side to spend the rest of the day in the boat.

When my husband worked at the local hardware store, Bomber would often arrive at the farm utility just prior to lunch, having had a swim, and being ready for a ride home.

You will be thinking that this dog should have been tied up more often. He often was, but if he looked as if he was in the mood to sleep on the mat at the back door, I would weaken and let him off the chain. When I turned my back, he would be gone.

Many times, I've driven into town and gone straight to the jetty to find Bomber. He would have had his swim, and at my call, he would bound into the vehicle and smile at me as if to say, 'Thanks for getting me.'

But while Bomber was something of a traveller, he was certainly no musician. We have a family of five and all are musical so we formed an old style dance band. During practice sessions at home, when the trumpet hit a certain key, Bomber would lift his head and howl, doing his best to accompany the player. He certainly was not in tune, though.

One quiet evening, when I was attempting to tape the Last Post for an RSL dinner, my son would get to a certain place in the music and Bomber would join in. This came out quite clearly on the tape. We eventually recorded the piece inside and Bomber was not on the final tape.

TUCKER-TIME
Mrs AM Turnbull, Cleve

Biddy was my father's dog, a border collie.

One day, when my father was riding near the boundary fence, he saw two sheep just inside the neighbour's paddock. One was ours and one the neighbour's. My father sent Biddy around these sheep, but they disappeared up the gully and out of sight over the ridge.

After a considerable length of time, Biddy returned. She had one sheep with her. It was the one with our brand.

Another day, this clever dog was in the laundry and she was trying to attract our attention. She was jumping up at the butcher's knives and killing-gear hanging up in there.

When my father followed her outside, she had all the ration sheep yarded.

She must have thought it was time to have some fresh meat.

THE THIEF

Stuart Clements, Kimba

Our large, yellow dog called Tiger has one fault. He is a thief.

We keep meat in the workshop in a fridge, but the plastic bags of meat started disappearing. I blamed my wife for giving too much meat to the dogs, and she blamed me.

One morning, however, the workshop door was left open and we became suspicious. We decided to keep watch, and, before long, Tiger came out with a bag of meat.

On investigation, we found the fridge door shut. He also used to get bags of meat out of the freezer at the top of the fridge.

Apart from that one time, he always closed the workshop door behind him.

A LITTLE LEG-LIFTING

Mike Hayes

At dog shows, they sometimes have a 'Dog Most Like Its Owner' category. It goes hand-in-hand with the Man's Best Friend Philosophy of dog-owning. Basically, without dogs, humans'd be . . . well, just humans. This yarn outlines another memorable collision between the human and canine universes. The bare bones of the yarn come initially from that inveterate tale-teller, Matt Crowe, whose memorable wine bar in the little village of Gundaroo, New South Wales, has been mentioned in my despatches before. Like most of Matt's yarns, I can't vouch for every detail. All I can say is that the people involved exist and if things didn't actually happen this way—they should have.

I reckon there are two things in life which come under the heading 'A Total Bloody Waste of Time' and that's politics and trying to work out which breed of sheepdog's the best! Looking back, if a bloke had to pick one particularly wasted afternoon out of an otherwise fruitful existence, it'd have to be that Election Day down the Dag Butterers' Arms. No, I can't quite remember which year it was, but it was quite a few Momentous Democratic Decisions ago.

Elections—whether they be Federal, State, Local Council or even Pastures Protection Board—tend to follow a seemingly ageless pattern in the bush. I don't mean the outcomes although, God knows, they always seem to be fairly predictable. What I mean is more the time-honoured drama that unfolds as the locals drift in to cast their votes.

For instance, back in those days, you could bet your boots the Back Creek brothers'd be the first into town to vote. Just like every bush town usually has a 'back creek' and therefore a Back Creek Road, they probably all have an equivalent of the Back Creek Brothers. What probably set our two apart from the rest is that you'd only ever see Vin and Doug in town together on polling days. Doug you'd rarely see in town at all.

They reckon he had a crook back from a lifetime of toiling away in shearing sheds or along fence lines, and couldn't work anymore. Like a lot of bushmen, he was scared stiff of doctors and hospitals and never did much about his back apart from half a lifetime of intensive Penfold's Therapy—trying to kill the agony with frequent applications of fortified wine. In between flagons, he kept to his bed for weeks on end. That's why it was always an experience to see him on Election Day. It wasn't an experience you'd quickly forget, either.

Vin, on the other hand, would breeze into town from their little slab shanty every few days to check their box at the post office and maybe pick up one or two essential domestic items such as food. According to local legend, on each trip Vin would stock up their larder with two meat pies.

'He takes 'em home, cuts 'em into four and they have a quarter each, once a day. That does 'em for tucker,' my informant (usually grossly unreliable) swears. It may or may not have been true. Both brothers looked like they hung from coat-hangers, rather than walked, so perhaps that's all they needed to keep them going.

Vin and Doug were drunks of the old school. Remember back in the old days, before people who indulged in a bit of excess kidney-flushing were said to have had Alcohol Related Problems? Drunks were just drunks—somewhat larger-than-life bods most notable, in small country towns after closing time, for being able to walk sideways while wheeling

60

a bicycle. Drunks also used to sing a lot. Vin and Doug still did, especially on Election Day.

Drunks also used to argue. Vin and Doug still did, even more so on Election Day. Between them they exercised what you'd call Division of Labour. Vin performed the vocals, Doug starred in debating. Doug was what you'd call a Bar Clearer. He could involve a total stranger in a passionate argument on the most obscure subjects and within minutes have everyone else in the place hurriedly gulping down their port and lemonades and suddenly finding excuses to leave early. And that's how it went on that Election Day back in 19 . . . whenever it was.

About mid-morning, when most other early voters had been driven home by Doug's invective, poor old Harvey Drench came barrelling along in his old ute, with a team of motley sheepdogs, some of them vaguely resembling kelpies, chortling in the back. Harvey had been up to the school to vote and, like all other civic-minded electors, had called in for a quiet heart-starter before going about his normal, more productive business. (Harvey was in fact a chicken sexer and part-time crutcher . . . both pursuits eminently more worthwhile than voting).

It must have been the unseasonably warm weather, or something, but unlike the other early starters, Harvey was silly enough to actually become involved in conversation with Doug. Vin, just for the record, was sitting innocently on a stool under the hookey board, quietly crooning old half-remembered Tex Morton ballads to himself. Using hindsight, I suppose the subject under discussion would have been pretty predictable, considering the mutts bouncing about in the stock crate of Harvey's ute, harmonising closely with Vin's warbling.

'They're noisy bloody dogs, you've got there,' Doug observed belligerently.

'Aww! They're just itchin' to get going. We've got to move a big mob of sheep for a bloke up at Starpost,' replied Harvey, enjoying the first caress of Stone's Green Ginger Wine around his tonsils too much to realise that he'd taken a bait.

'Some of them look like kelpies,' Doug continued, closing one eye to focus a little better. He was obviously still feeling, not quite believing, his good luck in actually nuking someone prepared to discuss the subject further with him.

'Yup. Most of them blokes are out of that little red bitch there. Bought her up in Armidale. Best bloody working dogs in the world.'

Doug knew which line of attack he should take now! His reaction to Harvey's claim about his kelpies produced a look like the one Doug could well deliver if someone had spat into his glass. Off they went.

Doug suddenly developed an intense hatred of kelpies and started waxing lyrical about all their aberrations . . . which basically added up to the fact that they weren't worth a pinch of what-he-said compared with his own personal collection of prize collies.

Like I said, Harvey's brain mustn't have been functioning properly, because he waded in and decided to defend his mutts. A few other voters who'd stopped by began to deliver their excuses most emphatically and moved towards the door.

'See ya later. Gotta take the kids to footie.'

'I'll see youse blokes around. The Missus'll be worrying where I am.'

'I'll be goin' too, fellers. Me mother-in-law's coming to visit and I'd like to be there to greet her.'

Although Jeff behind the bar looked as if he, too, would like nothing better than to go and greet his mother-in-law—or anyone else's for that matter—he abided by the ethics of his noble, self-sacrificing profession and chose to stay on and keep Doug and Harvey's glasses brimming, just in case they suddenly dehydrated. Over under the hookey board, Vin changed from Tex Morton to Buddy Williams with the vocal dexterity of a 'Julio Inglese'.

It went on all day. Voters came, drank briefly and fled, but still the argument continued.

'Bloody kelpies. They're gutless. A kelpie won't take on a big wether. They just drop to their bloody bellies and cringe.'

'Bull! A bloody collie just gives up and pisses off. And they get nasty when they get older. You find a sheep killer and you can bet it's a flamin' collie that don't know the difference between that and honest work.'

'Honest work? On a hot day, a bloody kelpie's just as likely to leave you halfway across the paddock and go for a swim in a bloody water trough.'

By late afternoon, even Jeff the publican was starting to flag. He sat in a corner, just ticking up the tab as the two contenders helped themselves from a bottle on the bar. After a Violet Crumble Bar health lunch, old Vinnie had abandoned his repertoire of Chad Morgan favourites and had dropped off.

There must have been a sudden wind change, or something, because all of a sudden, Harvey, who wasn't exactly spot-on in the sobriety stakes by then, suddenly seemed to come to his senses. While Doug spouted more anti-kelpie abuse to a couple more incautious souls who'd ventured into the bar, Harvey suddenly placed his glass firmly on the counter and tottered out to his ute where even his dogs, uncharacteristically quiet, showed signs of mental exhaustion. Rummaging around under the driver's seat, he careened back in, carrying a tiny red kelpie pup, about six weeks old.

'Here, Doug,' he intoned slowly and deliberately, 'I've heard so much balderdash from you on how bloody good your collies are, I reckon it's time you put your money where your mouth is. Take this pup—it's out of me good bitch—and bring it up like you do your precious collies. Feed it, train it and then see how it turns out. If it isn't ten times better than your dogs, I'll go He.'

Harvey's surprisingly generous gesture apparently struck a chord with Doug. Gently taking the pup from his opponent, he cradled it in his gnarled hands and actually started snivelling.

'Jesus. That's a decent thing to do, Drenchy. You're a reasonable sort of bloke—apart from your poor taste in dogs.'

And off they went again, hammer and tongs, Harvey defending his bitch's honour and Doug vitriolically predicting how useless the pup would be, despite the prospect of it enjoying the most expert training available in the land. He needed both hands to gesticulate and threaten violence with (not to mention emptying the occasional glass down the throat), so he stuffed the dozy little pup down his flannel singlet. After a couple of minutes the little bloke stopped wriggling and complaining and dropped off to sleep in the cosy warmth just above Doug's spare tyre.

Now, those of you who've taken a cold drink or two on festive occasions will be aware that prolonged sessions tend to put something of a strain on one's renal system. That certainly proved the case with Doug who suddenly felt an urgent need to empty his bladder.

'Hang on,' he belched to Harvey. 'I'll be back in a sec. I just wanna go out for a quick slash.'

For a waste disposal system as abused as Doug's, the hike out the back to the Gents' had always been a fairly ambitious project. Being an old hand at such personal crises, Doug knew better than to attempt it. There was hardly anyone around at that late hour (it was almost dark), so he floated out the front door onto the verandah for a quick piddle into the deserted main street.

Breathing in great lungfuls of fresh air as though close to nine hours of steady wading through four or five bottles of Mind Stealer had made him forget what it was like, Doug looked blearily at the distant hills, unzipped his fly and prepared to do what he had to do.

Engrossed in drinking in the wonders of the evening (while trying hard to maintain his equilibrium), he pulled out one of the forgotten pup's front legs and eased the strain on his bladder. Naturally, it wasn't too long before he started feeling distinctly uncomfortable. The discomfort became so intense that Doug was moved to look down to investigate its source.

It must have given him the shock of his life. A minute or two later, a pale-faced Doug came back into the bar, stone cold sober. He didn't say much, just something about growing claws in a funny place. And he didn't finish his drink. He just pushed his glass towards Jeff, gently shook Vin awake and helped him out into the dusk towards some spot further along the main street where they'd tethered their ute earlier in the day. It took a while for the full story to filter through to the rest of us.

'I bet that'll put the old bugger off the grog once and for all,' someone observed.

But it didn't, you know. He just gave up voting.

THE CAMP PIE TIN
J Woolford, Murray Town

My cousin offered me a brown kelpie named Peter. When I asked if he was any good, my cousin said, 'Too right! Whenever we throw out a camp pie tin, he goes out and rounds up the sheep.'

I hope the younger generations know what camp pie is. It was the greatest stand-by in the cupboard before refrigeration. We used it when-ever there was no fresh meat. The dog was very good, and gave me many years of service.

PART 5
ALL IN THE LINE OF DUTY

They won't just stick to sheep work either. They'll round up chooks, do a spot of nursing, ringbark trees, save humans, face the terrors of motorbikes and storms, not to mention getting shot on the job . . . all in the line of duty.

SUNDAY SINNER
Mike Hayes

It's a sad fact of life that working dogs, once described to me by an old-timer as the 'greatest source of free labour we've got', don't really spend an idyllic lifetime loping in slow motion through the long grass on sun-drenched fields. Out bush a great many of them lead miserable existences. The old tropical saying 'A dog, a woman, a mango tree—the more you beat them, the better they be' is adhered to far too strongly throughout rural Australia.

Oh sure, it's rarely deliberate, malicious cruelty. As far as the dogs go, it's more an odd philosophy declaring that if you treat your four-legged work-mates too kindly, they'll go soft on you. The blokes who spout it will usually be, as they speak, fondling a tubby, wriggling puppy in their gnarled hands. If you regard the bushman's relationship with his dog as a working partnership, their often brutal attitude can perhaps be explained, but not necessarily excused, by recognising that bush life is just as hard on people as it is on dogs.

If anyone's aware of the place they personally hold in Australia's heritage, it's the people up in the Snowy Mountains. It hasn't been easy to hang onto it, either. In the late 1960s, the mountain people lost what they regarded as their inalienable right—ready access to the spectacular high country where they'd grazed their herds for generations. The legislation and official restrictions which accompanied the creation of the Kosciusko National Park not only prevented them taking their stock up there any more—it physically cut them off from the places they felt set them apart from the lesser mortals of the flat country. Those soul-stirring high plains had been as much a part of their being as the genes they inherited from the hardy pioneers who first trickled into the area in the 1840s and dotted the flats with their slab and bark huts, hoping to shelter their tough families from the savage blizzards that whip the mountains between April and October.

These days the mountain people grumble bitterly about losing the right to ride freely into the high country to lose themselves in its magic like they did in the old days. They'll mutter grimly about not being able to fatten their stock anymore in the fragile environment of the mountain pastures: 'We were up there for yonks. If anyone knows how to protect the flamin' environment, it's us!'

But deep down, you get the feeling that aspect doesn't worry them a fraction as much as just not being able to wander at will in the secluded places they once called their own. If they really wanted to go back up there, they could, although they'd have to swap the rolled swags, elastic-sided boots and stocky mountain ponies of old for backpacks, sneakers and ideologically sound bicycles. They don't bother.

The mountain people these days have accepted that stock work is no longer the honest livelihood it once was. Relatively few still farm seriously or profitably. Instead, you find the descendants of one branch of a pioneering family negotiating real estate deals with trendy yuppies anxious for a toehold close to the snowfields. Young people jangle cash registers in local supermarkets, peer from behind bank counters or pursue their studies in far-off Sydney. Only a dwindling number of old-timers still cling to the pioneer style of living. You reach their modest fibro homesteads along winding, rutted roads, shuttered off from the outside world by hard-to-open, twisted steel gates.

They've not changed. Nor have their dogs. As is the case throughout the bush, the first sign of life the visitor encounters is the assortment of canine workers bouncing enthusiastically at the end of their chains in front of their oil drum and hollow log kennels scattered around the higher points of the home paddock out of flood reach. The mountain people always let their dogs have their say before emerging from their own kennels, leaning cautiously on their gates until they work out who the hell you are.

Like their owners, a lot of the old dogs have seen better days. Most are in semi-retirement, let off occasionally to help round up the killers or maybe being allowed to pile squabbling into the back of the ute to check the pregnant ewes somewhere up the back paddock. They're kept more out of habit than for any firm husbandry reason.

Like all bushmen, the old mountain stockmen talk tough about their dogs: 'What that useless bugger needs is half an ounce of lead—fair between the eyes!' But all of them seem to hang onto old mates and not entirely for sentimental reasons. Those old dogs, like the clapped-out old nags dozing under the willows along the creek, are living reminders of another, freer, wilder time.

'First thing I do in the morning is come out here and check under the tank to see if old Caesar's still with us,' rumbles the old-timer, limping painfully over to the stand and squinting into the gloom. Caesar, bony and proppy in the rear, stiff with arthritis, his ears patchy and misshapen and his frosted muzzle grizzled and moist like his owner's, staggers out, his skinny tail moving ever so slightly and his eyes bleary in the sudden light.

'Shoulda put him down years ago. Just couldn't bring meself to do it.'

A cross bred pup appears from nowhere and bulldozes its way through our legs to bounce cheekily in front of Caesar. The old dog barely moves, but dispatches the upstart with a low, bubbly snarl and promise of a nip. The bewildered pup, glancing fearfully over his shoulder, scoots back to the safety of the sheds, his feelings badly wounded. Caesar creeps back to the comfort of his wheatbags under the tank stand.

'Funny thing about a real good dog like Caesar,' observes his owner, 'none of his offspring were ever any good. Mad as cut snakes.'

By the time we make off for the house, Caesar's head's on his paws again and he's drifted away, back to the dreamy days when he could shoot like an arrow across a paddock, turn a thundering mob and slot them neatly into any yards you'd nominate.

'I just let him keep going. So long as he's not in too much pain, I'll just let him be,' explains the boss, almost apologetically. 'Y'know, on a warm day, he'll still do his rounds. He checks all his favourite spots round the sheds and up the hill. Only difference these days is that it takes him all day to do it. And he sleeps for the next three to recover.'

Caesar actually represents the old bloke's own mortality. You can't escape the impression that the morning he checks under the tank and finds the old dog still and stiff in the frost, he'll turn around and seriously consider packing it in himself. But for now, Caesar and the other dogs are still part of his well-established lifestyle. Perhaps in the Jindabyne pub, or around the relative sophistication of a barbecue fire at a local property, he and the other old-timers will continue to swap stories about the dogs— good and bad—they've all owned at one time or another.

'You know what it's like,' Lanky Cauldron once explained, 'you get into a session like that and soon it's one bloke shouts a round . . . another bloke tells his dog yarns.

'A mob of them were stuck one night like that down at the Snow Goose in Adaminaby. It was Dan Trembath's turn to shout and fate gave Lew Fletcher a turn at spinning a dog story.

The only thing Lew and I agreed about was that I'd never been able to breed a decent dog myself,' Lanky recalled morosely. 'I never really knew whether his had been good or bad.'

Lew, on the other hand, had few qualms about the excellence of his personal mutts. To make his point, he started reminiscing about the time just about every able-bodied bloke in the mountains had headed up to Snowy Plain for the annual pre-winter muster. They pressed their luck a bit. They'd mustered most of the sheep—about 5000 of them—but still had another 800 to go, when the weather closed in. The ominous sky, which had been darkening all afternoon, seemed to lower over the alps. It would snow like buggery once it got dark. You could almost hear the temperature drop. There wasn't much wind at first. In fact, when the first snowflakes started to dance in front of the stockmen's eyes, conditions were deceptively calm. The musterers huddled inside the hut for a quick conference. It'd be too easy to get caught if a fully-blown blizzard moved in.

After they got together in the hut it didn't take long for the wind to join in the game and the flakes were soon hissing evilly against the draughty walls. It was then, according to his own account, that Lew came up with the perfect solution.

'I told them I had a bloody good dog with me and if they hung around and concentrated on finding the missing 800, I'd pick up the bulk of the mob and move them down the mountain out of the snow to the stock reserve. Me and that dog kept 'em together nicely. In fact, once we'd moved them off the mountain, things weren't too bad.'

It's like that in the high country. A blizzard can be snarling away at the top, but lower down it's mild and calm. Lew continued his saga while, over at the bar, Dan haggled with the barman about his change.

'It turned out to be a lovely, clear, moonlit night. In fact, it was so bright that after the dog and I got them to the reserve, we had enough light to count the mob. And guess what? They were all there.'

Dan juggled the round over and plonked the glasses onto the little table in front of the troops.

'Yep!' clucked Lew, taking a generous pull on his fresh beer, 'he was one hell of a dog.'

Solemnly, Dan raised his own glass and bellowed to the throng, 'Here's to Lew. From now on his name's changed. After a claim like that, Fletcher is officially known as Stretcher.'

And what about the mountain dogs who were so good in the yards, they could even do up the gates?

'You've heard the yarn, haven't you?' asked Lanky Cauldron, 'about the bloke who reckoned his dog was so smart that he could pen a mob of sheep, push the hurdle gate shut himself and even jump up and put in the little wooden peg to keep it shut? The only problem was that those little pegs had a habit of fallin' out and if that happened, the bloody sheep'd get out.'

Some other bloke, who'd been listening all night without saying much, suddenly snorted with contempt.

'Piss weak. Don'cha know anything? Round our way, we train dogs properly. Once they get the sheep in and the gate shut, they piddle on the little pegs, wait for the moisture to swell the wood, then they put the bloody things in. That way, they never bloody well fall out!'

But there were dogs whose ability no mountain man would ever question. Such a toiler was old Tom McGufficke's Sunday. His feats were frequently discussed, from back in the days when stockmen roasted their backs and fronts alternately against a roaring fire of twisted snowgum limbs, yarning away the long autumn evenings at the mustering camps. Nowadays, Sunday's name is more likely to come up when the remnants of that same dashing band of riders reminisce quietly around a similar blaze in someone's Saturday night backyard, where the flickering flames allow them to relive those older, wilder times and where, for a moment at least, the ever-encroaching outside world stays hidden away in the darkness.

'Remember that time old Tom and some of the blokes got caught by the rain on their way to Corryong?'

McGufficke and the others were performing an annual chore, moving a big mob from the New South Wales side across the mountains and the Murray to Victoria. They'd moved most of the herd across the river when the weather broke. With the worst of the trip behind them, the mountain men might have been expected to shrug it off and continue on the relatively short leg to Corryong, but all of them were aware that some of the mob weren't accounted for.

The river, fed by the runoff from a whole night of rain, rose quickly, then leaked out a thousand brown fingers across the flats. Daylight showed their instincts had been right. In the middle of the rushing flood, a sorry band of cattle could be made out stranded on a temporary island a couple of hundred yards from the main mob. Tom McGufficke decided it was indeed a job for Sunday.

He didn't need to explain too much to the dog. Sunday threw himself enthusiastically into the torrent and was soon reduced to a small black dot, heading determinedly across the muddy ocean. Eventually he pulled himself from the water on the island, paused for a few seconds to shake the excess from his coat and then hurtled forward to do the job required. The cattle didn't argue with Sunday. He soon coaxed them into the floodwaters, then plunged in behind them and didn't let up until he'd headed them in the right direction, straight over to the Victorian side. As the exhausted cattle finally dragged themselves to safety, they were expertly picked up by a couple of the stockmen and driven over to where the rest of the mob waited in the drizzle.

'Hey, Tom,' someone called. 'Where's Sunday? Is he with you?'

McGufficke checked quickly around him, but there was no dark shadow trotting quietly behind him. A wider check showed no dark form resting awhile in the shelter of the river gums. A few more hurried checks with the other drovers and it soon became apparent that Sunday was no longer with them.

The cattle had started moving off southwards of their own accord and the stockmen couldn't hang around for long. They dallied as long as they dared, all of them avoiding the boss's gaze as they looked in vain for some sign of their brave little mate.

'Well, that's it then,' McGufficke sighed finally. 'The poor bugger's gone down in the line of duty.'

'He was a pretty good dog, though,' someone muttered before they all wheeled their mounts and took up their positions for the last leg of the drive.

It took a few more days to get rid of the mob in Corryong and spend some time propping up a bar or two, swapping a few yarns with mates they hadn't sighted since last year, before the mountain men turned their horses' heads towards home. It wasn't too long, however, before word got around that old Tom had received the surprise of his life when he leant

71

from his saddle to open the last gate into Leesville—and was greeted with great familiarity by Sunday.

'Jesus, Tom, you musta been glad to see him. What did'ja do?' someone asked him when he recounted the incident later in the old Jindabyne pub.

'I gave the old bastard the biggest hiding of his life,' Tom muttered. 'That'll teach him to bloody well leave me like that.'

As Lanky philosophised: 'It didn't matter that old Sunday had swum the flooded Murray and crossed the alps just to get home. You expect that from a good dog. But you never expect him to shoot through on you.'

A BIT OF A SHOW-OFF
Max Nitschke, Keith

Most dogs work for just one master. If anyone else tries to reproduce the commands they know, or tries to give them a task, they usually react with disdain—and go off and lie under a tree. Sometimes, they'll just be confused and not understand what it is that another is trying to tell them to do. So it's an unusual dog that will work for absolutely anybody.

Enter Trixie, who was used by all the neighbours in the Marcollat district in the south-east of South Australia whenever they had something their own dogs couldn't handle. At lamb-marking time, she was particularly sought after. Lambs are difficult to control because they tend to run blindly in all directions. It takes a special kind of dog to keep calm with lambs and not rush them. So they called in Trixie.

But she was good with everything. In fact she was a bit of a show-off. At shearing time, when all the sheep were penned up and she didn't have anything to do, she would come down to the house and work on the white rooster. Whether, because of his colour, she thought he needed shearing too, no-one knows. But she would separate him from the hens and nose him right up to the shearing shed, then inside the door—much to his displeasure. The old rooster would be cackling with annoyance and the shearers and everyone in the shed would laugh.

This dog would not only work anything on the ground, she was also a good retriever in the water at duck-shooting time. She'd swim out, half stand up in the water to get her bearings, then grab the duck. If it was still alive and it dived, she'd go underwater after it, then swim back with it in her mouth and drop it at my feet. She was better than any Labrador.

She'd also do her sheep work under remote control. I could stand here on the front verandah and send her out to the far paddock to bring in a mob. She'd go out in the direction I pointed, then at a certain distance look back for further instructions. If she couldn't see me clearly, she'd stand up on her hind legs for a better view. If she still couldn't see my hand signals clearly, I'd use a long stick. Whichever side I was pointing to, she'd go until she found the mob and brought them right back in.

I also used to start her off with a mob of ewes and lambs that I was sending to market. They'd be in a paddock about two miles from the yards, and they are really slow to move because the lambs get separated from their mothers and the mothers fuss around. Anyway, it would get to smoko time, and I'd feel like a cuppa, so I'd leave Trixie to carry on alone. When I got back to her, she'd still have every sheep and would be a good half mile closer to the yards. She would never leave any behind because she would only go the pace of the slowest sheep. Too many dogs will push them and make them scatter.

Trixie was a border collie, and I must have had her thirteen or fourteen years. I've had kelpies, but I always reckon border collies have a few more brains. I didn't have to teach her anything. It was sort of born in her. She started work when she was three months old, and was nearly a professional straight away. As a pup, she worked like an old dog, and she was just as good in the yards as she was in the paddock.

I really missed Trixie when she was gone. You only get about three good dogs in a lifetime. She was gentle and good with kids, but tough. With her son, she'd kill kangaroos when it was time to stock up on dogs' meat. They'd jump off the ute when we came across a big scrubber. Those big scrubbers don't run very far—only about 100 yards and then they sit up—but they'll fight. Those two dogs would catch them and kill them every time, and never get hurt.

They worked as a team. One would goad him in front, and the other would go and give him a bite on the bum. When he was turning around, the other would go in and give him a bite. This would go on for a fair while, then when they got tired, they'd lie down in a pool of water for ten minutes and have a good spell.

Then they'd both get up and start working on the roo again, until eventually the old kangaroo would tip over. Then they'd go and give him a bite in the throat. Yet they were never dogs that would hurt sheep. In those early days, there were plenty of kangaroos, and you fed your dogs on them.

I reckon those days were especially good for dogs. It was fairly wet here and you couldn't get out in a vehicle. If you wanted a mob of sheep in, you walked. While you walked, you could train a dog and the dog could hear everything you said. Since I've had motorbikes, I've had nowhere near as good dogs. Bikes are so noisy and we rush and tear around with the dogs on the back yapping and barking. I miss old Trix, and those days.

DOWN THE BLOWHOLE
DC McCracken, Elliston

My late uncle once owned, amongst his various sheepdogs, a small black and grey bitch named Winnie.

Winnie was absolutely sheep-obsessed. She would become excited at the mere mention of the animals.

On one occasion, when mustering with her master, who was on horseback, she came back to him in a very agitated state. She indicated that she wanted him to follow her.

He eventually did and she led him some distance away to a limestone blowhole several feet deep. Down it was a sheep. The sheep was rescued unharmed and Winnie returned to her mustering duties with an air of self-satisfaction and relief.

THE FOX HUNTER

Joy Nunan, Port Pirie

My story is over thirty-five years old. We were living on a mixed farm and my father used to breed fat lambs for export. The foxes were bad. They tortured and killed many baby lambs. To combat them, he used to poison them and go spotlighting.

One day, a young dog came to our place. We were unable to find his owner, so he stayed. Quite a good worker he was too. He also loved spotlighting and became excited as soon as we picked up the gun.

The problem with him, though, was once a fox was sighted, we were unable to keep him on the truck with us. We lost several of the distant foxes that he was unable to run down. He would jump on top of the near ones and roll over. My father would have to shoot the fox as it lay under the dog. After the fox had been shot, the proud laugh on the face of that dog was a sight to behold.

Knowing the law of averages, however, my father realised the dog would have to stay home. He was tied up on a hefty farm chain. The next time we went shooting, it was without Mickey and consequently there was not quite the usual amount of excitement.

We duly rounded up our fox. Believing Mickey was safely at home at the end of his chain, my father pulled the trigger.

I don't remember what happened to the fox, but it seems Mickey had broken the chain and was just outside the spotlight. He collected some of the shot in his front leg.

These days, he could have been saved, but thirty-five years ago, I do not know if the expertise was available. Even so, there was not enough money available to take 'just a dog' to the vet. So, a few days later, to relieve his suffering, Dad shot him. We were all very sad and missed him terribly. I guess it must have hurt my father the most as that was the second time that he had had to put down his favourite dog.

THE CASANOVA CHAINSAW

Mike Hill, Cape Jervis

We were short of dogs on the farm in 1966, so for $40 I bought Ringo and a bitch from Cec O'Leary, one of the local characters. Cec's parting words to me when I collected the dogs were, 'If ever you want to get sheep out of a gully, say to Ringo "Go get 'em". Then he'll run to the nearest tree, jump up and grab a low-hanging limb with his teeth, swing in the air and make funny howling noises. The sheep will then get out of the gully.'

Cec was a good yarn-spinner, so I laughed and told him to pull the other leg.

Anyway, one day I had a pile of sheep that I had to get out of a particularly steep gully. I had been trying to move them for a while with no success. I remembered Cec's words. When I checked no-one was looking, I gave the command. 'Go, get 'em, Ringo'.

Sure enough, to my open-mouthed surprise, Ringo ran up to the nearest tree, grabbed hold of a branch and swung there, letting out blood-curdling noises. The sheep were so terrified, they bolted out of the gully.

Because no-one ever believed me when I later told this story, we have recorded Ringo doing his trapeze act on film. Apart from that one peculiar working method, Ringo was a perfectly normal dog. A big border collie cross with longish hair, he was in fact a very good worker.

However, he had a couple of personal habits which I suppose could be called faults. He loved wood. The tree-swinging trick was, I suppose, a part of this affinity with wood, but it went further than that. He had a compulsive desire to ringbark trees. Whenever he had a spare minute, he'd be out in the paddock stripping bark off trees from the ground to as high as he could reach. He loved the stringy-barks and would pull great long strips off. It was a common sight to see him hard at work, being urged on by two of his favourite bitches barking excitedly. You could always tell where he'd been by the piles of bark at the base of every tree. He killed hundreds of trees, something I'm not the slightest bit proud of. This environmentally-damaging habit caused him to be banned from nearly every farm in the district.

Ringo even ate the whole front out of his kennel, so that the roof collapsed. After that, he used to lie on the roof. He completely wore his teeth out. They were just tiny white stumps by the end of his life.

All of his pups, and there were an awful lot of them in the district, but I'm coming to that, had the same destructive habit. People put up with them, though, because they were excellent workers. But it did get to the stage where we ran out of homes for the pups. So we used to take them to pet shops in the city. One day, not long after having delivered a litter, I was listening to a talkback programme on the radio. An irate woman came on. She said she had just bought a pup from a city pet shop.

'People should vet these dogs,' she said. 'My pup's just ringbarked all my trees.' I suppose I shouldn't have laughed. But it had to be one of old Ringo's pups.

By now you are wondering why we allowed this renegade dog to wander the district chomping through trees and siring pups everywhere. The truth is, he was impossible to tie up. We used to tighten his collar until his eyes bulged, but he had a thick neck and smallish head in comparison, and he would just slip his collar every time. You would just finish tying him up, feeling as though you were cruel making the collar so tight, and be walking to the ute. He'd be right behind you before you had even reached the vehicle. We would lock him up in a shed, but he would chew his way through the door. He had teeth like a chainsaw.

The other undesirable characteristic of Ringo was that he was a sex maniac. We lived on the top of a range of hills which flattened out and ran down to the sea. Ringo's beat extended down to the coast, along the hills and almost to the local town—a good five miles in all directions. Within that radius, he took it upon himself to service every on-heat bitch.

Every litter of pups born during his lifetime had the unmistakable stamp of Ringo. Other male dogs would stand aside when Ringo appeared, and let him go about his business. He was so notorious as a seducer of females that farmers would lock up their bitches when they were on heat behind thick doors. This didn't worry old chainsaw Ringo. He'd be through the door in a flash.

One day a bloke rang me to say he'd caught Ringo hanging around his bitch and that he had locked him in a shed and nailed a piece of weldmesh in front of the door.

'It couldn't be Ringo,' I said. 'He's asleep on the verandah. I can see him.'

The poor bloke went to check his shed. Ringo had eaten through the door above where the weldmesh stopped—about three feet up.

I wasn't one of the most popular blokes in the district. Understandably, sheep men got pretty sick of their working bitches always being pregnant, so they'd take a gun to him. Time and time again, he came home with buckshot up his arse. That would quieten him down for a while. But after we had picked out the shot and the wounds had healed, he'd be at it again.

Eventually, he was peppered with a bit too much lead. He developed a hernia in his rear, and became too sick to go on his visits. He would lie in his hollow under the house and sleep.

Every now and again, though, we would hear a lot of barking and scuffling from Ringo's pad. We'd go down and have a look, and there would be old Ringo, hard at it. Because he was too injured to travel to his girls, they came to him. They would arrive two at a time and he would dutifully deal with them, before watching them trot off out the gate again.

He died of his injuries at the age of twelve.

A STRAY SAVIOUR
Kate Heron, Kimba

This is a true story told to me by my grandfather. The morning was calm and warm. It would be pretty hot before the day was through, the boy told his pony as he fixed the slip rails behind the cows he had just yarded.

He must hurry. His pony had to have breakfast and so did he before he rode to school. Suddenly he saw a black and white dog out on the flat. He went over towards it, calling gently, but the dog withdrew into the scrub.

The property already had three sheepdogs, so it was only to be expected that the boy's father did not greet the news of a stray dog with any enthusiasm. He merely commented that an eye would have to be kept on the sheep in case the dog got too hungry.

Two mornings later, the dog appeared again, lying half a mile away on the flat. The boy again called softly and gently to the dog. This time, the dog began to crawl towards the boy on its stomach whimpering as it came. Five yards away, it stopped. The boy didn't move. He just kept talking softly, with his hand outstretched. With a quick wriggle, the dog put its head under the outstretched hand.

That began an inseparable friendship that lasted as long as the dog. After a great deal of persuasion, the boy's father said the dog could be kept—especially after he discovered the dog would work sheep and cattle equally well. Nobody ever claimed the dog.

During the Depression years, many farmers had been forced to leave their properties and find work in other areas, such as Whyalla, then a boom town. It was later discovered that the dog's original owner was one such family, but the dog hadn't settled into city life. When he returned to his old home, he had found it deserted. Hunger and thirst had forced him to move from farm to farm only to be hunted on until he arrived at Yeltana.

The dog was named Mukksy after a murderer who killed a taxi driver, shortly before the dog did the same with several chickens. Although he was not permitted to go to school, Mukksy would set off each afternoon, regardless of the weather, to meet the boy on his way home. At thirteen, the boy left school to work at Buckleboo Station. He took the dog with him.

One day he was mustering straggler sheep with the manager when he hit the limb of a tree at full gallop and was swept from his horse. The manager did not notice the boy's disappearance until much later. It was near sunset when the dog, which until then had been keeping flies away from the boy, left.

When the dog joined Mr Miller, who had been droving the sheep they had found that day, it seemed so agitated that Mr Miller realised something was wrong. The manager hadn't seen the lad either, and they both knew the dog normally wouldn't go anywhere without him.

Mr Miller left the sheep and began to follow Mukksy who raced off in the direction of the injured boy. It was almost dark and mid-winter.

It is doubtful if the boy would have survived the night if he hadn't been found.

This boy was my grandfather—and he still loves his dogs more than his wife.

THE EYE OF THE STORM

Syd Nosworthy, Lucindale

When Ray Nosworthy set out to muster a remote property, he followed a well-established routine. He rode to the mustering hut, dropped some food and went on with his kelpie bitch, Brownie, to muster the sheep.

Having scoured the big paddock, he started the mob for the hut. The routine was to place the mob in a section of fenced laneway, string wire across the mouth and spend the night in the hut ready to resume the journey next morning.

All had gone smoothly—until mid-afternoon. Brownie gave the first indication of trouble. Like many dogs, she was afraid of storms and Ray noticed she was tending to abandon her normal role of trotting slowly at the rear of the mob. While still keeping the sheep headed in the right direction, she kept returning to the proximity of the horse.

The reason was soon apparent. The skies darkened and before long thunder could be heard. Lightning and thunder coming ever closer were obviously disturbing the dog but with the hut in sight, Ray thought he would get the mob safely in the lane.

However, the leaden skies brought on premature darkness and at the same time rain began to fall. And how it rained. Great gusts of water, cascading down, reduced visibility in short order from yards to nil. In the frequent lightning flashes, Ray saw that the sheep had broken and scattered. He could not see the dog and his calls were drowned in the wild rolls of thunder and the drumming of the pelting rain.

Abandoning the sheep, he rode to the hut expecting to find Brownie already cowering there. She wasn't. He turned his horse loose, lit the old lantern in the hut and called. There was no response. Leaving the lantern in the doorway to attract the dog's attention, he lit a roaring fire, stripped off his sodden clothes and strung them up to dry. After a meal, he still could not attract Brownie, so he reluctantly gave up and climbed into the bunk. The storm was still raging and the rain was unceasing. He was up at first light. The storm had passed but he could see in its wake great sheets of water across the flat landscape.

Saddling his horse, he could see knots of sheep on high ground in the lane. Approaching he could see that all the sheep seemed to be in the lane on the higher ground—a subsequent count revealed they were all there. His surprise did not last long. As he neared the mouth of the lane, he saw Brownie, half submerged in water, patiently watching the lane to see no sheep wandered out.

He could only marvel firstly at her skill in getting the sheep into the lane and the amazing devotion she showed to her task by spending the night in conditions she found completely terrifying. When he reached her, she could scarcely move. Shivering and stiff, she had obviously remained at her post for hours. Knowing the sheep were not likely to escape through the water, Ray picked up the dog and carried her on the saddle to the hut.

Brownie was put in front of the re-activated fire and gradually thawed out. She ate a few scraps and appeared to be ready to work. The rest of the journey was across high ground and the sheep were in their paddock by about midday.

It was soon obvious that Brownie had not escaped the ordeal unscathed. She became listless and was patently ill. Ray carried her on the saddle until they reached home where he bedded her down. She was very sick for some time, but after patient nursing, recovered. It was not a complete recovery, however.

Brownie's lungs had suffered some damage and for the rest of her life, she wheezed and coughed with almost every movement. Although she learnt to canter for short distances, Ray realised she would never be able to work in the paddocks again. She became, instead, an honoured pensioner. But she wasn't keen on idle retirement, and wasn't happy.

However, Brownie was in luck. Ray's brother, Frank, suffered from a chronic heart condition that restricted him to walking pace only. He and Brownie fitted their lives together. She could yard the killers from a small paddock and she soon learnt to bring the cows in for milking twice a day.

Perhaps her most skilful function, though, was with the chooks. Poultry in those days was still very much a luxury. Frank reared a large number of cockerels and kept the homestead, friends and relatives supplied. They were free-range buds and his problem was to catch them. Gathering the fowls with some wheat, he would lunge at the cockerel of his choice with a piece of wire.

Brownie picked up her cue at once. Circling the bird, she quickly closed on it, pushed it over with her nose, and without disturbing a feather, placed one paw on it and held it until Frank arrived to pick it up.

Hundreds of times over the years she carried out this task, without ever harming a bird.

THE RABBIT COLLECTOR
Mrs AM Cox, Carrieton

I cannot imagine life on the land without at least one or two sheepdogs about the place. Regardless of their value as workers (they are better than an extra man up in the rough country) they are really great companions. I am on my own and fairly isolated most days, so I appreciate having them sprawled on the lawn or the back doormat. This is my favourite story about a faithful worker we know.

Increasing rabbit numbers were causing concern on our property, so we spent our evenings shooting by spotlight. A friend offered his assistance which we gladly accepted as he was a good shot—an experienced fox shooter.

He arrived in his utility, which was equipped with safety bars, and also his dog—his constant companion.

After about three hours, we had reduced the rabbit population somewhat, and being frozen to the marrow, decided to return to the house for a warm-up by the fire and a hot drink. The rabbits were thrown in a heap on the back lawn to be dealt with later, and inside we went.

When we went out to farewell our friend, about an hour later, we found that his dear old dog had laboriously loaded every rabbit back onto his boss's ute—and was standing guard over them.

What a job! He had jumped down, picked up a carcass, jumped up and dropped it, then gone back down for another one. He had obviously decided that those rabbits belonged only to his boss.

AS GOOD AS ANY YARD

Dick Mills, Kanmantoo

I thought you may like to know that I once saw my cousin, Bruce Mills, bring in a mob of sheep using eight dogs together. Eight dogs! Usually one is enough trouble for the average sheepman. Bruce had his dogs bring in the sheep in order to catch one, but he did this in an open paddock, without the use of a yard.

This was no trouble for Bruce. He held the sheep against the fence with each dog sitting, evenly spaced, under perfect control in a semicircle around the sheep while he went in and caught one. The dogs were as good as any yard.

THE BANTAM'S REVENGE

Chris Collins, Meningie

Fred was my first sheepdog when I went away jackerooing. He was a sort of big, gallumphing, lumpish, black and white kelpie sheepdog—a bit clumsy, but he showed a fair bit of ingenuity right from the word go. I remember the manager at the station where I was working finally coming to me in absolute desperation one day.

'Look,' he said, 'you've got to do something about your dog. It's plucking all our chooks.'

And it was true. All the chooks were running around with no feathers on them . . . just bald chooks everywhere. They didn't like it much. They went off the lay.

He was just a pup at the time and tied up on a dog wire. He would grab the chooks as they came past, sit down with a chook between his paws and tear its feathers out. When it was suitably bald, he would put it down and look for the next one. He was quite quiet about it. He must have clamped his foot over their heads to stop them squawking. I never actually saw him doing it, but there were always feathers around his drum.

From that unpromising beginning, Fred actually went on to be a very good sheepdog. But it turned out that the chooks more or less got their revenge, through a poultry namesake in the shape of a motorbike.

Fred had come back with me to the family farm—I must have been about nineteen—and I'd bought my first motorbike. It was an old BSA Bantam and I paid thirty dollars for it. There wasn't room for a carrier on the back of it, so Fred used to sit on the petrol tank in front of me. I used to use it to go down to the other block which is about twenty miles away.

On a hot day, Fred would leap off the bike, jump into a trough and then get up in front of me. It wasn't bad—a hot day, and a wet dog in front of you. It was a bit of free airconditioning. He got to the stage, though, where he didn't like motorbikes.

I had just done the bike up and it went pretty well. We were heading down the road, with old Fred all wet and dripping, and I was enjoying the cool blast of air. But then, his wet tail sort of crept over the side of the petrol tank and headed towards the engine. It made contact with the spark plugs. We were doing about fifty miles an hour down a dirt road. Fred sort of went all stiff and arched his back and leant against me. When he did that, I got a charge too. So there we were, old Fred and me, roaring along the road, both rigid. We ground ourselves to a halt on the side of the road and fell off the bike. It took a bit of coaching to get him back on it after that. He finally did.

In the meantime, I'd decided the old, fixed-seat on the bike was a bit rough, so I made up a frame and put a spring-action seat on the bike. It was off an old German motorbike and it pivotted at the front and had a couple of springs underneath. It moved as the bike moved underneath you.

So we finally got Fred on the bike again and with the new seat we headed out over the big veldt grass clods on the place. It was a bit rough and bumpy. I didn't realise it at the time, but as the seat was rocking up and down, the little gap between the petrol tank and the seat was opening up and closing. It went from about half an inch to about two inches, and then it would close again as I hit a bump. Well, a very delicate part of Fred's anatomy rattled down between the seat and the petrol tank. I can still see Fred now, with his cods caught between the tank and the seat ... poor old Fred, he was galloping on the petrol tank, but he couldn't go anywhere until we hit the next bump, and it let him go.

I never, ever got Fred back on that bike again. He wouldn't go near it. For the rest of his life, he preferred to run.

PART 6
NINE LIVES

And they don't give up easily either. Country life can be pretty harsh and the dogs come in for their share—harsh conditions, harsh masters and terrible accidents. They seem to survive it all.

EVERY YEAR FOR THE
REST OF HIS LIFE

Don Stevens, Port Lincoln

We lived on a farm in the foothills, and Toby used to get the cows in every morning when he heard my father's alarm go off at 5 am.

In the evening, when my mother took the basket to collect the eggs, he would, without being told, again go and collect the cows.

Being in the hills, Toby used to go to the highest point and then sit, looking all over the valleys and other hills until he saw where the cows were. Then he'd bring them in at a steady walk.

On one occasion, we had arrived home in the buggy from the Clare Show, thirty miles away. It was 10 o'clock at night. Father said he wouldn't bother about milking because of the time.

Toby met us and jumped up on the hub of the front wheel to greet us, and then he went over towards the cowyard.

Dad said, 'If that old bloke has the cows in, we will have to milk them for him.'

Sure enough, he had the cows in and was lying across the gate to keep them in.

One time, my mother, who hates snakes, was killing one on the front verandah. Toby hated snakes too and always killed them if he could. Mum growled at him and told him to keep away. In the instant that Toby's eyes flashed towards Mum, the snake must have bitten him. He killed it, but Mum didn't know he had been bitten until quite a while later when she went outside and found Toby prostrate.

Father was at the neighbour's place working the team. Mother rang and told the neighbour to tell Father that Toby had been bitten by a snake and to come home.

The neighbour went out to Father, waving and yelling, 'Go home. The baby has been bitten by a snake.'

Father unyoked the team and rode home on one horse, only to find out it was Toby, not the baby.

They searched through an old doctor's book for remedies for snake bite. One was: 'Strong black coffee—as strong as possible.' Father, using a spoon got some into Toby, who was by then unconscious.

Toby did survive but at the same time of the year, each year for the rest of his life, he was affected by that snakebite. He was unable to get up in the morning without being helped.

It got so bad that Toby would be down for several days before the effects of the bite wore off. Father finally had to put him down as he was a man who did not like to see animals suffer.

THE SAMOYED BITCH
Dr Ron Baker, Yankalilla

When I was working as a vet in a Victorian country town, I knew a farming couple who had a Samoyed bitch. They had owned her for quite a few years. They were a typically tough Aussie couple, dairy farmers, who were also pretty tough on their dogs. The dogs would be chained up to their 44-gallon drum kennels, chucked a few bones at night, and if they didn't work as they were meant to do, they copped a piece of 'four by two' over the head.

The Samoyed, although the daughter of a kelpie working bitch, looked almost pure Samoyed, her father's breed. Because she was pretty, she had been kept for the children to play with. She was silvery-white, long-haired, with a typical curling tail and lovely greeny-brown eyes. Only a few black flecks in her hair indicated she was not a pure-bred. I had been treating her on and off over the years for various things and had always liked her.

One night, I had a call from Jim, the dairyman.

'I want you to have a look at my dog,' he said. He sounded quite insistent. I arranged to meet him at the clinic.

Well, I was quite shocked. This once beautiful dog was a sad and sorry sight. Her hair was falling out. She was skinny and there was pus coming out of her vulva. I diagnosed her as having an infected uterus, and could treat her only by operating and without too much delay. Jim, however, said he wanted the dog put down. He said he had never liked the dog. The children were all in the car and were in tears, but he was insistent. 'Put it down,' he said.

I told him that for $150 I would be able to cure her. 'You've got plenty of money,' I said. 'Go on, she's a lovely dog.'

But Jim left the surgery with clear instructions that I had to put the dog down. I was terribly distressed. This dog had a beautiful nature, and I just didn't want to do it. So for the next five minutes, the Samoyed and I just sat looking at each other. I had tears in my eyes and, as true as I sit here talking, she had tears welling in her eyes.

I said to this dog, 'Look, I just can't put you down.'

I rang the senior vet in the practice and explained the situation: that despite being instructed to dispose of the dog, I couldn't. I asked him if I could spend some of his money and save it, and then find it a home. Definitely not, was his answer. The only way around it was to ask the owner if I could operate, and foot the bill myself.

I rang him and put that to him. He still said, 'No. Put the dog down.'

So I got the syringe out of the cupboard and filled it with Lethobarb, the euthanasia solution, to do the job. I sat down on the floor with the dog, the syringe in my hand, and we had a chat with each other for ten minutes, trying to talk through the problem. And that dog cried. It had tears running down its cheeks and was making sobbing noises. I am sure it knew what was going on. I cried too.

Suddenly, I stood up and thought, 'Blast it! I'm in this game because I care about animals.' So, I did the operation and thought, 'To hell with the consequences.' I saved the dog.

Extraordinarily, while I was in the midst of the operation, the wife of the dairyman rang and said they had reconsidered their decision and that I could go ahead, if I could find it a home. That was a relief as I wasn't sure how I was going to face the ethical problem of having disobeyed a client's instructions.

When the Samoyed recovered, I gave her to a sheep farmer who was a friend of mine who loved dogs and was happy to help out with a home.

Some months later he approached me, absolutely overjoyed. 'That dog is one of the best sheepdogs I have ever had,' he said. 'She's an eyeball dog, but she's good in the yards as well as the paddock. Thank you.'

She also had become the special companion of the sheep farmer's spastic grandson, who lived on the property, giving him special warmth and friendship to cope with his difficulties.

Whenever I visited that farm, that dog never forgot me. It was always very clear we had a very special bond. She knew I'd saved her.

BACK FROM THE DEAD

Denis Adams, Apsley

Taffy came into our family as a pet for our kids. Since we'd sold our farm, we had no need of sheepdogs and by no stretch of the imagination could anyone see Taffy as a sheepdog. His mother had been a Welsh corgi and his father an Australian terrier. The result was a dumb, suspicious, grovelling, ginger-haired, yellow-eyed mutt. Every time he was let off the chain, he'd vanish, so in an attempt to cure his ways, I desexed him. This was a complete waste of time as it was not animal lust that lured him away from home, I discovered, but a compelling love of nature. It was the poetic, Welsh side of him coming out. What other dog will sit for an hour, admiring the play of light on a pool of water, or watch chickens for hours on end without a base motive? What other dog will paddle quietly about in a farm dam, his face aglow with pleasure as he watches baby ducks?

It got a bit lonely driving a tractor out in the pine forest, so I weakened and sometimes took Taffy with me. The pleasure proved to be his, rather than mine. His nuisance value outweighed any fleeting pleasure he gave me.

One day I was working scrub land up for pines, using a heavy plough with two rows of fearsome-looking serrated discs. It was almost inevitable, I suppose, for him to get run over. By the time I managed to stop, there was no sign of him—just a neat swathe of freshly-ploughed sand.

Then, as I watched, the sand stirred and a bewildered-looking dog rose out of it. He sat there awhile, swaying a little, with blood oozing from his ears and a dozen deep gashes in his body. One front foot had been cut in half, right down the middle, and I could see he had broken ribs. As to his internal injuries, I could only guess.

I had no gun with me and I could not bring myself to kill him with the back of my axe. I decided to wait until he began coughing blood, then there could be no further excuses. By some miracle, though, it seemed his lungs had avoided damage, so I rolled him in my jacket and took him home. After two weeks in bed, he had made a complete recovery without any help from vets.

During his illness, I noticed a great change come over our formerly dopey dog. He began showing gratitude when I brought him his invalid fare of bread and milk. It seemed the accident had triggered off some previously dormant part of his brain. Taffy rose from his sick-bed, a reformed character. He was suddenly a faithful, courageous and intelligent dog.

Overnight, he blossomed into a first-rate sheepdog. He became a great hunter as well and was unafraid of dogs twice his size. He also seemed to have telepathic powers. On the day of the Ash Wednesday fires in the south-east, he began acting in a most peculiar way. An hour or two before the fire started, Taffy was terrified and began looking for places to hide. I remember asking him jokingly if there was something that he knew that no-one else did!

About three years ago, he decided that his race was run. He hadn't been well and was spending more and more time in bed. Finally, he only seemed to come out to eat and drink. The time seemed to have come for a replacement.

The new pup had hardly set foot in our yard before Taffy made another amazing recovery. From then on, if anyone paid the slightest attention to the pup, Taffy was on the scene, shouldering it aside to claim all the attention for himself.

Our battle-scarred old Taffy still soldiers on. He can still run, though no longer very fast nor far, and his left legs now seem to take longer strides than his right ones. But he's still going!

THE TWO-LEGGED BATTLER
C Gerschwitz, Minnipa

While showing signs of becoming a good working dog, Bob became the devoted and protective friend of Ann, our twelve-year-old daughter. Roaming the farm together, learning to swing on the swing, slide down the slippery-dip and ride with her on the motorbike were just some of the escapades of these two.

If Ann had a lolly, cake or ice-cream, there always had to be one for Bob as well.

Bob was a very ordinary black sheepdog of no special breeding. Due to his clumsiness, he gained broken leg number one at the age of six months. Using our bush first-aid, the leg was crudely set with bark and bandages. Daily, he chewed it off.

In desperation, we sought help, and the leg was set in plaster. Again, he chewed at it. To discourage this, we placed a pantihose leg over his head, exposing only his eyes and ears, and removed it only for him to eat. Callers at the farm found this very funny.

Broken leg number two came some weeks later when he overbalanced while riding on the back of the ute. We followed the same procedure, but it was a different leg.

Once recovered, he would watch for the school bus each afternoon at 4.30. Bob would then walk down to meet Ann, eat the remains of her school lunch and then have a race home. Ann rode her bike and Bob ran.

Eventually the time came for Ann to live in Adelaide to complete her schooling. The dog fretted at home and the child fretted in Adelaide. There was always a joyous reunion at holiday-time. However, the ritual of waiting for the school bus continued for many weeks. Bob would watch until the bus drove our of sight, then he would slink back home quite dejected.

He continued to be either a wonderful help or a damned nuisance working the sheep. He would spend his leisure time while Ann was away romping with the pet lamb who was in fact a fully-grown sheep. They would take turns to see who could knock whom over.

Broken leg number three came when he ran under our road-grader. He had his spine crushed as well. The kind thing to do would have been to put him down. But with a child in Adelaide threatening to run away from school if anything happened to Bob, and the fact that he was such a battler, we decided to nurse him through.

Complete with mattress, pillow and sleeping-bag, and all the tender, loving care in the world, Bob was kept as comfortable as possible. He had to be turned regularly and his limbs moved about to help circulation. Sore days, he was very miserable and howled a lot. Eventually he showed signs of wanting to drag himself around.

A local doctor agreed to X-ray Bob and discovered about four inches of bone missing in his spine. He offered to place a steel plate in Bob's hip and pin the spine, but at the time, it just seemed too expensive.

As time passed, Bob could be helped to sit up. Through all this he was always happy and seemed to understand whatever we said.

It became an ordeal to milk the cow. I had to wheel Bob in the wheelbarrow down to the cowyard, milk, carry the milk home and return to wheel Bob home again. I had to do this because Bob, in an attempt to come with me, would drag his hindquarters along the ground. This would wear sores on his legs.

On wash days, he lay on his mattress near the clothes line. When I worked in the garden, he had to be right next to me.

One day, as I was busily weeding, Bob dragged his foam mattress near to me. He shuffled around on it, seemingly unable to find the right spot. Jokingly, I said, 'Well, if you're not comfortable, go and get your pillow.'

He looked at me for a while, then dragged himself off to where the pillow was, brought it back and lay down again.

He shuffled and whimpered for some time, reminding me for the hundredth time that it would have been kinder to put him out of his misery.

'Well, if you're still not comfortable, you'd better go and get your rug,' I said.

So he once again dragged himself off and returned with the sleeping bag. With misty eyes, I made him as warm and comfortable as possible. He slept there in the warm sun for some time.

Bob eventually amazed us by starting to walk again—not on four legs, but on his two front legs. His terribly withered hindquarters were held in the air, just as if someone were holding them up as in a wheelbarrow race. This enabled him to get wherever he wanted to go and eventually he could put one hind leg on the ground and hop along a bit.

When he tired, he alternated between two and three legs. Many people came to see him 'walking'. We wish we had taken a movie of him.

Bob's end came on a hot day when he attempted to get involved in some sheep work. Although we searched well into the night, he couldn't be found. Being a cripple, it turned out he had had to take the long way round. In the heat, he had perished although he was only about 100 yards from a water trough at home. We didn't find him for some time.

HOUDINI HOUND
Wendy Treloar, Cummins

Oscar was a bitser. No other description could possibly fit his pedigree. Now that he is dead, we can reflect on his past glories. Oscar had no particular tricks, pranks, or begging-on-his-hind-leg stories . . . his was just a lifelong saga of staying alive.

As a young puppy, he was friend to all the Fitzgerald children. For some time, Oscar seemed content to bask in the spoiling, but one day, he was put into the back of a farm utility and driven around the paddocks to check the sheep. From that day onwards, he was free!

He discovered he could jump up without the driver's knowing. Thus he escaped the indignity of being dressed up in doll's clothes, or being pushed around in an old wicker pram. He leapt aboard at every opportunity and with the wind whistling past his ears he sniffed the smell of sheep, female dogs on nearby farms, emus, kangaroos and rabbits.

The Brooker farm was some twenty miles from the Fitzgerald homestead and on one visit, Oscar was accidentally left behind. He waited until sundown, then he set off. He sniffed all the tracks until he found the correct road and arrived home weary and footsore, but triumphant. He gave the worried family his most withering look and flounced out to his kennel.

From then on, Oscar roamed.

He scouted in the large nearby creeks and one winter was washed away under the bridge and downstream in a flash flood, twisting and bumping into the huge logs. Waterlogged, he eventually made it to the bank and, caked in mud, lay there, exhausted. The hard, setting clay saved his life. When he was examined by the vet, having managed to struggle home days after the searching was over, it was found his neck had been broken. It took weeks to get rid of the clay.

Recovery brought more adventures. He chased a fox into its hole. A terrible thumping was heard, and clouds of dust escaped from the hole. Out came the fox, but no Oscar. Spike Fitzgerald waited and whistled and dug deep into the lair. Poor Oscar. Surely he would be dead. Spike returned later in the day with a shovel to dig out the dog, but there he was, trotting home across the paddock, limping, ears drooping, bloodied and torn—but alive.

A passing kangaroo was an instant invitation to fight, especially as Oscar could leap sideways in the air like a fighting cock. It always confused the roos. Oscar would leap from his box on the motorbike as he went past.

At night rabbits, too, blinded by the spotlight, were good fun for Oscar. Oscar could leap and pounce simultaneously.

On his more manly excursions, he wandered one night across the road to Uncle Bas Fitzgerald's place. Not wanting his dog's pedigree to be mingled with Oscar's, Uncle Bas fired off the gun. Oscar was shot through his socks, ears and tail.

After his recovery, the kids dressed Oscar up and put earrings through the bullet holes in his ears.

Oscar accumulated all sorts of mates, and after one hot day's excursion, he and a friend took refuge in the shearing shed where some watered-down Lucijet was left. Oscar's mate slaked his thirst on the watered-down mixture, but Oscar drank his neat. His mate keeled over and died, but Oscar licked his lips and looked around for more.

Leaping into the farm truck during harvest involved a different form of risk. Only Oscar survived the slipping forwards of a bulk bin. It squashed his mate.

The truck backed over him, but the sandy soil under the tyres caused him to be only a bit squashed. After a rubdown, Oscar staggered to his feet once more.

Eventually Oscar's escapades took their toll and he retired to his kennel daring, with a toothless growl, anyone to come near his territory.

The battered old dog's life ended but the kennel is still underneath the pine trees.

ALL FOUR BACK
ON THE GROUND

Syd Nosworthy, Lucindale

When John Corbett arrived home with two border collie pups, he bedded them down in their kennels under restraint. The pups soon voiced their resentment of this treatment and as the sounds penetrated the kitchen, Mary, John's wife, remarked: 'It sounds as though we're in for some country music—a Slim Dusty concert.' Unwittingly, she had christened the pups.

Slim grew to be a tall, rather rangy dog. Dignified and aloof, he gave unswerving devotion to John, but treated with the utmost disdain approaches from anyone else.

Dusty was a complete contrast. Affable and gregarious, he soon learnt how to cajole the tastiest household morsels from Mary and developed a rotund figure not conducive to the rigours of a working life. He would obligingly work for anyone, but at a very leisurely pace, He was adept at backing round a building or any reasonable cover to keep out of John's view, but as the tail of the mob approached the gate, he would appear to hunt the last few sheep in and stand by for any plaudits that might be forthcoming. John was well aware of Dusty's habits but happily tolerated the friendly rogue.

'My dogs,' John always declared, 'are willing. Slim's willing to work and Dusty is willing to let him.'

A brush with a motor vehicle injured the youthful Slim and thereafter he carried one hind leg. It detracted little from his capacity for work and his speed around the paddocks invariably left Dusty floundering in his wake, floundering, but happily unconcerned.

One shearing season, however, Slim was again exercising his propensity for chasing motor vehicles. His collar caught in the wheel stud of a passing truck and he was whirled once around with the wheel and smashed heavily on to the bitumen surface. John, helped by the distraught truck driver, carried the unconscious dog to a makeshift shelter. Outwardly, there were no obvious injuries, but it was quite evident he had suffered serious injury—so evident that some observers suggested John should 'end his misery'.

By next day, Slim was conscious, but incapable of movement. He gave no response to John's presence and appeared quite oblivious of the milk and tasty morsels thrust beneath his nose. Dusty proceeded to give the performance of his life. He sat beside Slim and his soft whining and rapt attention not only told his concern, but he was obviously exhorting his friend to respond. He did respond, if only by a slight flicker of an eyelid.

Finally Dusty's pragmatic streak surfaced. He gobbled up the food, clearly thinking, 'There's no point in wasting it'.

Another factor was involved in Slim's eventual recovery. It was Julia Corbett, who had been a toddler when the pups arrived at the farm. They grew together. From the outset, Dusty and Julia were soul mates. Rolling and romping joyously on the lawn, their pleasure in each other's company was clear.

Slim watched these antics from close by though at first tending to shrink away from Julia's advances. But he did unbend, and she was the only person in his life to whom he did unbend. Mary wasn't prepared for Slim's reaction one day when she reprimanded Julia and the child cried out in indignation. A menacing snarl from Slim gave a clear message of his views.

The day after Slim's accident, Julia came home from school and rushed to look at and comfort her friend. An infinitely feeble movement of his head and an even more feeble twitch of his tail proved that Slim was aware of her. Although he ignored the saucer of milk she proffered, he did attempt to swallow when she dipped her small hand in the milk and pushed it into his mouth, letting the drops fall on his tongue.

This ritual was repeated over and again throughout the weekend until he was swallowing milk squeezed from a sponge onto his tongue. Although Dusty kept up his daily performance, ending as usual with his determination to maintain his own strength, he was excited and delighted when Slim did raise his head and lap the milk from the saucer.

It took Slim about three weeks to recover sufficiently to struggle into a half-crouching position and ultimately to sit up and eat the food and drink on offer. During most of that time, he lay almost inert, but when Julia sat beside him gently stroking his head, his eyes and tail marked his appreciation.

It was a moment of jubilation when Slim finally struggled to his feet and after a few tentative, staggering steps began to walk with greater surety.

'Dad!' called an ecstatic Julia. 'Look, he's got all his feet on the ground!'

No-one ever knew what anatomical miracle had occurred for Slim but for the rest of his days he was back on four feet and never again carried that hind leg.

PART 7
KNOCK-OFF TIME

*And when it's time to go, some are still hard at it while
a few 'lucky' ones might get to retire. One thing's for sure,
it's more a beginning than an end—they live on through
their offspring.*

JUST A GENETIC HICCUP
Mike Hayes

Not all that long ago, when I went out to seek a replacement for Wally the Wonder Dog, I (naturally) got into quite deep conversation with the owner of the particular pup we eventually roped in to our Rural Empire.

'Y'know,' he reminisced, 'there was a bloke round Starpost way who never let a young dog have a go with his sheep until it'd spent at least a year as a rabbiter. I've noticed meself that if a dog's been a rabbit dog, he usually does all right out in the paddock.'

Purists might disagree, claiming a dog who has a taste for bunnying could easily be distracted while working if a rabbit happened to cross his path in mid-muster. I really don't know. Wal was a hopeless rabbiter. Once, when confronted by a ravening baby rabbit, he sat there shivering and whining and his sheep work was almost acceptable. But that bloke's opinion reminded me there are working dogs other than the sheep and cattle variety in the bush. The honest rabbit dog seems to have gone out of vogue these days, but back in pre-myxo times, we often had more of them about the place than sheepdogs.

I'm also about to break the rule about never giving dogs human character istics. Anyone who's worked with one knows a dog's talents are entirely canine and it's unfair to treat them like people. However, how many of us have also thought to ourselves, 'I wonder what the little brown bugger's thinking?'

Old Sandy stirred on the cushion and half-heartedly attempted to re-position his rear end without awakening fully. The briquette fire was really pumping out the heat and Sandy's bum was getting uncomfortably hot. It felt a little like the old days, when he'd pick a nice shady spot to doze in the morning and, inadvertently having slept away three-quarters of the day, would wake to find the sun had shifted in the sky and he was quietly broiling himself.

Sandy chuckled in his sleep. Mrs Porter, who'd been diligently knitting an Essendon football club beanie for one of Nelda's boys, reached down and touched him gently.

'Shhhh!' she crooned softly. 'You're having a nightmare.'

'Nightmare be buggered!' thought Sandy to himself. The nightmares had gone long ago, coinciding with the time he'd been turned over to Mrs Porter and endured the long petrol-fumy trip from the bush where he'd been born, to the geriatric comfort of leafy Caulfield. The nightmares had always been part of the old days, along with the freedom and the thrill of the hunt . . . and the kids.

Sandy half rolled further away from the heater and, thankfully a bit cooler, drifted off in his mind back to those old days.

Sandy hadn't started life as a kids' dog. He'd been born, rather unexpectedly one quiet October morning, under 'Crackers' Hunt's woolshed.

Sandy's Mum was a grizzled old fox terrier bitch—not the dwarf, yappy ones you seem to get everywhere these days, but a stocky, medium-sized black and white dog called Annie. She may well not have been 100% foxie at all, but round those parts of western Victoria, that's the breed she was known as. Hunt half-heartedly tolerated her as a relatively long-serving member of his huge pack of rabbit dogs. Like most of the mutts, she was allowed free range of the bare, dusty acres of Hunt's front paddocks. Only the savage ones, the Alsatians and boxers, were tied up, and then only since the Shire sent Crackers a threatening letter after old Jim Polkinghorn's horse was spooked by a few marauding dogs on its painful way up to the Bluffs where Jim spent his time laying rabbit and wild dog traps.

Hunt hadn't earned his nickname without reason. Periodically, usually after a demented drinking bout, when the locals referred to him as 'moonstruck', he'd randomly select a few members of his canine rabble, tie them up by their hind legs to the low limb of the sheep-killing tree, and shoot them.

Later, in a fit of remorse, he'd drive all the way into Melbourne, select a few unwanted strays from the Animal Hospital and return with them to keep his pack numbers up. Crackers fed the dogs better than he fed himself. Every time he slaughtered a killer, he'd wrap only a handful of chops and bung them into the icebox for himself. The rest he'd diligently boil up, to kill any hydatid tapeworms, and distribute to his hordes.

His initial reaction to the Shire's letter had 'moonstruck' him too. After tying up the malefactors, he selected a few innocents from the other bony hounds around the place and summarily executed them.

Sandy's puppyhood had been filled with memories of Hunt's little quirks. That's when the nightmares started. The frightening thuds of his shotgun and the unmistakeable smell of blood in the dust engraved themselves on his consciousness at a very early age. At night, or during his exhausted puppy-dozes during the day, he'd mentally act out the one thing he feared most—seeing Hunt's dusty boots making their way to wherever he dreamed he was hiding, watching the big gnarled hand reaching into his hiding-place, hearing the click of the long, glinting stick he carried . . . waiting for the thump.

Not that Crackers was particularly brutal to Annie and her litter. He seemed to be especially intrigued by the pups. Quite often, he'd stop whatever he was doing when he worked in the yards or the shed and come over to inspect the wriggling, round bundles of new life. He'd cup them in his hands, run nicotine-yellowed fingers along their backs and hold them up to his face, examining them closely.

Sandy never found out why Hunt was so interested in him and the others. He never got to leave the property. He never heard the pub talk down at the Criterion in town, eleven miles away from Hunt's rundown selection.

'They reckon Crackers Hunt's got a litter of dingoes out of one of his mongrel bitches.'

'Yair. Jim Polkinghorn reckons an old warrigal musta snuck down out of the Bluffs one night and slipped her one.'

'Fair dinkum? Crackers don't wanna let the wildlife people hear about that.'

'No. Or some of his neighbours. Those big old wool cockies up past Ringworm Springs'd be onto him like a shot.'

'A shot? More like a whole lot of flamin' shots.'

Sandy heard none of that. He just sucked nourishment from his mother's dugs, wrestled with his siblings and made sure he was deep under the woolshed whenever he sensed that Hunt was on one of his rampages.

Eventually, Hunt's secret did reach unwelcome ears. One morning a government car lurched into the yard. Two men in suits spoke briefly to Hunt and they all came over to where Annie was feeding her litter under the woolshed water tank. Sandy sensed the animosity of the two oddly-dressed strangers. He also sensed the aura of fury that was starting to emanate from Crackers. Sandy knew. Soon there would be loud thumps—and the smell of blood in the dust.

Quietly, he backed away from his mum's belly and slid into the darkness under the shed. The other pups sucked on. There were the thumps. The strangers loaded four small, still bodies into a sugar bag and threw it into the boot of their car. Crackers stewed for the rest of the afternoon, then finally went into the house for his shotgun. More thumps. More blood and dust. After sundown, when Sandy finally emerged from his hiding place, he found Annie missing. He went hungry that night, and next morning. Late in the day, Hunt found him curled up under the tank. The madness in him having gone, the cocky picked up the little tan-coloured pup and spoke surprisingly softly to him.

'You poor little bastard,' he muttered. 'You poor, unwanted little bastard.'

When Crackers turned the pup over to us, Sandy was about a year old. Hunt made no secret of his ancestry.

'An old black 'n' white foxie I once had, got herself knocked off by one of Jim Polkinghorn's dingoes—probably when we were sawin' logs up at the Bluffs,' he explained. 'He'll be a good rabbit dog and you won't have to worry about him and sheep. He's too small to get into any of that sort of caper.'

Crackers' uncharacteristic generosity had been prompted by a chance meeting we'd had with another member of his motley crew of canines. Half a dozen of us had gone off after school to dig out rabbit burrows. In those days, before myxo decimated the rabbit population around our way, we discovered that rabbits proved a useful way of relieving the poverty so many valley people lived in. Our inventive mother found out we could get 2/6 a pair for them from a chiller operator who toured the district buying bunnies for the markets in Melbourne. In summer, especially, we were able to hurry home from school, grab an old mattock and a couple of shovels and earn what seemed to us a veritable fortune by doing the rounds of the thousands of massive rabbit warrens in the volcanic country up behind the village. Our modus operandi was simple. We'd watch where the rabbits ran when we disturbed them as we approached their warrens, then set to digging them out. In the soft soil, it was an easy matter to follow the tunnels and just before the end, reach in, grab the residents and despatch them quickly with a twist of the neck.

It would have been a lot easier with a good rabbit dog, but we got by. For a short time, we experimented with ferrets, but found they invariably ate any victims they found in the burrows, then curled up and went to sleep. Sometimes we'd be able to dig them out wasting valuable rabbiting time but often they'd get so far into the bowels of the warrens that it'd be impossible to find them. The only thing we could do then, to avoid getting into strife for arriving home after dark, was elect one of our number to sit up—sometimes half the night—beside the burrow, waiting for the ferrets to wake and report back for duty. No, dogs would have been far more useful than ferrets but, seeing we were making do on our own, we never actually got round to looking for one—until we fell in with Crackers.

On this particular afternoon, we were heading down from the Bluffs with twenty or so dead rabbits hanging head down from our Scout belts when Bruce suddenly called out: 'Hey! There's a dog stuck in the dam.' The dam in question was a water supply reservoir for the village. It had concrete sides and we knew from past experience how difficult it was for man or beast to scramble back up the smooth slope if they ventured into the water. The dam was heavily Cyclone-fenced to ensure no mishaps occurred, but it seemed that this time the dog—a large black, white and brindle pointer—had found a way through.

When we scrambled down, climbed the fence and investigated further, we could see he'd been there a while. His claws were worn away and his feet bleeding from trying to drag his way out of the reservoir. The poor old dog was knackered. He wouldn't have lasted another five minutes. Bruce slid the rabbits off his belt and we joined it to ours to fashion a lifeline with which we could lower him down the concrete slope towards the rapidly tiring dog. He managed to get a good grip of the long floppy ears and we soon had the dog safely grassed.

It took a couple of phone calls to work out who owned the pointer, who happened to be named Mackie. Crackers Hunt claimed the dog and asked if we could take him over to his place. He couldn't pick him up himself because he didn't have a car and was too busy lamb-marking to spare the time to walk.

We returned Mackie to his owner (quaking a little inside because we'd all heard the stories about Hunt's craziness) but instead of going berserk, as we'd been warned he might, Crackers went over to the shed and came back with Sandy.

'You little buggers'd probably find a good use for this little tyke,' he growled. 'He's no good to me and it'd probably do us both a favour if you give him a home.' That's when he explained Sandy's pedigree. We unquestioningly accepted his assurances about the unlikelihood of the little dog worrying sheep. After all, wasn't he all we'd ever needed? At last we'd got a dog. Our rabbiting enterprise would now be able to move into top gear.

About six weeks later, old Jim Polkinghorn brought the news to the village that he'd driven by Crackers Hunt's place and noticed all the dogs seemed to be dead. The gossip really started flying when the police from town went to investigate and found Hunt had indeed taken his shotgun to the lot—including poor old Mackie. He'd saved the last cartridge for himself. I remember the adults talking late at night about Crackers having had a wife who'd moved out of the district years before.

'That's when they say it all started. He wasn't a bad sort of bloke before then.' But by then us kids weren't all that interested any more and had forgotten most of the gory details—and so, I suppose, had Sandy.

The little dog's nightmares did indeed stop when he moved in with the kids. The small, light tan pup with pricked ears and white-tipped, cocked tail discovered an idyllic world, far removed from tank stands, shearing sheds and nightmarish thumps. He was allowed to sleep on an old blanket on the wide verandah which fronted our cottage. There were no terrifying sounds or frightening smells. There were always at least two feeds of rabbit and bones a day. In winter he was even allowed in to doze by the open fire before everyone went to bed. But, best of all, there were the afternoon excursions Up The Back to hunt rabbits.

He'd dabbled in the sport a few times in the last few months. Hunt's lack of control over his dogs meant Sandy and a few older dogs had been free to explore the back paddocks, relishing the tantalising smells along the sheep paths and wallaby tracks and occasionally thundering helter-skelter, with hysterical barks, if a rabbit happened to spook in front of them. But it hadn't been nearly as exciting as rabbiting with the kids. Sandy had no terminology to express it but, really, he'd found Heaven on Earth up there on the flat-topped volcanic bluffs behind the village, where the wind rattled through the uplifted arms of the dead trees, ring-barked fifty years earlier by the first selectors, and where the tussocks grew over exciting tunnels down which a keen young rabbit dog found limitless adventure.

The kids had originally only wanted a dog that would spook rabbits from out of their squats in the tussocks and drive them in panic to the warrens, from where they could be excavated. But for Sandy, that was never enough. The dingo side of him would allow him to leap forward from a standing start like an arrow. In a few short, frantic yards, he'd grab a fleeing rabbit by the scruff of its neck. A quick shake and the bunny'd be history.

The fox terrier genes in Sandy had a hunting edge to them, too, but they also saw to it that he insisted on taking over the actual digging-out of the warrens. In true foxy style, Sandy would scrabble frantically through the soft earth until he could snap up the quivering rabbit at the end of the tunnel. In larger warrens he was even able to wriggle down the burrows and drag their occupants out one at a time. Unlike the ill-fated ferrets, he never snacked or went to sleep on the job. Over the years he developed one or two proud scars from where we'd accidentally nicked him with the mattock or the edge of the shovel when he got in our way, so keen was he to better our efforts at digging out the warrens.

Then there were the foxes. With their scalps fetching seven and six a pop at the police station in town, Sandy opened a whole new world of wealth to us. He occasionally kept them pinned in the warrens where he'd chased them, but mostly he'd run them down and subdue them in a welter of raised hackles, bared teeth, splashing saliva and frightening savagery. Invariably in a head-on confrontation, one of the kids would have to drag a slavering Sandy away from his quarry in order to recover enough of the fox to prove it did, indeed, once possess a scalp.

At three years of age, Sandy's mixed breeding didn't appear to be in any doubt. Sure, he was small—about half the size of a normal warrigal—but his build, his colouring and his jaunty tail bore no resemblance to any fox terrier anyone in the district had ever seen. And there was something else about Sandy that suggested that quite a bit of the domestic dog in him had been suppressed. He'd never look a human straight in the eye. He never played with the kids. Whereas in his puppy days, he'd bounce around with us with humour and enthusiasm, he now embarked on his daily hunting trips with a lope and a look of guilt about him. It was obviously not just fun anymore. Deep within him a small voice was telling him that hunting was fair dinkum—something a true professional never just fooled around with.

Looking back now, it was also fair to say that Sandy was never a particularly obedient dog. He never really responded to a command. To get him to stop doing something, we'd just about have to drag him away physically. If we wanted him to follow us, we'd have to move off first, hinting that perhaps there was something better along the track. He never responded to whistles. He did what he damn well liked. The kids didn't really notice it, I suppose because in those days, what we wanted and what Sandy wanted were pretty much along the same lines anyway. The perpetually guilty look was perhaps the strangest feature of the little dog. Apart from never really obeying us, he'd never really done anything to feel guilty about—not then.

The crackling, brown days of summer passed slowly. During the Christmas school holidays we usually went Up The Back later in the day, when it wasn't so bakingly hot. Sandy slept under the house where it was beautifully cool. They were deep sleeps, completely free of the nightmares that had disturbed his rest as a pup.

That particular holiday break, a new influence entered Sandy's life. Lady was an eighteen-month-old rabbit dog—mostly fox terrier—not unlike what we imagined Sandy's Mum, the ill-fated Annie, would have been like. Sandy accepted her inclusion in our hunting ranks without rancour. He even allowed her to take over his spot on the verandah, although by then he actually preferred the hiding place provided by his comfortable little depression in the dust under the house. And out across the hills, Lady proved an efficient partner to the little dingo cross. When they flushed out rabbits and foxes, they worked as a team, herding them towards the appropriate warrens where the two of them took half the time to dig out their quarry.

With the extra money we earned from our rabbiting, we were able to transform the drab paddock at the front of the cottage with exotic garden plants, imported all the way from Melbourne. We even extended our formerly desperate water supply—complete with a fish pond—and built a bush-pole pergola which helped make a sad mockery of the other dusty front yards in the village.

The vegetable seeds we sent away for produced proud ranks of tomatoes and rambling pumpkin vines, welcome additions to a monotonous diet of mutton, rabbit or yabbie in those days when a camp pie, lettuce, grated processed cheese and half a tomato were considerd a gourmet salad, and the blatantly American hot dog was prosaically referred to as a 'sav and roll'. Sandy and Lady's contribution to our improved quality of life was greatly appreciated, even by the smaller kids.

And so were their pups when they arrived. Our Mum allowed Lady one litter before sending her to the vet in town to be 'fixed up'. There were three in the litter—two nondescript bitches, which we managed to palm off on other families interested in emulating our rabbiting successes, and a strapping chocolate and white lad we named Pongo.

Pongo seemed to have inherited none of his father's characteristics. He was large for a fox terrier—even the mongrel strains we accepted as pedigree—and he looked nothing like a dingo. Our family group became the top rabbiting team in the valley. Where Sandy on his own had been impressive and Sandy and Lady had been perfection, Sandy, Lady and Pongo were the ultimate.

We couldn't really claim to have had a hand in it, despite the quality of our hunting team, but about the time Pongo was coming into his own, rabbit numbers started to fall off. It was all due to the myxo plague doing its grisly job with silent efficiency. Uneatable sick and blind rabbits, oozing pus from their eyes and nostrils, started to outnumber the healthy ones we once sent away to market. The chiller stopped calling. The easy money dried up. No-one wanted to risk serving up one of those pathetic, emaciated creatures for Sunday lunch.

Lady and Pongo settled down to a less vigorous existence—happily accepting a greater emphasis on just being kids' pets. We still went on regular rambles Up The Back and often returned with the odd fox or two, but life was becoming less feral for us. Besides, the older kids were starting to go to high school in town and didn't get back home during the week in time to fit in much outdoor activity. Sandy suddenly found himself with time on his paws.

At first he took out his newly developed frustrations and resulting bad temper on Pongo. On the occasional afternoon we elected to go bush, a dam of emotion and instinct would burst somewhere within the little dog's psyche. Out there in his element, it'd sometimes prove too much and often he'd break away from the chase, or even from a battle with a fox, and turn savagely on his son.

The fights were terrifying. Pongo, although a gentler soul than his old man, was much bigger and, if not in the same league in terms of savagery, at least wasn't going to be one to stand by and be done over. He knew about self-preservation. Sandy, with his inbred savagery, never gave quarter. We'd drag them apart, take them home separately on leashes and keep them away from each other for a week while they sulked, their mouths swollen from the taste of their shared blood.

About then, the complaints about sheep-killing started coming in.

Sandy drank deeply from the four-gallon drum under the downpipe. The taste in his mouth stirred uncomfortable memories. It reminded him of loud noises, strange stillnesses and that frightening smell mingled with dust. Today's trip Up The Back hadn't been much better than the last. Although he wouldn't admit it to any other dog, Pongo seemed to be starting to get the better of him. Perhaps it was because he was larger—and younger.

Sandy had originally planned to go straight back under the house and try to sleep off the pain and discomfort of his newest wounds. But for the moment he just savoured the water in his belly and sniffed the still night air. It was warm and dark. From above the village, along the flats before the ground started to rise upwards to the Bluffs, he could hear the sheep calling to each other. Their bleating was full of the insecurity and half-panic which always tinged their conversation. It was strange that he'd only just started to notice them.

Back in the only half-remembered days at Crackers Hunt's, he'd grown accustomed to their greasy smell, tinged with that same aroma of fear they always exuded. You could hardly miss it when you lived under the shearing shed. Whenever Crackers brought his sheep in, the smell permeated the whole universe, the fear component getting even stronger as he put them through the confusion and, sometimes, agony of the sheepyards.

In Sandy's adolescent hunting years, the sheep and their smell had still been there. The dusty grey forms fleeing in terror ahead of the dogs and the kids as they crossed the paddocks on their way Up The Back had provided momentary distraction, but nothing more. He'd never needed to pay much attention to them. In those days, the rabbit and fox hunting had been everything.

Occasionally they'd come across a dead one Up The Back. The smell then had been far more interesting. First there was the heady stench of decay and something had replaced the fear—something far more satisfying and more in keeping with the feelings that flooded his being after a day's rabbiting. But these days, Sandy found himself paying more and more attention to them. There was an air about them that even quelled much of the occasional anger which caused him to vent his confused wrath on Pongo. Yes, sheep definitely required closer scrutiny.

The last light went out in the cottage. Barely noticing Lady's exhausted snore from the corner of the verandah, Sandy slid quietly past and sneaked quickly down the track towards the Marsdens' place. He didn't know why, but somehow he knew what he planned to do wouldn't sit well with the humans asleep in the cottage. He'd always had the feeling that they disapproved of him. As he'd grown older he'd found it more and more difficult to feel at ease in their presence.

He slid under the chicken wire and almost ran slap bang into Darkie. Darkie was the Marsdens' kelpie. Sandy hadn't had a lot to do with him until recently, when they'd met during a Progress Association meeting outside the village hall. They'd both observed protocol by weeing on a clump of tussock and boldly scratching the dust over it with their hind paws. Then they'd circled each other, with just the right amount of hackle-raising before sniffing suspiciously at each other's rears. Darkie's scent explained to Sandy that the kelpie wasn't a bad sort of bloke after all. He was never really keen on stacking on a blue and was more than happy to comply with any suggestion that they go for a bit of a wander up around the hills.

While the humans had continued to snarl at each other inside the hall, the two dogs poked leisurely around the community precincts, emptying their bladders on various landmarks, sharing a whole variety of fascinating smells and generally relishing each other's company. They even terrorised Warren's chooks for a while and studied a distant mob of sheep through the ringlock fence at the back of the houses. It could have gone further, but a shrill whistle from down near the hall turned Darkie's head and, obeying another instinct totally alien to Sandy, he trotted compliantly back to his boss's ute. Sandy followed him down more out of loyalty to his new mate than anything else.

But that had been in the early days of their relationship. Tonight, like on other recent nights, they had a whole program planned. Together they breached the barrier of the ringlock fence, Darkie sailing over and Sandy wriggling under a loose bottom strand. Darkie took the lead. He knew his way around the paddocks, although not generally in the dead of night. He cast wide to where he knew the sheep were camped. This late there was no bleating from the mob. Sandy could smell their peace of mind. It didn't last long. Darkie had reached the apex of his cast. They weren't Marsden's sheep, so the mob didn't know him personally. But they knew his kind. To humans, kelpies and other sheepdogs were merely animals with an instinct to work. To sheep and other animals, something within their scent and presence gave off the clear warning that they, like all canines, were just another predator.

The mob shifted to its feet and started warily back towards where Sandy crouched. They maintained a fair amount of order, not yet completely dominated by panic. They sensed rather than saw Darkie moving back and forth in the darkness where they'd been dozing. They didn't realise Sandy was there in the tussocks until, about the same time, he saw their leaders in the gloom.

Darkie had them well held. He used their reticence about venturing any further in Sandy's direction to guide them quietly to the eastern corner of the paddock where he jammed them conveniently into the V formed by the two fence lines. Darkie dropped back to press the stragglers in. Unable to progress in any direction, the sheep stood motionless and confused, still not really aware of their plight. Sandy was ready.

He came like an arrow, his ears flattened against his head for speed, and plunged into the forest of legs, which started shuffling and stamping with the first realisation of terror. A young ewe, about a year old, just a two-tooth, put her head down and Sandy took her on the cheek. The suddenness and speed of his strike pulled her down. The sheep were all small-framed Merinos and Sandy's lack of stature suddenly wasn't a drawback, especially considering the ferocity of his attack.

Behind him, Darkie barked a couple of times, excited by the sudden aroma of blood. But the excitement wasn't strong enough yet to override his basic instinct to hold the sheep. The killer in his genes lay further below the surface than with Sandy.

Around the growling dog and the wildly kicking ewe, the mob spilt.

Sheep jumped over Sandy's back as he relinquished hold of her cheek and burrowed desperately into the inconvenient woolly wrinkles protecting her throat. A bigger ewe would have shaken him off by now. Suddenly, Darkie blundered through the sheep, allowing them to escape. Slightly ashamed of what he saw as his dereliction of duty, he leaped about behind Sandy, panting and woofing noisily in the confusion and dark. Below Sandy's front paws, the ewe suddenly stopped struggling. Darkie was now beside him, inhibitions gone, slurping thirstily at the dark fluid gushing around them. Sandy growled the traditional warning: 'Piss off. I'm here first.'

Darkie, a little hurt but mindful of protocol, dropped away and went around to the rear end of the ewe, where she'd voided her bladder and bowels in terror. He worried at the soft area in front of her udder. Sandy moved his attention to the ewe's flank, burrowing through her soft insides in search of a morsel of liver or kidney. They both sensed the intruders at the same time.

To Darkie, the smells and sounds were familiar. The bright light that momentarily blinded him was very similar to the two on the boss's ute, and the stronger one he carried on the front seat to shine out fox eyes before sounding the gun at them. In fact, the smells coming from beyond the light grew even more familiar. There was the boss . . . and another like him.

'Fucking hell. It *is* bloody Darkie!'

To Sandy, the smells and noises were to be interpreted differently. Sure, there was the aroma of man. And although the light wasn't exactly shining directly in his eyes, he knew it to be a human force. But distinct among all the smells and sounds was the oily menace of the guns they carried and the distinctive click of them being straightened. They were smells and sounds from his puppy days. Soon there would be those heavy thuds—and that smell, not unlike the strong scent arising in invisible waves from around the dead ewe.

Sandy stayed on his belly and slid backwards into the tussocks, keeping low and quiet until the sudden brightness thrown from the spotlight had passed. He wondered at the way Darkie stood bolt upright with his tail wagging and his tongue lolling stupidly, gullibly waiting for the humans to reach him. Then Sandy started silently back towards the village. As he strained back under the bottom wire of the fence, he heard the single thud behind him. The cockies in the valley held several meetings to discuss the sheep-killings. The first one was called more than a week after Bill Marsden sadly accepted the task of destroying Darkie.

'The best bloody dog I'll ever have,' he commented later.

But Darkie's demise hadn't ended the killings and maulings. Two nights later, in the very same paddock, another three ewes were killed. Two had been lightly snacked, but the third seemed to have been slaughtered and left. Us kids didn't get to go inside to the meetings. Our parents went and we could hear the angry shouts from inside the hall while we clambered over the playground equipment.

'I'm losing my best bloody studs. I paid nearly a pound for most of 'em.'

'Well, it's not my dogs that are killing them. They're tied up all the time whenever they're not workin'.'

Notices appeared in the local rag, the *Express*: 'Let it be known that any dogs found wandering on Rocky Hill will be destroyed. Signed, Clem Manly,' and 'Poison baits have been laid at Wattle Glenn. Signed, Alf Darby.'

The threats stirred up dog owners and parents alike. A lusty debate about the dangers to young children followed the warning from Alf. For a while, Jim Polkinghorn enjoyed a boom time. However, despite his efforts, no dingoes or wild dogs were trapped on any of the afflicted properties and the sheep-killings continued. Saddened cockies begrudgingly put down their own dogs, just to keep the peace, amidst widespread accusations. And still the killings went on.

It took a while, but us kids started working out who was really to blame. We didn't twig at first when Sandy showed hardly any enthusiasm for jaunts Up The Back. The little mongrel was generally too knocked-up after his nocturnal jaunts to show much interest in daytime activity. He stayed under the house whenever we were around at weekends and holidays but sometimes, when we came back from school, we noticed Sandy wasn't around. If we decided to go up in the hills, Pongo and Lady would obligingly fall in behind us and we'd give Sandy up as a bad job. Then, up in the back country, way out of sight of the village, we'd suddenly find him loping guiltily through the tussocks, so preoccupied that sometimes he wouldn't notice us until we were almost upon him. The penny started dropping when, on too many occasions, we'd find him dragging a hunk of fresh meat around, or sniffing a ripe carcass hidden behind a fallen tree. By then, Sandy had his secret caches well organised.

We really knew what was going on after a couple of occasions when, once we'd reached the all-surveying vantage point of the Bluffs, we'd see a mob of sheep spilling in terror across a distant paddock and maybe catch the merest glimpse of a fox-like form slicing through the middle of them like a small red shark. Fox-like, indeed. But foxes didn't hunt sheep like that.

When you're ten or eleven, it's hard to know what to do in a situation like that. True, old Sandy wasn't what you'd call a kids' pet. He'd grown far too secretive and feral for that. But he'd been with us a long time. He'd been part of our young lives for as long as most of us could remember. At that age we couldn't be noble like the cockies who'd been prepared to sacrifice their own dogs in their desperate attempt to find the sheep-killer. Someone had got *Dusty* out of the school library. Most of us had read it. We knew the rules. That fictional dog's life seemed a close parallel to Sandy's, but the big difference was that Sandy was our dog. If anyone expected us to dob him in—well they just didn't understand the bond that exists between kids and dogs, even grumpy little psychopaths like Sandy. The thought of him being found out terrified us. He'd been a mate for too long.

It seems amazing now that the oldies never twigged. I remember big, bluff, Alan Grey dropping round and guffawing in his honest, loud voice, 'If yer don't watch out, that little dingo-lookin' bloke of yours'll be out killing sheep like that other dawg.' Our hearts stood still that afternoon.

Sandy didn't kill sheep all the time. Like Crackers Hunt, he only seemed to be gripped by the madness occasionally. In winter, especially, he tended to stick fairly close to home. Then, with spring and lambing, he broke out again. This time our Mum sprung him with a half-chewed lamb. I don't know if she put two and two together at first. Maybe she just thought it was his first offence. However, it proved the first step in Sandy's undoing.

Mum could be a hard woman. The bush tends to do that to people, but she had a soft spot for dogs. After telling us in hushed tones what she'd discovered Sandy doing, she ruled that he could no longer have a free rein. Sandy had to be tied up. It didn't last long. No dog enjoys being chained up and that genetic hiccup in Sandy made his plight even more pathetic. It wasn't just that the sudden loss of freedom took the fire out of his eyes. It was as if a life force had drained from that wiry little tan body. Even the cocky tail dropped in defeat.

'Sometimes I think it'd be better if we had him shot,' Mum'd say with increasing frequency. We quailed internally, but we knew she'd never have it done. Dog people are like that.

God knows where, or even why, she dug Mrs Porter up from, but one Sunday she arrived in a car carrying a special wicker basket to relieve us of our prisoner. She examined Sandy closely and said in that funny baby talk a lot of city people revert to when addressing dogs, 'Well, Sandy, are you going to come and keep little me company?'

Sandy went along quietly. He obviously wasn't exactly heartbroken at leaving our company. Like I said before, he was never particularly affectionate and probably thought we'd let him down pretty badly in the long run, anyway. It didn't really explain, though, why the almost-forgotten spring returned to his step as he pranced up into the back of the car, ignoring any suggestion that he use the wicker basket. Crikey, even the tail was back up at the top of the mast.

As the car growled away in a roll of dust, I experienced a feeling of relief that stays strong in my memory, even today. Maybe Sandy experienced the same thing. Anyway, there were never any more sheep-killings.

Before drifting off completely, Sandy recollected briefly how closed-in he'd first felt at Mrs Porter's. Oh, the accommodation and the catering were fair enough, but the dark house with its benign, apathetic smells and that tiny backyard . . . But at least the nightmares stopped.

Oh yes, back there with the kids, after the confrontations with the sheep, they'd started again . . . just like those of his puppy days, only even worse. The thumps, the still bodies, the smells . . . only this time he knew they were coming for him.

It had been even worse when he was on the chain. Then he'd had little to do but sleep . . . and dream those terrifying, guilty dreams. That's why he hadn't worried about coming away with the old, sweet-smelling human. At least she wasn't a threat. Maybe she could take him away from the nightmares. And she had. They'd gone.

Old Sandy breathed a heavy sigh and Mrs Porter looked over her glasses at him again. 'Still having bad dreams?' she asked again quietly.

'No way,' thought Sandy to himself.

Outside, cars hissed through the drizzle. The radiation from the briquette heater was just right for an old retired hunting dog . . . even an old retired half-dingo. As he slept, his only dreams were pleasant golden ones, full of excited puppy yelps from young humans, and rabbits hurtling desperately through the sun-kissed tussocks.

GOOD ALL-ROUND
Wally Karger, Vale Park

This is a true story of the life of a pup. We lived on a farm in the Adelaide Hills, running about 200 sheep, three cows, seventy chooks and ten geese. We trained Lassie from a six-week-old pup. Obedience was important, so she learned to sit and come at once. She also learned to pick up small articles and to put them into our hands, or in a bucket, or on a chair, wherever we told her to put them. We always gave her a small crumb or cornflake as reward.

Before she was six months old, she was able to bring me a pair of pliers, a screwdriver or a box of matches. She could even bring them out to where we were working in the paddock. Later, she learned to bring some sheep shears so we could treat fly-struck sheep.

In 1955, a bushfire burnt us out and we were broke. Lassie had become a sheepdog which we could lend to our neighbours. Our own sheepyards had been destroyed in the fire.

I had to go to work off the farm and Lassie would lie with no interest in sheep until 6 o'clock on Saturday morning. Then she would be at the door and I'd just say 'fetch the sheep in' and after I had lit the fire and had breakfast, the sheep would be waiting at the gate to go into the neighbour's yards. She was both a yard dog and paddock dog and rarely left a sheep behind even in the rough hills or scrub.

She was good with the geese too. If they wandered, my wife just had to say, 'Lass, the geese are on the road'. Very slowly, the geese would then be driven back to the dam where Lassie would watch them for an hour, sometimes not even allowing them out of the water.

Our neighbour, Murray, had Dorset Horn cross sheep and we had black-faced Suffolk rams. Murray's lambs always seemed to crawl under the fence and would join up with our black-faced ones. We always tried to drive them out before they got boxed up.

One Sunday, Murray phoned and told us to watch Lassie who was over on the hill. There she was, very slowly, walking between fourteen big weaner lambs of Murray's and our mob. While the lambs were feeding, she worked them gently towards the fence. Then she put them through the hole and moved them up into Murray's yard where she lay and watched them with her head on her paws.

Lassie knew our three cows by name; and once introduced to visitors, could single them out and drop a ball at their feet if she was asked to.

One of her last chores, at the age of fourteen, was particularly memorable. We were irrigating from the River Murray. I had left my rubber boots down in the lucerne where the sprinklers were.

I was tired and weary, so I said, 'Fetch my rubber boots, Lass'. The poor old girl loped down to the lucerne, and after ten minutes appeared with one boot.

I repeated the order and she brought the other to the door. By this time, it was almost dark, but there were my boots.

The look she gave me almost said what I was thinking, 'My time is almost up.'

When I decided we must put her down, I went to find her. She was curled up in her kennel in our garage, already dead.

STIFF AS A BOARD
Bill Hewett, Balaklava

Jock was a wedding present—a ball of black and white fluff, with plum pudding spots on his nose.

With practically no training, except basic 'come', 'go', 'sit,' 'stay,' 'speak', he seemed to know exactly what was needed, and by the age of six months, was an almost perfect sheepdog. For nearly sixteen years he performed almost everything expected of him and he still enjoyed putting chooks back in their house when they escaped. But he developed some annoying habits.

As he got older and slower, he needed a spell and a drink more often. It didn't save any time giving him a bowl of water in the yards. He had his own pet trough 100 yards away and took his time going and coming.

Jock never slept in a house or shed or drum or kennel. Even in old age and in mid-winter, he would still sleep flat out on his side in the middle of the yard. It was not uncommon to go out on a frosty morning and find him snow-white, covered in frost, and as stiff as a board.

I would pick him up and prop him up against the silo on the sunny side.

He would slowly move around it, following the sun, until he had thawed out enough to walk away for a feed and drink and a look in the sheepyards to see if anything was happening.

One cold day he did not thaw out. We had lost the best friend and helper our family had ever had.

BUGGA-YA
Maxine Brown, Padthaway

Rick, our part-time workman, friend and farmhand, was always intrigued at the names Bob, the dog, answered to, particularly 'Bugga-ya'. So I wrote a poem in explanation. He was such a loyal, loving old dog and he really did think as one with my husband, Terry—so much so that when he was very deaf in later years, he still knew exactly what to do and did it well, without commands.

Of course, if the sheep did need to go into a different paddock from the one Bob thought, it took much waving of arms and carrying on to attract his attention and get the message across. This was a rather exhausting exercise and frustrating too.

When Terry was talking to stockmen, travellers etc., Bob would stand alongside them with his head just touching Terry's leg and with his head down, listening but not moving for ages—or as long as it took the discussion (sometimes hours!). Occasionally, when they laughed, he would look up and give a doggy laugh too and then go back to his listening.

He was a great yard dog and good in trucks. Once we unloaded a triple-decker semi of lambs from interstate. They were cold and slow, so Bob had a big job to move them. He forgot he was in a truck, and not the yards, and jumped clean over the side of the top deck. He was so very sore and sorry, but survived.

Bob's one fault was 'women', and when life got boring, he would take off. It's funny how a dog knows a bitch is on heat ten to twelve kilometres away. People got to know him and he managed to calm their fury and persuade them to feed him, or just give us a ring. Most times though, he would just turn up at home next morning.

I think people eventually realised how good a sheepdog he was because there seem to be lots of longish-haired, black sheepdogs about—much valued by their owners, and looking a lot like Bob.

Before he went deaf, he was shrewd enough on these conjugal errands to get off the road and hide in the grass when a vehicle approached.

He was eventually hit by a vehicle when he could no longer hear. There was some comfort knowing that he died having done what he enjoyed most.

We really miss old Bob. He really was like one of the family.

'BUGGA-YA'

The working dogs were Bob and Sal
The farmer's friend, his own best pal
But puzzled stockmen wondered how
They got the name of 'Bugga-ya'

Bob was priceless, loved to work
But hot days tempted him to shirk
A cool sheep trough a tempting lurk
And worth the threat of 'Bugga-ya'

Together they worked just as one
But in his haste to see it done
Bob would often 'beat the gun'
And answered then to 'Bugga-ya'

Now Rick came working to the farm
Admired the dogs with all their charm
But then he found to his alarm
This dog responds to 'Bugga-ya'

When travellers and stockmen leaned on the gate
Bob, in his wisdom, kept close to his mate
Listened intently, willing to wait
Never a whisper of 'Bugga-ya'

Bob grew old and could not hear
Still worked the sheep, his love most dear
Commands ignored though men were near
He couldn't hear that 'Bugga-ya'

But still his faithfulness excelled
He knew his boss's mind so well
It saved them having then to yell
And give commands of 'Bugga-ya'

But Bob was still a boy at heart
The lure of sex was strong in part
He visited his doggy tart
'Now where's that dog gone? "Bugga-ya"'

Six miles away we found him dead
A vehicle had hit his head
Happily we know he's bred
Lots of little 'Bugga-yas'

We miss our trusting faithful friend
His daughter now the sheep does tend
Our neighbours all his offspring send
To work their sheep with . . . 'Bugga-ya'

THE OLD DOG TAKES GLORY
Angela Goode

On our place there is a funny-looking black and tan kelpie called Roy. He's missing a few teeth and his bark is a bit hoarse, because, at ten, he is a fairly senior fellow.

Now whether it's because he has just become a father of nine to the bitch down the road, or he's suffering dementia, Roy has suddenly started backing sheep, that trick of jumping onto their backs to push them tightly together in a yard or race. He has never shown the slightest tendency to such extravagances, being instead the type of dog that silently stalks the sheep with his rump in the air and his elbows and head low to the ground, hypnotising them with his rather bulbous eyes.

So it was with great excitement that we all ran up to the shearing shed during crutching a fortnight ago to witness this great event. The boss was fairly glowing with pride. 'I don't know what's got into the old fool,' he kept saying.

Just to fill you in, comparatively few dogs will back sheep and those that do are highly-prized. A dog that is good in the paddock and also works well in the yards is known as a utility dog. They can command prices around $1000. We weren't about to sell the old chap, but it did turn out that there was to be an inaugural yard-dog event at the local show. Of course, Roy had to be entered.

'It's just a bit of fun,' we kept hearing. 'We won't get anywhere.'

But we did notice that the old dog was secretly being plied with duck eggs and milk, and more than once we heard the boss murmuring to him, 'Now you won't let me down, will you old man?' The boss believed the duck eggs would help his concentration and stamina.

So last Saturday, earlier than was good for us, we set off for the show. Roy's black coat was gleaming with all those duck eggs, but his tan eyebrows were drawn together slightly in puzzlement at all the fuss.

The showgrounds were still quiet when we arrived. The judging of cakes, flowers, showgirls and cattle had started and of course the horse events were in full swing. Around the yard-dog arena, a knot of dedicated dog people had gathered. A maze of yards had been set up, with a truck and a menacing-looking race leading to it.

The first competitors got under way—lean, professional-looking dogs, dispatching their sheep slickly into the truck. Then came the young dogs who found the whole occasion a bit of a romp. They raced and yapped and scattered sheep all over the ground, while their owners whistled and shouted and grew red in the face. The rules forbid swearing, otherwise I reckon we would have heard a bit of paddock language.

Roy, oblivious to the pressure on him, lay at the end of a piece of chain in the shade of the ute. The public address system in the distance was droning on, calling viewers for the showgirls, and announcing the winners of the classes of polished hacks. In the tin shed that served as the show pavilion there was excitement because the cornflour sponge had been won by a man. And my chocolate slice had scored. But there was no time for such frippery.

'Dog number 15,' said the man with the loud hailer in the dog ring— and the stomach butterflies surged and my palms sweated.

Roy and the boss strode into the ring. The boss looked a bit tense, but Roy was just looking around for some sheep to work. With the familiar command 'Go back', Roy leapt into action, brought the sheep into the yard and whizzed them down the race. The old boy even managed a few of his wheezy barks, and the spectators could see he was missing a few teeth.

The judges scribbled on bits of paper and the boss, sensing that things were going well, hissed between his teeth for Roy to 'Get up' on their backs. That would be the clincher—and after all, it was the whole reason we had brought the senile old fool.

But Roy wouldn't have a bar of it. He smiled up at the boss and wagged his tail to show he understood, then turned his back and went on with forcing the sheep up the race the way he had done it all his life. Nevertheless, although it was a good, clean display, we felt let down. We even felt a bit cheated that his new-found talent had been such a fleeting thing.

The judges sitting beneath their umbrellas on the back of a ute in the ring finished adding up the numbers. Up they went on the board.

'Crikey! The old fool has got into the finals!' we all shrieked.

And when the finals were over, Roy ended up in fourth place. It was all a bit of a thrill and old Roy danced around the boss as he was patted and fussed over like he never had been before. His tan eyebrows were still drawn together in puzzlement though. He thought he was only doing his job. Anyway, that night the old celebrity rode home in the front of the ute—something that had never happened before.

Now the boss says he'll try competing again, and he's excited about Roy and Rhubarb's pups which are due in a fortnight because he says, with such a champ for a father, they should be little beauties.

In the district even now there is talk of more yard-dog trials and who will take the laurels. The school is going to put on trials as part of its annual fundraiser and twenty blokes have got their names down. This is the new sport all right... and I suppose it's as good a way as any to distract us from the miserable spring rains and the fact that the crops are withering.

But all I'm worried about is whether I can keep up the supply of duck eggs.

FOLLOWING INSTINCTS
Roy Hentschke, Blyth

In the 1930s, a drover was given ten pounds to train a border collie pup for sheep work.

An uncle of mine rescued her from the drover who was beating her for disobedience. He swapped her with an uncontrollable no-hoper.

The bitch was called Minty. She was one of the best all-round sheep-dogs I can remember.

When six years old, her former owner recognised her at the saleyards. My uncle immediately offered her back, but the former owner realised that if she had not been rescued from the drover, she may well have been dead. Instead, he said he would like a pup from her next litter.

When the litter of five pups arrived, Minty showed signs of sickness. When they were four weeks old, she carried them in her mouth, one by one, to a rabbit warren about 300 metres away.

My uncle returned them all to the kennel. He fed them and bedded them down.

The following day, the performance was repeated. Minty died not long after completing the task. This remarkable dog, knowing that death was imminent, had followed her instincts in making sure there was a source of food for her pups.

125

As a young farmer, I had one of her pups, Boxer, who became a good trial dog. I still have this blood line in my own dogs, fifty-two years later. They still have the 'eye' and ability that distinguished Minty.

GOODBYE LADY
Mrs John Schwarz, Taplan

His heart was heavy as he replaced the rifle behind the door. She had been a faithful companion for more than twelve years.

He had left it until almost dark, so that as the cold metal point touched her forehead, he wouldn't have to see those dark brown eyes of trust, imploring him for help.

It was during the last shearing, when she was on the back of the ute, heading out to bring in a new of mob of sheep, that a roll of barb wire, used for mending a fence the week before, had got entangled in the hair under her hind leg.

Part of the wire had cut into the bare patch of skin. The hair had to be cut, as well as the barb, to finally free Lady. The resulting wound never healed. Although she licked it daily to keep it clean, it always seemed to be weeping.

She seemed to lose the will to fight, and just lay waiting patiently, in a hole she had scratched for herself in the carport, beside the house. Barely eating, she would only lick at a dish of water. But she was alert to the end, always holding up her head, following keenly all the comings and goings of her friend, the boss.

He knew it was the kindest thing to do for her, but still he had put it off, hesitating to make the final break.

The boss wasn't the only one with a lump in his throat the next morning when he broke the news to the family. No longer would she be around when the ute was backed out of the shed. No longer would her warning bark be heard when a strange vehicle came up the track.

But later that day, Lady's freshly-weaned grandson rode in the ute on the boss's lap, to check the maiden ewes.

More Great
WORKING
DOG
STORIES

HISTORY OF THE KELPIE
Olive Hargrave, Yarrawonga, Victoria

In about 1869, John Rutherford, a highly respected pastoral pioneer and Yarrawonga identity, was sent a pair of top breeding dogs by his brother who lived at Dunrobin, Sutherlandshire, in Scotland.

The working ability of the Scottish dogs with sheep was excellent, but they were poorly equipped to handle the harsh conditions of the colony. So John Rutherford, who lived at Yarrawonga Station and was a fine judge of animals, set about improving the breed.

From the Scottish dogs, Rutherford bred Moss, a smooth-haired, prick-eared black dog with a splash of white on his neck. Moss is regarded as the grand-sire of the kelpie breed.

In 1869, another grazier, George Robertson of Warrock Station near Casterton in Victoria, imported another pair of breeding dogs from Scotland.

From his breeding program, he produced a bitch which was later to be called Gleeson's Kelpie after Jack Gleeson of Murray Downs Station, Victoria, who acquired her in exchange for his horse.

Jack Gleeson named the bitch Kelpie after the mythical Scottish spirit that was supposed to frequent fiords and rivers on stormy nights, and make itself apparent to those about to drown. Usually appearing in the form of a horse, the spirit itself was sometimes regarded as harmful.

Messrs Elliot and Allen of Geraldra Station imported yet another pair of dogs from Scotland in 1870. Mr Elliot was a brother-in-law of George Robertson of Warrock Station. The dogs were named Brutus and Jenny, and their matings produced Caesar, Laddie and Nero. A mating of Caesar to Gleeson's Kelpie produced a bitch called King's Kelpie. Moss was mated several times to Gleeson's Kelpie and King's Kelpie. It is now generally considered that it was from these matings that the cross was established from which all good kelpies evolved.

Laddie was mated with King's Kelpie and produced Sally. Moss was mated with Sally and a pup from the litter, a jet black, prick-eared, smooth-coated dog like its father, was given to a station hand named Jack Davis. He named his pup Barb after Barb, the hardy black racehorse of African descent that won the Melbourne Cup in 1866.

One of the pups from a mating of Moss and King's Kelpie was Clyde. When Clyde was mated with one of Walter King's bitches named Gary, the litter produced what many consider to be the best working dog of all time, a dog named Coil.

In the Sydney sheepdog trials of 1898, Coil was worked by Jack Quin and in the preliminary trial scored full points from a possible 100.

That evening, he was run over by a cab and suffered a broken leg. The next day, Coil went into the finals with his broken leg hanging loose and, again, was awarded a perfect score. This feat has never been equalled.

The world's first sheepdog trials are believed to have been held at Forbes, New South Wales, in about 1871 or 1872. The winner was a bitch named Kelpie, daughter of another bitch, imported from Scotland.

Yarrawonga has every reason to be proud of its heritage as the birthplace of the kelpie breed, through Moss, one of its most famous sons—the first link in the breeding chain of Australian working kelpies and barbs.

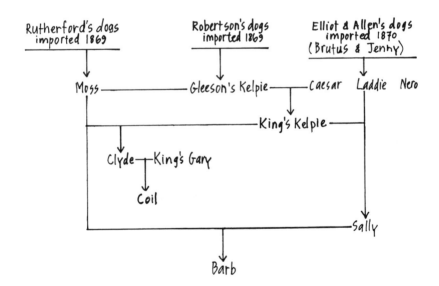

GETTING ACQUAINTED
Geraldine Boylan, Port Lincoln, South Australia

Between 1988 and 1991 I worked as a counsellor with rural communities. Having been raised as farm girl I was well versed with the position held by the farm dog on the farm. To my joy I found nothing had changed over time. Traditions reigned supreme, or should I say the place held by the farm dog did.

I quickly recaptured my former knowledge and set about to put it into practice. To give the dog his or her rightful place—he or she runs the farm and knows everything about everything that goes on, and if you make it with them then you have made it for life.

On arrival at a farm I developed the habit of winding down my car window and spending time quietly getting acquainted with the 'Boss' of the farm or with the 'Boss and his or her supporters'. They never let me down. They always rolled up to give me the once-over.

I learned much from observing these dogs. Sometimes I established a relationship quickly. A few words had them literally eating from my hand. At other times the inspection was more comprehensive—the wheels received the usual 'sniff and wee' treatment before I was given so much as a stare. Once the look in their eyes went from watchful to mellow, I learned to open the door and to sit quietly and allow the personal inspection. Mostly I found that after sniffs and a few licks, I'd made the grade.

After a while I learned to place the dogs in three categories—the wary, the smoochers and the rude. The wary dog often remained aloof, watchful and tense until I earned his acceptance. Thank goodness this type was scarce. At times I looked for a correlation between the tenseness of the dog and the tension on the home front, but I found no support for this notion.

With quiet talking the reserved dog could eventually be won over. I remember one occasion when I sat in the car and calmly explained the purpose of my visit to the dog; I explained I was the 'good guy'. I was not the bank manager. At that moment a head came around the shed corner and a voice said, 'I'm glad about that. I wasn't coming out—until I heard you say that.'

The smoochers were pushover dogs. Thank goodness they were in plentiful supply. My affairs with them were mutually satisfying.

To explain the third category I need to tell a story. One day I called at a farm and as I went through my usual performance a young pre-school lass came and swung on the house garden gate. Immediately she joined the conversation, giving a rundown on the dogs together with some strong advice.

'Watch out for Brucey. He's rude.'

Ignoring the dogs, I climbed from the car to join the child. Just then this dog thrust his head between my legs.

'See, I told you to watch him. He's rude.'

During the three years, I found many such dogs. Indeed there were more rude dogs on farms than any other types. They seemed to take great delight in actions which defied all words and which rendered unexpected and immediate embarrassment.

But in a way I respected these rude dogs. Their instincts still ruled supreme despite their training and complex skills. Even though they were totally obedient and submissive to a boss in the paddock, they were still masters of themselves. Politeness, the mark of civilised society, could never be trained into these dogs. They had everyone at their mercy. Any visitor with a superior air and an expensive suit could be humbled with a good sniff in the crutch.

Throughout the three years I never ceased to be in awe of the knowledge, and the silent stories, that were communicated through the farm dogs' eyes.

The dogs often made it clear what was going on, what was the state of the bank balance, how depressed were their owners. If a farm was falling to pieces you'd often find half a dead sheep dragged on to the verandah, holes dug all around the house and dogs and their mess lying around everywhere. There'd be a general air of decay as the dogs extended their territory into that of their owners who no longer were able to take an interest in disciplining their dogs and drawing boundaries between dog and human.

You could see loneliness in the eyes of these dogs. They were no longer working—all the stock had gone. They were starved for company as the wives were out working and the kids had left home to look for work in the city.

There was an air of resignation in a lot of these dogs' eyes. They'd throw themselves at you with a sort of desperate joyfulness, happy to have company, but looking for leadership and purpose once more to their lives.

PART 1
TRIBUTES

- *Paying respect*
- *An insight into the life of a working dog*
- *The value of a good dog*
- *Their work*

TOUGH COUNTRY, TOUGH DOGS

Peter Clarke, Kununurra, Western Australia

I used to work as overseer on Tubbo Station in the New South Wales Riverina. Tubbo was a sheepdog's paradise with up to 35,000 merino sheep of fine quality.

There were good-sized paddocks for the dogs to have a decent cast around, big yards, big numbers and big mobs. Struth, the Tubbo woolshed is 102 stands and to fill her up with 3,000 woolly sheep, good dogs were needed. Many a time I saw old Bob's dog Humphrey back a running mob of wethers 200 yards up through the yards and way through the shed, turn round and back them in the other direction as they ran in.

Sheepdogs! The outstation overseer ran anywhere between fourteen and nineteen dogs at once. His ute was a mobile dog kennel and butchery, with kelpies, border collie crosses and the odd collie thrown in—all different sizes, different ages, and different levels of ability.

The ute sides were strung with roo legs and old sheep that made up the tucker for these dogs. His job involved a lot of droving and mustering of lines of sheep of similar age from various paddocks into one mob and taking them the 30 miles into the shed. Mobs of 4,000 were common and even bigger mobs of 12,000 weaners were handled by dogs on Tubbo.

It is a skilful team of man and dog that can count through a gate 3,000 to 4,000 sheep, keep tallies, direct the odd young dog and keep the ants out of one's boots all at once.

A dog is a man's best friend. My top dog was a kelpie-New Zealand border collie bitch called Lucy. Sheep were her life. In winter when the ice was on the puddles, she'd have a good swim, then jump up on the ute ready for work.

She would sit on a whistle or wave of a hand away across the paddock. She would work on a wing or tail a mob for miles with no directions. She worked on when her body wanted to stop—130 degrees or more in the sun, pads worn and cracked and troughs miles apart, but she never let me down. Never. She was my friend and my helper. I couldn't have done the job with only my four dogs if Lucy wasn't there. A dog is worth five men and Lucy worth five dogs.

I told her through a veil of tears how much I loved her as I buried her after a 'pig dog' fought her to death. My wife and I were off the property and arrived home to be confronted with our best friend ripped to pieces.

When she needed me most I wasn't there but she was always there for me. I feel I let her down. That's what really hurts. She was killed three nights before we were due to move to Texas Downs where Lucy was going to retire, as no dogs were used there.

QUEENIE WITH THE DASHING TONGUE

Louella Vaughan, Mogilla, New South Wales

A droving friend of mine, Ted, had a red kelpie called Queenie. On quiet command she would be sent to turn the head or bring up the rear of the roving mobs.

In the full heat of summer, far from dams and creeks where cattle often break and run, I've seen Queenie work to hold the mob until she was staggering from thirst and exhaustion. Ted's hardy old Akubra would then quickly be adapted to make a water bowl to revive her.

At home after the evening meal was finished, a chair would sometimes be pulled up—'but not too near the table'—for Queenie. The mock kissing game which ensued would keep us all amused as the bespectacled, leathery face of the drover would tease his sleek, seal-like kelpie.

Her head would bow in false and knowing modesty, her eyes turned upward coyly at her owner, watching for that opportunity for her dashing tongue to make contact with the cheek that came so temptingly close, then jerked away. Affection masked by chastisement would follow: 'By Jesus, Queenzy, don't you go kissin' me.'

Her head would drop and the kelpie grin would turn to a Mona Lisa smile as she played the game over and over again and just now and then had a win, only to be called a 'dirty old thing'.

After the games, she'd be rewarded with a bone off a plate and would depart with a majestic air that indicated she really did understand the meaning of her name.

Somewhere in Queensland they took a mob. The day was hot, the grass was good and the herd had spread for what seemed like miles. Queenie was sent to bring the mob to check. She was on her way a 'long way back'. The rate of the dust rising from the road told Ted that a car was coming at a furious pace. He reckoned the driver would slow down when he realised the front stragglers were part of a mob. But he did not.

Too far away to warn Queenie, but close enough to witness the impact, Ted's heart missed a beat as he saw that she was hit. In rage he picked up a rock and hurled it at the passing car, shattering the windscreen. Still the driver did not bother to stop and Ted's curses were drowned out by the engine's roar.

Mounting his horse, he urged it through the settling dust to where Queenie lay.

'Sweet Jesus, why?' he whispered.

He took his pocket knife from its pouch and crouching over Queenie, slit her down the side. She had been heavily in pup and he thought one might just be alive.

The souped-up car and angry young driver returned with policeman in tow. The drover's weathered face was stony and white and the dust on it was wet and smeared from sweat—or tears.

In his trembling hands he still held the knife and in the other a fine, fat, lifeless pup, one from a litter of eight, their helpless bodies spread on the ground.

The copper cleared his throat and addressing the young driver said, 'Push off, son, you got off light. A bloke's dog out here's worth a man or three.'

And helplessly he stared at the scene of my friend, the still puppies and the corpse that was once our beautiful Queenie.

OWING A DEBT TO DOC

Geoffrey Blight, Narrogin, Western Australia

The day Charlie had to have Jenny put down was a bad day. The near sixteen year old bitch had slipped on the motorbike and mangled her legs. Charlie's son rushed her to the vet, then had to phone home and tell Charlie the worst possible news.

'Have him put her down,' was all Charlie said. The ageing sheep farmer sought the seclusion of the woodpile and for several hours moistened chips, remembering the years he'd spent with the old quarter-dingo kelpie-cross.

They'd shown them! On more than one occasion the extraordinarily tough old dog had shown what real dogs were made of. Never a sheep or other could call her bluff.

Even third prize in the State Yard Championship had dismayed the perfectionists, who had until then little time for the rough coated, often noisy dog that beat the living daylights out of any of their glamorous collies if they annoyed her. She always did things her way despite the loud protests from Charlie and threats to knock her bloody block off.

She'd had a good number of pups, some good, some a bit rough, but Charlie had kept a couple—Misty and Doc. Misty was good-looking, won a trial and was very obedient, but Doc was a bit too much like Jenny, hard to handle, wanting things his own way all the time, not to mention a bit rough on the sheep at times. He was inclined to give them something to remember if they didn't see it his way, but he was tougher than King Gees.

Charlie might not have kept him if he hadn't lost old Jenny and had a tragic poisoning of nearly all his dogs. So he was kind of stuck with Doc, if he wanted to keep the old part-dingo line of which he was so proud.

Doc was not just part-dingo, he looked and acted it—a big, funny kind of yellow-orange dog that prowled rather than ran. All Charlie's mates told him to get a better-bred dog and nearly succeeded when Charlie bought a very expensive but rather gutless border collie called Big Bob. Sure he worked trials well, but the bastard was useless at home. 'Weak as piss,' Charlie would say as an excuse to keep Doc to handle his 10,000 wild and woolly jumbucks.

When the wool prices collapsed in '89, Charlie's accountants told him to buy some cattle 'to balance things out'. Charlie got a herd of 30 Hereford-cross cows and calves. They were station bred, big wild buggers.

They may have been cheap for their size but they had rarely been handled, if at all, and were calving. Shifting them was nearly impossible. They went mad at dogs and a vehicle didn't do the job. Charlie found himself walking, leaving Doc, Big Bob and Misty on the ute, trying a bit of the old shoo shoo to get them out after they were delivered.

He thought he was going fine as he'd made it halfway across the paddock. He was at least twenty chain from the ute when a cow accidentally trod on a young calf belonging to a big, crumple-horned biddy of a cow, who immediately started to bellow and run around in a frenzy at the calling of the distressed calf.

Charlie had a weak heart. He'd been told many times to take things more easily and had been on medication for several years. When the big cow swung toward him, he was frightened. He couldn't run as there was nowhere to go. A second cow joined the act, threatening and running. Charlie couldn't turn around, or they'd have him. He roared and backed off hoping for something to defend himself with. There was nothing. More and more the cows stirred up, getting closer and closer to him. It was only a matter of time and he knew it.

A lot went through his mind in those seconds as she lined him up— desperation, fear, noise, as the whole herd psyched itself up. When she rushed, Charlie just shut his eyes, grimaced and hoped he could bear it.

The ground shook as she came the last few yards. Suddenly, over the bawling came an unexpected, deafening, howling bark. Charlie only caught a glimpse of a leaping orange flash close by, being showered with dust and dung as the cow changed course to meet a much more threatening intruder.

When he looked, Doc had latched onto the nose of the cow and hung on. Charlie retreated. First slowly then, turning, weak heart or not, he half walked, half ran to the ute, knowing they still could get him if they wanted to. The noise told him the whole herd was joining in.

The cow swung Doc frantically to and fro trying to get him off, finally crashing him to the ground and rolling over him as he tried to take her with him. At last, the big cow bludgeoned Doc off, tossing him mercilessly skyward and charged again.

Doc, now badly injured, retreated slowly, barking and growling with every step. He bluffed to delay another charge. He could have escaped to the ute easily but he didn't. Legs broken, face badly damaged, cut and bruised, he stood his ground, letting Charlie, not game to look back, grasping his chest, finally make it to the ute. Big Bob sat staring at the action from the safety of the tray.

Exhausted, Charlie now looked back and saw the cows continuing their attack on the badly limping, still rebellious Doc. This motivated Charlie to start the ute and charge into the fray, separating the maddened cows from the bleeding, broken dog.

Charlie was born tough, had lived tough and there were rules. There is no room for crippled sheepdogs on farms. Therefore, you put them down. Charlie knew what the vet was going to say. He was ready for it. After all, it wasn't the first time. There had been Jenny, but she was old. Doc was only five.

Halfway to the vet's, he decided there was no harm in trying. Especially if it was only a couple of hundred dollars. He looked at the mutilated form breathing heavily on the seat, covered in blood, and wondered if two hundred would have been thought too much if it had been Charlie there—and it sure as hell could have been.

The vet looked at Charlie funnily, as if he had changed or something, when he found himself explaining how bad and expensive it was for so little chance of ever being right again. That is, if Doc even lived. The old man muttered something about owing the dog a chance. At this stage the vet was unaware of the morning's drama and Charlie sure didn't want to spend the rest of the day on the woodpile again.

Word gets around, especially if you're a popular bloke, and Charlie was one of those. After 24 hours, it was clear that Doc would survive though he'd be crippled. Charlie sat on his front porch as day broke, stroking the swollen, rugged head and plastered body and thanked his best friend for life. He wondered what it was that had brought Doc to his rescue and left the so-called 'good' dogs safe where they'd been told to sit.

His thoughts were interrupted when the noise of one, then two TV choppers came out of the gloom and settled in his front paddock. It would be a long day. There would be many more cars and crews wanting to know the secret of their bond. A bond only a few men have with their best friends.

Doc lives on, awarded the State's two highest bravery awards. No man is more proud of a crippled, ugly, orange sheepdog than Charlie.

REAL DOGS
Nicola Laws, Qakey, Queensland

They always baulk at the door, a lifetime of lessons returning to them. People enter buildings, dogs stay out. Strong hands pull at their chains—or the more usual baling twine—dragging them inside.

The vet's surgery is a strange territory of unfamiliar smells and noises. There's an enclosing by roof and walls. Working dogs always think they're in trouble when brought here. Why else would they be made to come inside?

They make up over half of the small animal caseload of the mixed rural veterinary practice at which I work. For me it's possibly the most enjoyable half. We call them Real Dogs—dogs that work for a living. They present us with a spectrum of problems: routine heart worm checks, vaccinations, emergencies like snake bite, baitings or broken limbs. Or those niggling farm dog worries—flea allergy, ear haematoma or mange.

What do they have in common? Looks that won't win them any beauty contests, a rangy body shape, a patch of hair missing here or maybe a broken tooth or crooked ear there. They also have a stoicism rarely seen in other breeds; and an inbuilt trust of humankind, despite only the occasional pat or kind word.

Some are canine Jekyll and Hydes. The same dog we can do anything to at the hospital will eat us for breakfast should we step on their turf. All show a boundless, enduring energy and level of fitness. If a blue or a kelpie can't find trouble, then they're quite likely to go out and make it.

Snow was quite typical of his kind. Then six years old, a kelpie type, pale-eyed and with a coat so sandy it was almost white, he was one of five dogs that enabled his owner to run a cattle property single-handed near Cecil Plains, Queensland.

The district was flood-bound a few years ago, with many properties cut off for up to a week. Snow certainly picked his time to get sick. His

140

owner, a person I had come to respect for his care and concern for all his dogs, rang for advice. There wasn't much to give—start a course of injectible penicillin, keep up the fluids and bring him in as soon as the track was passable.

It was several days before I saw Snow. He was a walking anatomy lesson, so thin that every bone under that staring, dehydrated coat was visible. He had been depressed for days, not eating, and had begun vomiting. The lack of urination suggested kidney failure. The only dry thing at Cecil Plains that week must have been Snow's bladder.

Over the next few days that dog took everything we could dish out to him with good-natured acceptance. Blood tests, intravenous fluids, injections, bladder catheters. The vomiting stopped and he began drinking and urinating litres of fluid. We sent him home, despite the long-term dark cloud over him. Blood results had confirmed severe non-compensating renal failure.

We were never certain of the cause. The farmer had been draining radiators on the property that week, and the rain had resulted in some of the sludge pooling near Snow's kennel. Radiator additives can be very toxic to kidney tissue, and may be quite palatable to dogs. It all seemed to fit together.

I get to see a lot of dogs, and hear a lot of dog stories. Some are real characters or have performed acts of bravery. But there was something about Snow, and dogs like him, which strikes a chord. It's their quiet toughness and ability to survive, with maybe a little help from veterinary science, and that greatest of healing devices—a tincture of time.

Snow comes in every year. He's just a slip of a dog, and still drinks a lot of water. But he can do a day's work when asked. I've always got an extra pat for him when I see him. Because to me, he's a real dog.

THE DOGS OF OLD GLEN HELEN

Bryan Bowman, Alice Springs, Northern Territory

When, in 1938, I took over Glen Helen from Fred Raggatt, he had an old dog called Whiskey and an old bitch called Rosie. Rosie was mothering her last litter of puppies.

Raggatt at first insisted on killing all the pups and leaving the old dog and Rosie with me as he was leaving the Territory for good and going to live in Adelaide. Eventually, however, he agreed to leave three pups.

In three months, the pups—Bully, Snowy and Daisy—were following me through all classes of stock work, though admittedly I sometimes had to carry one of them home in front of me on the horse after a very long day.

Nineteen thirty-eight was a dry year on the north side of the Macdonnell Ranges but in January 1939, there was a big monsoonal rain causing high floods in the Fink, but this didn't dampen the dogs' enthusiasm. We crossed the horses over the Fink in a relatively shallow spot with the water just up to a horse's withers. The dogs not only swam the river but once waterborne, attached themselves to any horse hanging back.

Ten inches fell in one week, followed by a further six inches in February. By April there were plenty of cattle ready for market and we started mustering. We got most of the cattle easily without having to get out of a walk very often.

However, there was a big white cleanskin bull who defied all efforts to put him into the mob. The rest of the mob was complete and ready to move into the trucks with one day to spare, so we decided to make an all-out attack on the white bull. The white bull was well known to the Aboriginal stockmen from Raggatt's time, and usually ran on the slopes of Mt Razorback.

Our plan of action was to hold a mob of quiet cattle on one of the open flats at the foot of Mt Razorback. Two boys were to go round and turn the bull down onto this flat and I was to wait in a strategic position with the dogs.

It worked like a dream. The bull came trotting along with a stock boy to the right and left of him and I joined in with the dogs in the centre.

However, as soon as the bull saw the other cattle and horsemen, he whipped around like a polo pony and headed for his old haunts on Mt Razorback. But at this point the dogs sailed into him. Bully had bull-terrier blood and usually went for the nose. The other two were typical blue heelers and maintained a merciless attack on his heels.

Confusion reigned for some minutes. Bloodcurdling roars of fury came from the bull and an occasional yelp of pain from the dogs. Bully went sailing through the air like a football and I thought it was curtains for him, but he picked himself up and joined the heelers in their ferocious attack on his heels. At this point the bull admitted defeat and ran to the other cattle for protection. Once into the mob he soon quietened down and duly went up the loading ramp in Alice Springs.

Nineteen thirty-nine was a good season and with the assistance of the dogs the whole herd, including the big cleanskins, was branded and the fats disposed of. War had broken out in Europe and a military camp had grown up in Alice Springs bringing restrictions on sending cattle out of the Northern Territory. The good rains of 1939 were not repeated in 1940, which proved to be one of the driest years on record.

By November 1940, cattle were dying along the Fink and it was apparent the whole area had to be destocked within walking distance of the Fink. Most of this area had been completely eaten out. It had been overstocked for years in Raggatt's time, but there had been no alternative to this as he had no other permanent water.

We had opened up two wells on the west side, one on the Dashwood and one on Stokes Creek. It was 45 miles to the nearest well on the Dashwood, a long walk without water for weak cattle.

However, we achieved this feat by waiting for the full moon and travelling through the night. There were minimal losses. We put the cattle together on the Fink about two days before the full moon, gave them a good drink at about five o'clock in the afternoon, had supper and moved off into the copper and gold sunset with the moon now well above the horizon and the dogs bringing up the rear. If at any time a cow or a calf lay down in the scrub, you would hear a commotion and a calf would rush past you back into the mob while the dogs, looking very pleased with themselves, would be eagerly looking for the next one to hang back.

We moved some 2,000 cattle from the Fink area and saved that country around the Fink from being knocked around during that terrible year.

The end of this story is sad and one for which I blame myself to some extent. One very hot day in January 1943 I had to go down to No. 8 Bore to meet Jim Bullen, who was bringing cattle out to stock his Derwent Station. We had killed for rations the night before and the dogs were gorged with blood and offal from the beast. With this in mind I carefully chained the dogs up before leaving, but when I got about two miles down the Dashwood, I saw them following me. They had very small heads and could usually pull their heads out of any collar if they really wanted to. It was getting late and I didn't fancy going back and tying them up again. I decided to let them follow and hope for the best. When I got to the bore there was no water. The dogs were nowhere in sight and I thought they had most likely returned to the station. But in fact, being so full of meat, they had knocked up and must have been lying down somewhere in the scrub.

When I got back to the station and they were not there, I got a fresh horse and a couple of waterbags, and with one of the stock boys went looking for them. But I never saw them again.

I have tried since then to establish a good breed of cattle dog without success.

The day of the cattle dog in the Centre for mustering is over, but they are still used a bit for yard work. This is due to two factors.

First, dogs of today ride too much in Landrovers and utilities and their feet get too soft. A day's work in the Ranges is all they can stand.

Secondly, most of the mustering is done today with helicopters and there is no way dogs can adapt to this kind of work except that one of the disabilities of helicopter mustering is that once cattle get used to the chopper, they are apt to go into thick clumps of scrub and lie down. There is then no way the chopper pilot can shift them.

A couple of good dogs could get them out pronto, but it's hard to see how this could be coordinated with the helicopter. I have never heard of it being tried.

MR BROOKS AND BLUE

Jeff Baldwin, Wangaratta, Victoria

An old man as I remember him, Mr Brooks was the last of the bullock-ies in our area, the Dandenongs, between 1920 and 1930. Contrary to the popular image of bullockies, he was not loud-mouthed, nor did he swear. Instead he was a kindly, softly spoken man who got things done quietly and efficiently. To my knowledge he had always been a bullock driver.

I daresay he sensed my love for bullocks and dogs, and that's why I was allowed to tag along.

Mr Brooks and Blue, his kelpie cross Queensland heeler, probably had some influence on the choosing of my career. I was allowed to follow along behind the wagon (bare feet in the dust or mud) and turn the wheel that operated the brake! Being allowed to do this probably changed my ambition from being an engine driver like every other young boy at the time, to becoming a bullock driver! (I suppose at 73 years of age I still am a bullocky at heart. In the farm shed hang the bullock yokes an old teamster gave me years ago and I still have the ambition of breaking in my own team.)

When Mr Brooks was yoking his bullocks for the day's work, Blue would heel the bullocks with such ferocity that they would just stand and watch him, too frightened to move away and avoid the yokes being put on.

These days it's hard to visualise an old man yoking up a team of between twelve and twenty bullocks single-handed and without yards, but that's what Mr Brooks did with Blue. The dog would stand by and watch, until asked to take action on any beast that would not get into line.

After the team was yoked and hitched to whatever load they were asked to pull, Blue really came into his own. Bullocks are like humans—they will bludge if given the chance. When this happened, it only needed Mr Brooks to say 'Baldy', 'Ring', 'Brindle', whatever the name was of the offending beast, and Blue would slip in behind the 'bludger', usually unseen, and provide the necessary incentive to correct the bullock's laziness.

In most cases it was not necessary for the dog to heel the guilty bullock because as soon as Mr Brooks spoke its name, it knew what the result would be should it not respond.

I have been working dogs all my life and still am. When I set the gates a certain way, a bitch will muster a 150-acre paddock; when I rub the knife on the steel, a dog will bring in the killers; when bringing up the house cows, the dogs will leave the dry cows behind—and so it goes on. Most farmers have dogs that respond to a given situation.

However, on reflection over the years, Mr Brooks and Blue seem to me to have been the most perfect combination. The dog Blue made it possible for that old man to carry on his profession right up to almost the end of his life. He never had to rely on other people, and more importantly, he did not draw on the public purse for social service, pension or whatever—thanks to Blue, who only ever asked to be fed.

100 MILES BACK TO PATA
Ruth Payne, Victor Harbor, South Australia

We were living on a farm at Pata near Loxton. The boss had a mob of sheep on a property at Pompoota near Murray Bridge, which he checked regularly with the help of his dog Tinker.

One day the boss went to Pompoota and then decided to sell the sheep at the next market. He left his dog with a neighbour until his return.

Back home at Pata, he was up early next morning to do the milking. He missed his usual helper, but out of habit called him anyway, saying, 'Fetch the cows, Tink!'

He was utterly amazed when out from a sheltering bush crept his faithful dog—footsore and weary but ready to work. Tinker had walked 100 miles to get home.

REPAID IN FULL

Mavis Appleyard, Warren, New South Wales

When he was sixteen, my husband Doug found a man ill-treating a young kelpie bitch. After an altercation he took the dog with him and kept her.

He called her Janet and she filled the void in the lonely life he led on a huge sheep station. She quickly became a wonderful, reliable worker, mustering huge paddocks, drafting, penning up, yarding and doing shed work. She knew what to do before she was even told to do it and Doug and she were inseparable.

One day working in the shed at Butterbone Stud Park, Doug was frantically busy and was very annoyed with Janet because she kept disappearing and had to be repeatedly called from under the shearing shed.

By nightfall when he knocked off, Doug was exasperated with her and she finally crept out looking very guilty after much angry calling. In the eight years he had owned her, she had never let him down or left his side when they were working. When she made it obvious she wanted him to check under the shed, he did. In a corner, where the sheep under the shed could not walk on them, were thirteen squealing newborn pups that she had produced between taking mobs in, yarding, penning up and taking sheep away.

Janet repaid us in thousands of ways in her thirteen years for being rescued from a cruel owner by a young boy.

She was a very shy dog and did not like children near her and generally gave them a wide berth. However, after a lot of rain I couldn't find our fifteen month old son. Hearing his annoyed squeals from near the swollen creek, I ran down there and found Janet running between him and the water bumping him sideways away from the water.

She looked very relieved to see me and quickly disappeared and left me to collect him.

LEARNING MY PLACE IN LIFE
Margaret Williams, Yandina, Queensland

Thirty years ago I was governessing for Christopher and Shirley White on Pembroke Station, between Roma and Surat, Queensland. I learned a few valuable lessons while I was there.

One day Ringo, the prized red kelpie sheepdog belonging to Christopher, was knocked down by a car, damaging one of its front legs.

That night, by sheer coincidence, I fell in the bath, hurting my ankle.

Next morning, Chris bundled Ringo and me into his car and drove us 28 miles to the Surat Base Hospital for medical treatment.

The medical superintendent attended to the dog first!

HE FOUND FAME IN THE END
Geoffrey Blight, Narrogin, Western Australia

Gus had been a top trial dog in his day, with wins in four States. He was a short haired tricolour border collie, South Australian bred and a first generation import of the Scottish Merle that had won the British National title in the seventies. Gus had been runner-up six times to the Dog of the Year in Western Australia, but although he had done well in both field and yard trials, he'd never taken the top award.

He started life as an impossibly headstrong dog, which led to his being sold cheaply in Western Australia, where he enjoyed success under a rigid boss. With age and pressure, he had a few heart problems and was declared past it after failing for a year to show form and even the will to stay on the trial ground. It was decided he should be put down.

A very intelligent dog, he'd attracted the eye of an old contractor, new to dog trials, who had owned only one dog for most of his forty years working on farms. Gus had sired some good pups so after a little pleading and much talk about it being a waste of time, Gus was spared and moved to another home. Everyone involved in dog trials was critical of the newcomer for spending time on a has-been dog who had learnt to quit. 'They don't come back,' was the catchcry.

Old Gus started a new life as a sheep contractor's dog, which entailed handling ewes and lambs daily in portable yards—a very different lifestyle and pressure from handling three wethers in trials.

His new boss nearly gave up when he first tried to force Gus to work. The dog attacked his arm, then returned to the box on the ute. The boss continued on with the job using a couple of rather thick border collies to draft and mules.

Gus sat on the ute for several days, never attempting to work, and it looked as though all the advice had been right. Then one day, the other dogs made a mistake and there was a bad break of lambs they couldn't hold.

No-one noticed old Gus drop down, but when they finally headed the breakaways, they became aware that very few sheep had got out of the yards. Most of the 800 ewes and lambs had been blocked by Gus who was sitting, covering and holding with great skill.

Nothing was said to the dog except a few calls of 'good dog'. As the pen was closed, he hastily returned to the ute, ignoring any encouragement from the workers to return.

It was the first sign that he still had a bit of will to work, so Gus was allowed to just watch without ever being pressed to do anything. It was soon noticed that he had a habit of joining in when things weren't done to his liking.

If the sheep wedged in the entrance, he would drop down, circling, and, with extraordinary skill, go forward to shave off a break and push them scurrying deep into the pen, followed by a well-directed barking push that would pen the resisting ewes and lambs.

He would be seen to circle the incoming flock and collect runaways, weak or blind sheep. Even though ignored, he would bring them in with a skill not often seen, but he still refused any communication with his boss.

One day, his new boss watched with concern as Gus attempted to remove three lambs stuck behind a gate. Their heads were caught in the ringlock fence. Gus, realising they wouldn't back out, gently took each of the week-old lambs by the hind leg and dragged them back around the gate, letting them go to trot off, bleating, to the ewes standing waiting, stamping their defiance at the dog.

The final turnaround came one hot night as the boss sat watching TV.

The doors were open to invite a breeze. As he dozed he was awoken by shuffling on the verandah. He looked up to see an old ewe backing through the kitchen into the lounge, followed by old Gus who was looking at the boss for signs of approval. He'd obviously found the old ewe on the road and decided it should be brought to somebody's attention.

When the boss offered the dog an outstretched hand, this time Gus did not ignore it, or bite it. After helping load the ewe onto the ute, he returned to sit by the boss and the television.

There was an amazing change from then on. The contracting team suddenly had a very skilled look. Gus got dinkum once left to his own resources to fit in and showed some longtime sheep farmers skills they had never seen before. And no-one tried to correct or tell Gus what to do.

The new boss had recently taken up dog trialling, but wasn't doing very well. He had never worked on three sheep. He was used to the pressure of coping with irate farmers in a hurry with plenty of barking, shouting and kicking. Time after time he would be disqualified from a trial for everything from walking backwards to patting the dog. The only time he had completed the course, he had received a score of one, despite his best efforts to imitate the champions, including Gus's former owner.

There was much curiosity among the dog triallers when they saw Gus had been entered again. They'd watched for a year when he failed all over Australia, running away despite being offered everything, including pockets full of meat lumps to try and start him.

The new boss had never even tried to work three sheep with Gus in case the bubble burst. It was a very quiet and subdued bloke who walked out onto the ground with Gus following. Everybody held their breath. The siren went, but Gus pricked his ears and headed for the three wethers.

It wasn't the greatest run, but he tried. That in itself was a miracle as the new boss, rather than command the dog to perform, appeared to follow him around the ground.

Over the next four years, they made the finals of many open trials, not achieving more than an odd place and a fourth in the State Utility Trial, but the pups the new boss bred went on to do it all and Gus became Western Australia's top sire.

Gus became well known in schools and hospitals and was the mainstay in a publicity stunt for the Perth Royal Show when, in a team of six dogs, he drove sheep right through the centre of the city watched by a crowd of 20,000 people, and was featured on all four TV news reports.

Gus worked rabbits, ducks, geese, goats, cows, horses and even roos. He became one of the State's best known sheepdogs, even appearing on BBC television. But Gus had arthritis and it was taking a toll. X-rays showed his joints were welded and he was in pain, despite much treatment. In his fourteenth year, he could no longer work. He had to be lifted into the ute. The time was getting near. He was left at home now, to sit in the drive and organise visitors.

JILL, MATRIARCH
OF CHAMPIONS
Bernard Doyle, Tenterfield, New South Wales

After some experience on sheep and cattle properties, and eight years in the dairy industry, I took up sheepdog trialling in 1957.

At this time I was employed with the Queensland Department of Agriculture and Stock at Winton. About that time we purchased Lava Jill from Mr Jack Forest of Oakleigh, Longreach. Jill was Herdsman bred from Sheba and by Chappie.

We moved from Winton at the end of 1959 and at our first attempt at the Brisbane RNA show in 1960 or 1961, we won the open trial against fairly strong competition. Jill was a determined hard worker and was placed second at the Queensland Championships when aged thirteen years.

She displayed her talents early. My wife Dulcie reared batches of up to 500 laying pullets at the back of our Winton residence. When the small percentage of cockerels in one of these batches was becoming evident (by comb, wing and tail feather development), someone left the gate chain loose.

Soon after, to everyone's surprise, Jill arrived at the back door of our house with all the conspicuous cockerels under control. She had forced the gate and drafted the baby cockerels from the 300 pullets. Jill was eight months of age and had not shown interest in stock at the time.

We are still breeding fairly closely to Jill's bloodline and right now have great grandsons and great grand-daughters working successfully. Kynoona Tess, one of Jill's progeny, now nine years old, has won several open trials and placings from a relatively small number of trials attended.

Tess and I were selected to represent the Queensland Working Sheep Dog Association Inc. at the recent televised *Australian Sheepdog Challenge* conducted at Werribee Mansion near Melbourne. I am a life member of the above Association and am deeply grateful for being selected. The series was broadcast on ABC television as 'A Dog's Life'.

The results of the grand final for those of you who didn't see the program were: First—Doug Connop of Bridgetown, Western Australia with Glenromain Dinny. Second—Sid Cavanagh, Rochester, Victoria with Marlowe Benji. Third—Greg Prince of Dubbo, New South Wales with Rosedale Turbo.

You may be interested in a few points from an article I wrote in 1983 for the *Queensland Agricultural Journal* on the care and training of working dogs.

Select pups from keen, hard-working parents of proven bloodlines. Pups from some bloodlines will exhibit a keen desire to work at first or second sightings of sheep. From others the pups may be eight months or older before they exhibit this desire. It is good to see pups show an early urge to work but excellent dogs have developed from both early and late starters.

Before the command sessions are started the pup must have a name. One syllable names are best since they have a sharp inflection. Throughout a dog's life it will respond best to commands if its name is used occasionally to obtain added attention.

The trainer can assist the pup by watching its facial expression and encouraging it if he sees uncertainty. Should he see stubborness he may have to scold to the degree necessary.

At the early sessions off the lead allow the pupil a few chances to obey each command. The trainer should stay calm and keep the pup's confidence.

During training 'body talk' is important. It can be an effective aid should the pupil show uncertainty. The trainer can do much to help by using exaggerated body movements.

Most working sheepdogs in Australia originate from strains of 'heading dogs'. Their dominant instinct is to go to the lead of stock and gather them. They should be encouraged to cast out and to keep recasting as more sheep are sighted. It cannot be overemphasised that practice makes perfect. Working dogs are no exception. They keep on improving with practice and guidance.

HOW DID SHE GET THERE?

Doug Harkin, Maryborough, Victoria

I tell this story in an effort to solve a longstanding mystery. Between 25 and 35 years ago, I saw a border collie bitch lying beside the road at the intersection of the Talbot–Wareek and Maryborough–Avoca roads. The latter is now known as the Pyrenees Highway. This intersection is eight miles west of Maryborough and nine miles east of Avoca.

After about two days the dog moved some 300 yards down to our house. It was very noticeable that one hind leg had about six inches cut off it. This looked to have been done by a mower or a binder. The dog's leg appeared to have been professionally repaired so I thought she must be a good dog and made every effort to locate the owner.

After feeding and watering her for a couple of days, during which she was very shy, I showed her a mob of sheep in the yards, but she did not seem interested.

I took them back to the paddock and called her. She very reluctantly followed me. When they were in the middle of the paddock I said, 'Go way back', and waved my arm. She flew around them with that particular hop and skip owing to one short leg.

She stood up behind them and as I waved my arms she followed every order. From that moment she was my adoring slave and never left my side. If I was in the house, she would lie on the verandah and wait and listen. If I went out the back door she would be there in a flash. Wherever I worked she would curl up nearby but never let me move without her. When she knew which paddocks the sheep were in, and where the gates were, she could practically do all the sheep work herself. While travelling in a vehicle she was alert to danger and would warn the driver with a

153

short whimper. At the house she announced a visitor with a single bark.

If I went away for a few days she would lie under an old sofa on the verandah and only eat enough to keep herself alive. When I came back she was back to her usual self.

My uncle once said, when trying to capture her attention, 'She won't take her eyes off you. She thinks you're bloody marvellous'.

We were inseparable for years and when she died I was very emotionally upset. She was the best and most faithful dog I have ever had in 70 years.

I have often wondered how she was left there—obviously not deliberately. Perhaps a truckie got out to inspect his load, and did not miss her on getting back. Surely, somewhere, there is someone still alive who knew of a marvellous border collie with three legs lost in that area. If so I would love to hear from them.

PART 2
AFTER YEARS OF WORK TOGETHER

- *The bond that is formed*
- *Trust*
- *Mutual respect*
- *Shared lives*

SANDSOAP

Ron Kerr, Borroloola, Northern Territory

Forty years ago this year I was tailing a mob of bullocks a few miles north of Bourke, New South Wales, along the Darling River at Mays Bend.

The bullocks had come from Nockatunga Station on the Wilson River, south-west Queensland. There were 1,250 head and after droving them for months from Nockatunga, they were well handled and the grass along the Darling was knee-high and green. We were waiting for the Bourke Meatworks, run by Bunny Tankred, to have enough room in the yard to take the bullocks.

It was a drover's dream tailing bullocks on tall green grass alongside clear running river water, compared to the country we had come over, with raw sand, dust, flies and scrub. Already the bullocks were starting to camp only two hours off night camp, about a mile off the river where we would ride night watch.

There were five of us in the camp—a horse-tailer, cook and three of us with the cattle, all taking turns to watch the cattle at night on open, soft ground free from gullies, logs or stumps. The spot for night camp was mostly picked by the cook and horse-tailer—a place where the night watchman had a chance to go with the lead of the cattle if they jumped. And this mob had done plenty of that for the first week out of Nockatunga.

But now they were like milking cows and could be handled by one man. That's why that day I was on my own with the bullocks. It was my turn to tail the cattle.

I left the night camp at daybreak, with my corned beef and damper in the saddlebag and a quart pot on the other side of the saddle as I wouldn't be back to the camp until it was time to bed down the bullocks at dark that evening.

That night I wouldn't have to take a night watch and I was looking forward to a good night's sleep as everyone else in the camp would be sleeping most of that day. It was about dinnertime or midday when the cattle camped along the hollow in the river bed, so I put the quart pot on to boil.

When the horse, tied to the tree, started moving about, snorting now

156

and then, I walked over to check if there were ants about, or whatever else might be upsetting it.

About twenty yards from the horse was a black and tan pup about two months old, and that poor I thought he'd have to stand twice before making a shadow. I felt like getting a good, strong stick and putting him out of his misery. He had big, sad eyes and wasn't frightened to look me in the eye with both of them.

I tried to pat him, but he got up and moved about ten feet away. I tried again. He moved away again. I said, 'OK, you independent bastard. I've got a quart pot boiling away and I've got no use for a dog, as we've never had dogs in the camp.' I went back to making the tea.

Getting my corned beef and damper out of my saddlebag, I'd just sat down when I heard something behind me. Looking around, there was the pup with his big, sad eyes sitting under the shade near the horse. I thought, 'I'll win this dog over to my way of thinking.'

Breaking off some corned beef, I walked over to him, getting on the upwind side so he could smell the beef. It was no go. He could smell the meat all right. I could see his nose twitching, but he wouldn't come to me or let me touch him. It was just those big, goggle eyes that said nothing.

I threw the meat towards him. It hit the ground about six inches in front of his nose. I think it was still moving when it disappeared and I saw the lump snaking down the pup's throat. There was not even a wag of the tail. Just those big glassy eyes looking at me, or at something above my head.

I had finished eating as much corned beef as I wanted and still had plenty left over. From habit I always carry more corned beef than I need in case there is trouble with the cattle. You may miss a mealtime and beef was not short in this camp; and the more you ate, the better you were paid.

So, going to my horse to check out the cattle, I emptied what leftover food I had not far from the dog—who never made a move towards the meat. Riding away, I looked back. The pup was eating, so I left him to it and rode around the bullocks.

Half an hour later I was sitting on my horse under some shade overlooking the bullocks camped along the grassy hollow when the horse tried to get a look behind him. I turned around and there was Big Eyes sitting under a tree twenty yards away. This went on every time I moved. The pup moved like he was some sort of tail-light.

About 3 o'clock the bullocks were on their feet starting to feed. I was kept busy working the bullocks out of the river, making them feed out over the river flats towards the camp. It was near sundown when I looked to see if the pup had followed. Sure enough, there he was, even though his eyes looked the biggest part of him.

Just on dark the horse-taller came out and gave me a hand to put the cattle on camp as he could then take my horse out to the others and hobble him, and bring back another night horse. With the cattle bedded down, I picked up my swag and took it over near where the night horses were tied up. Although I wasn't watching that night, I had to be up and on a horse if the cattle jumped.

The horse-tailer came up with the last night horse and asked where the bony, big-eyed pup came from. I told him he'd been following me at a distance all day along the river and I didn't want to chase him away as he might run into the bullocks and spook them. And as he was over near my swag I'd try to catch him and tie him up that night in case he put the cattle on their wheels.

The horse-tailer said, 'If you can fatten him you might see that he has a bit of breeding in him.' I said the breeding might be a long way in and the way he eats beef we might need the whole mob to fatten him. But the horse-tailer said, 'He's a black and tan kelpie and could be close to pure-bred and they don't bark much unless they're made to bark.'

That night when I went to my swag with a piece of fresh cooked corned beef, I was going to try to catch Big Eyes and tie him up with one of my swag straps. I started feeding him little bits of meat at a time. Each piece was gulped down but I still couldn't get a hand on him. At last I gave him all the meat. The way his gut came out you could see where the beef was.

A few days later, we moved off with the bullocks to the meat-works yards. There our long trip from Nockatunga finished and Big Eyes was there twenty yards behind me all the time.

From there, I looked up my brother, Frank, who was camped with his droving plant at North Bourke. Me and Big Eyes camped with Frank for a week or so, then a mate of mine came along looking for someone to go with him up on the Culgoa River towards the Queensland border mustering sheep for shearing.

So next day, me and Big Eyes left for Kennibree Station walking a plant of horses. Big Eyes wouldn't get up under the wagonette with the other dogs, so he followed me behind the horses for the 40 miles. By now, he was in my shadow all the time and I could put my hand on him. But he never wagged his tail. He just lay down and looked at me like I was stupid.

My mate Wally Smith said, 'He's a one-man dog if ever I saw one and if you just give him time, he'll make a worker and a good one at that. But you want to call him a name, and one that someone can't pick if you lose him. Big Eyes is too close to his looks.'

A few days later, we were washing our clothes down at the creek and Wally said, 'Have you worked out a name for the dog yet.'

I said I'd tried every dog's name I know and there was still no reaction. As I had a cake of sandsoap in my hand for washing, I said I might as well call him Sandsoap. The dog stood up and wagged his tail for the first time. Smithy said, 'That's close to his name. Call him Sandy.'

The reaction was now from the ears and tail.

Smithy said, 'Make it Sandsoap. It's harder for someone else to think of.'

So, Sandsoap it was. I now had a dog with a name and one I could pat, tie up and which had meat over his ribs.

For the next two days of mustering sheep, Sandsoap never got any more than ten feet from my horse, but he jumped up and down when Wally's dog went around the sheep.

Wally rode around the mob saying to me, 'Has Sandsoap taken any interest yet.'

I said, 'He goes ten feet from the horse and I go the rest. And he's supposed to be a sheepdog.'

Next morning, we were taking shorn sheep back to a paddock. I said to Wally, 'I'll tie this Soap ad up as he might cause trouble.'

Wally said, 'No. Bring him along. These shorn sheep're hungry and they'll take some holding until we get out onto some grass country.'

There was a small holding paddock near the shearing shed with about 1,000 shorn sheep, all snow white. Wally said for me to go down and open the gate and try to steady the lead of the sheep when they went through.

I opened the gate and out came the sheep. Now to steady the lead.

There was no lead. They were all round the horse, under the horse's belly and I was trying to get the horse to the outside. Finally reaching the outside, I looked for Sandsoap. Was he still in the middle under the sheep? I noticed that Wally's dogs must have blocked the lead as the dogs were starting to turn them back.

Getting to the lead, I saw Sandsoap doing about 30 miles an hour right across and just under the noses of the sheep. To give him moral support, I yelled, 'Stick it into 'em, Sandsoap.'

That sent him mad. He went around the lead and down the other wing. About 40 yards down the wing, he turned and came back, bringing the other point of the wing around and across the lead. I got out of his way as the lead came bolting around the rest of the mob. I sat there on my horse and couldn't see a thing. There was a red cloud of dust 50 feet in the air.

Wally came around the other side of the mob covered in red dust, saying, 'That dog's starting to work.'

I said, 'He's gone mad and deaf. I can't call him back.'

Wally said, 'Don't try. He's ringing them back onto the fence and will stop ringing soon.' Sure enough, the dust was lifting as the sheep pulled up. Out of the dust came Sandsoap, his tongue almost on the ground and the goggle eyes were like fire. Watching the sheep, he almost ran into us before he saw us.

Wally said, 'I'll bet anything he's a born lead dog, a dog that wants to work on his own. Catch him, and hold him until I bring the tail up. Let the lead go for a while, then we'll give him the lead to work.'

By now, we were coming into grass country and the sheep were settling down, but still moving and spreading. I let Sandsoap go. His tongue was still hanging out, but he trotted across the tail of the mob, stopped once, looked back, then loped off up the wing. Later we could see him trotting back and forth across the lead.

The shed cut out three weeks later and I stopped on the station as overseer for the next three years. Sandsoap started as a jackeroo pup and went on to he head stock dog.

I saved some money, bought a truck and went back droving.

Sandsoap was well known around the drovers' camps and I had a mob of cattle to bring from Quilpie in Queensland to Bourke, about seven to eight weeks' walk.

My brother Frank had 5,500 sheep heading down the Darling to Wentworth. He needed a lead dog, and as I didn't need Sandsoap with cattle, he went to the Vic border on a job he liked best.

We both arrived back at Bourke about the same time, where Frank gave me news about Sandsoap. Having finished the job to Wentworth, and coming home back up the road along the Darling, Sandsoap fell off the back of the truck and hanged himself.

Frank said he was in a hurry to catch the punt over the river at Louth before the operator headed for the pub at Louth, where it would be hard to make anyone hear you after dark. One of his men had got out of the truck to check the load and found Sandsoap hanging. He unhooked him and put him off the road.

I didn't miss the dog much until I had nearly 8,000 sheep going down the Darling and across to Swan Hill on the Vic border, some three months after Sandsoap was hanged. I crossed over the punt at Louth and was going down the west side of the Darling.

I was at Dunlop Station with 8,000 sheep, very little feed and a mob of sore-footed dogs, when a fellow from Dunlop Station came down the road on horseback and with a dog. As he came level with the lead of the sheep about half a mile from the tail, I saw a dog branch off and go across the lead of the sheep. The bloke I had up on the other wing near the lead started coming back and the bloke that was to pilot us through came on down to the tail where I was. We both arrived on the tail of the mob about the same time. The station man said he'd left his dog up the lead as it was the only place he'd work. My man said he was a good lead dog, too.

Me and this station bloke rode along behind the sheep, him telling me about his dog in the lead, and me telling him about my dog Sandsoap, and how they worked very much the same. You didn't see much of them, but you knew they were up there as the lead, was being kept square across the face and every now and then the lead would be bumped back. Everything Sandsoap could do, this bloke's dog, Bandy, could do, and I was beginning to think that this bloke was a parrot. I thought there wasn't another dog in the country that could work as well as Sandsoap. Everyone that knew him reckoned he was the best dog they'd seen.

We were pulling into dinner camp and I said to this bloke, 'Pull your dog in, mate, and give him a blow and a drink.'

He said, 'He'll come in when the sheep start to camp.'

I felt like hanging one on him because Sandsoap wouldn't leave the sheep until the sheep had started to camp. Then I thought, 'How did this bloke know that I never told him.' And I said, 'Do you want to sell him? I could use a good lead dog and you could buy a good dog for five pounds.' So I offered him ten quid. He said he was not for sale.

Just then, the dog came from behind. I couldn't believe my eyes. The dog was the same colour black and tan, had the same goggle eyes. The bloke called the dog Bandy and it was heading for him. I was at the fire twenty yards off the line the dog was taking when the bloke called out, 'Bandy'. I called, 'Sandsoap'. The dog stopped and came straight for me, jumping all over me.

The bloke from the station said, 'You must have a way with dogs. That's the first time I've seen him go near anyone else.'

I said, 'We've been talking about the same dog all morning.'

He said, 'It can't be. You said your brother had him when he was hung.'

'That's right,' I said. 'But it was only 25 miles back along the road to Louth where he was supposed to have been hanged. He must've been unconscious when they left him. How long have you had this dog?' I asked him.

He said, 'I came five months ago and I was here about a month when the dog turned up. He was very sick and couldn't eat much.'

He asked how long it had been since my brother was through here. I told him it had been three months and three weeks.

'Are you sure he's your dog?' he asked. 'Prove he's your dog.'

I said, 'You send him around the sheep and I'll stop him within ten feet without calling his name.'

He sent him. The dog just started to gallop and I gave a sharp whistle. The dog went down to ground. I said for him to send him again. This time I let the dog get further away, and I stopped him again. Then I said, send him. You stop him by name.'

I sent him and he called him, 'Bandy', then again, 'Bandy'. I let the dog go until he was at the sheep, then whistled. Down went the dog.

The bloke got up and said, 'He's yours, all right.'

I said, 'Yes, a bloody ghost dog.'

The station bloke left the camp minus Sandsoap, but with twenty pounds in his pocket. After that, Sandsoap was known as the ghost dog around the drovers' camps.

He was run over by a truck out of Broken Hill in 1958. That time he didn't return.

CHANCE

Robert Ellis, Duckmaloi via Oberon, New South Wales

In 1941 my father went to war. He was in the 8th Division which was devastated during the fall of Singapore, where he died.

He had a two-tone tan kelpie dog named Chance, who besides being a good sheepdog was also his very good mate. We lived during this time on Round Hill, a property at Eugowra owned by my uncle. Round Hill was three miles from Eugowra on the Cowra railway line.

Each day a motor train came from Cowra to Eugowra, arriving at 9.30 am and departing at 4 pm for the return journey. On leaving for the war, Dad's first trip was on this motor train, leaving from a point at Round Hill where his family and dog saw him off. I was at this stage not yet one year of age.

We lived for a further two years at Round Hill, where each day Chance went down to the spot where my father boarded the motor train. He always left, rain, hail or shine, just on 4 pm and arrived just before the train went past. He stayed there for a further ten or fifteen minutes before returning home.

He wouldn't work for my uncle or anyone else after Dad had gone.

Two years later we shifted into town, where, again when loose, he left our house about 3.30 pm and trotted along the railway track until he came to the site where he always lay down waiting for the train to go past.

After it had passed he waited about ten minutes, looking down the track, and then slowly trotted off home again.

This went on for a further three years until one day, old and sick, he didn't return.

He was found dead, where he last saw my dad.

I still have descendants of Chance today. They display the same devotion.

HAPPY FATHER'S DAY
Geoffrey Blight, Narrogin, Western Australia

It's a few years ago now, just two days before Father's Day. The phone rang, summoning me to Busselton Hospital, 200 kilometres away. My father had just been admitted, unconscious after collapsing at his home.

A third generation sheepman, Dad had retired three years earlier after being struck down with a heart attack on the family farm. After a short hospital stay Dad had hung up his boots and took Mum, who was also in poor health, and they went paddling together in the sea, to live out their remaining life.

For Dad, that break away was not like him at all as the farm had been his beginning and, simply, his life—a life totally dedicated to the simple devotion to his family of three, and twelve grandchildren.

Also a life of love and dependence on the land, the sheep, the dogs and the horses that he had shared his 67 years with. All these he left behind after that first hospital stay.

What we didn't know, because he told no-one, was that he had cancer and he felt he owed it to Mum, something she had desired, something she had earned over 44 years—a rest and some friends to talk and share a break with from the never-ending battle of the problems the man on the land faces.

And so they went, not looking back as they said goodbye, everyone not really understanding but still happy for them, all bar Rusty—and Rusty missed Dad.

For Rusty was an ageing farm dog, a big, red, long-haired mongrel kelpie who had worked with Dad every single day for about nine years. Dad was a hard master—the dog went on the chain at night, he was not allowed inside and he did as he was told. But Dad loved him and he shared those working days with him, morning to night. Every hour of light they were together. Fencing, driving sheep, whatever it was, there they were, the old ute, Dad and his dog.

There was nothing for a dog like Rusty where Dad was going, only the chain, and that wasn't the way a man likes to see his best friend end, so they had to say goodbye.

Rusty worked those three years, a bit here, a bit there, but it wasn't the same. So often I would find him sitting on the disused old ute, just looking, just waiting, just hoping.

At the hospital they told me that they had already done investigative surgery. Dad had massive abdominal cancer, his bowels were blocked. He had been fitted with artificial pipes and bags, but his chances of more than a few days were very remote. Mum wanted me to tell him rather than the doctor. She felt I might be more of a comfort to him.

Because of the drugs and the operation Dad was too dazed to talk to that day. I had shared the ride with my sister to the hospital so I was obliged to borrow my father's car to return to the farm, and then drive back again on Father's Day, to see him through to the end.

The car sat in the yard next day and an old dog strutted around and around it, ever watchful, looking and waiting, fighting any canine that was game to draw too near. The scent was strong, his hopes were up but the hand or the voice never came.

I lay awake all night and pondered on how and what to say to my father. 'Thank you, Dad. I love you, Pop. Goodbye. God bless and Happy Father's Day,' but nothing came and with dawn I just felt confusion and sadness as we prepared to leave.

A phone call from Mum told me that Dad was being allowed home for an hour to share Father's Day with his entire family, who by now had begun gathering, and still the words wouldn't come. 'Remember the old days, Dad. Don't worry, Dad. We won't forget you, Dad.' They just weren't right.

Dressed and ready to go as dawn broke I stood by the car door, looking down on the ageing dog while waiting for all the family to get themselves settled in the car. The sad, disappointed eyes still searching, looking, hoping, pleading.

I opened the door and for what reason I still don't know, I told the old dog to get in. The ears came up, the scent was stronger, it had been a long time since he had sat in there. Maybe, just maybe.

All hell broke loose when my well-dressed family now had to share space with the hairy old dog.

'Why in the name of fortune does he have to go. There's no room. Don't be stupid. Get that dog out of the car.'

The spur of the moment idea didn't enjoy any support and matters didn't improve when we reached Busselton.

'What are you going to do with the dog. There's nowhere to put him. He'll start a fight with Rex. Get him out of here.' And so, after three hours of hoping, Rusty was bundled into the garden shed, out of the way before we went to get Dad for that precious hour.

He looked very sick, very tired. He coughed blood every few minutes as he tried to smile and to be happy but he knew, he had known all along, that this day would come. At least he had made Mum happy these last three years and they had been happy, the walks, the swims, the grandchildren, the peace, time to remember.

We put Dad on a bed in the loungeroom, propped up with pillows. Grandchildren everywhere, muted chatter—'How are you? . . . Anything I can get you? . . . Hello, Poppa.'

Everyone wanted to speak but no-one could think of what to say. All were uneasy. I went for a walk on the beach. I could take it no longer.

Later they told me they were going to have some photos taken of the grandchildren with Pop when the barking started. Pop, needing something to say, asked to see Rex, Mum's pet labrador, which was making most of the noise. Mum let Rex inside. He sent things flying as he bounded around everyone, forcing them out of his way and so had to be banned outside to the shed, with a departing smile and a pat from Dad.

No-one had mentioned Rusty and Mum didn't know what to do as Rusty had never been in a house in his life. Dad never spoke of him but here, eyes shining at her, his old ears up, Rusty was pleading to be let out.

Twenty people stood in the loungeroom, the camera ready. They were about to take a picture we could all remember, one last shot of Pop and the family he loved. Everyone was restrained. They kept looking away, the words just wouldn't come.

Then another entered the room. He came quietly and fast, his head held high, the eyes glistening, ears up, now the scent was stronger. Between the legs he came. All stared but no-one said a word. The old dog only looked ahead, tail wagging, and then their eyes met.

Only the old dog moved, a slight bound and four hairy paws rested on the bed. Glistening eyes stared at each other in a silent room. As the long nose reached out, the soft moist tongue touched a hardened old cheek, the tears, shining and silent, joined together and rolled uncontrolled down a very sick but happy face.

It was then I met all the family walking quietly along the beach. They had left what was left of the hour to Mum, Dad and Rusty.

When we did return to the house it was time for me to take Dad back. Nobody touched or spoke to Rusty. He just sat by the bed and as we moved Dad into a wheelchair, out he followed.

Everyone was saying goodbye or volunteering to go back with him to the hospital, but Dad just smiled and thanked them and beckoned Rusty into the back of the car, asking that only he accompany us.

I could not say anything as we drove the four miles back. I just stole a glance occasionally at the strained faces looking forward, the old dog now standing on the back seat, his nose only inches from the old man's cheek.

Nothing whatsoever was said between man and dog. At the hospital entrance I lifted Dad into the wheelchair. He stared straight ahead. No words, not even a glance at Rusty. As I moved the chair back to shut the car door, the old dog sat, nose pressed hard against the glass. Still the old man stared ahead, now visibly upset and trembling.

For a moment I thought I might say something but could not. As I started to push the chair away an old hand suddenly came out and bony old fingers pressed hard against the glass. Their eyes met for the last time and in a moment not meant for me, the old man, tears streaming freely down his cheeks, mumbled, 'Goodbye, old boy,' and we slowly moved away.

They are both dead now. Dad was carried to his final resting place by his tearful young grandsons, his witness read solemnly and sincerely by loving grand-daughters. The man who believed 'Family is Forever' presented his credentials to his maker.

But on the last page of a family album that spans 44 years of a happy and very successful marriage is a picture of an old man, tears rolling down his cheeks, his hands outstretched to his workmate, his friend, taken in the loungeroom on that final Father's Day. A loving family left all the words to a hairy old dog to deliver and by the photo rests a card which reads:

Dad

A gift for today I have not bought
On this Father's Day our time is too short.
Forgive me then for hoping this way
To take you back to yesterday

When times were hard and times were good
The times we'd relive, if only we could.
The cold morning air, the midday sun
When twilight came our work was done.
So I've brought your mate who lived them too
Who like all of us, shares a love for you.

PINING FOR THE PAST

Mrs Mac, Lake Cathie, New South Wales

We had a small farm on the outskirts of Grafton. Our dog was a blue heeler named Rover.

When we got rid of the few cattle we had, Rover used to walk our big black rooster around the paddock all day long, every day.

One sad day my grandfather died. We then discovered that the dog was always missing between 10 am and 11.30 am every day. We used to wonder where he went.

The grave-digger who lived not far from us told us that if we were looking for Rover between these times, we would always find him lying on his master's grave.

I took a photo of him on my grandfather's grave and keep it in my collection.

FOR NO-ONE BUT DAD

Carolyn McConnel, Esk, Queensland

I was leaving Brisbane, where I had been working, to get married, and I wanted to give Dad something special in thanks for all he had done for me. In the *Queensland Country Life*, some kelpie pups in New South Wales were advertised for sale, but the ad said they could be railed anywhere in Queensland. I wrote asking for a black and tan bitch pup.

The office at the Roma Street Railway Station seemed deserted when I went to collect the pup, but finally a porter arrived to say he had found it, but as it had looked hungry, they had taken her down to the canteen and given her a feed.

To my horror, a large black belly with a head and four feet was handed over to me. It appeared she had eaten very well indeed and was in some danger of bursting.

By the time we had driven out to my parents' property at Ilfracombe in western Queensland, some 800 miles away, she was looking more like a pup and less like a balloon. Dad was very pleased to get her as his old dog was slowing up and it was time to start training a replacement.

He called her Coco as she really was a very elegant-looking dog. She quickly took to work and to riding around on the back of Dad's motor-bike, and she was very much his dog. She tolerated the rest of the family, but took orders from no-one but Dad.

The one thing that really stood out was her uncanny ability to know from what direction Dad was returning when he was away in the property's Cessna. A lot of other planes flew over every day, but she took no notice of them. When Dad flew off, she would go and camp in the shade somewhere.

Some time later you would see her get up and go out onto the area near Dad's office and she would sit peering into the distance. You would then know that Dad was on his way home. We would not hear the plane for a good ten minutes, but Coco always knew and she always sat facing the way he was approaching. Sometimes we'd laugh at her, knowing that Dad had gone west and there she'd be, facing east. But sure enough, something would have happened and he'd have had to go somewhere else and would be coming back from the east.

Even when he went to Brisbane for a few days, the day he was due home, about a quarter of an hour before he arrived, old Coco would be sitting outside the office watching for him.

Once he had landed she would wander down to the hangar to help put the plane away and just check he was back safely. Then she would camp outside the garden fence, keeping an eye out in case he needed her help with anything.

She really was a wonderful old dog, as loyal as any dog to her owner and she was sadly missed when she finally died of old age.

A LONG WEARY WAIT

Joy Combe, Crystal Brook, South Australia

My father got a young kelpie pup from a neighbour and we named it Brown Towser.

Before Jim and I were married, we used to go for long walks in the hills and Brown Towser pup liked to come with us. After a little while, she would usually get tired and Jim would pick her up and carry her. As a result, whenever she got tired, she would jump up into Jim's arms to be carried.

Jim went away with the RAAF during the 1939 to 1945 war. After several years, he came home on leave.

My father and Towser were bringing sheep up from the front paddocks past the house to the hills at the back. When Towser saw Jim, she left my father and the sheep, and dashed across to Jim. She immediately jumped up into his arms and stayed a few minutes before racing back to my father and the sheep again.

NOT ON SPEAKING TERMS

Denis Adams, Apsley, Victoria

When I went to Jabuk in 1952, one of our neighbours was Alan Ross, a man ahead of his time in the control of sand drift. He was one of the nicest blokes you'd ever meet, but even old Alan could be temporarily unpopular.

One day I found him hard at work in the sheep yards. And 'hard' was the operative word! Normally his large, plump sheepdog bitch Trixie did just about everything except work the drafting gate. This day, however, Trixie was not her usual, busy self. She was acting like a wife whose husband had forgotten her birthday.

She would half fill the yard, then pause to give Alan a dirty look.

'Come on, Trixie,' he would urge. Then, with a look that plainly said 'Humph', she would disdainfully run a few more in.

'What's up with Trixie?' I asked.

'Oh, she's not speaking to me today,' Alan told me, looking embarrassed. 'You know how humid and stinking hot it was yesterday, before we had that bit of a thunderstorm? Well, I was feeling so tired and crook with this damn boil on my backside, I thought I'd take a spell. I was lying on my belly out on the bed on the verandah.'

Coming from Alan, this was an amazing admission. Normally he ran rings around all us young blokes. He was a workaholic!

'Trixie was asleep under the bed,' he went on. 'Then all of a sudden there was a terrific clap of thunder. She got such a scare that she jumped up on top of me—fair on my boil!'

Alan, it seemed, had risen vertically some distance above the bed. With a howl of agony, he had lashed out instinctively at poor, terrified Trixie.

'I didn't mean to kick the old girl,' he told me sadly. 'I was sorry as soon as I'd done it, but she still hasn't forgiven me!'

NOT THE BEST DOG
IN HIGHBURY

Geoffrey Blight, Narrogin, Western Australia

Standing on the side of the road on a cool April afternoon never struck me as being the place I might hear a great dog story. So when a familiar ute pulled up as I herded a mob of crutched weaners into the paddock, I hardly could have guessed the outcome.

It was old Bill. I'd known him all my life. He was of my father's generation and Dad's mate. Dad's been gone ten years and I'm a grandfather, so old Bill is no longer young.

Bill never married. A very shy chap. I'd had many talks with him over the years.

'I've been reading your yarns,' he said.

I sensed there was something more. Bill wasn't the reading type, but as we talked he again came back to the dog story of mine he'd read.

'If I tell you a dog story, you won't laugh, will you?'

He didn't have to ask.

'I haven't told anyone in fifty years, but you might be able to tell me why it happened.'

Bill's old face, wrinkled with age, almost blushed and I wondered at his shyness.

Bill was the last of a family that had pioneered Highbury. We had buried his brother a fortnight before.

'Your uncle gave me a dog once,' he began. 'A black kelpie called Jack. Not the best sheepdog in Highbury, but he did me and we got on all right.'

The story I now repeat was told uninterrupted on the side of a gravel track that fifty years before had seen Bill, his old dad and Jack travel four miles to the Highbury siding at midnight. There Bill caught the train and went to war.

His kelpie Jack was his only possession and his dad promised to look after the wayward old bastard. He told Bill to take care and to come home as soon as he could. Bill stood at the train window and stared at the old ute's fading lights. He was filled with restlessness and fear as he left his father and dog in that dark railway yard.

Bill had mates going also. Soon the homesickness gave way to a sense of adventure. The whole world was before them, but not for long. War makes young men grow up fast and Bill was no different. He soon learnt about the fear and tragedy of the cost of lives. Unlike the others, he didn't have a girl back home, making him feel left out when the blokes spoke of getting back to their women. He used to think of old jack and wonder how he was going.

His mother sent letters. There weren't many and they were not very well written. They told him Jack was still Jack, still no better at rounding up sheep. Things seemed to be always grim. It was who had fallen or been injured, or how terrible the grain and wool prices were. But—they were from home.

Bill lost a close mate. Everybody did. There was no-one to tell. He wondered why he was there. He was sent to Queensland for retraining for the jungle. The Allied position was bad. The Japanese were advancing through New Guinea and already bombing Darwin. It looked like a certain attack on Australia.

Bill had not had home leave for years. Suddenly, he was told to go home and see his folk before being sent to the Islands. Not permitted to tell anybody, nor allowed to write or phone, he was issued rail passes for travel. The Defence Force didn't want troop movements known or recorded anywhere. It took Bill eleven days to get on the 'Midnight Horror' that would take him home to Highbury. Everybody was frightened and depressed. The war was going badly.

Even though he had been travelling for eleven days, it seemed an eternity to wait at Narrogin station. The people had a midnight cuppa and the slow Albany train passed through, on its way to Perth. The trains always passed each other at Narrogin, so the first there had to wait.

Finally they were rolling again. Bill stood in the rocking gangway looking out into the gloom, knowing that only a mile further was home—and Jack. It had been too long. No light showed in the darkness.

Suddenly Bill felt good. He was nearly home. He realised that he would have to walk back four miles, but what the hell. There weren't any guns here. Not yet anyway. How great it would be to see his parents and Jack. God, I hope he's still alive, thought Bill. He would be old now for a dog.

There were no lights in Highbury. No-one to meet the train. The train slowed and finally halted as the guard, with a lantern, jumped down to drop a solitary parcel. Bill jumped down into the darkness. There was no platform. The train immediately shuddered and began its slow choo, choo, choo before slipping away into the night. Suddenly Bill lived a magic moment of his life. He has never forgotten. It led him down the road to tell me fifty years later. About the dog who wasn't the best sheepdog in Highbury. The dog that jumped up to greet him in the pitch darkness that night and embrace him.

Bill was never an emotional man. Very much the opposite. Never one to have admitted a tear, but on this occasion, even as he told me fifty years later, his eyes glistened as he remembered.

'You know, I'm glad no-one was watching. I couldn't help it. I broke down and cried. You know that bloody dog was worth fighting for.'

Although he asked discreetly later, nobody had ever seen Jack in Highbury. No-one knew whether he was there when the midnight trains came in. It was four miles to where he lived.

'How was it,' asked Bill, 'did he know I was coming home?'

'Another funny thing,' Bill went on, 'after I walked home with Jack, I didn't wake the parents. I just went off to my room and went to bed. At daylight, Dad came in carrying a cup of tea.'

'I knew you were home the minute I saw old Jack this morning,' was his quiet way of saying 'welcome home, son'.

Bill said, 'He would never tell me why he made the cup of tea before checking, or whether he had ever brought over a cuppa when I wasn't home.'

Those were secrets Bill's father died with.

'That's why I never told anyone about Jack,' Bill said. 'I don't think they would have believed me.'

WEDDED BLISS
Marj Wood, Benalla, Victoria

Skipper was married to the boss long before I was. He wasn't very thrilled with my arrival and made sure I knew that the boss was *his*. In Skipper's opinion the management order was the boss, Skipper and 'her', a very poor third.

Early in our marriage I used to love riding in the back of the ute, with the cold wind blowing in my face as we roared along the narrow dirt roads. Skipper refused to ride in the back with 'her', choosing instead to sit on the passenger seat next to the boss.

When the stock crate was on the back of the ute, I'd squeeze through the gate and into the back, while Skipper sat disdainfully in the front with the boss.

Seeing the ute go past with the boss's wife inside the stock crate and his dog up front beside him, the locals decided that here was one farmer who had his priorities right.

TEAM EFFORT
Marina Hanstock, Parkes, New South Wales

My grandfather had two sheepdogs, Blue and Trixie. In May of 1942, Grandfather was lopping kurrajong to feed to the cattle. He fell from the tree and was badly injured.

Blue walked home, about three miles, while Trixie stayed with my grandfather and kept the cattle at bay. Every time my grandmother came outside, Blue would bark and run in the direction he had come from. After a while Gran followed Blue back to where my grandfather was lying. Gran had to walk a mile for help.

Three days later my grandfather died.

'NO DOGS!'
Kath Frost, Port Macquarie, New South Wales

An unprecedented wet occurred in far western Queensland a few years ago.

Because of the vastness and the low nature of the land, the heavy rains were very worrying for the landholders. To save their stock, great herds of cattle had to be moved miles to high ground. The task would have been impossible to handle without the valued and untiring assistance of the blue heelers that worked with the stockmen.

After days of hard driving, they finally got their cattle to the only high land for miles, and it was then that they found that they, too, were stranded. There was nothing they could do but free their horses, and settle down with their saddles and dogs to wait.

Fortunately, after a couple of days a helicopter flew to their rescue. The pilot got out of his craft and surveyed the dirty, tired and hungry stockmen with their mud-covered dogs. He yelled to them, 'G'day, fellers. Get aboard, but *no dogs!*'

The hungry and weary men, astounded at the thought of leaving their dogs behind, yelled back over the noise of the chopper blades, 'We don't go without our dogs,' and no threats or cajoling could make them change their minds. The pilot was, in the end, forced to concede to their demands.

These highly trained blue heelers were a very valuable asset to the stockmen, as well as being much loved. How could they have left them behind?

SCARLET THE PROTECTOR

Kerry-Anne Bourke, Tallawang, via Gulgong, New South Wales

When Scarlet was about sixteen weeks old and was being broken in, I was drafting some sheep. A neighbour's wethers, western-bred and 'crazy', had got through my fence. A few of these sheep ran into me and knocked me down in the yard. As quick as a flash, this miniscule pup pounced onto me, bared her teeth and barked like something possessed to keep the sheep from trampling me.

To this day, if I go into the yards, she walks between my legs barking and will not let the sheep come near me. I have told many people about this but wasn't believed until recently.

I was working at a friend's shed, and her husband was working next to me, penning up. Suddenly Scarlet jumped into the yard and began frantically barking from between his legs. We were both in jeans and she must have thought his legs were mine.

A LAST FAREWELL

Nyree Renney, Berriwillock, Victoria

As we headed off to Nandaly, we knew we had a sad day ahead of us. Pat Conlan, the father of a very close friend of ours, had died suddenly on the Sunday night from a heart attack at the age of fifty-three.

Arriving at the funeral, we weren't surprised to see five to six hundred people. Pat had been a pillar of the local community, a leading farmer in the district, a wonderful husband and father to six strapping sons.

However, we were surprised to see a sheepdog tied to the church gate. He was greeted by a few as they went through to the small country church and we decided he must have been Pat's working dog.

A few hundred people were standing outside the church and as the service conducted by Father Coffey went along, we all became more and more aware of the dog. Each time the congregation was asked to pray, the dog would howl. After a reading or eulogy was finished, he would howl again.

To this day, I feel a wonderment at the dog's action—although, after all, he had probably spent as much time with Pat as anyone. One certainly got the feeling that Patrick Conlan and his dog had been soul mates.

The dog continued on with the family to the cemetery and once again acted as though he were grieving for his master.

At the luncheon after the funeral, the dog arrived again and was put in the kindergarten playground. He was a little lighter hearted there.

Everyone who attended the funeral commented at some time on this dog and his actions. They also commented on what a moving and loving tribute to her husband it was for Marie to remember the dog at such a tragic time and give him an opportunity to say a last farewell to his master and very obviously best mate. It was the most moving funeral I've ever been to. The dog's name was Oscar.

COMPLETE TRUST
Mavis Ingram, Bega, New South Wales

This is a story about a very old working border collie dog called Socks.

Socks had a very sore front paw and had been carrying it for about a week. Paul and I had tried a few times to find the problem but as Socks didn't like people around him with a needle and scissors, we tended to let him go.

But another week passed and it was no better, so Paul held Socks's mouth while I had a real poke around with the needle. After about ten minutes of trying, I let his paw go and said, 'Socks, I just can't find it to get it out.'

Socks gave a whimper, looked at me and put his paw back in my hand. I knew I had his trust, so Paul didn't hold his mouth. I did some pretty hard and cruel squeezing and prying with the needle and at last a grass seed and heaps of pus came out from between his toes.

As I gave him a cuddle and pat he gave me a small growl as if to say, 'Thank you.'

That is the closest I have ever felt to an animal. I had his complete trust.

GOOD MATES ARE HARD TO FIND
Mark Thompson, Mapleton, Queensland

I remember the first time we met on the track
I was feeling down with me lot
And you wandered up to me fire
And tipped over me old quart pot.

Aw, I thought to meself—what an idiot
This mongrel will never do.
Then you took off the lid to me camp oven
And stuck your face in me stew.

You ate all of me freshly made damper
And gave out with a cough and a fart,
Had a scratch and a yawn, then you silly red prawn,
You leaked on the end of me tarp.

But there were some things you did quite naturally
That earned my respect and my trust.
Like that time we were out west and droving
That night when the cattle rushed.

I remember how me horse stumbled
You know, the new one, the grey.
I remember you standing beside me there
And keeping those cattle away.

Yeah you turned out to be a pretty good mate
In our travellings down the track.
Even the times that I swore at you
—You never answered back.

And I remember that late night in Walgett,
The locals thought they'd have a go
And beat up an out-of-towner, eh,
And help themselves to me dough.

Well, your free-wheeling style of fighting
Had them scurrying off like mice!
By Jeez, I was glad of your company
Even though you bit me twice.

Yeah, you've turned out to be a pretty good mate
You stuck by me all through the years.
You've always been here to protect me
When I've had too many beers.

But at times you could be kind of stupid
Like right now with your leg in a trap.
And there's still three days walk to the next flamin' town
That I can't even find on a map.

I wish I could think of some other way.
I wish I could do something else instead.
But I can't sit here watching you suffer,
When with one bullet you'll be quickly dead.

Don't lie there expecting a miracle
With that trusting look in your eye.
I can't even give you a decent last meal,
All we've got is a tin of camp pie.

For God's sake, stop your looking at me
I'm finding it so hard to aim.
But it's the only thing I know of
That will give you an end to your pain.

Well, there you go, now I've done it
And I'll have to write down somehow
How two good mates came to be parted
And why you're resting peacefully now.

PART 3
BRAINPOWER

Dogs unafraid to use their intelligence.

ELEVATED TO THE PEERAGE

Jim Kelly, Naracoorte, South Australia

Our Prince Charles arrived on the same day in 1948 as his royal name-sake. He was a fat and cuddly red kelpie pup with possibly a drop or two of dingo blood. If Charlie wasn't the pick of the litter, somebody else got an exceptional choice.

He learnt his name very quickly and was one of those amazing pups who seemed to know all he had to, right from the start. Except for the occasional ride in the old army surplus jeep, dogs had to do all their own footwork in those days. We always carried a stockwhip and galloped about a lot more than we do today. The young dog had no fear of the whip and seemed to develop a special relationship with Solo and Melody, the main stockhorses in our stable. On hot days, while our horses were tied up to the fence, he would stand in the horses' shadows, where the ground was cooler. In the middle of the day, this often meant lying under the tail of the horse, right next to the dangerous back hoofs.

As time went by, Charlie developed into the most outstanding dog of my life, both as a yard dog and as a paddock worker, with a big wide cast. He was a rarity in this age of specialisation of eye, bark and cast. He would work for any one of the family and as he grew older, was rarely tied up. We loved him with respect and admiration.

In the middle of the night in August 1955, when we had a team of Poll Shorthorn bulls on feed in the bull pens, I was awakened by Charlie barking at my bedroom window on the front verandah. We had a baby daughter in an adjoining room and were frightened the hullabaloo would wake up the rest of the household. I told Charlie in my gruffest, deepest, whisper to 'Go and lie down.'

To our surprise, he barked back. I said, 'Something must be wrong, he's trying to tell me something,' and leapt out of bed into a dressing gown. With a torch from the kitchen, I left the house by the back door. Charlie met me with a wagging tail as we walked down the path to the bull shed. As we got closer, I could hear banging, crashing and very heavy breathing. A gate had come open somehow and two bulls were fighting in a confined space. It was tricky and dangerous separating the heaving bodies and I expect Charlie barked and so distracted them long enough for me to push one through the gate and close the catch.

Prince Charles was a hero. The bruises to the bulls must have been superficial, as they won big ribbons at the Royal Adelaide Show a few weeks later.

I've spent my working life of some fifty years with animals. I've seen some remarkable behaviour where an individual has performed in special ways, either to solve a problem or bring attention to themselves, but always within the normal range of behaviour for its species. A cow that hides her calf, a draughthorse that pulls to the utmost of its strength, a sheep which always walks through a gate first so the mob follows.

They are displays of superior intelligence that make close contact with individual animals such a rewarding experience. But Charlie's behaviour that night was quite exceptional, outside the norm, even for a smart dog.

Consider his position. Somehow he became aware of the commotion going on in the bull shed. Perhaps he slept there, we don't know. Normal dog behaviour would have been to bark at the fighting bulls till something happened.

Charlie knew he could not fix the problem and must have known I could. When I scolded him for barking at the window, normal behaviour would have been to lower his tail and head and skulk away, yet he kept barking in a most defiant and unusual way, so that I got the message that he needed help. He kept the idea to deliver the message in his head, despite the scolding.

For me this was a unique experience that I have often contemplated. Down our way Charlie was almost elevated to the peerage, despite his colonial background. We addressed him, if time permitted, as Sir Charles.

NOT THE
NEIGHBOUR'S SHEEP
Hurtle Baldock, Buckleboo, South Australia

Undoubtedly the best dog I owned was my first, when starting on a scrub block after the war. He was a black and tan named Tim and although a slow beginner, was uncanny.

At shearing or crutching time, if we missed any stragglers he would bring them in, even to the point of delivering them right to the back door of the shearing shed. While mustering in the scrub he would find sheep I didn't know were there.

One day my brother and I saw three sheep on their own a quarter of a mile away. I sent Tim to bring them in. After running some distance he stopped and refused to go around them. After three attempts to get him to bring them in, we went to investigate.

We were amazed to discover they were a neighbour's sheep, with only their brands and six months difference in wool growth to set them apart from our sheep. I told my brother the dog could read brands!

Many years later when his hearing and eyesight had failed, I had to put him down, so I shot him while he was alseep.

NIGHT MUSTER
Zita Ward, Singleton, New South Wales

The following episode is a tribute to a black kelpie sheepdog named Nigger. During the late 1930s we lived on a farm which was situated at the end of the road, and well off the beaten track. It was a valley with a creek which forked into three separate narrow valleys. Each valley was separated by high, and quite rugged, wooded hills, mostly unfenced.

It was a very pretty place, quiet and full of tranquillity—except for the dingos which seemed to have arrived en masse very soon after we stocked up with sheep. Their attacks on our flock became so bad we were forced to yard all the sheep each night.

This proved a difficult task for us with only my father to do it, plus help from my eleven year old brother and me, aged sixteen. We had several dogs who would work well for anyone, but Nigger was a new, young dog being trained by Dad, and not allowed to go with us kids.

One night my father was called away from home overnight, which left only the children to muster. Our mother arranged to do the valley near our house, and since she did not ride a horse it meant walking a few kilometres into the rough foothills. She decided to take Nigger with her, hoping he would understand her inadequate instructions, in place of

184

Dad, who had a mighty voice and a whistle which carried a power of authority.

Just on dusk my brother and I arrived back at the house after yarding our mob, only to find our mother was not yet back. We rode up the valley to meet her and found that she had lost Nigger in the scrub. Obviously he had moved out of earshot as our calling and whistling failed to get a response.

By now it was quite dark. The area was so rugged and dangerous for anyone not very familiar with it that we were forced to give up and hope that Nigger could find his way back home. We had already lost a few dogs who had been enticed to follow the dingo pack and had never returned. Our father would be most upset if we lost Nigger as well.

About 9 pm we heard strange noises at the back gate of our house yard. There we found Nigger holding a small flock of about 50 sheep in a tight circle. This was an incredible feat for a lone dog to have shepherded his sheep out of that steep, rough country and several kilometres back to the house.

Nigger was quite knocked up and glad of a late feed. Needless to say we were overjoyed to have him back safely, and also to have the sheep safely home since more than likely they would have been victims of the wild dogs who persistently waited for a chance to maul any strays.

RED TED ALERT
Bruce Rodgers, Yeelanna, South Australia

When I came to this district 63 years ago, my nearest neighbour, PH (Mick) Wagner, had a sheepdog called Red Ted, which was from a red kelpie bitch by a border collie dog. Ted was a good all-round sheepdog, and had a lot of intelligence in matters other than working sheep.

We had a scrub block adjoining the Wagner farm, which had no improvements, and we were using Wagner's stable and horse yards, and camped in a hut near the sheds.

One night about midnight, Ted insisted on barking at Mick's back door, and would not stop when told. Then he went to the bedroom window and put his paws on the sill and barked more than ever.

Mick got out of bed and, armed with a hurricane lantern, went to investigate. The first thing he saw was his own two horses in the back garden, and he realised that our eight horses would not be far away. He found them beginning to tear open and eat some seed wheat which had been stacked in bags and pickled. Fortunately they had not eaten much, because a lot of pickled wheat would have killed them, and horses at that time were scarce and precious. My father said Ted was a very valuable dog and had probably saved us hundreds of pounds. We made sure the horse yards gate was closed correctly thereafter.

ONE YELL TOO MANY
Tresna Shorter, Katherine, Northern Territory

Despite his lack of training, Fella, being a border collie, had natural ability and knew instinctively what to do. This was more than could be said for the rest of us. My husband, who was more interested in wheat growing than dealing with animals, had little patience when it came to sheep.

In his impatience, it was not long before he started yelling at all of us for not being in the right place at the right time. I could take being yelled at a couple of times, but being a city girl and still learning country ways, I soon became annoyed. After all, I reasoned, we were helping him out during a labour shortage, weren't we. Where would he be without us? Foolishly, I expected gratitude, not abuse.

Eventually, he yelled at me one time too many and I turned around and started walking home. Next, he yelled at Fella, and to our amazement, Fella also turned and strutted home across the paddock with his crooked tail waving in the air.

Later, my husband had a good laugh that even the dog wouldn't put up with his rotten temper.

MY DOG ELS

Rob Williams, Albury, New South Wales

I won her in a pub at Blackall. She was mostly blue cattle plus something else. So that's what I called her—Els.

She was easy enough to train, but most of the time she'd do something else first. Being a patient sort of bloke, this didn't worry me too much.

I had two other dogs who were good workers and Els soon copied them. But she always included some other job as an extra. She believed she was a star. As it turned out, she was.

I got a job bringing down a small mob of cattle, all a bit rough, from Nardoo way, to Cloncurry. This is back in the fifties. The country was bloody dry and hot. Because I was broke, I took this on, on my own. Just three dogs, three horses and me. Any quids at the end were mine! I wasn't worried about condition. I was pushing them fast and me and my dogs really worked.

About two days run from the 'Curry, my horse Sampson caught his foot in a hole, fell with me pinned beneath him and he was trapped. I was too. I found out later that my leg was busted in two places and I was concussed.

I came out of it some time later with Sampson going wild every so often, two dogs sitting in some shade, but no bloody Els. She'd run off. I've had it, I thought.

Now this is what Els did. She ran all right—in a straight bloody line to the only two blokes within 50 miles. How she knew, I'll never know.

These blokes were fencing. They told me that this sweaty looking, tired dog came up, barking at them, and pulling at the pants of the bloke with the wire. He thought she was mad and hit her, but she kept circling, barking and running off. She did this four or five times.

In the bush, the real blokes get a feeling about things. I can't explain it. These blokes, God bless them, got that feeling. They got in their ute and followed her. It was only about six miles.

She led them back to me and I suppose that's the end of the story. Els should have looked after the cattle. She could have had a laze in the shade, but that dear, stupid bitch did something else—and saved my bloody life.

BLUEY WARNER

Mavis Taylor, Uranquinty, New South Wales

Bluey Warner, as the name implies, was a warner. If any stranger seemed the least bit aggressive, the dog would stroll over and take his heel gently in his mouth. But he had even more sense than that.

One day my two youngest girls went across to the neighbours' place to see their two mates. As with most children, they didn't use their heads. Away down to the creek they went to play in the water—a novelty as we hadn't had rain in ages. Typically, they just had to get in and get wet. The creek was fairly deep where they were and flowed into two dams before careering on down through our place.

Fred went out to milk, but Bluey Warner, who always had the herd waiting for him at milking time, wasn't there. This was so unusual, because you could nearly set the time by the dog. So Fred smelt trouble.

'Where are the girls?' he asked.

I told him they were over at the neighbours' place.

'Bluey Warner hasn't brought the cows in,' he said. 'Let's go.'

We went next door and told them the dog had not brought the cows in. And so the search was on.

Down at the creek we were met by four bedraggled children and a muddy dog coming up the track. They had climbed down into the creek and couldn't get out. The power of the rushing, rising water had been pushing them toward the dams. They had been four very frightened children on the brink of a tragedy.

They had called out, hoping to make someone hear up at the house. We lived about a half-mile from the creek and although we hadn't heard their calls, Bluey Warner had.

According to the eldest child, he turned up on the bank and they tried to get him to go for help. Instead, he crouched down and grabbed the eldest girl by her clothes and started pulling. This was enough to enable her to get a foothold in dry dirt and she scrambled out. She then lay down on the bank and pulled the other three out.

The children said Bluey Warner snarled and snapped at them. They couldn't believe his behaviour. We know dogs can't talk, but clearly they were getting a roasting from him, and a warning never to try playing in a swollen creek again.

READY TO STRIKE

Jeanette Osborne, Roadvale, Queensland

While Bluey and I were droving a herd of cattle along the road, one cow began to lag behind. I swung my whip, which promptly became stuck under my horse's tail.

When I had dismounted to retrieve the whip, my horse suddenly snorted and bolted. Spinning round, I came face to face with a huge brown snake rearing ready to strike me.

Bluey never hesitated. He charged in and tried to shake the snake to kill it. Instead he was bitten three times and died shortly afterwards. He had saved my life.

SHALLIE THE, FAITHFUL

Tim Hardy, Penong, South Australia

It was just before shearing and Shallie, my six year old red kelpie bitch, and I had mustered up the wethers on the scrub block 30 miles from the house.

We had put them in a yard for the night before going home. At 6.30 next morning we left home in the ute to drive the sheep home. When we arrived at the yards we found that the sheep had broken out, so we scouted around in the vehicle and found them on the edge of the 3,000 acres of scrub. I let Shallie out to drive the sheep back to the yards through about one mile of scrub. While she was doing that, I went back to the yards to get a motorbike so I could go back and help her.

On my way back to her I hit a tree root and fell off the bike. I landed heavily on my back, hitting a stone. I couldn't move my body or legs. I realised my back was broken.

Shallie reached me after about half an hour. She drove the sheep around me, but sensed something was wrong so left the mob and came over to me. She licked my face and then lay down beside me. I dragged myself about 30 yards along a fence but couldn't go any further because the wire cut my hands. So I just settled down to wait for the family to come looking for me. I knew it would be ages because they would probably think I had dropped into the pub on my way home, or something like that.

I decided to write a note on a matchbox and then hooked it onto Shallie's collar. I told her to go home 30 miles away, but she wouldn't leave me. She just lay beside me all day from 9.30 in the morning until 9 o'clock at night, when finally a search party with a spotlight found me. The only way they could spot us was by picking up the shine of Shallie's eyes as she jumped up and down. An ambulance came and collected me, and Shallie was taken home.

Next morning, when my wife called Shallie, she wasn't there. She was found fifteen miles up the road on her way back to where she had been with me all day on the previous day.

While I was in hospital for three months learning to cope with life in a wheelchair, Shallie would not go near anyone, even for a pat. She must have been fretting. When I finally returned home, she went back to being her old self.

Since that accident three years ago she has retired from sheep work and spends all her time alongside my wheelchair.

OLD BILL

Gladys Maddison, Macksville, New South Wales

Old Bill, a black and tan kelpie, was about sixteen years old at the time of this incident.

I was bringing in a flock of young ewes with their first lambs and it was close to dusk. The gate was awkwardly placed and Rover, an untrained puppy, was overenthusiastic and separated one ewe from the flock. It careered down the paddock with Rover in full pursuit.

Meanwhile the ewes and lambs went quickly through the gateway with a little encouragement from Bill. I fastened the gate. Rover had returned, but when I looked around for Bill, he had disappeared, so I went off to look for the errant ewe.

It was nearly dark by now. I tried to get Rover to guide me to the ewe, but he didn't understand. The paddock was rough and boulder strewn, so it wasn't easy to find one missing ewe.

However, I heard a distant barking at intervals, then silence. I went down the gully in the direction of the barks. Rover left me and I followed him quickly, knowing he would lead me to Bill and, I hoped, the ewe.

Imagine my surprise when I reached the two dogs to find the ewe up to her neck in a waterhole that was only her length in diameter. She couldn't get out but there was old Bill at the side of the pool, hanging onto her wool with his teeth, letting go, barking to attract my attention, and grabbing her again so she wouldn't sink.

It was quite an effort to haul her out as she was in full wool and water-logged. But all was well and after a short rest she went back up the hill to her baaing lamb.

It was all in a day's work for Bill. He retired a few years later as he was becoming deaf, but he lived to be 22 years old!

PART 4
A CUT ABOVE
THE REST

The champs

NACOOMA GUS—A LEGEND
IN HIS OWN LIFETIME

Lyndon Cooper, Kingston, SE South Australia

Over all the years I have been breeding and training working dogs, I have always found the true, all-round working dog the most fascinating and intelligent. He's the dog that can muster a paddock on his own, drive a mob of sheep to yards or homestead and also work in the yards when the mob has been yarded.

These dogs think for themselves. They seem to be able to work out where the stock has to go and they rarely get into trouble doing their work. Although I have great respect for a good yard dog, the all-rounder is the type of dog I enjoy breeding and working the most.

Nacooma Gus, my kelpie dog, a son of Bullenbong Mate, never ceases to amaze me with the level of intelligence he has. I remember one particular time a couple of years ago when I walked out from the homestead with Gus just on dusk. I cast him around a 60-acre paddock covered in thistles and dock to pick up a mob of 300 wethers that I had put in there a couple of days before to be drenched.

After about fifteen minutes, Gus returned without any sheep. I gave him some harsh words of advice and sent him out again to have another look. This time twenty minutes went by, but still no sheep and also no Gus. And it was getting quite dark. I returned home to collect the utility to look for the missing sheep and dog.

After driving around the paddock, I failed to find the sheep myself, so I headed for the gate into the next paddock which led into a laneway into the cattle yards. Much to my amazement, Gus and the 300 sheep were coming from the next 60-acre paddock into the laneway and out onto the track heading for home. Somehow the gate had been left open and the wethers had found their way into the next paddock.

Gus, obviously not being able to find any sheep in the first 60-acres, went through the fence and mustered the next paddock, found the sheep and knew where to take them to get them on the track for home.

At shearing time at our place there is always a lot of talk about dogs, some funny, some serious, but rarely does a shearer have to wait for sheep.

One year we had a new roustabout. He was fascinated with the dogs and the way they would cast out into the hills, muster a mob of sheep and bring them into the yards while we were working in the shed. Only on the very odd occasion would they leave one behind.

At about 11 am on the second-last day of shearing, the weather was looking rather threatening and one of the shearers suggested bring the last mob in. As I was busy wool classing, I took Gus out into the paddock and cast him out over the bracken-covered hills, left him to it and returned to the shed to go on classing wool.

After about 30 minutes, much to the amazement of our bewildered roustabout, over the hill and into the yards came this mob of sheep.

During lunch it started to rain, so we pushed these sheep into the shed. It was chock-a-block full. You couldn't fit another sheep in, but we felt very pleased with ourselves as it rained all day.

As we walked from the shed after knock-off time, the roustabout spotted approximately twenty sheep up on top of one of the hills. He looked at me and said, 'What are those sheep up on the hill there, Coop? Gus never leaves any behind, eh?'

Thinking very quickly, I replied, 'Well, he knew they wouldn't fit in the shed, so he left those few behind.'

Well, I can tell you that roustabout was the best publicity officer I could ever have employed because various versions of this true story circulated the local hotels for some time.

I know a dog may not be that smart, but for a dog that has won four State Farm and Yard Dog Championships, been in 56 finals and won 24 of them, represented South Australia in the National Titles four times being placed as high as third, as well as learning tricks like climbing ladders and walking backwards, I reckon he's capable of almost anything.

THE TRIAL

Garry Somerville, Mosman, New South Wales

This story told to me about 35 years ago is based on fact, but I have changed the names.

Ben had spent all his life in the bush, mostly as a station hand, sometimes as a drover. He had wandered about central Queensland and western New South Wales, never staying long in one place.

At 75 years of age, he was a bachelor, in good health, a teetotaller, a non-smoker and had spent the last three years as station hand for Mr Alex Davidson on Burran Station, near Wilcannia.

A pillar of honesty who worked hard from dawn to dusk, he was an excellent sheepman who kept to himself. His sole companion was his eight year old red kelpie Sailor. A keen lover of dogs, Ben had acquired Sailor as a seven week old pup for five shillings from a passing traveller. He had taken a fancy to the pup and thought it a good 'un. His previous dog had died from distemper.

Ben was an expert with dogs, and had patiently trained Sailor over the years to be an exceptionally good sheepdog. During this time they had become inseparable and Ben had never missed an opportunity to correct or encourage his charge. The results had been amazing—the dog understood everything Ben said.

Sailor bedded down every night in the shearers' quarters alongside Ben, some distance from the homestead. It was common for Ben to chat away to Sailor for hours on end. They were truly great companions. Of all the dogs he had owned, Ben knew he had an extra soft spot for Sailor, though he never let on. Wherever he went, his four-footed friend was always within scent distance.

Ben's boss knew them both well and considered them worth three men. When a job had to be done, these two could be relied on.

One Sunday, he remarked casually to Ben, 'The sheepdog trials are on at the showground next Saturday. Do you want me to enter you and Sailor when I'm in town today?'

Ben, no lover of crowds, hesitated for a moment, then said, 'OK, we'll give it a go.'

For the rest of the week Ben gave Sailor a good work-out with the sheep whenever the opportunity arose. It was uncanny how they worked. Ben never stopped talking to the dog; it was as if each understood exactly the other's thoughts. The companionship and unity between them was unique.

Ben knew Sailor could do well at the trials. But, he also knew they were both slowing up and even the long trip into town would be an effort for them.

When Saturday arrived Ben was up early and finished his chores in time to fit the harness of the horse and trap which his boss had given him permission to use. Today, Sailor, who usually trotted behind, was allowed up alongside Ben.

The Wilcannia showground is huge, surrounded by a picket fence, and when Ben finally arrived, the ground was crowded, with some competitors having come from as far as 50 miles away. The sheepdog trials were a popular event and everyone made an effort to be there. The entrance fee was one pound, with the winner's purse twenty-five. There were twelve entrants and Sailor had drawn No. 12.

Each competitor started with 100 points, the judge deducting points when the dog made an error. The dog and handler started from a common peg and, on a signal from the judge, the dog would be cast out by the handler to the opposite end of the ground where three sheep were standing.

The dog had to bring the sheep back to the handler as quickly as possible. It then had to take the same sheep through a drafting race and some 200 yards to a small bridge. Finally it had to drive the sheep another 200 yards, then put them in a pen. The handler then shut the gate to conclude the competition. The maximum time allowed was fifteen minutes. Points were deducted for slow work, sheep being off course, dogs overrunning and sheep breaking away from the dog.

Ben chose a cool spot on the outskirts to park the trap so Sailor could rest up a bit, away from the crowd, as he waited his turn. Ben and Sailor kept to themselves, Ben nodding occasionally to someone he knew. Most of the other competitors and spectators congregated round the start. Ben knew Sailor would need all the rest he could get if he was to put up a good show, so he was content to watch from a distance.

Promptly at 11 am, the steward blew his whistle for the first contestant. The crowd was silent and each competitor stood at the starting peg. The first three dogs of mixed breed were average and scored between 80 and 90 points each. The fourth dog, a huge black and tan kelpie, was very good. He made few errors and his cast was as good as Ben had seen, and Ben had guessed correctly when the score went up at 95. 'A tough one to beat,' he muttered to Sailor, who was still asleep under the trap in the shade.

The day wore on. Two other dogs scored 91 and 92, the others in the eighties.

The ninth competitor was Floss, a well-bred two year old border collie with good markings. A good-looking dog Ben thought, and one he guessed would be difficult to beat.

He had heard of the collie's exploits at previous trials. Both he and his handler were well known and raised murmurs from the crowd from their bearing. The dog sat upright and willing, a good sign in trial competitions. Floss's cast and lift were neat and straight and the only fault, Ben thought, was that the young dog overran a little. A polished performer, Floss brought the three sheep straight down the middle of the ground.

At the first obstacle the collie was faultless, putting the sheep through the race perfectly with a maximum score. Ben admired this dog; he was certainly a champion. He had an air of confidence about him, and he reminded Ben of what Sailor had been like some six years ago. He looked at Sailor and smiled.

When 98 went up on the board there was a tremendous outbreak of cheering. Ben realised then what they were up against. This Floss was a good one, better than any he could recall. He roused Sailor just prior to their turn. 'You'll do your best, old boy,' he whispered as he walked towards the start.

When Ben and Sailor arrived at the peg, a quietness settled on the ground in deference to their age. Sailor, with his white whiskers and muzzle, and Ben, stooped over slightly, were a direct contrast to the collie, Floss, and his handler.

Sailor sat quietly at the start till the three sheep were liberated at the other end of the ground. When they were standing steady, the judge signalled the timekeeper and Ben was given the signal to start. For about ten seconds, Ben hesitated so that Sailor could get the scent. This was going to be a tough one, Ben knew.

Suddenly there was a change in Sailor. He sat upright, listening with his ear back in an antenna fashion. Ben cast him out: 'Go way back, boy!'

Sailor, sensing he had to do well, was off like a flash and Ben, because of the obstacles, used a shrill whistle to guide him. It was a perfect pear-shaped cast and he came up smartly behind the sheep and, on Ben's whistle, halted directly behind them.

Sailor, as if by telepathy, delivered the sheep without fault in a straight line down the centre of the field. He was precise and neat, handling them quietly but with assurance. Never for a second did he give them the opportunity to be contrary. He was indeed master of the situation, and Ben knew Sailor had gained the maximum points for his effort.

Ben's hands began to sweat. Though excited, he kept a poker face.

Next Ben led the way round the fence with the three sheep behind him and Sailor taking up the rear. On reaching the drafting race Ben stepped into the car tyre placed on the field for the handler, who has to stay there till the sheep are put through the race by the dog. Until now Sailor had not made a mistake, but just as the last sheep was about to go through the race he veered a fraction to the right. It was only for a second, but Ben knew they had lost vital points.

From the time Sailor left the starting peg Ben had talked to him constantly, giving him encouragement and commands, and trying to keep one guess ahead of his dog.

After the race it was 200 yards to the next obstacle, the bridge. Ben encouraged Sailor by talking to him reassuringly; again, he could not fault his dog's effort. Once more he realised they had gained maximum points. He was at work on the sheep immediately the last one left the bridge.

With the final obstacle, the pen; some 200 yards ahead, Ben told Sailor, 'Good boy!'

There was, unknown to Ben, whose full concentration was on his dog, a silence around the ground as everyone sensed the closeness of the scores.

'Go back, go way fore, go back.' Sailor appeared to be on a string; everything Ben said, the dog did.

With the three sheep close by the pen and Sailor glued with his nose twitching in front of them, one paw raised as if to pounce, excitement reached its peak. Two sheep raced into the pen, with a slight movement from Sailor. One to go! Suddenly, for no apparent reason, the remaining

199

sheep ducked out of the edge of the wing. Sailor had him back and in the pen in almost the same instant, but Ben knew as he moved to close the pen that he had lost another point.

The crowd cheered and everyone except Ben and Sailor seemed to go mad. Ben returned slowly to his trap and quietly fondled Sailor's ear. 'You went close, boy. It was a fine effort.'

When the score of 97 was marked up, a ripple again went round the crowd. Floss had won by one point. No-one had dreamed that any other dog would come near to Floss's score. However, Ben's experience told him the younger dog had deserved his win, so he tried not to let Sailor sense his disappointment.

Floss's owner, knowing how close the result had been, finally broke away from his friends and walked over to congratulate Ben on the fine performance Sailor had put up. He, too, recognised a good dog when he saw one.

He was there some minutes with Ben, and when he returned to his friends he had a worried look and seemed at a loss for words. One of his friends joked, 'What's the matter, Alf? Anyone would think you'd lost!'

He didn't reply for some time. When he did, his voice shook. 'You saw how that old kelpie worked those sheep so close . . . do you know he's been totally blind for two years?'

STILL A CHAMPION
Allan & Annica Sutherland, Ballidu, Western Australia

Tessie was the typical retired sheepdog enjoying her last years with the luxury of little work and plenty of good food.

In her heyday, Tessie, a border collie, had been a successful trial dog in Western Australia. Eventually she had to be retired from trialling as she cunningly began to use her intelligence to escape discipline when competing. We would like to share a story from the time when she had become known as Old Tessie.

It was a chilly, moonlit winter night during seeding. A gate had been left open and the sheep, being sheep, had made their way out. Frank, the boss, had set out in pursuit with the eager old dog on the back of the ute. He returned some time later with neither sheep nor dog.

Meanwhile Allan had set out on the motorbike to help. After an hour of fruitless searching, he also gave up and returned the bike to the shed. As he headed back to the house he heard the twang of the fence as Tessie streaked through.

Allan was surprised to find Old Tessie had beaten him home with the sheep and was holding the mob at the gate of the house yard. Tessie had driven the mob of approximately 600 sheep for two or three kilometres.

Only days before this event, we had been considering putting Old Tessie to rest as her age seemed to be catching up with her and her health was declining. This display proved Old Tessie still had plenty of life in her.

SECOND IN COMMAND
TO BULLENBONG MATE
Nancy Withers, Naracoorte, South Australia

Before I had Mate I did not realise the things a working dog could do above the normal everyday ones. Mate educated many people who had worked with stock all their lives. He was truly an incredible animal and, although I have had many good dogs and some which come close, I doubt I'll ever see his like again. The trouble is that you can't obtain kelpies of pure old blood any more and a lot of them have been crossed with dogs of much less talent by breeders who don't understand them.

For the eight and a half years that we lived between Robe and Kingston, I did all the stockwork with the help of a station hand. We ran 1,000 cattle and 7,000 sheep. Most of the work was done on horses and the country was pretty rough. Without Mate and his offspring, I simply could not have managed. Tim, my husband, was constantly busy clearing scrub, fencing, sowing pasture and eradicating rabbits and weeds.

Mate was the foundation of my business. He introduced me to many new friends and my sport of yard trialling, which has taken me to many places. I became fascinated with the study of the genetics of the working kelpie and spent many hours learning where particular traits came from.

All my stud dogs are Mate's descendants. I am not ashamed to admit that a dog changed my life. This is how it all started.

A well-known kelpie breeder and friend of mine from New South Wales rang one evening and, after the usual chitchat, he asked if I would be interested in a seventeen month old kelpie dog which he had bred and an elderly man had reared for him.

My friend had recently suffered a very nasty back injury in a fall from a horse and was unable to work the dog and felt he would be wasted.

'He's not a bad-looking dog,' he said. 'Knows a bit, too. Could do your stud a bit of good. He's all sound old blood.'

Although the dog had never seen a sheep and I already had a potential sire, I decided to take him. His name was Bullenbong Mate, Mate for short.

He was despatched by train and arrived four days later. I first saw him in a large crate. He was a big, black and tan kelpie dog with a broad head and the darkest of chestnut tan markings. 'Hello there! You must be Mate,' I said.

There was no reply. Not a wag of the tail, not an inclination of the head. He just stood and looked back at me with as much pride as I've ever seen in an animal. And that was to characterise our relationship over the years. He was arrogant, proud and supremely sure of himself. An aristocrat.

Despite his four days' travelling, he was still shiny black. He was of medium to large frame with strong, although not overly heavy, bone. However, he had quite a short, straight tail.

We loaded Mate into the hatchback part of the car, and headed for home. Mate rested his broad head on the back of the rear seat and as I drove I glanced in the rearview mirror to see him looking in my direction. I said to my friend, 'You know, I think I'm going to like this dog.' Almost as I finished speaking Mate gave one deep 'woof'. We all burst out laughing.

So began the best relationship I have ever had with an animal. I have worked with animals most of my life and as a breeder and trainer of dogs I have handled hundreds, but Mate stands alone as the greatest animal I have ever had the pleasure of working with. When I write or speak of him, I claim no credit for his ability. He was an extremely well-bred dog, with some excellent station and trial dogs in his pedigree, well-proven sires and dams. In fact, Mate taught me more about shepherding sheep than I ever could have taught him.

Quietly intelligent and with that immense pride, he was a gentle and affectionate dog. However, he was difficult to work. He liked to think for himself and had an incredible memory. Those who worked with him, people and dogs alike, were left in no doubt as to his own opinion of his status—he was the best dog around and he was invincible.

For the first few months, I tried to instil some discipline. This proved a frustrating and exhausting task for both of us. All the positive commands were fine. It was things like 'come', meaning 'come straight away', which seemed to fall on selectively deaf ears. All the more annoying because he wasn't rushing off anywhere but merely proceeding in the opposite direction at his own steady pace. He absolutely refused to 'sit' and after many hours of anguish I settled for 'stop', which I persuaded myself had the same effect and even prided myself that he obeyed this command about 80 per cent of the time.

I could tell many stories about his cleverness finding and driving sheep in rough country, his fearlessness in the yards and his sense of humour, but if I had to tell just one, this would be it.

The first indication that all was not well with Mate, now three years old, was when he refused to eat, first one day, then another. We were busy crutching at the time and although I was concerned, this was somewhat allayed by the fact that Mate was quite happy to proceed with mustering and yard work, However, when he didn't eat for the third day and I noticed that he wanted to, but appeared uncertain to do so, I took him to the local vet straightaway.

The vet took his temperature and then examined him, pressing his abdomen firmly, but the dog did not flinch. It was decided to put him on medication and we proceeded home.

After two days he had not improved and was visibly losing weight. Once again, it was off to the vet and another examination. Once again, we arrived home with medication. At lunchtime, I received a call from my husband's nephew, Chris, who managed a nearby property. He was also crutching and had four crossbred ewes with half-grown lambs at foot which kept eluding the muster and escaping into a patch of thick scrub.

'Could you please bring Mate,' was the request. 'They're pretty tough and cunning and he's the only chance I have of getting them.'

I explained that Mate was ill, but agreed to do it, thinking I would carry Mate to the edge of the scrub and then let him go. At least he wouldn't have to run to get there. So off we went and after catching and saddling the horses, I mounted and Chris lifted Mate up to me where he sat in his favoured position in front of me in the saddle with his front paws braced against the horse's neck.

We found the ewes and lambs at the edge of the scrub and they shot away into it. Before I could lift him down, Mate leapt from the horse and was after them. The scrub was so thick that it was very difficult to walk through. Chris and I stopped at the edge of the scrub and waited. Soon the sheep appeared and were milling near our feet. Suddenly one ewe sat down, then another, heads stretched out flat on the ground in front of them.

'This is typical,' said Chris. 'Turn your back and they'll be off into the scrub as quick as a flash.'

We decided to tie the legs of the ewes which were down and did this as Mate held the other sheep. In the meantime, another ewe lay down and suddenly the one still standing bolted straight over Mate, knocking him aside in his attempt to stop her. He disappeared after her and the lambs took off in another direction. Muttering our disgust, we tied the other ewe and shortly Mate brought the last ewe back. He backed her the last few metres until Chris grabbed her. Then Mate turned and disappeared back into the scrub. Ten or more minutes later, he appeared with the four flighty lambs under control. He held them while we caught them and tied their legs. We left them to be collected by the four-wheel drive.

When Mate and I arrived home I offered him a drink. He wanted one but seemed too apprehensive to do so. I knelt down beside him and tried to coax him to take some water. He sat down alongside me, looked into my eyes, reached out with his paw and touched me gently on the arm. That was it! He was asking for help and I had to do something.

I rang a vet in Mt Gambier for his opinion and it was decided that I should take Mate there immediately to be examined. An operation was duly planned for first thing in the morning.

The dog was found to have had a blocked bowel, an extremely painful condition, which the vet said could normally be picked up in two days. Mate, however, so arrogant, so proud and so stoic, had worked every day and eaten nothing for nearly a week. I felt terrible that I had allowed him to work. Then I thought of Mate's ego and knew he would never have stood for not working without getting very upset in his kennel.

Mate hovered near death for several days. He was fed intravenously. On the fifth day after the operation, Mate could hold his head up and at last I knew he would survive. However, he was literally a skeleton with a starey black and tan coat. The hair was beginning to lift from his ears.

As usual, that afternoon, we headed off to the vet's for his intravenous feed. Chris had phoned to ask me to bring him something he wished to borrow on my way to town and, with Mate lying in the hatchback rear of my car, I pulled up near Chris's shearing shed. Chris and his dogs were working sheep in the yards and the dogs were barking as they forced the sheep into the race. I got out leaving one of the doors open and walked about 25 metres from the car.

Suddenly, Chris called out, 'Have a look behind you!'

I turned to see Mate coming towards the yards. He had dragged himself over the back of the rear seat, between the front seats and out the door. In doing so, he had reopened the cut in his side. As he came towards me he staggered and fell. Fluid trickled from his wound. He picked himself up again, moved a few drunken steps, staggered and fell as I reached him. Tears welled up in my eyes as I held him. Mate was *the* best dog in the district and *he* was coming to work.

It was three weeks before Mate was able to drink milk and another week before he could eat meat. Six weeks after the operation he started to improve.

Mate worked the stock on our property in South Australia for seven years. He also worked in the hills of the Great Dividing Range in New South Wales, the Riverina, steep river frontage country in Victoria and on several properties in South Australia.

We competed in yard trials in three States and he was placed in five State Championships. His descendants are worked in most States of Australia, and some work in Scandinavia.

Although Mate was a champion in the yards, in my opinion it was in the paddock, mustering rough country and shepherding sheep, where he truly excelled. He required very little guidance from me and often spent a great deal of time searching and mustering out of sight. His uncanny ability intrigued me and I quickly learned to give him a go and be patient when things were difficult.

ROCKETED TO STARDOM
Shirley Hands, Boyup Brook, Western Australia

After three weeks of shearing we felt a sense of release when the sheep were all mustered and the last day of shearing arrived. I felt thankful that the discipline of shearers' hours was almost over when I took that morning's smoko into the shed. I had no sooner put the food down on the side table than the boss looked over from the wool press and said, 'How about getting the straggler ewe out of the oat crop?'

Besides being the cook and 'bottlewasher', I seemed to be expected to be responsible for the mustering—although no-one formally said so. The crossbred ewe had never been called 'a straggler' before. She was a very old target. Each member of the household, from the boss downwards, had tried to muster her, but she and her two lambs had evaded us all winter.

She had been the subject of several dinner table mutterings along the lines of, 'I'll shoot the old sod'. All attempts to get her had failed and she still lurked in the 100-acre paddock where the crop was growing—about a mile from the shed. The oats, just coming into head, looked like an impenetrable green fortress.

I felt the task was hopeless, particularly when I looked at my youthful companion, a small black bitch with a sharp inquisitive face, pointed ears very wide at the base, four white feet and bronze markings around her smile.

Sunny, then a year old, had only begun her training at the onset of shearing, but she showed a lot of promise mustering chooks and had a keen eye.

With Sunny beside me I opened the gates into the yards and walked through five acres of bushland, and crossed the gully and hill before opening the gate into the crop. After half circuiting the paddock to the far side of the crop, I saw the cunning old girl, grazing quietly on the grass by the fence on the edge of the crop. Sunny, walking by my side, tensed as she saw her quarry.

Her eyes homed in on the ewe who looked up and saw us. She ignored our advance until we were within 200 metres of her then, gathering up her burly lambs, she set off at a smart canter along the firebreak.

As Sunny raced past them in a wide arc, intending to head them off, the ewe turned and, with her lambs, darted into the crop. Sunny, now only a metre in their wake, followed them. Ewe, lambs and Sunny vanished without a sound into the green forest. Their tracks were barely visible as the oats closed over their path.

Their sudden disappearance alarmed me. The crop stood five-feet high, a green wall of stiff resistant stems. I hurried along the edge of the crop, calling Sunny to heel. As I stopped at intervals to wait and listen, a terrible sense of foreboding overcame me. What if I never found Sunny? Lost and blinded in that terrible green maze she could lie down from exhaustion and die. How could we ever get her out? I ran along the fire-break, panting and calling. It was nearing midday and I had to leave to do lunch for the shearers.

When I reached the shed with the food in the esky, the shearers and staff were all collapsed on the floor as though lunch was finished.

I told them the terrible reason for being late, of losing my precious dog in the oat crop. After they wolfed down the lunch they all consoled me, promising that when they had shorn the last sheep they would come and help look for her.

After lunch we went into the yards to shed the last batch of sheep. Within the open gate of the entrance yard was Sunny, standing modestly behind her quarry. The crossbred ewe was cowed and beaten and her two burly lambs were somewhat less jaunty than before.

Sunny spent a successful and happy life demonstrating the techniques of timing and movement, but her mastery over the old ewe had rocketed her to stardom. From that day on she became top dog and sat beside the boss in the front seat of the ute.

PERCY
Bruce Rodgers, Merriwa, New South Wales

Percy was an orphan pup that Bob Telfer had reared on a bottle. Bob turned up at our place with him one day. 'Dog's name is Percy,' Bob said. 'Might be OK. Give him a go.'

207

Percy was starey-eyed, black and tan and gangling.

He soon shone as a lead dog and then developed other skills that found him half a mile from the mob with a handful of stragglers, or right behind you at a gateway when a push was needed. He could handle cattle as well as sheep, and I wouldn't have a dog any other way.

On the particular night when Percy showed just how good he was, there was no moon. The plains grass was as high as a man standing and the three of us, a truck driver, my wife and I, were straining our ears to hear the slightest sound of 40 Angus weaner cattle lost off a truck from Casino that had arrived around midnight. The truck driver had rushed up to our door, out of breath and out of sorts.

'The weaners are all out,' he said. 'Someone must have left the back gate of the yards open and I didn't shut the front gate as I reckoned I'd only be twenty minutes.'

On with the boots, out with the torches, off with Percy and into the ute. We blocked half the mob in the lane, but 40 had managed to beat us onto the reserve, which was three miles long and a mile wide, with four roads out of it. The furthest they could go was probably Cassilis, 26 miles on a main road west. The thought paled me.

I told Percy to hop out of the back of the ute, and cast him in the general direction of west and hoped for the best.

The driver grew more and more agitated that there was no sight or sound of the cattle for half an hour or more.

Forcing my way through plains grass, falling over stones and logs, I headed for the fence on the far side. Every now and then I could hear something, but nothing that gave me a bearing. After half an hour of this, I was ready to give up until daylight. The night was black and so were the cattle.

Then suddenly I heard them corning down the fence heading east. Bobbing down, I tried to get a count of their backs on the dull skyline. Missing the count but knowing there was a good number, I blessed my luck and followed. Luck had nothing to do with it. Old Percy was bringing them along alone and unassisted.

When they reached the crossroad, they had drawn too far away for me to give him any orders. He had more idea than I where home was, but he had to cross them over the east-west highway on a long weekend.

Heart in my mouth, and catching up with my wife, neither of us knew where Percy was or where he was heading. The sound of late night traffic on the road sent chills down our spines.

We reached the road to find no cattle and no dog. Venturing on up the lane that leads to the front gate, there was Percy—just floating along behind the weaners. If he could talk, he would have said, 'Where have you all been?'

The truck driver was ecstatic. 'That must be the best dog in the world,' he said.

'Could be,' I replied. 'I'm going to teach him to shut gates next.'

PART 5
MIND-READERS

- *Perception*
- *A bit of ESP*

THE MIND-READER
Tim Catling, Katanning, Western Australia

Scampy was a big, strong black dog that I owned in the late 1950s, or perhaps he owned me as I am sure he believed. He was a wonderful worker as well as a good mate. Sadly he was killed in his prime by a full drum of petrol being pushed off a truck.

He had one unusual trait, that of a mind-reader. In those days of farmers' first affluence for almost 30 years, all companies seemed to have travelling salesmen doing the rounds in the bush. My farm is split by the main road and most weeks two or three of these hopefuls would appear. Many were interesting people, but some only wasted one's time. It was this last group that Scampy seemed to be the mind-reader about.

If ever I was standing there wishing to myself that a particular salesman would leave, Scampy would always come along and pee on his trouser leg. This always had the desired result of the fellow leaving, usually quickly. How that dog knew I wanted the fellow to leave I never discovered, but he saved me many a boring time by this mind-reading.

I DREAMED NOT OF GENIE
C McConnel, Esk, Queensland

I had wanted a working dog of my own ever since I left school, and finally Dad thought I knew enough to train a pup. I had visions of a red kelpie pup, but fate has a funny way of doing things. A friend who bred kelpies told Dad he had a pup that would suit me as she was too timid for a man. She had been sold as a small pup but had just been returned as being useless.

I wasn't too impressed when I went to collect my dream dog as she had to be dragged out of her kennel. She was an odd grey and tan colour. Anyway, I was told that if she didn't work out I could have a pup from the next litter, so Genie came home with me. I called her Genie hoping that she would turn out to be just like her namesake and solve all my problems.

Actually, I think she created more havoc than any other dog on the place. Nevertheless, she turned out to be a wonderful old character, never a top dog, but a handy old dog and as loyal to me as could be, even if she had to break the rules.

For instance, dogs were not allowed in the homestead garden. I was sick at the time with some wog or other and had had two days in bed. I heard Dad calling Genie to tie her up, and finally he came in and told me not to worry—but that she had been missing for the past two days.

Just then we heard a slight thumping from under the bed. Looking under we saw old Genie. Somehow she had got into the garden and then crept into the house and under my bed. It must have been terrifying for the silly old thing—but she was looking after me.

PREDICTING HIS RETURN
Margaret Shine, Pigeon Ponds, Victoria

Nigger was a small black kelpie with long hair who was very devoted to my husband, Doug. Often when he was walking along, Nigger would be that close behind him that he would get clipped on the jaw with his boot—but he would still stay there.

At shearing times I used to do the mustering on a horse. Sometimes Nigger would come all the way to the particular mob of sheep I was to bring back. Most times, however, he would only go through a couple of paddocks and while I was opening the gate, he would be gone, back to the woolshed and his master.

Doug would realise he had left, so would send him back to help me. Nigger would find me all right, often a long way from where he'd left me, and he would stay till we returned with the sheep. When we got about 200 yards from the sheep yards, he would run into the shed and sit at Doug's feet, so Doug would have to come and yard the sheep.

Nigger used to have a kennel in view of our kitchen window. When it was lunchtime, he would give a couple of sharp barks as he watched up the road. I knew I could then dish up because Doug would be home in

213

about five minutes. We thought it was just because he had much better hearing than we had.

However, when Doug went fishing up on the Murray River near Robinvale, or to the Coorong in South Australia, he would be away for a week or ten days, and sometimes longer depending on the weather and the amount of fish he caught.

Doug never phoned to say when he would be back but Nigger always seemed to know the day he would be returning. He would be out of the kennel, give a couple of sharp barks, run around for a while, then settle down for half an hour or so. Then he would start the routine again.

When the children came home from school I would tell them Dad would be home that day. 'Watch Nigger,' I'd say. I could have bet the farm on him. Doug would come home some time late afternoon or even 10 o'clock at night.

Nigger certainly couldn't have heard the ute in the early morning when he started his barking and running.

At first Doug and the children didn't believe me, but as the years went on, Nigger's perception never let him or me down. It was a sad day for all of us when we lost him. I guess a dog like that you are lucky to have known, and to have owned, once in a lifetime.

PIP, THE MARRIAGE BROKER
Susan Martel, Gollan, New South Wales

My childhood memories of Pip are of an aged brown kelpie. Yet it is to Pip I owe my existence. It was he who sealed my parents' relationship.

Pip was my father's favourite dog. Dad, a young bachelor manager, had obtained Pip as soon as he returned from active duties in World War II. Pip was his mate and worked with him through drought, flood and ordinary times.

Mother, a tall, dark-haired, attractive young lady, was swept off her feet at the local Bachelors and Spinsters Ball by the handsome manager who, at 33, had somehow managed to avoid matrimony.

As young men of the land do, Dad had taken Pip when courting

Mother, who worked at her father's stock and station agency. I often wonder what Mother thought of this since, as I remember, she did not appear to be over fond of dogs. I recall that she wouldn't let us bring the dogs into the house, take them in the car or even allow them into the garden. Yet when family discussions turned to the worth of dogs, even Mum would become a little misty-eyed when Pip was remembered.

It was not until my parents' fortieth wedding anniversary three years ago that I learnt why Pip was such a popular dog. Dad related the story.

One morning at the property where he worked, some 30 miles from town, he came out to discover that Pip was nowhere to be seen. All staff were alerted to keep an eye out for Pip, since dogs die quickly from snakebite.

That night, Dad received a phone call. Pip had turned up at Mother's family home. What a good excuse to go to town! Dad happily drove the 30 miles of potholed road to retrieve Pip.

He seemed to be convinced that for Pip to walk 30 miles, he must have been trying to drop some hint about the stock agent's beautiful daughter. So Dad did the only sensible thing and asked for Mother's hand, there and then.

GINGER

Helen Best, Barraba, New South Wales

We had a regular shearer, John, who was a friend of the family. He always brought his dog Ginger with him while he was at our shed for the weeks of shearing.

After several years of shearing and crutching, Ginger was a welcome addition to our workforce and Dad began to rely on him being there.

One year, a few days after our shed cut out, we were surprised to see Ginger on the doorstep and ready for work. He had found his way back to Fairview, seven miles from the town, on his own.

On the Friday night there was no sign of our extra dog. He had gone home to be with his owner.

Thus the pattern was set. Whenever John went to a big shed and left the dog in town, Ginger came out to Fairview and worked happily with us. He always only stayed until his owner returned to town, be it Friday night, or because of a break in routine because of rain and wet sheep. Ginger always knew.

As 'our' dog grew older, the seven miles seemed to be too much for him, so he made the decision to make his home permanently at Fairview.

However, we never did know how Ginger could possibly have known when John got back to town. Did he sense it, or did he pick up the sound of his car?

SO SHE WOULDN'T BE LEFT BEHIND
G H Harkin, Halifax, Queensland

My father was a drover from 1910 till late 1960. He had numerous stories of working dogs, the kelpie breed mostly, as they were the dogs that knew the job well, were very hardy, reliable, intelligent and obedient to the drover's command.

He had been camped for a while between jobs. The red kelpie bitch had produced puppies and kept them near a tree, some way from the camp. The time came when Dad had to move off to pick up his next flock of sheep. He started to pack up and harness his horses.

Suddenly he noticed a small puppy on the track to the bitch's tree. He picked it up and returned it to the tree, but found that others were missing.

The dog apparently had noticed the movements in the camp signalling they would soon be off. She had taken it upon herself to load her puppies into a wire basket under the wagon—the usual place for pups when the droving outfit was on the move.

HE KNEW THE TIME

Lynette Pouliot, Horsham, Victoria

Tim was bought from the Horsham Saleyards back in 1962 for the princely sum of £2 17s 6d. Although only three months old, he was alert and easy to handle and it was obvious that our new black and tan kelpie had loads of potential.

It wasn't long before he was displaying the qualities of zeal, stamina, intelligence and loyalty which characterise the Australian working dog. During his ten years of working with sheep, Tim literally 'never missed a beat', his energy never waned and he didn't take one 'sickie'.

As a stock agent, my husband inevitably had various moves around Victoria, the first being from Horsham to Ouyen. On the day of our departure Tim went missing, only to be discovered several hours later sitting up in the cabin of the furniture van. This had necessitated jumping at least seven feet from the ground through a half-open window —no mean achievement—but he wasn't going to be left behind!

Summertime in the Mallee often meant working in extreme heat. This, coupled with harsh ground conditions, did not slow up our dog at any time. He worked tirelessly and unerringly, whatever the task.

The big monthly sheep market in Ouyen made for a long and busy day. Tim had a routine from which he never deviated. He went about his work in the saleyards from daybreak until 2 pm, which was when selling commenced. At that time, he would sign himself off, come home for a rest and later have his tea.

On the dot of 5 pm he would be gone again, back to my husband. Instinctively he knew this was the time to start droving sheep up to the railway trucking yards.

We never worked out how he told the time so accurately!

UNDERSTOOD EVERY WORD
WE SAID

L Lee Buckman, Gilgandra, New South Wales

We had never given much thought to retiring, but after receiving a good offer for the farm we decided maybe the time had come to go. Our only problem was what we should do with our dearly loved sheepdog and constant companion, Bill.

He was twelve years old and a bit old to start life again with a new boss, but was still very alert and agile. We wondered how he would adjust to life on the coast far away from sheep and the wide open spaces.

After the sale was completed we kept our sheep till within a few weeks of moving and then contacted our agent about selling them. The day the buyer came Bill did his job helping us to bring the sheep up to the yards and then he lay down in his usual place near the gate while we discussed prices and trucking arrangements. The buyer would be back for the sheep in two days.

The next morning Bill seemed very listless and just lay around in the shade. That night he wasn't even interested in his food, so we took him to his usual place in the header shed to sleep.

We had to bring the sheep up to the yards the next morning to load them up for their trip to their new home, but Bill just refused to come with us. Thinking he might be sick, we didn't worry him and got the sheep up without his help.

By lunchtime they had all been loaded with the help of the buyer's dogs and we waved them farewell and returned to the house to check how Bill was. He was dead.

We always said he understood every word we said, so perhaps he realised his work was finished and we didn't need him any more.

Bill's boss, my husband, died four years later. He missed the sheep and the wide open spaces. Retirement wasn't for him either.

SAM KNEW

R D McDonald, Kerang, Victoria

I feel I should not let the chance go by without telling this story of Sam. Now, I am not a writer or storyteller by nature, but I will put the true facts on paper and I think that should be of interest to many people.

Very early in the Dirty Thirties Depression, three young men decided to get out of Melbourne with all its troubles. One of these young men had worked in our district, so they made it their destination. They bought a horse and buggy which were very cheap in those days and off they set, seeking casual work and food as they travelled north.

One landowner gave them a dog for company. This was fine until they passed a paddock with sheep near the fence. The dog straightaway went quietly around the sheep and herded them to the roadside in quite good style. The dog kept doing the same thing each time they were near sheep.

The upshot was, when they reached our area, we were shearing and they did some casual work around the shed. I took notice of the dog and was impressed by his ability. I eventually offered them five pounds for the dog and they were delighted as five pounds was a lot of money in 1931.

The spokesman for the three was Sam Felling, so I named the dog Sam. Then his real work began. We quickly became attached and he would not let me out of his sight.

We had a property 30 miles away from the home property and I used to do most of the sheep work there. To muster this property meant riding the 30 miles with Sam trotting along at the horse's heels. Sam then would muster and help draft the sheep, never turning a hair. If necessary, he would follow me home that evening. He was truly a great working dog and he loved it.

However, there were plenty of good working dogs. The real part of the story is as follows.

As you know, the war broke out on September 1939. I immediately joined the forces. I went into camp on October 1939, which meant that I had to place Sam in good hands. My elder brother gladly took care of him.

Knowing that Sam was very much a one-man dog, my brother kept

219

him well tied up until he got a little bit settled before taking him around the sheep. Sam gradually adapted and seemed to like his new environment.

I was away for nearly three years from when I first took Sam to my brother. Sam by this time was quite at home there.

After returning from the Middle East, we got a few days' leave to go home. I arrived home late one Friday night and after greeting my family I enjoyed the strange feeling of a comfortable bed.

I woke early in the morning and was anxious to get out and look around. When I opened the back door, there was Sam on the mat. He looked at me a little guiltily, but as soon as I spoke and patted him, he was all over me, and until I delivered him back to my brother, he was glued to my heels.

To get to our place, Sam would have had to travel nearly 40 miles if he'd followed the roads. If he'd gone as the crow flies, it was at least 25 miles and he would have had to swim two major streams—the Murray and the Little Murray—and go through heavy red gum forests.

This was quite an achievement, apart from the timing of it all. It made me wonder if he had been uneasy when we were pinned down by shell-fire in the desert, or bombed and strafed at.

I know I probably haven't told this very well, but now I feel too sentimental to rewrite it or say any more.

PART 6
WHOOPS!

Heart in the right place, but sometimes that's not enough!

THE INDISCRETIONS OF
PETE THE PUP

John Sykes, Bordertown, South Australia

Pete the Pup was born of quite common parentage. His father belonged to our southern neighbour, his mother to our eastern neighbour.

Within a few years Pete the Pup knew the entire layout of the farm, knew where the gates were and, more importantly, the nature of Dad's way of doing things. This was supplemented by the way he understood my mother's soft touch. On returning from a hard few hours' work, he would always line up for a leftover chop bone or a piece of cake for morning tea.

I found out one day just how human a nature Pete the Pup had. It was at shearing time. It was hot and I was putting sheep in the shed, running them up the platform. I wasn't getting on terribly well. Sweat was flowing and my blood pressure was rising. I was standing at the bottom of the ramp waving my arms and generally shouting at the sheep.

Suddenly I felt a large grab on my ankle and, looking down, I noticed Pete the Pup just pulling his head out from between the rails. He was peering up at me. In his eagerness to move the sheep up the ramp, he had given one just a little nip on the leg to encourage them, nothing drastic, but just enough to get them going. Well! On this particular occasion, he had grabbed my ankle and when I looked down in amazement at him, the look on his face was most expressive. It said, 'I am so sorry, boss. I got the wrong leg. I didn't mean it. I just got the wrong leg.' He looked terribly apologetic.

Perhaps the greatest indiscretion was the day one of my sisters' future in-laws came to stay with Mum and Dad for a weekend. They had never met my parents and arrived on the Saturday morning from Melbourne in a large, white Mercedes.

Mum and Dad walked out to the car and while they were opening the door to allow the future mother-in-law out, Pete the Pup came to inspect.

My father was introduced to her by my sister and while they were shaking hands, Pete the Pup calmly walked between them and, lifting his leg, widdled down the future mother-in-law's stockinged leg. My father was extremely embarrassed, my sister was horrified and Pete the Pup had rather a sore backside for a few days.

BAILED UP

Tom Hordacre, Tenterden, Western Australia

This happened during the 1930s when I was a schoolboy.

The annual Christmas Tree at the Tenterden Hall was always a big event for the local children. A nearby farmer was to be Father Christmas. My father, being the proud owner of a model T Ford, would pick the old chap up at a prearranged point, close to his home.

The appointment was kept by my father. After a few minutes' wait, and no sign of Father Christmas, he decided to drive up to his home.

On arrival, the cause of the delay became obvious. The old gentleman, dressed in his robes, was home alone, frantically waving at the window to draw attention to his normally friendly sheepdog. The dog was loose and promptly challenged his master and held him prisoner in his own home.

My father managed to calm the dog and chain him up, then all was clear to leave with his passenger.

Father Christmas arrived a little late, but was made very welcome by the children.

'WHAT THE DEVIL'S GOING ON?'

Rose Bindon, Penguin, Tasmania

I woke to the yowling chorus of an intense cat fight directly under the floor. A full, bright moon lit my bedroom.

My mother was already awake, having thrown open her bedroom window. I could hear her saying 'Scat, scat' in subdued tones, so as not to disturb the rest of the family. The yowling continued.

With firm, determined steps and muttering under her breath, Mother, in her nightie, jumped into her gumboots and stomped down under the house. Her presence still did not stop the racket. So, with fierce determination, she let the dog, Katie, off her chain and gave her the order of 'Scat 'em, girl!'

Now Katie was a very intelligent dog, but with an askance look on her face and a wag of her tail, she waited for the order to be repeated—which it was, this time with a note of anger. Katie knew that tone and it meant Mother was to be obeyed immediately.

Whether it was the noise from the fighting cats or she misunderstood Mother, Katie took off up the home paddock, through the bush and across a few more fields. Within half an hour (a record time) she had every one of the dairy cows, plus the cranky horse, rounded up and running down towards the cowshed ready for milking.

By this stage Mother was yelling 'Get in behind!' Katie was barking hard and fast. The horse was snorting and neighing and trying to get away from the officious dog. Cows were running and mooing. The cats fought on. Pandemonium!

Dad woke thundering, 'What the devil's going on!' The rest of the children sat up bright-eyed at the window, watching and listening.

At the sound of Dad's voice, the cats stopped fighting. Katie came to heel—Dad's heels. Mother stopped yelling and the cows stood quietly in the shed yard waiting patiently to be milked. Peace at last—at 3.30 in the morning! No doubt the butterfat was down that day.

MOBILE HOME

Peter Hall, Glen Alice, via Rylstone, New South Wales

Tan is a striking black and tan kelpie that grew from a very fearless pup and now, as a dog, just lives to be with the livestock on our mountain valley property.

He was whelped at a particularly droughty time, and my wife Vinny, like most women in the valley, had a few poddy lambs and a very inquisitive poddy heifer calf, named Daisy, to feed each day.

The poddies would line up for their milk at the garden gate and so would the pup, so that he could sneak a lick of the excess milk from a few faces and generally enjoy himself.

Consequently, Tan, due to the daily ritual of feeding the poddies, grew into a very knowing young dog that was very keen on still licking Daisy, even though she had grown to twenty times his size. They were great mates, and you would often see the big poddy heifer happily getting her motherly grooming from the dog.

This was soon to change though, for the young dog had started to get very keen with stock and soon had to be chained up, otherwise he would muster everything back to the house.

The heifer, on the other hand, due to the persistent drought and the knowledge that the hayshed in the house yard was the best place to be, especially if she was given the odd slice of bread by Vinny, was never going to leave. The heifer would lazily walk over to Tan to have a drink out of his water bowl, get a motherly lick and then wander off again. Why go to the stock trough for water when Tan was so obliging?

Then disaster struck and the friendship was broken up for ever. Daisy had gone to Tan's water one day when I was shearing a few sheep in the nearby shed. I had chained up Tan and he had drunk most of his water after mustering the mob earlier. Daisy was persistent and moved about sniffing at the bowl. Tan was also moving about her. In doing so, he tied the sweetest half hitch around her leg with his chain.

Suddenly there was an almighty bellow and bang. I looked up from doing the long blow on my sheep and immediately ran to the door of the shed, the half-shorn sheep closely following me dragging its fleece.

In the tradition of a good 'Jolliffe' cartoon, there was the heifer, Tan and the kennel careering across the paddock. There I was trying to bull-dog the panicking heifer, calling loudly to the wife to help me bloody well free my best dog from under her bloody animal.

Tan survived to be the best dog I had. However, for months after this incident he had the habit of taking his water bowl into his kennel.

MAINLY FOR ENTERTAINMENT

Graeme Hobbs, Kojonup, Western Australia

When I came home to work on the farm in 1962, two dogs, Laddie and Peter, were in residence. Laddie was a border collie and Peter was a black mongrel of indiscriminate heritage. Passable dogs working sheep, they were kept mainly for their entertainment value.

Laddie would ride on the back of the truck travelling seventeen miles from farm to farm, constantly snapping at the overhanging branches of trees, spitting out the mouthfuls of leaves while waiting for the next branch. One day he misjudged, grabbed a branch and was left swinging in the air as the truck passed underneath him.

Peter loved chasing sticks, balls and stones. When the occasional travelling salesman called, Peter would work on him for some play. Finding a rock or half a brick, he would drop it a foot or so away from the visitor's toe. If nothing happened he would pick it up and drop it closer . . . and so on until at last it would land right on the end of the toe, much to the consternation of several salesmen. It would depend on the opinion we had of the products being sold as to whether we would warn them or not.

BARKING ORDERS
Noel Drury, Hynam, South Australia

At shearing time, everyone is busy. Nobody has time to talk, relax— or even open their eyes.

The boss went off mustering sheep with Rusty, the red kelpie. They got to the mob in the back paddock and the boss sent Rusty around the sheep.

Now Rusty was a very erratic dog. Half the time he does what he wants and not what the boss wants.

Time was short and Rusty was being difficult. The boss was getting very annoyed and yelling at him. The sheep were going all over the place and still Rusty was racing through them completely ignoring the loud roars and somewhat colourful demands from the boss.

After some minutes, the boss turned away from the scene in disgust. To his astonishment, he discovered Rusty sitting behind him on the motorbike, looking a picture of innocence.

The boss turned back towards the sheep and, to his embarrassment, discovered he had been barking orders to a big, red fox.

FRONT-WHEEL DRIVE

Kay Hole, Naracoorte, South Australia

Joseph is a gentle man. He loves his dogs and they will do anything for him. He has a passion for well-bred kelpies.

On the particular day I am going to tell you about, he was determined to spend some time getting his new charge, Zach, working, even though Zach's front leg was in plaster. The exuberant pup would in time replace old, wise Sally.

The day was bright and sunny, although there was a chill in the air which comes with the first balmy days of autumn. The cattle first had to be fed, so the gentle farmer went down to the paddock with hay on the back of the ute and the two dogs in the front.

It was customary for Joseph to put the ute in gear, jump on the back and slowly feed out the hay while the vehicle bumped its way across the paddock. Zach and Sally were left in the front. Sally was there to protect the little pup and make him feel less frustrated. The windows were closed but not quite shut to the top, so that the dogs could manage to get air.

Contentedly, the farmer began to throw the hay to the bellowing cattle. Little Zach ran from side to side in the front of the ute so he could get a glimpse of his dear master. Sally was happy to sit and wait. All was right with her world.

Joseph collected the last bits of string from the wispy pieces of hay still left on the tray of the ute, then he jumped to the ground and grabbed the door handle on the driver's side. It wouldn't open. Zach was tonguing at the window—'I'm a good boy. I stayed inside with Sally.' Sally was looking a little dismayed.

After trying the door on the passenger's side with no success, Joe realised that Zach had locked each door with his little plastered leg. The ute was heading for the neighbour's fence and Joseph could be seen from all directions.

He decided to go down on his knees, making sure that he was not visible from the road (a man's pride was at stake), and try to turn the front wheels with his hands. It worked! But how was he going to stop the thing? 'Ah, the drain across the middle of the paddock,' he thought—'I've stalled her in that plenty of times before.'

The old Datsun responded to his now not so gentle hands and headed for the drain. Helplessly, Joseph watched as the old bomb casually crawled her way through the drain and up the other side without missing even one beat.

By this time, Sally was looking through the window and wondering why Joseph was using his 'rounding up the sheep' language just for a simple little jaunt in the paddock, and why he didn't get in and drive home. She was getting sick of all this.

She was not the only one. Joe had to quickly pretend he was leaning on the ute as it lamely wandered across the paddock, because the neighbour just then was travelling very slowly through one of his paddocks trying to see what on earth was going on. 'He's gone,' thought Joseph. 'Right, one more try in the drain.'

'Damn. Through again. Blast, I wish that pup would stop his infernal yelping,' Joseph mumbled as he front-wheel-steered the ute to a huge pile of logs. He quickly threw one under a back wheel, but it was too small and the old Datsun once more headed for the neighbour's fence.

Joe then summoned all the bits of strength he had left and grabbed a huge log, risking angina and hernia, to heave it under the back wheel. It worked. The ute stalled.

In the meantime, quite a few very slow moving vehicles were going at a snail's pace along the main road as their drivers watched this crazy farmer trying to steer in this novel fashion. What was the wacky fellow trying to do? There he was yelling at someone or something inside the ute, throwing logs at it and steering it from a kneeling position while it got perilously close to the road fence.

The pup's training was postponed until the next day and never again were the dogs left alone in the ute.

OH! WHAT A FEELING

Doug Keith, Elmhurst, Victoria

The tray of the Hilux ute was rusting away, mainly due to the male dogs using it as a urinal. So I purchased an aluminium tray as a replacement and put it into storage for the time being.

In due course, when there were no other urgent jobs, I parked the ute near the workshop and set about removing the old tray.

The dogs dozed in the sun, occasionally opening one eye to make sure that they weren't missing anything important, but generally conserving energy until there was some real action.

Eventually all the rusted bolts were undone and I removed the old tray from the chassis, and dragged it some twenty feet away. I then got into the cab chassis to go and collect the replacement tray.

Instant action from the dogs! Decisions to be made! In an instant, habit took over and all four dogs dashed for the old tray and leapt on. Oh! What a feeling!

But as I drove away, their euphoria evaporated and you could see their expressions change to—'Trust a bloody Toyota to fall in half just when we're needed!'

WHAT AM I BID?

Ralph Dawson, Birdwood, South Australia

During my 40 years as a stock agent in South Australia, I spent fourteen years at Angaston. Very often I was required to attend the Gepps Cross sheep and lamb markets to assist in the drafting and penning of the various lots, and then to do some of the clerking of the sales.

I usually took my border collie Nimrod with me and he worked in the yards helping with the penning up. Often when we were selling, he would jump up on the walking plank above the pens and follow the agents along, watching the sales' progress.

On one occasion, he slipped past me and followed close behind the auctioneer. The auctioneer was taking bids from buyers in the race, and also from someone touching him on the leg. As bidding slowed, he glanced quickly down to see who was touching him, in readiness to knock the pen of lambs down to that person presumably in the pen below. Imagine his surprise to find that this person was Nimrod, rubbing his head against the auctioneer's leg. The eventual buyer was, of course, unaware that Nimrod had cost him several shillings due to his sham bids.

On the way home to Angaston, it was my unvarying custom to stop at a roadhouse just out of Gawler and buy two icecreams—one for myself and one for Nimrod.

YOU SILLY MUG
Arthur Finney, Broadbeach Waters, Queensland

It was early spring and as was usual I had risen at four-thirty. First thing was to send Patch, my faithful and ever-ready blue heeler, to round up the cows from the night paddock, driving them round to the yards for milking.

Meanwhile, I went back into the house for my usual early morning cuppa and piece of buttered bread. Coming down the back steps on my way to the yards, I looked over towards the night paddock. It was still shrouded in a light mist. In the half light I could vaguely discern the outline of what looked like a cow that Patch had missed. 'I'll give that dog the rounds of the kitchen when I get to him,' I thought as I walked over to the yards.

Patch had the herd penned when I got to the yards. He was just sitting at the gate waiting for me to shut them in.

When I scolded him for leaving one of the cows behind, he seemed quite perplexed, looking at me in the quizzical way he did when uncertain of my wishes. He baulked three or four times at going back to the night paddock. Ultimately, I had to really bully and threaten him before, with a very sulky manner, he trotted off to bring in the cow that I reckoned he had missed.

Had I stopped to do the right thing, I would have had a quick head

230

count. This would have saved me considerable later embarrassment, but being irate about the missing animal, I vented my impatience on Patch. I was certain I had seen a cow in the half light and morning fog.

There was no time to waste. Into the bails with the first six cows. Wash their udders and on with the machines. Get things moving, or I would be late for the milk carrier.

Then around the corner of the house fence appeared Patch, trailing, of all things, old Darkie. Darkie, my old draughthorse, was almost pensioned off and I had put him in the night paddock about a week earlier.

Patch slowly marched him to the yard gate. He then sat on his haunches and looked across at me with an expression on his face which seemed to say, 'There you are, you silly old mug, try and milk that one.'

RACING DOG
Barbara Shugg, Stratford, Victoria

We had heard of the oldest son borrowing Dad's car, and a younger son doing a bit of circle work around the front paddock, but were quite unprepared for the kelpie pup to take off in the farm ute.

It was towards the end of the '71 drought. The new black and tan was settling in nicely. He was showing plenty of eye and was very willing. The only command that he really understood, though, was 'sit'.

As was the daily procedure, the farm ute was loaded up with fifteen opened bags of oats. The young pup and the master climbed into the cabin and drove to the south paddock to feed the ewes.

The ute was put into low-range first gear and set in motion. The pup was left in the cabin while his master leapt onto the tray. Balanced precariously on the tail gate, he proceeded to trickle out the grain to the sheep, which were panicked into a feeding frenzy. The ute meandered slowly around the paddock for some distance and the frantic mob began to settle.

Suddenly, the motor roared. The ute bolted forward, sending the farmer flying off the back into the midst of his nervous sheep. The ute whizzed crazily around the paddock, bouncing in and out of potholes, scattering grain in all directions. The farmer and his sheep took off in hot pursuit.

The pup was of the 'when-in-doubt, sit' variety. The louder the boss yelled, the harder the terrified pup sat on the accelerator, the faster the ute bumped around the paddock and the more the bleating sheep panicked, chasing their food supply.

It wasn't until the farmer's voice ran out that the little dog ventured up onto the seat and peered out the window to see what was causing all the commotion. The boss, gasping gentle encouragement to the dog, finally managed to keep him off the floor long enough to catch his utility.

LOVED BY HIS OWNER AND NOBODY ELSE

Jenny Caldwell, Forbes, New South Wales

An old drover by the name of Mattie O'Connor gave me Wally as a pup. Wally was a little bit of kelpie and a lot of everything else. He grew up as most pups do, loved by his owner and nobody else—especially in my mother's garden and when trying to get the sheep through the gate.

Time went on and Wally thought he could do anything that was asked of him, so we packed a large chair and set off to a wether trial at Plevna, Trundle, New South Wales, which had yard dog trials on later in the day. Wally and I had never entered a trial before so this was a very brave move, more on my part than Wally's.

We were called to be eighth into the yards so we watched every move the others made, getting little tips on the fence from the veterans of this very male-dominated sport. The plan looked simple enough—fill the drenching race, then draft the mob three different ways and count them without physically helping your dog. Only verbal help and encouragement were allowed.

At this stage Wally, as you can imagine, was very hard to restrain as the excitement was all too much. There were dogs everywhere and I had quite a job to hold him. At this point I should add that Wally had a fetish for lifting his leg on every car tyre, every tree and every gatepost.

In the middle of the yards was a man who was to decide our fate, including whether Wally should be put to stud as a champion yard dog. There he was—crisp blue shirt, shiny riding boots and clean white moleskin trousers.

Our turn had come. The previous dog had been very well behaved and scored well. The bell rang to signal our start. I released Wally, and, well, he took off, jumped every fence, and was off behind utes and trees seeking other dogs. He had completely forgotten about the sheep. All thoughts of a blue ribbon vanished. The crowd loved this performance. The judge was not amused and I was getting very embarrassed and thought, 'this is enough.' I called out, 'Walter.'

It did take a while but then I saw a brown blur heading towards me and thought, 'What a good, obedient dog.' Wally, however, thought he'd take a short cut via the judge, who at this stage was looking a little flushed.

In his excited state and with all eyes on him, how was Wally to know that those white moleskins were not another white gatepost? Needless to say, Wally did not get a blue ribbon.

TEACHING THE APPRENTICE A LESSON

Neville Kajewski, Emerald, Queensland

My old friend Fred Wilson had a cattle dog called Ho, a wonderful worker and clever in many ways.

Ho wasn't just a good worker, he was Fred's mate and constant companion. I'm sure they knew each other's thoughts.

In the latter part of Ho's life, Fred bought a pup to train as a replacement before arthritis completely immobilised the old dog.

One day, Fred, Ho and the pup were yarding a mob of bullocks for dipping. According to established routine, once the mob was mustered Fred took the lead on his horse, allowing the dogs to bring them along while he opened the gates.

All was going well until a couple of bullocks decided they were going home. Under normal circumstances they would be no more than a nuisance to Ho. He would simply return them to mob with a couple of disciplinary nips to nose and heel, but he hadn't reckoned on the inexperience of the pup.

When the two bullocks broke away, the rest of the mob turned. The pup, thinking he should be behind them, went to what was now the back of the mob.

Ho's barking at the two breakaways stirred the pup to enthusiastic action. At full pace he ran back and forth behind the mob, barking furiously and occasionally diving in to nip a heel for good measure.

Meanwhile, poor old Ho was working as hard as his arthritic joints would allow. Facing him was the whole mob, defiant and determined to escape. He blocked one then another group of breakaways, sending them back to the mob with tails high and nostrils flaring—but as he regrouped the mob on one wing, a breakaway started on the other.

Ho's exertions spurred the pup to even greater effort. The atmosphere became charged with the fear of confused bullocks being pushed around by the two dogs working in opposition.

Fred watched for a while, hoping the dogs would sort things out, but he finally decided to add to the confusion and help Ho while he shouted threats at the pup like, 'Come behind here, you bastard' or 'I'll shoot you'. He rode around the mob, cracking his whip, turning back one then another, but he knew failure was imminent. The bullocks had had enough.

Suddenly, cued by some primeval signal, the whole mob revolted. They scattered in all directions, making it impossible for dog or man to control them. Ho gave up. He knew he was defeated and let the mob go. It really wasn't their fault anyway . . . now, where's that pup?

As the bullocks streamed away around him, Ho ran straight for the pup who, with tongue lolling and tail wagging as he panted in the shade of a bush, was very pleased with his achievement. But the pleasure was short-lived. Old Ho wasn't at all amused.

He grabbed the pup by the scruff of the neck and shook him as he would a rabbit, at the same time scolding him for his stupidity with savage growls. The pup's yelps of fear changed to whimpers of submission. Ho dropped him but mauled some more warnings. Completely cowered, the pup rolled onto his back, baring his neck and belly, and awaited his fate.

Disgusted, Ho turned away from him, lifted his leg and peed on the bush, then trotted away to join Fred, whose laughter echoed around the ridges as they started again to muster the mob.

PART 7
OVER AND ABOVE
THE CALL OF DUTY

Going beyond the brief

A DEDICATED PARTNER

Geoffrey Blight, Narrogin, Western Australia

It was spring in the worst year of my life. I was broke. Sharefarming wheat was going very poorly and we were involved in a legal wrangle over the land and the house we lived in. My wife was pregnant with our first child, so I was glad to get some crutching on a local farm about nineteen miles away.

It was a small place, only one stand in the shearing shed, an old house, an old man and an old blue dog.

There weren't many sheep, about 1,100 all told, which needed crutching and then they were to be sold. The farm had already been sold and the old man was moving into a home in Perth. He had no family, just his dog and he was to be put down when the sheep were gone.

Scotty couldn't go to the new home—they wouldn't allow it and he did have trouble with his bowels and smelt quite often. Some mad young roustabout had run over him the year before as he sat by the shearing shed. I believe the old man had threatened to kill the young fellow if he ever showed his face there again.

The shearing shed was very old and rugged. A stiff breeze could have demolished it. It even looked as though it was ready to fly away. The shed only held about 50 sheep in just two pens separated by a picket garden gate. As I kicked off, the old man explained his predicament and also asked if I'd mind, each time I finished a sheep pen, throwing the picket gate open so the still unseen dog could do the penning up.

Well I had heard a few stories, I had been shearing for a few years and seen a fair bit of action, but I guess I didn't believe any dog was going to do what the old man reckoned. Still, he was a nice old fellow so I thought, if I had to, I wouldn't mind penning for myself. I'd had it worse. As the old chap wasn't able to stay for some reason or other, when I had finished the first pen, I did what he said. But I still couldn't see the dog.

I reckoned it was taking me about one and a quarter minutes to crutch each sheep. When I straightened up and saw the pen full, I received a shock as I had not heard any noise through the closed gate in the front wall of the pen.

When the second pen was done I repeated the exercise. Same result.

I could hardly believe it. When I had the chance I directed a few how-are-you-mates to the bent old blue dog. He showed no interest in me whatsoever, even seemed suspicious of me, so I didn't push my luck.

The crutching lasted three days and was a piece of cake. The old dog had those sheep so well trained they penned more like milking cows than wild wheatbelt sheep.

I guess it was my praise for the old dog that made the old man ask if I would like old Scotty. He assured me that, although he could not run, he would still pull his weight for a while yet and as long as I didn't take him into the house, the smell wasn't too bad. He had visibly shown he wasn't looking forward to putting his dog down and no-one else wanted him. I thought he probably didn't know many people that well, having lived a very secluded life. The whole area had only recently seen extensive clearing, except for a few scattered properties, including his, that were the remnants of an attempt in the thirties to open up the land.

It was a few weeks later when the old man phoned and asked if I would come and take Scotty. He had to leave the next day. Scotty now became mine, but only till the next morning. By then, he was gone. I found him back at the now empty old house, looking pretty weary. That didn't stop him biting me as I tried, and finally succeeded in, pushing him into the car.

Next morning, I found he had slipped the collar and was gone again. I cursed him and swore he could go to hell.

After three days I relented. I took the gun and went back to the old man's former home, quite prepared to put him down rather than leave him to starve. He looked very old and hungry and surprised me by rising from where he had been sitting on the verandah and walking straight to the car, hopping in quite voluntarily.

Scotty didn't run away again but I didn't have much sheep work for him at that time so during the harvest, he just sat lazily around with our very useless labrador. They both passed their time killing hundreds of mice that were in plague proportion everywhere.

The harvest was a failure. By Christmas it was clear we would have to get out and go back to the sheep country I'd come from and go back shearing again.

I had about 600 mixed sheep running over 5,000 acres of sparsely cleared land on the cropping block where we lived. These would have to be mustered, which would take many days as they had spread all over the place in small mobs.

The weather was stinking hot, over 120 degrees on the back verandah of the tin shed type residence we lived in. I had thought I could probably catch the sheep at the three water points, though that would take even longer, building yards and shutting two points off. They might not even travel to the third water point anyway.

I was surprised when, just as the sun broke on Boxing Day, I became aware that a lot of sheep were bunching over some spilt wheat not too far from the house. It was a marvellous opportunity to just round them up and into the one yard we had. I was on foot with just Scotty, because it was too rough for a vehicle in most places, and I hadn't caught the horse. I sent the dog, fully expecting him to just pull them in.

As I have said, Scotty couldn't run and I soon realised that the sheep were going to get away despite my urging and swearing. Eventually, I hurled a stick at the dog, who wasn't going any faster than I was, which sure wasn't fast enough. Out of sight they went and I gave it up as a bad job and forgot about them.

The day was a real scorcher and there was no getting away from the heat. By mid-afternoon, the wife and I had settled for lying under the fan on the bed. I was nearly asleep when I became aware that large amounts of dust were drifting into the house, but we couldn't hear any vehicles approaching.

Staggering out the open front door, I was in no way prepared for what I saw. I had forgotten about the sheep and Scotty a good ten hours ago. I could not believe it. Here was what looked like 600 sheep moving very, very quietly and slowly up to the house, followed by a staggering, old, blue dog.

It was going to be a while before what had happened sank in. I swiftly took advantage of the muster and yarded them with total ease as the sheep seemed to quietly accept their capture. It was only when this was complete that I became concerned about the condition of Scotty—his staggering, his bleeding feet, his flanks tucked up and his fast and erratic panting. His eyes were sunken as he lay exhausted in the nearest shade.

In the next half hour I tried in vain to cool and calm and water him. It frightened me as he gulped and then shuddered in a fit as I withdrew the water. However, greater powers than either of us took a hand. While

I watched, believing that Scotty was very close to death, the wind came fast, followed by black storm-clouds bearing wonderfully cooling drops of rain.

Although the storm was short, it seemed to have the right effect. The dog lay motionless on the verandah, his breathing calm, and he now seemed able to cope.

Because of the rain, which is common to such hot climates, I had some trouble tracking what exactly had happened. It was obvious the old dog had continued that morning in his pursuit of the sheep, managing to keep them grouped to a north boundary for miles, before they had been turned and gradually pushed back. At times they would have had to pass through scrub and regrowth which would have presented any dog with trouble. He had probably seen no water at all.

Being then young, it would take me some years to realise the significance of that muster. As I worked and trained dogs I came to understand the incredible dedication that can be counted on in a dog when he has spent a lifetime sharing the job as a sole partner to a human being.

A DROVER'S MATE
Des Coombes, Coffs Harbour, New South Wales

Dan was a true drover's mate. I'm not sure how my father acquired Dan, whose parentage was never established, but many of the local experts reckoned he was a kelpie with a touch of barb in him. But there was no doubting his working ability.

My father often drove a mob of abattoirs bullocks from the Kempsey area and through the town of Macksville for slaughter, a distance of 50 kilometres. Dan was his only help. Without ever having to be told, Dan would block and direct the cattle in any problem areas along the way.

His reputation became so great that people would come out of their houses and shops in Macksville to watch Dan shepherd the stock through the town and over the bridge. If you know the town of Macksville you would realise how difficult the task was. Dan never missed a trouble spot or lost a bullock.

During the 1940s, when droving was the common way of moving mobs of cattle, a good cattle dog was a prized possession, especially when getting stock to abattoirs in a non-stressed state was paramount. On at least two occasions Dan was stolen, but each time an observant citizen would report to my father that he had seen Dan chained up at some farm in the district and Dan would be retrieved, happy to be back home.

My mother worked at a Kempsey cafe and often finished work late at night. When he wasn't away droving, Dan would lie on the doormat and wait to escort her home. He never was told to do this.

HOME DELIVERY

Madge Wilson, Clements Gap, South Australia

In the 1940s I lived near the railway line that went from Adelaide to Port Pirie. We used to have our daily paper, *The Advertiser*, thrown from the train by the guard at our gates in the paddock about a quarter mile away.

I used to carry my young border collie pup up with me to get the paper. As he grew I would give him the paper to carry back to the house. When he was older I started sending him to pick up the paper on his own.

Later, when he heard the train whistle which blew when it left the station, he would go off on his own, pick up the paper and deliver it to the back door. He did this for many years. He was a good sheepdog too, and was sadly missed when he died of old age.

SLEEPERS AWAKE

Patrick Boylan, Port Lincoln, South Australia

In 1937, my father was involved in a short-term contract as a drover with Goldsborough Mort. As well as his team of dogs, he employed the services of a workman named Charlie. Charlie's role was that of cook and camp-maker. Now Charlie, who was a model of virtue at first, soon showed signs of being a cupboard drinker. My father took it upon himself to ration the alcohol, but one particular day, Charlie, who was left behind to break camp, failed to catch up with the flock at the usual time.

Upon investigation, Charlie was located asleep in the horse-drawn cart. Closer scrutiny showed him to be very drunk and, despite every effort, he was unable to be roused. After some deliberation my father decided to assign his most reliable and loyal dog, Grundy, the task of looking after Charlie and the horse and cart. Grundy's lead was clipped to the horse's bridle and as the sheep moved along, my father would whistle up Grundy and Grundy would bring up the cart.

Later in the day my father's attention was drawn from Grundy and his role to the sheep. After a while, when he gave his usual whistle, no dog turned up.

After some searching he located the team. Grundy had gone up onto the railway line and the cart had become firmly settled between the rails. Being an intelligent dog, he had proceeded down the railway line. The continuous bumping of the cart as it went over the Sleepers still failed to wake Charlie.

MAYHEM IN THE KITCHEN
Nancy Hyde, Port Lincoln, South Australia

Uley, the property where we lived when my children were little, was about 30 square miles of rough limestone country on lower Eyre Peninsula. The house was about 100 years old, thick-walled, with small, paned windows.

Apart from growing good wool, Uley was home to a great number of kangaroos, rabbits and foxes, which the dogs, both border collies and greyhounds, were encouraged to hunt.

One particular day, Brian and the family were out collecting firewood not far from the house. I heard a bit of a commotion outside but didn't take much notice, thinking that it was just another fowl being taken by a fox. I was very busy making biscuits for a Mothers and Babies Fete and concentrating on getting another trayful into the oven.

243

The next thing I knew, a fox with all the dogs after it came hurtling through the opening in the garden wall. The dogs were right on its tail and it didn't get a chance to turn. It just jumped onto the woodbox outside my kitchen window, then jumped straight through the closed window. It landed in the middle of my biscuits, showering everything with glass.

So, there was this fox in my biscuits on the bench staring at me a couple of feet away. I screamed and ran out the back door in search of Brian and the boys, who had seen all the fun and were shrieking with laughter—that is, until they got nearer the house and could hear the mayhem. The dogs had raced into the kitchen as I went out. We stood back and listened to the clanking of broken china and barking and general pandemonium. Then Brian summoned me in. 'The thing's dead,' he said.

I went in to survey chaos. China, biscuits and dogs everywhere and in the bathroom was the dead fox tangled in my bath towel. On the wall were its toenail marks where it had desperately tried to get out of the window. It had upset my face powder in the process, which just added to the rest of the mess.

The dogs stood around very pleased with themselves for good work well done!

BIRTH ON THE JOB
Joyce Shiner, Albany, Western Australia

Sissy was a young red cloud kelpie who was supposed to be chained up at shearing time, but somebody forgot. She was close to having pups and there were other dogs to do the work, so it was thought best that she was rested.

From the cookhouse window, I saw her drinking at the bowl under the tap, then she disappeared. Hearing a puppy yelping I went to investigate and found a pup in her bed. Several times she came back for a drink, each time leaving a pup or two. Then she would race back to the shed again.

At lunchtime we compared notes and discovered that Sissy had worked in the sheep yards all morning, returning to the house between jobs ostensibly for a drink.

The shearers were amazed to see her litter of newly born puppies, and she hadn't even missed a beat in the shed.

CHAMP THE LONG DISTANCE LOVER

Richard L Mould, Naracoorte, South Australia

Nobody ever told us how Champ came to be on Lincoln Park Station, but it was clear from his intelligence, appearance and working ability that he was a particularly well-bred border collie. It was probable that he had been trained for sheepdog trials. However, he was too big and clumsy and he lacked the pace for a competition trial dog.

When handling sheep Champ could be controlled most successfully by whistles and hand signals alone, a routine foreign to our sheep station trained animals, who responded mostly to voice commands. On hearing a voice, in particular a raised voice, Champ would come straight to heel, and if the voice had any hint of menace in it, he would slink away. Indeed, he tended to be rather timid—far too timid for the rigour of sheep station work. This was in direct contrast to our mustering dogs, who were boisterous and somewhat rough and ready, not easily put down for long by voice or threat.

A good mustering dog is very fast and casts wide when heading a mob of sheep. Consequently the dog is quite often in the lead before the sheep realise it. Champ, on the other hand, tended to work too close, which meant that the sheep were being literally chased for a long time before being headed. This could have disastrous consequences if Champ became too tired to carry on or, as was his habit, to stop halfway to the lead and look for a hand signal. By the time he resumed the chase, the sheep would be over the horizon.

Mustering dogs had to be very tough, with a good constitution in order to withstand work day after day, week after week during the shearing, crutching or lamb marking seasons. In fact I had a black and tan dog called Whisky, who followed me for 70 miles in one day and he kept up with my horse the whole way. Champ, though, had tender paws, a soft constitution, and lacked the necessary stamina for mustering in large paddocks, some of which were over twenty square miles in area.

Our working dogs were short-haired kelpies or kelpie-collie crosses. But Champ, being a collie, had long hair which not only made him overheat in hot weather, but it also tended to pick up every kind of prickly vegetable matter imaginable. Therefore his coat would become a tangled mess of burrs and hair which, apart from hampering his movements, must have been very uncomfortable. To alleviate these problems, we periodically sheared Champ with the mulesing shears. After our dog shearing efforts he certainly did not look like a collie. Indeed, he only vaguely resembled a dog.

Since we used voices to control our mustering dogs, Champ would not work when other dogs were present. He had limited use as a mustering dog and he was useless for yard work because he could not tolerate large mobs of sheep at close quarters, yet he was brilliant when it came to putting a few sheep through a gate. This made us believe that he had been trained for trials rather than as an all-purpose working dog.

He was also very handy for carrying out the many station droving jobs such as taking shorn sheep away from the shearing shed, bringing mobs from outlying yards into the shearing or crutching sheds, and moving sheep when a watering point dried up. He was masterful at handling ewes with small lambs at foot. When a lamb breakaway looked like developing, he would crouch and stare at them. More often than not the lambs would decide that discretion was indeed the better part of valour, and they would turn and gallop back bleating to their mothers.

In fact he was so handy that we used to take him from Lincoln Park to Wartaka Station for shearing, crutching and lamb marking. Soon he was at home at either location. The two stations were 40 miles apart, half the journey being along Highway 1, which was mostly a gravel road in those days. This did not prevent Champ from making the 40-mile journey when a bitch came into season. If he was at Lincoln Park he used to make the journey to Wartaka. If he was at Wartaka he used to make the journey to Lincoln Park. How he knew when the bitches were in season from 40 miles away was a complete mystery to us.

We used to call Champ the Gentleman Dog because he always greeted us by sitting on his haunches, wagging his tail from side to side and extending his paw to shake. His manners when dealing with his handlers were similarly impeccable. But most of the time he kept to himself, avoiding trouble and keeping well out of the way of anything that might hurt him.

He avoided fights, but when cornered he would fight like a thrashing machine, and he won more scraps and sired more pups than any dog I have ever known. Indeed, Champ was a highly intelligent dog, adept at planning his moves and very adept at slipping his collar or breaking his chain when he needed freedom. In fact we had to tie him with an extra heavy chain and wide collar to control him.

When a bitch came into season on the other station, Champ used to plan his 40-mile trip to perfection. At some stage before chain-up time in the late afternoon, he would simply disappear. He would journey most of the night to the other station, when the temperature was cool and travelling was relatively comfortable. He would arrive at his destination in the early hours of the morning when his rivals were chained up. He could then carry out his courting free from interference by the other dogs.

One night my father and I were returning home from Snowtown sheep market. It was fairly late at night and we were still about twenty miles from Wartaka. Suddenly I caught the momentary gleam of a dog's eyes in the bushes. The presence of dogs running around in the bush always had to be investigated, so I reversed the utility and was about to swing around so the headlights would shine in the right direction to pick up the eyes again when suddenly I had an inspiration. I jumped out of the ute and called out, 'Here, Champ! Come on, boy! Come on, get up!' The command 'get up!' told our dogs they were about to get a ride and they would immediately jump into the back of the vehicle.

Next thing Champ came slinking out of the bushes doing his best to cover his stomach with gravel rash. He was on his way from Lincoln Park to Wartaka to do some courting and he knew he had been caught out and was in the wrong.

My father was all for making Champ run the remaining twenty miles. I protested, pointing out that somebody might pick him up and then we would lose him. It would be a more suitable punishment if we took him home to Wartaka and chained him up so that he could not carry out his courting. He would be so near to the object of his desires yet so far, and that would serve him right. My father agreed to this, and after chastising Champ for being a silly old fool to run 40 miles just to do some courting, we continued on our way.

When we arrived, my father grabbed Champ and chained him up before he could get anywhere near the bitch. It was Molly, my father's best working dog who was the centre of attention, and there was still time to lock her away before any damage could occur.

'I'll lock Molly up in the morning,' said my father. 'I can't have her in pup with shearing so close.'

Next morning when we went to work, who should be waiting at the garden gate but Champ. He had slipped his collar during the night and he greeted us by sitting on his haunches, with his paw extended, his tongue lolling from the side of his mouth, his tail wagging from side to side, and his eyes glistening. He looked extremely happy, which is more than I can say for my father. I was suddenly very glad that my father had chained Champ the night before and not delegated it to me.

Molly duly gave birth to her pups in the middle of shearing and the collie traits of her offspring were obvious.

Champ kept up his epic journeys for many years between Wartaka and Lincoln Park. Sometimes he no sooner made the trip in one direction than circumstances caused him to make a return trip in the other. Occasionally he forgot his manners and made the trip at shearing time. When this occurred his popularity was at zero level.

As for Molly, her litter of pups as a result of my father's inept chaining of Champ produced one of the best mustering dogs ever seen on the two sheep stations.

SANDY

Ian Burkinshaw, Benalla, Victoria

Tom McDermott was a drover and dealer who lived in Maldon, Victoria. He became known to me when I was a child during the 1930s through the dealings he had with my father, mainly buying and selling horses and hay.

Tom would often buy a mob of sheep and take them on the road (the long paddock) with Larry the van horse and Sandy. Sandy was a medium-sized dog, dark in colour, with sandy points. He always had his tail in the air.

The team had quite a reputation, especially in the potato growing districts of Bungaree, Newlyn and Dean, near Ballarat. It was on one of these trips that Sandy's ability stood out even more than usual.

Tom pulled in with the van and sheep to camp in a lane between two potato crops. There were only flimsy, three-barb fences on each side, not sufficient to keep sheep out. The cocky soon arrived on the scene.

'You can't camp here,' he said. 'Your sheep will clean all my potatoes out.'

Tom said, 'I'll give you a quid for every sheep found amongst your spuds in the morning.' A quid was a lot of money in those days, it could be equivalent to about $400 today.

The cocky was on the scene at daylight and to his amazement, not one sheep was amongst the spuds and it was obvious none had been in there during the night either.

Tom pointed to the little narrow track in the frost on the inside of the fences where Sandy had made his regular rounds during the night. Sandy's ability was such that Tom very seldom had another dog with him. The dog could handle 800 to 1,000 sheep quite capably on his own.

SOME DOGS HAVE TO DO IT

Peter Knight, Coonabarabran, New South Wales

It has only been in recent times that Hound has really found his niche in life. It came with the approach of Coonabarabran's annual show and the dog jumping competition. We decided to enter and do a bit of training, but Hound was absolutely hopeless. He just couldn't see any point to it and was not even the slightest bit interested in jumping over anything, unless it was a bitch.

The big day came and time for the big event. I was still caught up at the cattle shed tidying up the last of the Head Steward's jobs, cranky and stroppy as I am allowed to be for that one day. But off I went to make a fool of myself in the main arena. Hound was too busy shaping up to every other dog around to be the slightest bit interested in a stupid dog jumping competition.

The jump was starting to get quite high, but still Hound was more interested in fighting. As long as he was snapped back into reality for long enough to get him confused, we were fine. When I called him from the other side of the jump he just gave a hop and a skip over to the only familiar face he knew. Once we had worked out the psychology of the athlete in Hound, it was hardly a challenge.

Gradually, as the jump grew really big, the competition dropped off and there was less to sidetrack Hound. He actually started to realise what he was supposed to do—and, what's more, enjoy it. You could see he thought it was great fun showing off to everyone as he pranced around, tail high and adrenalin pumping. Besides, he had more attention from me than he had ever had. This was great fun, he reckoned.

I don't think we realised just what it takes out of a dog to be the top dog of Coonabarabran show. Hound pranced around for a bit with his blue ribbon round his neck. He offered a few cursory snarls to the other mere mortals, but you could see his heart was not in it. He made it to the bar with us while we had a celebratory drink but it was all he could do to lift his leg on the seating log and then curl up and go to sleep. He woke up in time to load the bulls at nine that night, then just slept in the passenger seat all the way home. Couldn't even raise a snarl at the trucks on the highway. It is a tough life but some dogs have to do it.

Hound was one of those dogs for whom the description 'man's best friend' was coined. A great mate, a lot of fun, just occasionally useful and a man wouldn't be without one for quids. He was just one of the many reasons that makes life so worth the pain that is often such a part of living in the bush.

They somehow make it worthwhile to put up with droughts one year then floods the next, prices as low as they can go one year then worse the next. Always there with a smile and never a complaint. May the Hounds of this world continue to help keep the sanity of Australia's rural folk. They work far better than any therapist.

BIRTH ON THE JOB NO. 2

Alan Werner, Jeparit, Victoria

Going back a few years I had a brown kelpie bitch called Snip. I also had a Willy's jeep that didn't have doors, which got me around the farm. Every time I started up the jeep, Snip would leap onto the front seat.

At one stage I had to shift a mob of sheep from one farm to another. Snip was very pregnant. After pushing the sheep along for a while, she hopped into the jeep, had a pup and hopped out again to go on with her job. After another few minutes, she hopped in again and had another, then hopped out again. She finished up having three pups on the front seat of the jeep during the trip.

Ten minutes after getting home and being put with her pups in the kennel, she produced another two pups.

That is what I call a good working dog.

PART 8
PULLING THE WOOL

- *Having a bit of fun*
- *Dogs using owners' weaknesses to advantage*

ONLY BRING TEN!
Les O'Brien, Alice Springs, Northern Territory

Like most blokes who run sheep, my dad always had a team of dogs to whom he devoted almost as much time and effort breeding and developing as he did to his sheep.

As in most teams the dogs were selected for particular skills such as mustering, yard work, shed work and even for something as simple as their ability to bark. This was desirable when he wanted a dog to keep the pressure on a mob to force it through the race while he worked at the other end of the race. Being a team, their collective talents contributed to getting the work done; but they didn't all work at once even if they wanted to. In order to keep them fresh until needed, they were generally kept tied up.

Dad had a particular dog named Mugsy that was good around the yards and OK for paddock work, so long as he had another dog to follow. If there wasn't a dog for him to follow, he would venture out only about 200 to 300 yards on his own.

One day an agent from the stock and station firm Pitt Son and Badgerys dropped in to inspect some wethers that Dad had in the house paddock. With the usual greetings and obligatory comments about the weather, they headed off to the shed to check out some paperwork.

The sheep were scattered around the paddock but a small group was relatively close by as Dad despatched Mugsy (the dog that just happened to be off the chain at the time). With a whistle and call of 'way back!', the dog sped off. As if it was an afterthought, he then called out, 'Only bring ten.'

When the men emerged from the shed a few minutes later, there was Mugsy with ten sheep bailed up in one of the open yards. Needless to say, the agent was more impressed with the dog than he was with the sheep.

Dad was still enjoying the joke, so he muttered something like, 'Yeah, but he's a bit slow. I don't know how many times I've shown him how to shut the bloody gate . . .'

'DIVIDE!'

Brian Richards, Port Pirie, South Australia

My story takes place in Two Wells, a small rural town about 40 kilo-metres north of Adelaide. It occurred early in the 1930s at the Two Wells Hotel.

A local farmer had acquired a new sheepdog and had spent con-siderable time and effort trying to train him to do his job. He proved to be pretty hopeless in spite of the efforts of his owner. His only 'skill' was to race straight through the middle of the flock of sheep then return to the feet of his master and look up in anticipation of some words of reward and a pat on the head.

One day the farmer had tied his trap to the hitching rail outside the Two Wells Hotel and left the dog sitting underneath whilst he entered to enjoy a 'couple' of drinks with his mates. Shortly after, an unknown farmer on his way home from the market at Gepps Cross, near Adelaide, called in to quench his thirst. He had noticed the kelpie sitting under the trap and had obviously been impressed with his looks.

After ordering a beer he struck up conversation with the patrons in the bar, enquiring as to who owned the dog outside. The owner spoke up and a conversation ensued about the possibility of the dog being for sale. The owner could sense a chance of making a few bob, which was pretty precious in that depressed era. He enthused about the dog to the stranger and after a price had been discussed the owner asked the prospective buyer if he would like a demonstration.

The other locals, having previously heard the tales of woe about the dog's lack of ability, also adjourned outside to watch the demonstration with great interest. There was quite a large mob of sheep in the paddock over the road and the two men and the dog wandered over and climbed through the fence, eagerly watched by the other men.

The owner sent the dog around, and at the appropriate time he waved his arm in the direction of the sheep and shouted, with great gusto, 'Divide'. The dog of course obeyed the command to the letter and the interested farmer was suitably impressed, quickly paid his money and continued on his way. The locals returned to have another beer and a good chuckle.

255

THE BRAND READER
Alan Kettle, Bundaberg Queensland

My story concerns a dog owned by a friend of mine, a dairy farmer with Jerseys, whose dairying country adjoined land grazed by Herefords.

My friend claimed his dog could read brands, and when the appropriate circumstances arose while visitors were on his property, he would demonstrate his dog's 'ability' with justifiable pride. The necessary circumstances occurred when some of his milkers would get through the fence and mingle with his neighbour's cattle. He would then set out to 'prove' his dog could read brands.

He would send his dog through the fence with instructions to bring in only cattle wearing his brand. The dog would then rush down and get in behind the mingled herd to drive them towards the home property. Every time, the milking cows would separate themselves from the beef cattle and head home, much to the surprise of the visitors.

Since the dog was of small build, he had to stand on his hind legs where the grass was taller to locate the cattle. This helped confirm the claim of 'brand reading' to the gullible friends.

Of course, the milkers, being anxious to get rid of their load of milk and always brought in twice daily by the dog, merely believed it was milking time when the dog appeared. Hence their trek towards the bails.

HEAVY OPPORTUNIST
Mrs J V Carey, Wilmington, South Australia

Since we live in the town, my husband has to travel to the farm each day, and he is always accompanied by our sheepdog Ace.

The dog is somewhat overweight and has to be lifted onto the utility each morning and lifted off at arrival at the farm. He would rather stay on the ute all day than get off by himself.

However, should my husband stop at the post office or shop and there are other dogs in the street, Ace can spring off, as nimble as you like, and join the other dogs. Marvellous, isn't it!!

UNDERSTANDING THE
WORKING SHEEPDOG
Arthur Shepherd, Paringa, South Australia

During 1923, a Mr Pocock drove my grandparents to our farm in the South-East in a 1923 Dodge motor car. Each evening my father debated evolution with Mr Pocock.

One evening my dad told Mr Pocock that in the next 100 years, dogs would learn to talk, because at the moment they could certainly understand English. Mr Pocock reckoned that would never happen.

Dad said, 'In the morning I will prove to you that my sheepdog Boxer understands every word I say.'

Next morning, Dad took Mr Pocock to a spot near the woolshed where they could overlook a sixteen-acre paddock. Two of my brothers and myself went along to provide the audience. Dad gave a whistle and Boxer came and sat in front of Dad about six feet away, looking Dad straight in the face.

Dad said to Boxer, 'Just over there is a sixteen-acre paddock. Somewhere in the paddock there are about 30 sheep. They are usually in one of the corners. I want you to go along the western fence, keeping about one chain from the fence. If they are not in the north-western corner, go down to the north-eastern corner, round the sheep up and bring them along the eastern fence.

'When you get near the next corner, there are two red gum trees. If you want to, you may cock your leg on one of the trees. Then bring the sheep along the south fence and hold them in this corner just here.

'Now get on your way,' Dad said, and waved his arm in the direction of the sixteen-acre paddock.

Boxer made off at full gallop, jumped between the wires of the fence of the sixteen-acre paddock and proceeded to do exactly what Dad had told him. He found the sheep in the north-east corner, brought them along the eastern fence and paused to cock his leg on the red gum tree. (When this happened the audience jumped with excitement.) Boxer then brought the sheep along the southern fence to the corner near us and sat down and held them there.

Dad turned to talk to Mr Pocock, but he had gone, absolutely frustrated and beaten, and did not utter a word.

PS—Boxer, the black, white and tan sheepdog, had been doing this same routine at least once every two weeks for three years!

AMAZING THE UNINITIATED
Max Williams, Exford, Victoria

It was my daughter, with some of her first job money, who bought Ralph for me. I've had dogs before Ralph, and good ones too—but Ralph was really something special.

A pedigree border collie, from trials and working dog parents, he soon showed he could carry on the tradition of his forebears. The breeder, Vern Sullivan, was keen to see new blood in the trials circuit, and sent up a couple of his mates to encourage me. So every spare chance, Ralph and I, and three sheep, sometimes more, were out practising.

Now, my story isn't about Ralph's trials career, but his career does have a bearing on it. Rather, it is about what any sheepdog worth its salt does, and that's drafting sheep.

Our sheep agent came one morning to draft out some lambs from the ewes, a mob of about four hundred. As he was going on to a bigger job next, he had recruited a chap from the office to help for the day. This chap was a nice fellow, keen to get stuck into it, and had obviously seen somewhere that it was done by hopping into the pen, flapping your arms about, yelling 'Ho, ho, ho', and generally working up a sweat, while a kelpie springs on the sheeps' backs, barking furiously.

Well, we'd just started the job when, thinking to have a bit of fun, I said to this chap, 'No, we don't do it that way. Ralph is boss here. We'll just open and shut the gate for him.'

I could see he was a bit dubious, but I just opened the drafting pen gate, said to Ralph, 'Get over, Ralph,' and the yard was very quickly filled. Ralph then was in amongst them, pushing them through, no blocks and no barks, while we just chatted.

I could see the office chap was pretty impressed by this, so thought I would jazz the next scene up a bit. As soon as the drafting yard was empty, I opened the gate again, and Ralph filled it up as usual. But now I played my trump card. Just as I was shutting the gate, I looked at Ralph and said, 'Ralph, I think we can get a few more in here. Bring another three.'

Now, I knew from my trials training that Ralph loved working three sheep, and that my chances of him bringing that many from the mob were pretty good. Sure enough, back he came, three sheep in front, and straight into the pen. If the chap was impressed before, then this time he was goggle-eyed.

The mood had grabbed me by this time, so while Ralph was in the pen pushing, I was saying things like, 'Steady on, Ralph, that's Karen and she's made a nice job of that lamb,' or 'Get that one there, Ralph, she's always been a smarty.'

On the next few penfuls, it was much the same. If I said, 'Get three more,' and Ralph came back with more, I'd just cover up by saying, 'OK, if you think they'll fit. You're the boss!'

All that was a long time ago now, and the agent later said that the chap couldn't stop talking about it back at the office—about how Ralph could even count.

Ralph is retired now. He's sixteen years old and his daughter does the sheep work. Ralph likes going shopping these days, so he can have the donut my wife buys him. He also likes lying in the sun.

When I first got Ralph, I said to my trials mates, 'Well, at least I know a bit about sheep,' and, 'This is what I'm going to teach Ralph ...' Both statements were pretty stupid. I had much to learn about sheep, and Ralph taught me more than I taught him.

I know Ralph's time is getting short now and that one day he won't be with us, But in another way, he will always be there—over drafting sheep and amazing the uninitiated with what a real working dog can do.

RUBY AND THE TAILS
D Wight, Parkes, New South Wales

Mulesing time is usually a pretty bleak and depressing time of the year. Around the lamb cradles as you go about your job, your knees freeze and the wind whistles through the sheep yards. It usually rains, and everyone ends up getting covered in mud and blood. Hour after hour standing in the same spot doing the same repetitive job, we tend to run out of yarns and jokes, told to distract ourselves. There are some great talkers among mulesers and shearers. The more mundane, repetitive and unpleasant the job, the better the yarns.

Last year was no different from any other. Everyone was arguing about who was next to pick up lambs. It was freezing and the flow of talk had stopped because we'd been going for a few days and had no fresh stories to tell. All around us, lambs were bleating as they searched for their mothers and a drink. But when your spirits get low and things are at their worst, something often happens which sparks everyone into life.

Ruby was the most useless dog ever to step onto the place. She was destined for the bullet, but on this particular day, she'd been tied up in the back of the ute to keep her out of the way. Her continual jumping as she watched ewes and lambs eventually broke the chain. With that, the idiot dog bounded off the ute with the sort of delight that only a farm dog can fully express.

Grinning wildly, she raced around the paddock, came back, did a lap of the ute, jumped a few yard rails, then dived head first into the pile of lamb tails just to the right of the lamb cradles. She tossed them into the air, rubbed her head in them, then grabbed a huge mouthful and belted off across the wet paddock, ducking and weaving all over the place.

Now as you know, lamb tails are much more than the severed, pathetic little ends of lambs. They are the actual currency of a sheep station. They determine how much the muleser will get paid for his days of work. And for the manager, they are his guide to working out the lambing percentage to show how well his rams and ewes have bred. You certainly don't want some dumb dog leaping into the tails and stealing any.

So when Ruby did just that, the muleser, Alan, dropped his shears and hurtled off after the dog. Everyone else stopped work and joined in on the chase too. Alan wasn't the sort of bloke who was built for speed, being round and fat. Nevertheless, he took off at top speed. The manager, the overseer and the jackeroo, who was me, followed. Ruby, after having watched all the other dogs working, and being tied up for so long, reckoned this was a good game.

She crouched, mouth stuffed full of tails and grinning. As we approached, she took off again, bounding wildly. As tails fell from her mouth, scattering all over the soggy paddock, Alan and the manager would make rugby dives for them and shove them into their pockets. It was pretty hilarious, but I didn't think it would be the right thing to laugh.

This stupid game went on for ages. Every time the dog had an empty mouth after scattering tails in the paddock, she would dive back into the pile, then exuberantly chuck tails into the air, before dashing off for more fun. Alan looked as if he would die from exhaustion—despite the rain that was falling, he was as red as a beetroot and really sweaty, as well as muddy and bloody.

Eventually we caught that stupid dog and tied her up again. We all had to comb the paddock for tails after work so the boss could count them and pay off the muleser. Alan didn't reckon it was much fun being diddled by a dog. The work is tough enough, he says.

Anyway, that night the boss loaded up the gun to shoot the useless bitch, but she was lucky. One of his city friends arrived just as he was cocking the gun and offered to give her a home. She is now just a fat, lazy pet which is about all she was ever good for. But we often laugh about the day she tried to rob Alan of his pay. And it was a pretty good distraction too.

CHEEKY SINGER
Betty Draffen, Macarthur, Victoria

Cheeky, our kelpie-cross, had been unintentionally conditioned to sing a song on command.

Whenever my husband sharpened his combs and cutters on the grinder during shearing, the harsh sound aggravated the dog so much that he howled. Eventually he obliged with a 'song' without the accompanying noise of the grinder. All my husband had to say was, 'Sing a song, Cheeky,' and he would throw his head back and 'sing'.

One weekend Bill left Cheeky in the care of his shearers who were staying at the Jerilderie Hotel while he travelled home to Geelong for the weekend.

In the early hours of the morning the shearers stealthily took Cheeky up to their room and invited him to 'sing a song' to disturb another group of shearers with whom they had a score to settle. Cheeky's loud tenor voice disturbed them all right—as well as the publican.

I'm pleased to say it wasn't Cheeky who suffered any consequences. His friendly nature no doubt ensured that.

PART 9
ALL IN A DAY'S WORK

A SMALL BLACK OUTLAW
WITH AN HONEST HEART

Margaret Glendenning, Everton, Victoria

I am not sure where Dot came from. She just arrived. I was only a child and I welcomed her without hesitation into our family of animals and people.

Somehow, however, I gained the impression that she had been suddenly and desperately in need of a home, had been passed from hand to hand in search of one. There was something about her previous owners moving right away from the district in mysterious circumstances and with great haste. Such details didn't trouble my curiosity for long— it was not until later years that I began to wonder about her life before she came to live with us.

A small, black kelpie with alert brown eyes, she was not young. Polite, but slightly reserved at our first encounter, she settled in easily with us, though she ignored the hunting dogs. Dot proved to be a good paddock dog, and useful in the yards. She never barked—no use ordering her to 'push up' and 'speak up'. Still, she managed to get her woolly charges right where she wanted them, without uttering a sound.

The hidden talents of our new helpmate did not become apparent for some time. One late afternoon my father stood watching a large mob of sheep stream through the gate past him, heading for the open paddock. One of the animals caught his eye as it leaped upward to canter off towards the hills.

'Should have had a look at that one,' he said as he stepped forward and pointed to the rapidly retreating wether.

I had been idly watching Dot where she sat behind the fence rails. I saw her galvanise into instant full speed, shooting out under Dad's arm like a little bolt of black lightning. In no time at all the indicated sheep was back almost at our feet, unhurt, but on its side and helpless. Dot held on firmly with absolutely no intention of letting go.

I watched her in action many times after this demonstration. We only had to quietly say 'that one' and point. She never failed to bring her quarry silently and quickly to us. We used her to single out a 'killer' for the table or to capture an animal out of the mob that may have needed our attention.

A neighbour, watching her performance one day, laughed and slapped my father on the shoulder. 'Got yourself a duffer dog there, Jack!'

I didn't understand that remark. To me, a duffer was someone who unintentionally made errors, a bit of a bungler. Dot was no duffer—she didn't make mistakes. Her neat responses never wasted time or energy and I was sure she understood every word we said.

Time passed. Dot grew old and a little deaf. Like many aged dogs, she seemed to hear what she wanted to hear without any trouble. I was older, too. I knew now about 'duffer dogs'. I recalled how she would sit at dusk, tense, quivering, with some unknown excitement, staring at the moon rising over the distant hills. Was she remembering happenings of her past life, or was I just inventing them for her? I could well imagine the scene. The vehicle furtively hidden in trees by the fence, the hushed whispers and shadowy figures. The barely heard, low whistle. An elusive dark wraith silently dropping sheep one by one, standing over them until they were collected. Another farmer complaining angrily after finding a dozen sheep missing when next he tallied his mob.

Dot slipped her collar one night. I doubt she knew what hit her on the nearby road. We missed our little duffer dog, our small black outlaw with the honest heart, and I was not the only one who cried.

WELL TRAPPED

Nigel Smith, Tamworth, New South Wales

In the 1950s and early 1960s my father was one of the best known drovers in the Southern Tablelands of New South Wales. His droving entourage consisted of a horse and sulky, a wagonette and draught-horse, an offsider (usually me or one of my brothers) and, most important of all, Baldy.

Baldy was one of the biggest border collies that ever graced the sale-yards and his reputation as an exceptional working dog had spread far and wide. He was constantly called on to pass on his genetic code, from which Dad made good beer money.

When I was ten, Dad and I were droving a mob of sheep on the immediate outskirts of Goulburn. We were coming up to a T-junction on a main road. I suggested to Dad that one of us should go ahead to make sure the sheep went the right way. Dad said not to worry as the sheep had been that way a few times and knew where they were going. When the sheep turned the wrong way and started heading into the town, I didn't make any comment.

Dad was whistling and yelling for Baldy but he was nowhere to be seen. He made some very rude comments about Baldy and told me to cut through the paddock and bring the sheep back. They had by this time spotted the nice green feed that masquerades as householders' lawns and gardens, so there wasn't a lot of time to lose. I bolted over the fence and took off, dodging the briar and jumping the horehound.

Suddenly I had the triple sensations of falling, darkness and then immersion. I struggled for breath and grasped for something to cling to. What I found was warm and hairy with smelly breath.

Baldy and I were in that cold disused well for over two hours before we were rescued. Dad had spent those two hours rounding up the sheep from residents' backyards, no doubt cursing us both.

Baldy obviously had not had Dad's optimism and had judged the sheep would head in the wrong direction. He had taken off across the paddock only to fall through the rotten timber that had been used to cover the well. It was probably fortunate that I had fallen in too, otherwise we would never have found him.

On the other hand, I am not sure that I would be here today if he hadn't already been in there. He helped keep me afloat, warm and unafraid.

LETTER FROM MAURINE
Cecilia Howard, Clontarf, Queensland

The letters of my late sister-in-law Maurine Needham came to light when we were cleaning out the family home recently. In the late sixties, she was working on a sheep station in south-west Queensland and she wrote describing the dogs' routine.

... There are twenty-one sheepdogs on this station and they are tied up until 3 pm when the cook lets them go. When they see her coming, the din is unbelievable. They all start yelling and howling to 'let me off first'. Not that it makes any difference as they all trail after the cook until the last dog is free. By then she has twenty deliriously happy sheepdogs all over her as she tries to untie that last dog.

As soon as they are all free they go hell for leather through the yard and over to a medium-sized laundry tub which is always full of water. This tub holds four dogs—just. So in splash the first four and there they sit up to their chins in water and drink and drink. The other seventeen meanwhile are falling over each other round the edge of the tub trying to get their share of the water. Then out charge the first four over to the wood heap. Round and round the blocks of wood they go until they find a block to their liking and then do three widdles each.

In the meantime, the next lot hop in and for ten minutes or so there are dogs sitting in water, dogs drinking and dogs widdling—quite a humorous sight.

'I SHOULD BLOODY WELL THINK SO'

Marj Wood, Benalla, Victoria

One afternoon, after a day's drenching up at the yards, we were putting the final mob of ewes away. They had to go through the small paddock next to the lane, across the lane and into a fresh paddock. So they wouldn't go charging off up the lane, the boss stood in the lane to direct them across.

'Keep the dogs with you,' he commanded as he went off to open the gate and stand in the lane.

Whenever we had Jo and Ben working together, they were very difficult to control as they kept trying to prove to each other how good they were, how rough and tough they could be and how much better each was than the other. Keeping them behind me I could feel them making little darting movements of escape, so I had to continually snap, 'Behind, Ben', 'Behind, Jo', 'Come behind', 'Behind!'

The boss opened the gate and the ewes flowed across the lane and into their new paddock which was knee deep (on a sheep's leg) in green grass. (After eighteen months of terrible seasons this picture is but a distant memory!!)

Some ewes put their heads down and started eating immediately and others did happy little sproings through the gateway. Neglecting my duty, I was busy watching the sheep and not the dogs. The boss's irate shouting brought me back to the job in hand with a thud. Ben and Jo were behind the mob trying to put them through the gateway all at once and the poor ewes were getting rolled and bowled over in the dirt.

'What do you think you're doing, you -*/ ¢.#,' he shouted.

Ben and Jo immediately fell to the ground. The boss kept shouting. Genuine regret was the best policy I thought, so I fell to the ground too. Ben looked over his shoulder and saw I was getting into trouble, so he slunk back beside me and leant on me.

Noticing Ben was gone, Jo looked back and scurried over to join us, giving me a couple of quick slurps with her tongue in sympathy. The ewes slowly got to their feet, the dust settled and the final ewe went into the new paddock. The boss looked at the =*#@¢# who were all still in their 'we're very sorry' positions and shouted, 'Come behind!' Ben and Jo hurried to obey and I followed. We all sat at his feet looking very repentant.

'I should bloody well think so,' he said crossly, but then, unable to stop himself, started laughing.

'We're forgiven,' noted Ben, jumping about the boss. Seeing me still sitting there he nudged me with his nose. 'Come on, you can jump about now. He's not cross any more,' and he and Jo flung themselves about the boss, tails wagging and barking happily.

A LIGHT CASELOAD

Anne McLennan, Derby, Western Australia

The working dogs of the north deserve some recognition for their courage and character. They generally live shortened lives up here, what with all the hazards of their work and problems caused by living in the tropics.

Bodie was one of the funny old canine characters I knew. He was a blue heeler cross, mainly white in colour with blue spots. His short, thick neck and stout head were appropriate for his work with cattle, especially bulls.

He was a bit of a fighter too, probably encouraged by his young stockman—owner. A fighting/working dog is a status symbol among these cocky young men. Bodie's ears had that well-chewed look of a seasoned fighter—a bit like a boxer with cauliflower ears.

His owner, Ion, nicknamed Weevil, was head stockman at Mt House Station. He and Bodie were out in the stock camp at Spider Bore. Each night Ion would tie the dog to his suitcase next to his swag, more as a gesture than a secure tether. It did the job and stopped him from going off scavenging or fighting.

That evening dingos were heard while the men ate their meal and discussed the next day's muster. As everyone settled into their swags for the night, tired after a long day's mustering, and with the fire beginning to die, Bodie became restless. Weevil, too tired to care what it was all about, drifted into a deep sleep.

Suddenly Bodie took off with suitcase in tow. A dingo had wandered into the camp looking for food. The poor old battered case with its half-hearted latches burst open, Weevil's clothes scattering everywhere. Bodie was oblivious to the now empty suitcase still bouncing and sliding wildly behind him. His only interest was in having a decent punch-up with the dingo.

He and the suitcase raced past the fire, which was now only a pile of glowing coals. As he did so, the suitcase knocked over the tin of petrol the cook used as firelighter. The petrol burst into a ball of flame ensuring everyone was awake. Some of the men had to leap from their swags to avoid the out-of-control case as Bodie continued his chase undaunted.

The dingo dived under the chuckwagon trailer and galloped out the other side. Bodie was in hot pursuit . . . until the case hooked around the wheel and pulled him to a tumbling halt.

Weevil reckoned he'd use another tether after that.

PRIDE'S SHORT CUT
Phillip Clerici, Sale, Victoria

During the 1930s my late father-in-law, Arthur Taylor, then proprietor of the Ensay Transport Service in far East Gippsland, had a kelpie cross named Pride. The dog had been a bit of a champion in his day.

One day Arthur and Pride unloaded a few sheep near the transport depot for transfer to the saleyards just around the corner.

The local pub, The Little River Inn, was en route to the saleyards, so Arthur popped in for a quick glass, leaving Pride to attend to the sheep.

Pride must have felt left out, because he directed the sheep through the front door of the pub and headed for the bar. However, the bar door was closed, so he continued with the sheep down the passage, through the hotel and out the back door. He continued on to the saleyards after his 'short cut' without losing any of his charges.

A TERRIER FOR DIRTY WORK
Brian May, Pine Creek, Northern Territory

Many years ago I had a small farm about five kilometres west of Pine Creek. I had a few buffalo cattle, geese, ducks, chooks, goats and a mob of pigs.

Once they had been fattened, I used to take about ten pigs each week to the abattoirs in Darwin in the back of my Toyota ute. I used to have to muster these pigs on foot to get them to a small holding pen from which they would go up a ramp and into the vehicle. It would take at least five hours to load these pigs on a Sunday afternoon.

It turned out that my wife wanted a small house dog—a fox terrier. We went to Darwin to get this dog. It was to be hers alone and I was given strict instructions that I was to have nothing to do with it. So I sat back and watched the little fellow grow up. My wife called him Panda because he had black patches over his eyes. When he was fully grown he stood about eighteen inches high.

Panda would always come up to me and whimper as though he wanted to go to work with me. One day I went off to load the pigs and Panda indicated he wanted to go with me, so I asked my wife if Panda could come.

At first she said no, but when I said I would keep him in the front of the ute and that he wouldn't get dirty, she agreed. We got to the paddock where the pigs were grazing. My son was with me as he was quicker on his feet. I backed the ute up to the loading ramp and wound the window down about eight inches so Panda would not get too hot.

Mustering the pigs on foot was exhausting. I could see Panda in the ute jumping up and down with excitement as we got the pigs closer. Next thing, out of the window came Panda. My heart just about stopped as I know and you know what a fair sized back-fatter pig can do to a dog, and I knew what my wife was going to do with me if anything happened to the dog.

Panda headed straight for the lead pig, grabbed him on the ear and steered him, with all the others following, straight into the pen, up the ramp and into the back of the ute. Panda was running up and down on their backs, barking and going completely mad. He loaded all the pigs onto the Toyota in ten minutes. I quickly grabbed him out of the pen. He was covered in dirt and pig manure and looked a real mess—but what a dog!

My wife went right off her head about his state but I managed to calm her down and eventually she let me use Panda every Sunday to load the pigs. I have seen a lot of working dogs over the years, but none with guts like this little one. What a worker—he saved me hours.

DON'T FORGET THE CHOOKS

Lloyd Collins, Nyngan, New South Wales

Shearing was in progress. During the midday break, my dog mustered the whole poultry mob of twelve hens and one rooster and took the chooks a distance of twenty chains to the shearing shed.

He was holding them at the sheep yards waiting for me and the shearing gang to return, presumably thinking we had overlooked them.

THE WRONG WHISTLER

Frank Condon, West Ryde, New South Wales

Bob was a good cattle dog. Whenever Dad whistled for the cows to be brought in for milking, Bob would do it.

We also had a pet rosella parrot named Joey who, like most parrots, liked to mimic things he heard. So, one clear moonlit night at about 3 am, Joey decided to mimic Dad's 'fetch the cattle' whistle. Bob, obeying what he thought was Dad's whistle, immediately began to round up the cattle.

The family was startled awake by drumming hooves and lowing cows, at a time when cows, like people, should be sleeping. Dad quickly called Bob off and proceeded to curse him.

It was only later when we heard Joey doing his new whistle that Dad realised he had misjudged Bob.

A WHIRLWIND AT THEIR HEELS

David Griffiths, Port Lincoln, South Australia

When Mo first indicated his desire and ability to work in the sheep yards, I thought I had a freak. Then I discovered that Australian silky terriers have several original families and that they had been bred as working dogs. Mo proved that to be true.

During the latter years of my farming career, I owned three dogs—two paddock workers and the diminutive Mo. With a pedigree longer than him, he was eager to work and afraid of nothing. During drafting, after every 50 or 60 sheep he would come through the race to be sure I was there—checking I was doing my job as he was doing his.

Woe betide any ewe that doubted his authority and hammered him against the fence. With teethmarks on her nose, she would have a whirlwind nipping at her heels in the best blue heeler tradition.

At the end of the job Mo, dirty and often bruised, would be carried to the house to be cleaned up and praised. He was the best yard dog I ever had.

A CLERICAL ERROR

R H and H F Cherry, Armidale, New South Wales

We were droving a mob of sheep which had to be loaded on the train at the old Tamworth trucking yards. It was peak hour in the afternoon. We had traffic lined up on both sides of the sheep.

I had a little border collie bitch, a keen worker of whom I was very fond. I decided to let her off to give me a hand. Just as I did, a car overtook all the others and hit her. Seeing what had happened, my very irate husband cantered back on his horse swearing, abusing and calling the driver all sorts of names. The driver had his back to my husband because he was busy explaining his actions to me.

When he turned to face my husband, the cursing suddenly stopped. My husband's mouth fell open. A sudden look of shock replaced it, then just as quickly he said, 'Well, I don't care if you're Jesus Christ himself, you should be more careful.'

You see, the driver was a man of the cloth.

My dear little dog died of her injuries.

HOT TIPS FROM PEPPER

Pat Stewart, Helena Valley, Western Australia

My late husband ran a shearing shed to which thousands of sheep came for shearing for most of the year. The sheep were mostly big wethers for export to Kuwait. The pace for men and sheepdogs was very hectic.

Many fine sheepdogs worked for us, but one conspicuously stands out in memory—a black and white kelpie cross we aptly named 'Pepper'. He was an excellent yard dog and could also bring in a mob from the paddock with the minimum of fuss—two attributes that do not always go together, as sheep men will tell you.

However, Pepper had another string to his bow—he was an excellent dog trainer. We often had little pups coming on to learn the sheep business. Like a clever teacher, Pepper would show them by example just enough to learn, and yet give them sufficient scope for their natural instincts to be expressed. He would gently bite them if their misdemeanour was small, or yank them away if it was a significant error. If the learner was doing well, Pepper—at such times he always seemed to have a self-satisfied look on his face—would retire and watch placidly in the background. He was always watchful, though, in case his own talents were required again.

UP TO ME TO BRING IT OUT
Jim Kelly, Naracoorte, South Australia

I'm a miserable old sod who hates to spend money, so when some breeder offers for nothing a kelpie pup from working parents, I'm inclined to take the chance. I've had some considerable success too.

I sometimes think the owner is more important than the dog's pedigree.

My latest hand-me-down pup is now fifteen months old, and I'm at the stone-throwing, bad temper stage, when Chip's exuberant energy is almost more than I can handle, but, as from her first look at sheep a year ago, it's all there. The instinctive desire to work a flock or herd and the desire to please the boss. It's up to me to bring it out.

THE MASTER SPEAKS
Jean Birrell, Longueville, New South Wales

There was an old farmer down Bombala way who had the best sheepdogs in the district. No-one could come near them.

When asked how he did it, he said, 'Well, first you have to know more than the dogs.'

WITH AN EYE
ON THE CLOCK

Keith C Kidd, Youngtown, Tasmania

Every afternoon at 4.30, Bounce, my crossbred border collie, would find me where I was working out on the farm. He'd always go through a ritual of lying down with his four legs in the air for a scratch on his stomach. His joy would be almost too much for him to stand. The mood then would have to change and I would become stern and tell him to go way back and get the cows.

Away he would go flat-out, and half an hour later he would arrive back at the cowshed with the cows.

The mornings would be different, He would always take my neighbour's cows in first because he started milking at 4.30 am. He would then come home and have my cows in the cowshed at six-thirty.

This routine went on for years, through the whole milking season.

PART 10
TOUGH AND UNPRETENTIOUS

Unpampered 'real' dogs

STRETCH GOES TO
THE BIG SMOKE
Greg Standfield, Bourke, New South Wales

We were mustering bullocks for the next Dubbo sale on the flood plains of the Darling River just out of Bourke. As usual I had brought along my bold red and tan kelpie Stretch, usually a sheepdog, but quite capable of blocking up a mob of cattle.

We had the mob together when the lead started to head through a break in the fence and up an old irrigation channel, so I sent the dog to turn them back. He did so but in the process copped a kick in the hind leg from one of the 1,200-pound bullocks, breaking it badly about half-way down.

The local Department of Agriculture vet tried valiantly to set the break, but after a number of casts it appeared that the leg and joint would require pinning. As I was soon going to visit the folks in Sydney, where veterinary facilities are more advanced, the local vet suggested I take Stretch with me and have him attended to there.

We planned meanwhile to take Stretch to the local hospital, sling the radiographer a carton of beer and hold Stretch down on the X-ray table so that I only had to present the dog and the X-ray to the vet in Sydney and thereby save a few dollars (knowing how metropolitan vets charge).

So, off we headed to Sydney for a few days with the dog in the back of the ute. He seemed to enjoy the trip, with all the new scenery, but didn't go much on the traffic jam on Parramatta Road and decided to jump out (broken leg and all) and stretch the legs whilst the cars were pulled up. Other motorists looked somewhat surprised as he christened a few of their tyres and then jumped back into the ute.

After a day or so in Sydney, I decided to head to the vet's. A very flash clinic confronted us, neatly landscaped and painted very white. Nevertheless we headed in, me in my boardshorts and T-shirt (so as not to look too conspicuous) and my 'thinner than your average city dog' on the end of his eight-foot chain.

Well, talk about smell the gum leaves on us. We were on the end of some strange looks as we took our seat between a pure white Samoyed with an ingrown toenail and some other huge, overly pampered woolly dog called Heathcliffe, who was in to get his teeth cleaned.

As I was about to take my seat, one of the owners of these dogs commented on my 'nice looking country dog', which 'needs a feed'. Whilst acknowledging the compliment, Stretch went to the end of the chain and nonchalantly cocked his leg over all the *Women's Weeklies* neatly stacked on the coffee table near a settee. Obviously he was trying to convey some sort of a message to his pampered city cousins, but he certainly embarrassed me—not that I really wanted to read a magazine anyway.

After a short while the receptionist beckoned us to the counter. 'Name, please,' she said.

I replied with my name and address.

'No, no, not your name, the dog's name,' was her reply.

'Oh, his name's Stretch, but he's not real good at signing the cheque,' I replied.

With these formalities over we again took our seat, Stretch giving the other dogs a complimentary growl as we sat down.

Finally the vet came out to greet us.

'You don't want him to get away, do you?' he commented, looking at the rusty eight-foot chain attached to his worn leather collar.

'Oh, it's the only chain I've got,' was my response.

'We have little plastic leads at the door for you to use. Remember that next time,' he said, putting us quickly in our place.

Eventually, after the dog had to spend a day and a night at the veterinary hospital and me having to part with a large sum of money, Stretch was returned to me with the customary, 'Here's your Daddy come to pick you up.'

'Just give me the dog,' I said.

As we were leaving the surgery, walking past even more pampered hypochondriac pooches and numerous shelves containing dietary dog food for those canines with an obesity problem, I could imagine Stretch saying, 'Let's get out of this place.'

Footnote: Stretch with his mended leg soon after came second in the Open Yard Dog Trials at Brewarrina.

THE REVIVAL OF OLD JACK
AT PAT RODDY'S PUB

Stan Harris, Wauchope, New South Wales

In early 1946, after losing the six best years of my young life with the RAAF in World War II, I realised I had to get started again to catch up; and also that I would need to work hard, so work hard I did.

I also realised I could not work for a boss, so with my knowledge of the meat trade, I took on a butcher's shop in Gulgong which was going at an almost give-away price—which was all that I could afford anyway. It wasn't long before I realised I needed a good working dog.

I had become friendly with Mr Charles Niven of Springridge Station, from whom I used to purchase fat lambs and who later was to prove a very good friend and mentor when the going became tough in the drought of 1946–47. During a yarn over a cup of tea in the shop, I asked Charles where I might find a good working dog.

'I have a good old dog out home,' he replied. 'He's now too old and slow for a long day's work and his heavy coat's too hot for him on hot days. I'll bring him in for you.'

The next day Charles arrived with the 'old' dog in his utility and presented him to me, giving him a pat on his head.

'He's a good dog and his name is Jack,' he said.

Jack charmed everyone with his personality. He also charmed me as a worker. He knew every trick there ever was to know with sheep, cattle and people. I think he could even tell the time. He would be at the slaughter yards when needed to yard up. He would be at the holding paddock before anyone arrived and would have the sheep in a corner, and at what seemed almost the same time be at the butcher shop to keep any stray dogs out of the backyard. He knew every word we said and a lot more.

Jack just loved to ride between the mudguard and the engine of our old 1939 Buick Coupe. Somehow he had psychic vision or mental telepathy with me as he would be waiting in his position ready for me to move off even before I left the shop.

About fifteen months later, when the business had built up and I was almost too tired to continue, out of the blue I was made an excellent offer for the business at a huge capital gain which provided us with a wonderful 'bank' for our road back to prosperity. So we moved on for a short period to Gilgandra; and of course, Jack came too.

We left Gilgandra in late July 1947 with all our possessions in the old Buick, and jack in his usual seat on the running board. We were on our way to Wellington.

There had been an enormous frost that morning. The sun was warm, but the wind was cold. About eight miles out of Wellington I looked down to see Jack and soon realised the poor old chap was frozen stiff. I stopped the car, took him in my arms and placed him in the front area with my wife and daughter, Colleen. They rubbed him and wrapped him up but he didn't seem to be coming round. We raced the old Buick to Wellington where I knew that at Pat Roddy's Railway Hotel there would be a big log fire in the bar.

When I took jack in before the fire all the old hands—drovers, sheep and cattle station owners (it was sale day)—gathered around. One old chap said, 'I think you've lost your mate, soldier.'

Then someone else said, 'No, not yet. He just blinked his eye.'

A great whoop went up when Jack's front leg began to shake a little. What tremendous interest ensued as he gradually came to life, until finally he wagged his old tail and snuggled against me, with a look up to me that said, 'Thanks, boss, I'm OK again.'

Someone asked his name and I proudly replied that his name was Jack and that Charlie Niven had given him to me. Of course Charlie Niven was so well known throughout those areas that great yarns flowed about CA Niven and dogs during the drinking session that followed. Jack was toasted many times in hot rum and the merriment continued until it was too late for us to travel further, so we stayed at Pat Roddy's pub.

Jack spent the night in the garage with the old Buick, snug as could be in a corner which backed against the pub's donkey boiler, and the girls from the kitchen carried all the goodies out to feed him. What a charmer he was. What a day.

The next day we headed off for Coneac Station, owned by my wife's brother Hilton McCarthy. It was mustering time and Jack and I enjoyed helping out. When we moved on to Kempsey, we left Jack behind and he endeared himself to all at Coneac. A great number of good working dogs were bred from Jack and I think the breed has been established and continues even to this day.

Eventually Jack became really 'old' and stricken with arthritis (from the freezing at Wellington?). He died leaving us with many wonderful memories.

CAST IRON SOCKS
Des Richardson, Broken Hill, New South Wales

This is an amazing but true story about a border collie who has been working in and around shearing sheds in the West Darling area of New South Wales and Western District of Victoria.

The dog's name is Socks and he is owned by Mr A Norris, a shearing contractor, of Coleraine, Victoria. Socks is now ten years old. He had a pretty normal life up until he was about three years old. Then his adventures started.

He was tied up in the back of a ute outside a hotel in Coleraine when someone decided to take the ute for a joy ride. The ute was found three days later, parked on a beach just outside Portland. A woman noticed the ute on the beach. When it was still there the next day she notified the police. When the police arrived, they found Socks locked in the front.

When they opened the door of the ute, the poor chap jumped out and urine sprayed out of him everywhere. He was blown up like a balloon. The police couldn't smell or see any urine in the front of the ute. They reasoned he hadn't urinated for the three days he was locked in the front of the ute. They were amazed that a dog could go that long without urinating.

The next chapter of Socks's life was when he was about five years old. He was working at Devon Station between Broken Hill and Wilcannia. One day when he was walking through the engine room, a small child patted him which made him happy. He started wagging his tail, but the smile soon went off his face. He had got too close to the motor and his tail had got caught in the flywheel which spun him around a couple of times. He hit the cement floor on his way around and then his tail came off,

282

leaving a stump of raw meat and bone about two inches long. When Socks realised what had happened he got up and went straight outside and started fighting with the nearest dog he could find—as if to blame him for the pain.

Socks was taken to a Broken Hill vet who cut off the stump and pulled skin over it. Now he looks a bit of a dag, especially when he is wet.

About two years ago, Socks fell off the ute between Broken Hill and Wentworth and was missing for eight or nine days before he was found at Kudgee Station, just off the main road. He had skin off him all over, his sores were infected and he had a dislocated hip. He took over four months to recover from that escapade.

This amazing old dog is still one of the best dogs working around the woolsheds that I have ever seen.

I'LL TEACH YOU A LESSON
E A Unger, Parkes, New South Wales

Nigger could claim no pedigree of any kind. However, between us we managed to do all the necessary work with my sheep in spite of his occasional mistakes.

In true public spirit I had ploughed a firebreak with a disc plough. This naturally left a furrow. To avoid thistles and grass I followed the furrow on my motorbike—with Nigger perched on the small platform behind the seat.

As inevitably happens when you are proceeding slowly, the front wheel fouled the edge of the furrow. Consequently I found myself flat on the ground and pinned by the bike.

Nigger, who had been thrown off, quickly summed up the situation. Before I had a chance to move, he lifted one leg and in true dog style, baptised me before slowly trotting off towards home.

I HAD GOT MYSELF
A BEAUTY

Shirley Joliffe, Mitchell, Queensland

I had been working in a newsagent's whilst my daughters were at school but as soon as they finished, I decided to return to the bush and mustering.

A young friend offered me his cattle dog, Ned. She was a medium-sized, cream and tan bitzer with kind brown eyes, floppy ears and dew claws as long as a parrot's beak.

At first Ned got in everybody's road when they were saddling up their horses by bringing sticks and stones in her mouth and dumping them at their feet. It wasn't a promising start.

The mob of cattle we had was stroppy. One broke away and I yelled, 'Fetch him back, Ned,' and she was off like a shot. Ned was a heeler and after a couple of death defying circles, the cow headed flat-out back to the mob—with Ned floating through the air like a trapeze artist on the brush of the cow's tail.

She came back puffing and wagging her tail. 'By cripes, you're a good dog, Ned,' I told her, realising I had got myself a beauty.

The cattle took some settling down, but we moved off with Ned looking anxiously for another breakaway. One of the boys cracked the whip and my quiet old horse nearly stood me on my head. The boys laughingly told me Ned had grabbed my horse by the hind leg when the whip cracked.

So came Ned's first hiding. I grabbed a switch. She cowered down, crawled over to me and took her punishment without a whimper. I gave her ears a tug telling her never to do that again and put down the switch. She promptly bent down, picked it up and proceeded to carry it along in her mouth, jogging beside me.

Ned always rode in the back of the truck with much glee. This day I heard a yelp and, stopping, found Ned getting up out of the dust with blood pouring from a cut over her eye and half her bottom lip hanging down. You'd swear she had just gone ten rounds with Cassius Clay.

'Cripes, Ned, you'll need cosmetic surgery for your looks, but we're miles from anywhere,' I told her.

She blinked at me through her bloodshot eyes and wagged her tail as if to say 'she'll be right, mate'. So Ned carried her dribbly lip for the rest of her life. Her head healed up fine.

I tried desperately to prevent Ned having puppies, but somehow she mostly outsmarted me. One day I went to fix a fence and when I came back to the truck, Ned was lying underneath it with one very dead, skinny little puppy.

'Ned, he's dead,' I said. 'We're going to have to leave him.'

She looked at me, picked the puppy up in her mouth and jumped up into the truck. She carried him faithfully in her mouth the 55 miles home. When I went to remove him, she clung on tightly for a while, then hung her head and let him go. Ned's old eyes watered. And so did mine.

LEFT IN A PIT
Stephen Vagg, Barmera, South Australia

An ex-livestock transport driver living at Burra in South Australia's mid-north walked from his house one day to find both of his kelpie dogs showing signs of having eaten snail bait, which had unfortunately been left lying around.

The old dog was near death. The younger pup, however, didn't appear to be so bad. On phoning the nearest vet at Clare, the owner was advised to bring the pup to the surgery immediately.

On the way, he briefly stopped at the saleyards and 'finished off' the old dog with a humane blow to the head with a large shifting spanner. He left him in a pit used for disposing of dead sheep. The pup was then taken on to the vet and, following treatment, duly recovered.

Twelve months or so later, while at the Burra sheep sales, the dog owner noticed a familiar-looking kelpie working sheep. He asked a fellow truck driver where he had acquired the dog.

It was revealed how the new owner had come across the dog about a year before, trying to extricate itself from the sheep pit in which it had been left, presumed dead. After the original owner explained the situation, the dog was returned to him, none the worse for the experience except for a permanent lump on the head.

Subsequent discussions with the vet indicated that the blow to the head may have saved the dog's life as during unconsciousness its system slowed, possibly providing better resistance to the poison.

STITCHED WITH STRING

Valda Farmer, Gawler, South Australia

During the Great Depression of the 1930s, my sister and I lived on a wheat farm twenty miles south of Bordertown, South Australia. We walked two miles to a little bush school at a siding called Wirrega. On the way we would always see dozens of kangaroos in the paddocks along the roadside eating the wheat crops. Unfortunately, the local cockies had to shoot them. Our father and his brother would ride out on horseback and, with the help of our kangaroo dog Bluey, would help round them up for the shooters.

On one occasion when Bluey had bailed up a huge six-foot old man kangaroo, he went in a bit too close. Before Dad had time to shoot the roo, the dog was slashed right down his stomach by the powerful back legs and claws of the roo, which was sitting right back on its tail.

Dad lay Bluey over the horse's rump and rode home as carefully as possible. When he got to the house we watched as he quickly found a big needle and string. After pushing Bluey's intestines back into place, he stitched the wound together. All this time Bluey didn't whimper or move. He just watched Dad with sad eyes.

We thought Bluey could never survive, but with loving care he did recover and once again ran with Dad and the horse after kangaroos.

A SYMBOL
OF OUR STRUGGLES
Patty Cahill, Moora, Western Australia

Bitchie never would have won a beauty contest. She was a rotund blue heeler with a sagging belly and spindly brown legs. But despite the massive proportions of her body, her head was refined, with a white star in the middle of her broad blue forehead.

Even as a young dog Bitchie was overweight, but it never stopped her from working. My husband Kym owned a station in the goldfields. Often times were tough and money was scarce. In desperation we'd drive around to the various windmills where the feral goats came in to water.

Bitchie would take a flying leap off the ute and get stuck into the fleeing goats. One day she caught thirteen, which was a record. Kym took the goats to town and the money he received for them was used to buy our groceries.

I still get shivers up my spine when I remember her bravery with the great white bull. He was a mammoth-sized Brahman cross, who'd run free all his life in the station country and never seen a human being before.

Earlier in the day we'd managed to throw the bull down and hobble him, but when we came back for him, he jumped up and charged towards our camp where the horses were tethered.

Kym let Bitchie go. Just as the white bull crashed into the yards, narrowly missing our horses with his massive horns, Bitchie latched onto his ear. He screamed in outrage and galloped away from the yards. Bitchie was flung repeatedly to the ground as the bull twisted his ugly head in anger, but she refused to loosen her grip. She managed to slow the bull down just enough so that we could get in close and rope him to the ground.

Her body was bruised and she limped for days afterwards, but at the time she was so proud of herself and sat down on her heavy haunches with a lopsided grin on her face.

Bitchie battled on with us, but later we sold the station and Bitchie retired. She got old and sick, but just before we were going to have her put down, she fell into an underground tank and drowned.

287

Bitchie was more than a dog to us. She was a symbol of our past history—our struggle to survive in the outback and our battle to keep ahead of bank managers and interest rates on the farm. She was a battler like us. When she died, a part of us was gone; a part that could never be recaptured.

SEARCHING FOR HIS TRUCK
Stephen Foott, Swan Hill Victoria

The following is the true story of Butch, lost from a stock crate at Tailem Bend at 2 am one Friday morning.

Unaware that Butch had climbed through the bars of the crate, the driver returned to Swan Hill. All hell broke loose when it was discovered Butch was missing as he was a third generation truck and paddock dog.

I rang my brother, Peter Foott, who was working in Adelaide at the time. A day later Peter located Butch in the caravan park at Tailem Bend. Happy to be amongst friends again, Butch took up residence with Peter's family at Marleston, which is close to Adelaide airport.

But Butch was terrified of the sound of the jets taking off and landing. Returning home from work two days later, Peter discovered Butch had jumped over a six-foot galvanised iron fence and had disappeared. Peter rang the RSPCA and reported Butch missing. A search began and two hours later Butch was located ten miles from Peter's home, sitting in front of a service station apparently waiting for 'his' truck to come along.

After work one week later, Peter discovered Butch was gone again. This time he had chewed his way through a flyscreen, got into the flat, smashed another flyscreen and escaped. Both windows had been open at the time. Peter rang the RSPCA, reported Butch missing and returned to Swan Hill for the long weekend. Sadness and disappointment prevailed and we gave up Butch as lost forever.

On his return to Adelaide, Peter once more rang the RSPCA. A terrified Butch had indeed been sighted running through the Adelaide traffic, but no-one had been able to apprehend him.

To Peter's amazement, three days later the RSPCA rang to inform him that Butch had turned up at the Noarlunga Abattoir, 27 miles from Adelaide. It was a location he had been to only three times. The last time had been two weeks previously, and wasn't via Adelaide, but over the punt at Wellington.

The drover at the abattoir had come to work early in the morning and found this red dog very tired and footsore at the gate. Immediately the gates were opened the dog had run to the truck ramps. The drover realised the dog was lost and rang the RSPCA.

Since his experiences in metropolitan Adelaide, Butch intends never to get left behind again, as he now sits beside the right-hand-side wheel of the truck after it is unloaded.

PART 11
NOTHING ELSE MATTERS

The job comes first

IN THE HEAT OF THE NIGHT

Ian Waller, Beaufort, Victoria

I began my jackerooing in 1970 on a large property near Hay in the Riverina. I obtained my first working dog soon after arriving. It came with the name of Flea, because it was the runt of the litter. It was a small, hardy, black and white dog with impeccable breeding—out of Spec by Darky! She learnt her trade quickly and became a loyal and faithful friend. The name Flea, however, had a few variations—and it wasn't long before she answered to Fleabag and, later in life, Old Bag.

For two months during winter, a friend and I were at the outstation shearing shed living in the old shearers' quarters. Our job was to muster ewes and lambs for marking.

The hut that I slept in had a door that would never shut properly, so Fleabag was able to sneak in and sleep under my bed. To help keep out the cold on the frosty nights, I had borrowed a heavy jute woolpack from the shed. It was a very effective blanket despite the smell of wool and its weight. However, it turned out to be a bit too effective.

I started to notice that Fleabag's performance in the paddock was deteriorating. She was knocking up more quickly than I would normally expect. I could not work it out.

After discussing this with my friend who slept in the hut next door, all became clear. He told me the dog never got a chance to sleep. Because of the heat, weight and smell of the woolpack on me, I was having vivid sheep dreams. He could hear my commands of, 'Way back, Fleabag,' and piercing whistles throughout the night while I was fast asleep. The dog kept tearing out the door and barking way off in the distance trying to find the mob I was dreaming about. This was happening two or three times a night. No wonder the dog was worn out next day.

I decided to forgo the woolpack, so the dog could get a decent night's sleep.

STILL CIRCLING

J Griffiths, Beaumaris, Victoria

Bob's owner was Snow Anderson, who lived in the Terrinallum district of Victoria, which suffered a devastating fire about fourteen years ago.

Bob was well known and loved. He was reaching an age when some people thought he had run his time and could be put down.

On the morning of the fire, Snow told his wife he was going to move his stock—1,600 sheep and 200 cattle—onto a bare paddock. He took Bob to help him.

While they were there, the local fire brigade came by, called Snow over and told him a big burn was coming their way. Snow was an officer in the fire brigade, so he immediately climbed up onto the truck to help fight the fire. He didn't give Bob another thought.

While Snow was away at the fire, a wind shift turned the fire over Snow's farm. His wife and children knew what to do to save the homestead and surrounds.

The firefighters worked all day, then had the heartbreaking job of shooting injured animals, and securing what was left of the properties. Late in the day, Snow returned home exhausted. His wife persuaded him to have a meal before he went out to shoot his injured stock. Snow took his gun and set off to complete the tragic day.

When he reached the paddock, Snow found his old dog, Bob, still circling the sheep and cattle. They were all safe, but Bob had burnt the pads on his paws. Snow picked him up and took him home, where the family nursed him back to health and to live out his life to the full.

Sadly, this did not occur as Bob was hit by a car a few weeks later, but not killed. Snow and his wife nursed him again.

Three weeks later, Bob began to make an unusual bark. Snow said, 'I'll go and see what's troubling the old fellow.'

When Snow got to him, Bob crawled up on Snow's knee, nuzzled him and dropped dead.

Snow cried, and years later when we relate the story we still get a lump in our throat and tears in our eyes.

WORKING MOTHER
V T Mengler, Tenterden, Western Australia

Tootsie had about eight pups which, unfortunately for her, decided to appear just when our shearing began. As everyone knows, sheepdogs are required to work very hard at shearing time, but with Tootsie facing motherhood, and then actually becoming a mother, she was put on 'maternity leave'.

For a few days she and the puppies were shut in their netted-in pen with kennel, food and water available. The puppies spent most of the time feeding or sleeping. However, this did not suit Tootsie. She heard the sheep and the men working in the yards, so on the first day her pen was opened for her to have a run, Tootsie worked out her own plan.

I was cooking in the kitchen but when I went to the back door I found that Tootsie had carried each pup about fifteen metres and placed it carefully on the back door step for me to babysit. She had already sped off to the shearing shed.

I put the pups back in the kennel, close together for warmth. As soon as lunchtime came, Tootsie dashed into her kennel, fed her brood, drank lots of water and was ready to go back with the men after lunch to work. She did the same at afternoon tea time and the routine continued for the rest of the shearing.

I always kept an eye on her pups in her absence.

A LUST FOR WORK
H J Treasure, Cowra, New South Wales

I have never known a dog enjoy his work so much. When it was over you felt like apologising to him. Choc had the look of a deflated balloon as he slunk away to his kennel to wait for the next job to begin. While waiting he always lay with his feet crossed like an old man. I don't know if this was body language for confidence or some other thing. But he always did it.

Choc could move across a sheep's back with the footwork of a dancer, or move under their bellies like a half-back breaking from the scrum base. He would use his front paws like hands, loading sheep. And as he grew older and stronger, he used his shoulders too.

Single out a sheep in the mob and he could catch it. His eyes would never leave the animal after he had singled it out. Find a lamb on the wrong side of a fence and he would stay there all day if necessary to guard it, belly low to the ground and eyes never off the face. Pick up a knife and sharpening stone and the killers would be under your feet in a few moments.

They say a dog is man's best friend. When things are going wrong as they sometimes do on the land, the dog often seems to sense it and stands as close to you as he can. Then he'll sit on your boot and lean against your leg to get a little closer. Somehow this always seems to make things a little easier.

DUTIFUL BLUEY
Anne Donovan, Wellington, New South Wales

Bluey, a blue heeler, grew up with our daughter Mary. When I put her in the sunshine in her pram, Bluey would station himself beside her and allow no-one and nothing to go near her.

As they grew older they were inseparable. One day I told her about Bluey and how he minded her in her pram. Unknown to me she took her dolls in their pram outside the gate and told Bluey, 'Mind my babies, Bluey.' She then went off and spent the afternoon about her business and forgot all about the dog and the dolls.

Later that evening at feeding time, Bluey was missing. Suddenly Mary remembered her dolls, and there was Bluey still on guard.

One day Mary and her dad rode into the saleyards with cattle. They left the horses and saddles in an unused stockyard, had lunch and then went to see the stock being sold.

During the sale we got a message that an interstate transport had got out of control at the creek and rolled at our gate. We hurried home to see what could be done to help. The horses and saddles ended up being left at the saleyards overnight. Next morning, Bluey was there—still on guard.

I'M NOT YOUR BLOODY DOG

Heather Edwards, Padthaway, South Australia

This is dedicated to pregnant wives who help in the sheep yards, where husbands turn into monsters—but quickly turn back into husbands once the job is done.

PARTNERS

I sit here in the protective shade assuming
   that soon my instant obedience to a command is looming.
I look and see just where the boss is now at
   is he scowling under that old felt colander-like hat?
Yes, his face *is* taut as his voice rasps out to me
   doesn't he notice my sad whimpering, my urgent plea?
Oh, for a rest for my time is not so very far away
   I should give birth soon, so please hurry on the day.

Yet faithful always and certainly eager to please
   I balloon forward into the mob with a certain unease.
My swollen belly hinders as my legs clip the top rail
   but I'm determined to yard these ewes and I will,
I will avail!
So up the race I go with seemingly lightning speed
   but the boss thinks I'm slow and he's even more peeved.
I'm in the wrong place (again!) so I'm definitely told
   whatever happened to the days when I was worth my weight in gold?

Mingling dust and words scatter freely overhead
   I ache, heart pounding, with legs of jellied lead.
But the job must be done now and the drafting complete
   for the boss is always right and he must never be beat.

One stubborn old ewe with slaughter on her mind
  decides to block the race as a futile protest for her kind.
Blasphemies and hat fly high as he finally loses his cool
  and berates me more profusely as a useless, fumbling fool.

'That's it, I've had enough!' I want to scream.
  'I'm hot, dusty, tired and, yes probably useless in this team.'
Instead, silently simpering I snatch the toddler and flee the strife
And call back dejectedly, 'Remember, I'm not your bloody dog,
  I'm your wife!'

BOSS DOG

Alan Green, Mt Gambier, South Australia

Having worked as a wool classer throughout southern Australia for many years, I have had the opportunity of seeing many great sheepdogs in action. The one that sticks in my mind was a beautiful dark red-brown kelpie with a distinctive white ring around the butt of his tail. He was aptly named Ringo.

In one particular shearing shed there was a race behind the catching pens which was partitioned off with gates that slid up on a counter balance, similar to a window. These gates were finely balanced and could be slid up with a minimum of effort. Ringo would go ahead of the sheep, put his nose under the bottom rung of the gate, push it up, and then come back across the sheeps' backs to force them forward. I am sure, had he been tall enough, he would have pulled the gate down again.

Ringo's greatest act was filling the shearers' catching pens. As is usual when the shearer's pen is down to one sheep, he calls out 'sheep ho' to have the pen refilled. Ringo would appear flat-out as soon as he heard the call and walk down the shearing board in front of the catching pens until he came to the pen with one sheep. There he would sit until the boss came to pen up.

If the boss didn't appear quickly enough, Ringo would find him, grab his trouser cuff and give it a good shake. He would walk past pens with two or more sheep and always propped at the pen with one sheep.

At times there would be two or more close calls of 'sheep ho', and Ringo would always stop at the first pen with one sheep. I never saw Ringo make a mistake in the six years I saw him work.

One of Ringo's greatest assets was that he would work for anyone. His owner often lent him to growers to help with dipping, lamb marking and so on. As soon as Ringo worked out the movement of the sheep through the yards, which he learnt very quickly, there was no need for orders or instructions. You just left it to Ringo.

By the way, for those who claim you spoil a sheepdog if you make a pet of it, Ringo would sleep on the end of the boss's bed and always travelled in the front of the ute. The best sheepdogs I ever saw were those treated as pets and made part of the family.

BREAKING IN THE
NOVICE WIFE
Margaret Jones, Bathurst, New South Wales

Being relatively new to country life I thought it a novelty to put on the gumboots and head for the hills to round up the sheep. My job each day was to move them from an 80-acre paddock, and the thrill of putting them through a double gate into the home paddock to graze on the new oats was tremendous. At the end of the day I had to move them out again.

After a couple of weeks of sometimes taking an hour or so each time, and after the neighbours took pity on me and sent their dogs over to help, we thought it about time to buy our own working dog.

We asked around and decided to talk to old Cliff, some 50 kilometres from home. Cliff showed us three dogs which he in turn put to work with a whistle here, a word there or the wave of an arm. The decision was made. I asked the price of the rather scrawny, unattractive, plain brown dog that was our choice—'$300,' said Cliff.

My husband didn't blink an eyelid so I kicked him, mouthing, *'Three hundred dollars,'* thinking he must have thought Cliff said thirty dollars. My husband told me to write out the cheque, which I found very hard to do for that boring-looking dog.

We took Sally home and all the time I was thinking what a huge waste of money it was.

Within the next week my life became very busy and moving the sheep twice a day became tiresome.

I would run past Sally sitting in her kennel on my way to pound the paddocks, thinking to myself, 'All that money for a dog and look at me, dirty, tired, cranky and totally unfeminine.' After another few days of this I couldn't go on any longer. I took the chance and took Sally with me, not knowing what to do or say to a fool of a dog. We walked to the top of the hill so we could see the sheep. I bent down and told Sally to bring them to me. As she disappeared over the hill I knew I had done a very stupid thing and that one of many unpleasant things was about to happen.

The dog would run away and there would go our $300. She would push the sheep through the fence to the neighbour's place, which would mean more money for repairs—or, worst of all, she would kill them. In my panic, I started towards home, not knowing what to do nor how I was going to tell my husband I had lost the new $300 dog.

When I turned back I saw the most beautiful sight. Six hundred sheep were heading straight for me with the most wonderful brown dog at their rear gently bringing them in. Still not knowing what to do, I ran in my gummies towards the gate and minutes later every last sheep was where it should have been with Sally standing there looking at me with her lovely big brown eyes. She had taken minutes to do what had been taking me hours.

I gave her a huge pat and much love and ran back to the house and rang my husband. 'Why didn't you give Cliff $600 for the dog?'

SORTING THEM OUT
Roy Postle, Pittsworth, Queensland

I was droving about 200 cattle from Toowoomba to Pittsworth when this event happened.

At a little place called Broxburn there is a watering point for travelling stock. The property either side of the stock route was owned by the Day brothers, who had a dairy and milked 45 to 50 cows. When I topped the rise, I saw that their dairy cows were just about home to the yards. However, two of my cows which had already had a drink were wandering off to join them.

I told Spot to get around them but they were in with the milkers before he could head them off. Without me telling him to do anything else, he went through the mob, found one cow and brought her out. Once clear of the milkers, a couple of good bites and she was on her way back where she belonged. Back he went again, and sure enough he did the same with the other cow.

While all this was going on, I was at least a quarter mile away, but the Day brothers were on the yard rails watching.

When I caught up to move the cattle on they called me over. They said if they had not seen what Spot had done they would never have believed it. And with a bit of a grin they asked if I would sell him. What would you think?

RELIABLE DART
Linda Irwin, Casino, New South Wales

Dart was a red kelpie owned by W J (Herb) Dunn and was descended from the first dog he brought to the far north coast of New South Wales in about 1910. There are thousands of kelpies up there now and most owners would claim they are descendants of Dart.

While Herb and Whispering Jack, an Aboriginal stockman, were asleep under a tarpaulin, their mob of 200 bullocks 'rushed'. Hearing the roaring noise, they mounted their horses bareback and galloped after them, hoping to eventually catch up and turn them. They were surprised to go only two kilometres before finding the panting bullocks and the dog standing quietly. Dart had gone, without direction, and turned them into a two-rail fence.

Herb often took mobs of cattle, mostly young or bullocks up to 1,000 head, through Casino with its many streets, lanes and empty blocks. He would steady the lead, and Dart, needing no instructions, would keep the mob moving by racing up one side, peering through the moving legs, and when the cattle broke away on the other side he would race around the tail and bring them together.

Herb often had to take cattle over the Richmond River at Coraki. He would notify the punt operator who in turn would warn travellers that the punt would be disrupted on a certain day.

One particular day Herb, with Hilary Lulham, a lad of sixteen, mustered 400 young steers and drove them to the landing area to get there just on daylight. Dart and 25 head were first on, and with a few whistles, Herb directed them to an area away from the punt landing. Each trip took half an hour. Dart met each load and kept the mob together without any further directions. The whole operation took ten hours and it was dark when the cattle were driven to a holding paddock.

SNIP THE RIDER
Gloria Godlonton, Bellingen, New South Wales

Snip was very active like his mother and took some controlling while young, so I commenced his training on a long lead. He proved to be a most intelligent animal, faithful companion and an excellent sheepdog.

He rode on the back of my horse even at the gallop. He moved to the front of me where I held him securely with one arm when the pace got really fast.

Out in the paddock when he was on foot he would put his paws onto my boot in the stirrup whenever we came to bindies or when he was getting weary after a long day. I would bend down and slip my fingers under his collar and he would leap onto the saddle blanket via my knee.

I always had to use a long saddle cloth as my mare Flight would not stand for the claws of his front paws. His hind legs on her rump did not seem to bother her after the first few rough rides Snip and I endured.

THE APPLE DOG

Stan Mentha, Mt Barker, Western Australia

In about 1955, we had around 1,500 sheep, but our main income came from an apple orchard. We exported about 5,000 cases of apples to the UK and the Continent annually, so the orchard and the fruit were very important to us.

We lived 60 kilometres from the sea and during summer we always liked to take the children to the beach at the weekends—but summer was when black cockatoos were a menace to orchardists. They would fly around in flocks of up to 200. Cockatoos will destroy apples at the rate of around one case per bird per hour, so in one hour, 200 cases of apples could be lost.

We trained our sheepdog Brandy to chase the cockatoos out of the orchard and he became so good that if a bird landed in the trees he would be there in a flash, barking and hunting it out immediately.

It was lovely being able to go to the beach knowing our fruit exports were safe. Brandy was worth many thousands of dollars to us.

SKIPPER

Kevin Clarke, Geraldton, Western Australia

This working dog story is about Skipper, a part border collie, bred by Sergeant Sanderson in Adelaide in 1960. Skip was my only dog and one of the few that I could draft ewes and lambs with single-handedly. This event happened on a sheep property I was overseeing south of Tintinara, South Australia.

We had prepared for crutching and were waiting for the team to arrive. Out of the blue, they turned up at 9 pm and asked if they could get under way at 7.30 the next morning. Obviously they couldn't, not without sheep in the shed.

I thought about it for a while and decided to night muster with Skip. I had a mob of about 500 four-tooth wethers reasonably close to the shed, so I tried for them.

I first drove the boundary and got the mob ringing. I then let Skip out with the usual command of 'fetch 'em up'. I drove well ahead, stopping occasionally to hear Skip barking when he turned the wings. Four gates and four paddocks later, we had them in the shearing shed yards. We pushed enough of a mob onto the grating inside the shed to start the first run in the morning.

Skipper was a brilliant one-man dog for both paddock and yard work. Although not good in the heat unlike the kelpies I owned later, he was patient with ewes and lambs and boisterous and fast with bare shorn wethers.

CHIPS WAS DOWN
Neil Finch, Balranald, New South Wales

It was two days before shearing and time to muster the big wethers about ten miles away in a paddock of some 8,000 acres covered in huge river red gums and thick spiky lignum bushes. Chips, my black and tan kelpie, and I got the sheep into a holding paddock in readiness to walk them to the yards the next day.

Next morning was cold, there had been a few points of rain overnight and the ground was slippery. Chips and I arrived at the yards in the old ute.

When Dad opened the gate of the holding yard, the sheep, for no apparent reason, took off wildly in all directions.

Quickly I jumped on my motorbike which we'd left at the yards overnight. Repeatedly kicking, I tried to start it. By this time the wetness from the seat had soaked through my jeans. I could see my companion standing by, the well-mannered dog that she is, waiting for the bike to start first before jumping aboard.

I tried again and again, continuously kicking, but to Chips's disappointment, the contraption still wouldn't start, I checked the choke and key, then kicked again, and suddenly the roar of the motor echoed through the tall gums. As soon as it started, Chips was on behind.

There was no time to warm up the motor. I pulled the stiff clutch lever in, slammed it into first gear, the chain gave a wrap and at high revs we took off, ripping up the sticky dirt and weaving in and out of the trees. As I found fourth gear, I realised I had lost my partner somewhere in the take-off. There was no time to go back and get her.

Jumping logs, crashing through lignum at full speed, I worked my way to the front of the mob. A clearing in the scrub was a help and I was gaining fast. But at that crucial moment, the chain came off, jammed and I came to a sudden sideways skidding halt.

I jumped off the bike and tried to head off the runaway woollies on foot, but my rickety knee couldn't keep up the pace and let me down. The sheep went running on. I raised my voice and loudly yelled words that most haven't heard before.

I gave up and turned to make my way back to my bike. Then a smirk came on my face. There was Chips, still coming along. This was my last chance. She went right on by me with one purpose in mind—just to head the mob. She gave me a cool, sideways glance as if to say, 'You wouldn't wait for me, so I don't need you.'

After already running close to a mile, her ears laid back, Chips, trying to run faster, really pushing herself, kept on going straight ahead. She knew where to go—my best mate, buddy, friend, my girl Chips. She rounded the sheep up and gained control of the mob in no time.

The wethers soon settled down and walked the miles that led on to the Sturt Highway where some travellers paid us the courtesy of slowing down for the sheep with a friendly wave. Many other idiots paid no attention to signs or travelling stock. Still, we reached the homestead sheep yards, and shearing was done with Chips, the all-rounder, continuing her great work in the shed as usual.

PART 12
A MIND OF
THEIR OWN

Doing it 'my' way

A RATTLER ON THREE LEGS

Bill Donovan, Wellington, New South Wales

Old Jim was a drover with the best team of working dogs in the Back Country—that is, if you can take Jim's word for the fact.

'See old Biddy there,' said Jim. 'She's the best all-rounder I ever owned. Works wide in the paddock, jams 'em in the yard. Could put a bee in a pickle bottle.

'She's going to pup to Fred Scott's dog. Fred's dog is a fancy worker. Won a few dog trials too. Biddy has never thrown a bad pup yet.'

So I duly lined up a deal with Jim for the pick of Biddy's pups.

When the day arrived for me to take my choice of the litter of eight fat, grub-like creatures, I carried them a few metres from the kennel and placed them in a row. It has been ingrained into dogs from eons past to select the best pup first and take it back to the safety of its kennel—something to do with the survival of the fittest. Anyhow, the pup that I took home wasn't my choice, it was Biddy's. I've never known this method of selecting a pup to fail.

He grew up to be a playful nuisance, always in the wrong place at the wrong time with his tongue hanging out showing his teeth in a silly sort of grin as if he had a joke he would like to share.

The first time I took him around the sheep it was a freezing cold July day and he ran around puffing steam. One of my offspring said, 'You oughta call him Steamtrain, Dad.'

A man would feel a clown yelling, 'Go way back, Steamtrain,' so I compromised and called him Rattler, which suited him because he turned out to be a rattling good dog.

When he was being trained the property was infested with American burr grass (also known as spiny burr grass and many other names that I dare not write). It is a shocker on working dogs and Rattler got the habit of carrying one foot whether there was a burr in it or not.

One day a stock agent came out to inspect some sheep and after watching Rattler working them for a while he said, 'That dog would win at Molong Sheep Dog Trials. He has a lot of class, but you'd want to scrub him up a bit. You get points for appearance as well as working ability.'

I nominated Rattler for the Open Championship and took him to 'Le

Fleur Dog Salon' to be spruced up. The young lady got me all flustered and nervous when she called me sir. The last time I was called sir was when I was pulled up for a roadside breath test on the way home after my mate's bucks party.

What with trying to explain that I wanted Rattler prepared for the dog trials and not knowing exactly what preparation was needed, I got her quite muddled. She kept looking at the dog and then at me as if she was comparing our IQs. By the look on her face as she ushered me out, the dog got top marks.

When I went back to collect Rattler, he was as shiny as a new billy can, toenails lacquered, teeth polished and—the most indignant treatment for any dog—shampooed. While I was leading that fancy looking hound out of the beauty parlour, I was wishing I was invisible. I felt like a police inspector sneaking out of a house of ill fame.

The trial ground was a hive of activity with the intercom drowning most other sounds. When Rattler's turn came, he performed like a true champion. Still displaying his old habit of carrying one paw, he finished the last turn and penned the sheep.

There was a pause on the intercom, then the request—'Would the owner of dog number 123 come to the secretary's office, please.'

When I arrived the head bloke said, 'I am sorry to inform you, sir, your dog has been disqualified because he's lame and we can't have lame dogs competing in sheepdog trials.'

I answered, 'He's not lame. That's a bad habit he got when I broke him in when the burrs were bad.'

The judge looked at me and said, 'This is my thirty-seventh year of supervising dog trials. I thought I had heard everything. Now you come along with a story like that. I tell you the dog's lame and I'd advise you to take him to a vet.'

It's annoying to tell the truth and not be believed, so I answered in my most indignant voice, 'He doesn't need a vet, he needs an animal psychiatrist to get him out of his bad habit.'

As I stormed out of the office, I overheard the remark, 'Someone needs a psychiatrist, but it's not the dog.'

HEAR! DOG!

Margaret Glendenning, Wangaratta, Victoria

Bluey's goin' deaf, ya know.
　　Why, just the other day
I whistled him to block some sheep,
　　He looked the other way.

Two hundred wethers charged the fence,
　　Stampeded past the gate.
That dog just sat and stared at me
　　Until it was too late!

He wagged his tail, and watched 'em go,
　　They didn't stop until
They reached the scrubby cover
　　On the far side of the hill.

Those sheep were wild as mad March hares,
　　Long legged brutes, and cunning.
Don't know how he would've turned them,
　　He'd have had to do some running.

Yesterday he got the cows,
　　Came strolling in behind them.
The young bull wasn't with the herd,
　　Way back, boy, go and find him.

(Jersey bred, and nasty,
　　Don't trust him, stay on guard.
He hates all dogs and chases them
　　On sight, across the yard.)

Blue ignored my signal,
　　Looked positively dreamy.

Is he going blind as well?
  I'd swear he didn't see me.

I had to fetch the bull meself,
  I was careful not to cross him.
Last time he tangled with the dog
  He'd charged, and tried to toss him.

Poor old dog'll have to stay
  At home, take life at ease.
His biggest worry from now on,
  To shift to scratch his fleas.

Couldn't have him working stock,
  He'd be useless anyway.
I'll have to pension Bluey off
  To dream his life away.

Just look at the old codger go!
  He's jumped the garden gate.
You'd almost think he'd heard the scrape
  Of food fall in his plate!

School bus is early home today,
  The kids are loudly cheering.
Bluey's there to meet the boys—
  Too bad about his hearing!

WITH GREAT DISDAIN

Peggy Hodgson, Dalwallinu, Western Australia

Jock was trained very easily considering that he had four young children to untrain him and many distractions. One of his great strengths was his absolute love of sheep work. Once he learned to cast and take a flank, he wouldn't stop working. We had to tie him up or he'd be out rounding up any sheep he saw, whether ours or the neighbours'.

In his work, Jock was completely autocratic. He was a one-man dog who would occasionally and, with great disdain, condescend to work sheep for me. I had to learn my place though. He would allow me to drive him to the paddock and tell him what was wanted and then I had to shoot through. The moment I tried to drive a flank or help in any way, he'd turn the sheep the wrong way or push them through the wrong gate, just to show me who was boss. I suppose I could say we could work together . . . as long as I played twenty-ninth fiddle!

Left on his own, with instructions, he worked well for me, if somewhat distantly, but I always had to pick him up in the ute afterwards and bring him home according to his union rules.

My old father-in-law, who considered himself a good man with dogs, was helping us at shearing time and he took Jock out to the paddocks to help bring sheep up to the shed. Time lapsed and no sheep appeared. A search party was about to be launched when father-in-law showed up.

Shamefacedly he asked if someone could come and help him as— 'That bloody Jock has boxed up all the sheep in the married couple's house yard and made a real Charley out of me!' He had too.

The boss did his quince and had it out with Jock. 'Get those bloody sheep out of there and up in the yards or I'll kick your backside!' he yelled.

Without so much as a cringe, Jock flew into action and the sheep were in the shed yards in no time. Like I say, he was a one-man dog.

PUTTING A DAMPENER
ON THE DAY
Robert Pratten, West Dubbo, New South Wales

When leaving for work in the mornings in the Landrover, everyone would be keen and fresh for work. The dogs would hear the gate click and their chains would crash against the upturned iron scoops and drums which were their kennels.

Released from their chains they would rush off to soak the leg of the windlight tower or tennis court corner, then chase a couple of chooks and when I got into the Rover, they would leap into the back. Axes, sheep dip, tucker box and wire flew in all directions as they scrambled for a place.

Now Tiger, who did not like being the same as everyone else and who refused to copy what all the other dogs did, had been bounding all this time round my heels. So when I rested my arm along the side of the door to look back as I reversed (no rear vision mirror) I would feel a damp warmth spreading from my elbow and realise the horrible truth. Tiger had done in the back of the ute what he should have done earlier.

The only reason this dog ever survived was because he was friendly, faithful and would work, although mostly in the wrong place.

KEEP THE LANGUAGE
PLEASANT, PLEASE
Wendy Muffet, Wirrinya, New South Wales

Wal, our border collie–kelpie cross, is one of nature's gentlemen. With his 'softly, softly' manner he has a deep-seated loathing of anything resembling roughneck colonial behaviour. He is always first choice when quiet handling is the order of the day, and so got the nod the morning we mustered the AI ewes.

All was going well until we hit the yards. We were on a fairly tight schedule and the boss was getting a bit frustrated with Wal's 'ever so gently' approach. 'For God's sake, Wal, *push 'em up!*' he bellowed.

Wal stopped in his tracks and looked back at us with a pained expression on his face, as if to say, 'I hope he's not going to start that ill-mannered yelling again.'

'Well, don't just stand there looking at us, you useless ******!! Push those *bloody ewes up!*' roared the boss.

I don't know if it was the volume of delivery or the aspersions cast on Wal's family tree, but this poor behaviour simply could not be tolerated. He calmly padded over to the fence, jumped out of the yard and hopped up onto the nearby ute.

You can imagine the effect this act of mutiny had on the boss. With steam coming out of both ears, he told Wal loudly and explicitly (far too explicitly for the purposes of this yarn) what he thought of collies in general and Wal in particular.

Wal's response? He stood up, delicately turned his back on this tirade and sat back down again, gazing wistfully in the direction of the house yard where such 'paddock language' is not tolerated.

What could we do but laugh—and let one of the rough and tumble kelpies off to finish the job, leaving Wal to recover his bruised sensibilities?

THE EASY OPTION
LEFT DAD BOUNCING
Peter Waterhouse, Maya, Western Australia

About 30 years ago when I was a small boy, my father used to take me out kangaroo hunting with his two dogs Nip and Trixie.

It was too difficult to shoot kangaroos because we had a lot of regrowth bush on our farm, so he used kangaroo dogs instead. Those two dogs used to kill up to 80 roos a month, saving most of our crops in those hard times.

One Saturday afternoon the two dogs bailed up a boomer, well over six foot tall. My father decided to grab the tail of the roo to make it easier for the dogs to pull it down. Nip's neck had been stitched up a week earlier after being kicked by a roo, so by holding the tail, Dad hoped to make the dogs' task safer.

Just as Dad got hold of the huge roo, a smaller one hopped by. The dogs sized up Dad's roo and then looked again at the smaller one. They quickly decided to chase the smaller roo. This left Dad at the mercy of a very angry boomer which was keen to get hold of the creature hanging onto its tail.

Two hours later he was still holding on. After yelling for his dogs and bouncing around behind the boomer for all that time, he was exhausted.

His dogs returned wagging their tails as if nothing had happened. Dad couldn't afford to yell at them in case they took off again.

Eventually he persuaded the dogs to kill the boomer and he was able to fall back for a rest under the tree—that I had been up the whole time.

180 KILOMETRES AND ACROSS THE MURRAY
Joe Mack, Loxton, South Australia

Ginger was a nondescript, medium-sized mongrel (retired sheepdog) belonging to an elderly couple in Barmera, in South Australia's Riverland.

His virtues were faithfulness and a placid nature. But his owners were old and growing feeble so, in the twilight of his life and amidst heartbreak, they gave Ginger to folk in Mildura, in the Sunraysia district some 180 kilometres distant.

Six weeks later, they were amazed to find Ginger, bedraggled, footsore and lean, at the back door! Enquiries revealed that his new owners knew of his disappearance, but had not wanted to alarm his previous owners by advising them, feeling somewhat guilty at not knowing what had happened to cause their new charge to vanish soon after arrival.

The whole story eventually unfolded, something like as follows. A truck driver used to commute regularly between the Riverland and Sunraysia districts and stay overnight with his lass at the Barmera Hotel.

He was travelling near Lake Cullulleraine, west of Mildura, when he stopped to study a brown dog in distress on the roadside. The dog responded by jumping into the truck through the open door, so the

313

truckie watered the dog and drove on, wondering what to do with his companion, who was now quite contented.

On this particular journey, he had to detour via Loxton and then continue around Moorook, Kingston and Cobdogla before getting to Barmera. Between Pyap and New Residence (out of Loxton), the dog became agitated. The truckie stopped the truck, whereupon the dog headed for the nearby River Murray and vanished.

To reach Barmera from there, the dog had to swim the river and navigate through territory foreign to him.

SAGACIOUS LADDIE
Ken McCarthy, Heathcote, Victoria

This story about a brainy sheepdog from Daylesford appeared in the *McIvor Times*, Heathcote, Victoria, on 27 February 1890. It was reprinted from the Creswick *Advertiser.*

SAGACIOUS BRUTE

A remarkable instance of canine sagacity occurred at Kangaroo Hills on Friday last, the hero of the occasion being Messrs Tankard and Gordon's well-known sheepdog Laddie.

During the last two months Mr Gordon had been in the habit of taking at the end of each week a parcel of 60 or 70 sheep to a certain butcher in Daylesford. Last week however, he missed doing so, and the dog evidently thinking there was something wrong collected about 100 sheep from one of the neighbouring hills and set out with them himself, apparently for the usual destination.

Mr Gordon was away from home at the time, but returning an hour or two later, he missed the dog and the sheep.

Mrs Gordon remembered having seen the dog watching the sheep about the house at one time during the day, but did not know what had since become of them.

Proceeding on the road, however, Mr Gordon observed tracks of sheep going in the direction of Daylesford and following them up came upon the sheep about two miles from home, with the dog in charge—and conducting them—the day being hot and the sheep heavy—slowly along.

Laddie seemed delighted at the arrival of his master, but had to submit to being turned back.

Having given his orders, Mr Gordon returned home, and the sheep and dog followed in due course.

THIRSTY FELLOW
Beryl Parish, Stuarts Point, New South Wales

We had a cattle dog called Sam, a border collie–kelpie cross. He always followed my husband to the yard when he milked the house cow. My husband would always squirt some milk into an icecream container for the animals after he had enough for the household. Sam would have a drink and then the rest was brought to the house for the cat. When the container was empty it was left at the back gate for the next day.

One afternoon Sam must have got thirsty because I looked out the window and saw him pick up the container in his mouth and take it out to where the house cow was feeding and put it under her udder. Then he sat and waited, but she walked on after a few seconds. Not to be outdone, Sam picked up the container again, followed the cow and did the same thing. She didn't understand of course, and kept walking away until Sam gave up.

TARZAN THE SNAKE KILLER
Glenn Bradley, Bowraville, New South Wales

Tarzan was a ferocious snake killer. In the early days red-bellied black snakes were around in large numbers when there was much more timber and rubbish for them to hide in. Quite often they sought the sanctuary of the houses, so it was an asset to have a dog that would seek out and kill snakes.

On one occasion my father carried a load of wood into the house and threw it into the fireplace. Out crawled this big black snake, spitting and rearing straight at him. A hoe was handy and he chopped a hole in the floor killing the creature.

Tarzan would leap in, grab the snake behind the head, shake it viciously, release it, jump back and then leap in again, repeating the process until the snake was dead.

Death adders were also around in large numbers. They are sleepy,

315

docile animals that will not get out of the way, but if you touch one they will flip over like a flash and you are history as they are deadliest of all.

Tarzan took a death adder one day, did not handle it quite so well and that was the end of him.

WITHOUT INSTRUCTIONS
Hilda Harkness, Esperance, Western Australia

When we were living in Langkoop, Victoria, some Department of Agriculture inspectors arrived on the farm to do a spot check for footrot and lice. The paddocks were too wet to travel in by utility, so the inspector and Woof were riding in the tandem trailer behind the tractor.

As we approached a mob of lambing ewes, Woof—without any instructions and to the amazement of all—leapt off the trailer, singled out and caught a ewe with lambing problems.

He was also very clever at picking out and catching flyblown sheep.

SCENTING THE WAY
Tom Robinson, Wilmington, South Australia

My dog story comes from an era when working dogs really earned their tucker. It was during the war years when petrol was rationed and prior to 'Ag' bikes. At that time, we had two female working dogs, sisters named Brownie and Kitty, and they never worked on the same side of a mob of sheep.

Dad and I were mustering various paddocks to get together fat lambs for railing to Gepps Cross market. Hammond was the railway siding at which we loaded and it was located in about the centre of our property.

Our first job on this particular day was to take a mob of sheep from a paddock six miles west of the siding. As we got them out on the road, one of the sheep wouldn't walk, so we loaded it into the back of the utility.

We left Brownie to take this mob of sheep to Hammond. We then drove to the railway yards, unloaded the sheep that wouldn't walk, and proceeded to another paddock that was located six miles east of the town to muster the sheep held there. Having completed this task, we then walked them towards the railway yards and were about one mile from Hammond when we met Brownie with her mob.

The local Postmaster at Hammond later told us that he saw Brownie bring her mob into the town, every now and then going ahead and smelling the ground to find the scent of our ute. In the middle of the town she turned the mob at the crossroads and detoured up to the railway yards (where we had unloaded the lame sheep) and not finding us there, again turned the mob and followed our tracks back through the town with the sheep, turned at the crossroads and proceeded on to meet us.

Nowadays, the increase in road traffic and public liability insurance risk would not allow such a feat as this to occur.

ANYONE SEEN ROVER?

John Griffin, Toorak Gardens, South Australia

My father farmed happily and desperately on the drought-haunted Willochra Plain in South Australia, from the late twenties till the end of 1949. Then, with the same sad lack of foresight which had marked our family's history on the land in Australia, he sold up in 1949 and moved south so that we could live closer to secondary schools. He wasn't to know that the Korean War was about to break out, sending wool prices through the ceiling.

Our sheepdogs were always locally bred kelpie–collie crosses. Good workers, intelligent, reliable and able to take their instructions from my father as he drove his yellow buckboard behind the sheep. We were a small operation with just one dog at a time.

We took our sheep for shearing to Boolcunda woolshed, north of Hammond. It was there, in 1948, that our dog mysteriously disappeared and we never saw him again.

Rover—the dogs were always Rover—was with us in the morning

when we went to Boolcunda. The sheep had been driven there the previous day. When we packed up to go home that night, Rover was missing. He had been a reliable dog who always came home and we couldn't understand it.

Months later, the agents who handled our wool contacted us. Rover had been found in Japan—squashed flat in a bale of wool. It seems he had done a bit of adventuring in the old woolshed and had explored his way into the wool press. Rover gained some notoriety as the first dog from Hammond to travel to Japan.

However, the Japanese buyer, finding a flattened dead dog in his bale of reasonably good wool, had not been very pleased.

NOT SO USELESS
Bruce Mills, Tumby Bay, South Australia

Tiger was a black and tan kelpie owned by a family who lived in the rough hilly country of the Gawler Ranges. The two sons of the family were very competent motorcycle riders and rode their bikes over rocks and through scrub at a furious pace when mustering sheep.

Tiger was a large, heavy-boned dog and not suitable for carrying at speed on the petrol tank of a bike, so as soon as the going became rough he was pushed off and expected to follow. Now Tiger, being an intelligent animal, decided that if the boys were going to take all the exciting work he might as well go home—so he was branded as lazy and useless by his young masters.

It was shearing time at their station and I happened to visit. The father of the family suggested we go for a drive to check waters. It was a hot day and when we reached the tanks and yards we noticed about fifteen unshorn sheep a short distance from the trough. The sheep raced off and Tiger was sent after them and soon had them stopped. After giving them time to settle he walked in and started the sheep towards the yards, but at the first bush, one old ewe ducked underneath and stopped. The rest kept going. Tiger tried to fetch the old ewe out but she only shrank lower. Meanwhile the other sheep had curved off and were getting away.

Tiger left the ewe and turned the rest back only to see the old ewe take off in the opposite direction. Leaving the mob, he raced around the ewe once more, only to have her dive under another bush. This time Tiger showed his frustration and rushed under the bush at the ewe and she went right to ground.

Backing off, Tiger circled around the mob and drove them back to the ewe lying in the bush and waited and panted and all the time watched his sheep. After a while, the sheep mooched off and the old ewe got up and went with them. Tiger circled around them once more and guided them slowly back to the yards where he helped yard them.

So this is the useless, lazy dog, I thought. We had just witnessed some most intelligent work. Nine out of ten dogs would have either left the old ewe behind or stayed with it and let the rest go. Not only that, but Tiger's instinct to bring all the sheep to the ewe had overcome his training to bring the sheep to his master. He had in fact driven them directly away to collect the cunning old ewe.

BEYOND PRICE
David de Bomford, Forth, Tasmania

In the late 1920s my family lived on a farm on the old Surrey Road at Romaine, south of Burnie. My father owned a female border collie sheepdog which he had trained to drove sheep unaccompanied. On one occasion when he had bought sheep at the Cooee saleyard, my father sent them on their way and left the dog to take them home—a distance of about five miles.

My father had business to attend to and returned home via a different route. When the dog did not arrive with the sheep at the expected time, he went in search of them. He found them about halfway home and wondered why the dog had taken such a long time. An explanation was provided later by a local farmer who had seen the dog alone with the sheep and had watched her at work.

There had been a lame sheep in the flock and rather than hustle it along, the dog would allow it to have a spell at frequent intervals. She would let the rest of the sheep wander on but she was careful not to let them get too far ahead. She would bring them back to the lame one, gather it into the flock and urge it on a little bit further. Again and again she shepherded the sheep to and fro, all the while taking care to ensure that the lame sheep was given sufficient rest to allow it to continue.

Although the continual rounding up of the sheep and the backtracking with them must have wearied the dog, her patience never flagged. Her efforts not only kept the flock intact but ensured that the lame sheep did not just make the journey, but did so with the minimum of discomfort.

The farmer was so impressed with the dog's capability that he offered to buy the dog for a substantial sum of money. My father would not sell her. She was beyond price.

PART 13
AT THE END
OF THEIR LIVES

GIFT TAKES ON THE JOB

Charles Vosper, Gympie, Queensland

The old dog was curled up in a ball. He was barely alive and shivering like hell. I don't mind telling you, tears came to my eyes when I saw him there. I knew old Darkie had moved his last cow in off the paddocks. As for the pup, Gift, I think he knew too, because he just lay there with his head resting on his front paws.

I told Peter about Darkie and he asked me to take him to the vet and have him put to sleep, but to bring him home and lay him to rest where he belongs. It was one chore I wasn't looking forward to, but it had to be done. After breakfast I found Gift was still there beside his old mate. He was a bit put out when I put Darkie in the truck.

That afternoon I let Gift off the chain, but he just didn't want to work. I had to get the herd in with some help from my wife. Gift had found the spot on the bank above the main yard where I had buried Darkie. He had a bit of a dig and sniff around it but wouldn't come away and leave him. He stayed there for three days, as if he was waiting for Darkie to get up.

On the fourth day I went down to the milking shed and had switched the lights on and was putting the rinse water through the machines when I had this feeling that something was watching me. There, standing in the half light, was Gift. He was crawling along down low on his belly and sort of crying. I took his head in my hands and said to him, 'I know, mate. I miss him too.'

You know, if I didn't know better I would reckon that dog knew what I said, for he seemed to liven up a bit. I gave him the order to 'go forward' and away he went. From that day on he never looked back. It was a real treat to watch that young dog working. The old dog had surely done a good job as a teacher.

THE EXPERT

Linda West, Wagin, Western Australia

There is always a power struggle between a farmer and his dog, but none more drawn out and obvious than that between Gus and Jim.

Gus was the runt of the litter, destined to rejection by everyone including his mother—until Jim decided to give him a go. Working on the assumption that he was used to having to struggle for everything he got, Jim thought this dog might just prove to be tough and tenacious. He was right. From the word go the struggle for supremacy between the two of them was a seesaw affair. Watching from the sidelines it was obvious that the dog thought he had won every round—and equally obvious that Jim thought he had. To the rest of the world it was plainly a rare thing—an equal working partnership between man and dog.

There was never any doubt that Gus was a star in paddock or yards, but at the house he was a problem, and the problem was his terrible appetite. He seemed to spend his entire life striving to get enough nourishment to make up for what was lost as a pup in the litter. He was extraordinarily clever at opening doors and jumping to great heights on slippery surfaces to steal anything edible lying around. Food was left out by a new, unsuspecting wife. Whole legs of mutton cooked and left to cool for the never-ending supply of cold meat disappeared from a closed kitchen.

Blame was sent flying around at all two-legged inhabitants of the house—accusations of tricks being played, tall stories of enormous blowflies carrying things away—until the greasy trail and paw prints were found. Gus again! He would open the kitchen door, jump up to the sink and drag his prize away to eat it amid the squashed area of garden reserved for his dining. Raw meat of course was a favourite and unloading groceries on a Friday afternoon had to be planned around the dog. Meat and other edibles first and all at once, or he would be in the car and off with a kilo of the best rump.

Gus was supposed to retire at twelve, but nobody told Gus. He continued ruling the roost and no other dog could topple him from his place. Everyone still depended on him but he did less running and more riding in the front of the ute. The young dogs were sent out to do the long stretches and he was called on for expertise and close work. He was beginning to lose his hearing and his sight, and arthritis had taken its grip on his back legs. Still he kept going. If the boss's boots and hat went on, Gus was still at his heels.

Gus retired himself at sixteen and took over the front verandah of the house. Every now and then as a mob of sheep went past he would wander out and scatter them to the four winds by being in the wrong place at the wrong time. The young dogs still gave him every respect and never challenged him. He was still top dog.

This was made obvious one day in the yards when two humans and three dogs were trying to funnel sheep through a gate. All was despair. The air was thick with dust and profanities, with sheep going everywhere and dogs becoming confused.

Through the dust, just in the nick of time, came the Expert, this time in the right place at the right time. The sight of him cheered the humans and galvanised the dogs into efficient action. He had sensed the confusion from his throne on the front verandah and had come to set us all to rights. He was very conscious of his own cleverness. We often caught him with a smirk on his face when he was proven correct. This was one of those times. Once he had sorted us out and had the sheep running through the gate, he took himself back to the house, pride and smugness in his every step.

AN OLD DOG RUMMAGING
THROUGH HIS MEMORY
Paul 'Shakey' Brown, Mackay, Queensland

I sit here on a small beach. My memory wanders at leisure over the years looking for clues. An old man introducing his memoirs. No longer wearing a young man's clothes, I resemble more an old dog the family owned rather than an old man.

He was a cattle dog and, of course, they called him Blue. He was never brave but in his youth he had an amount of cunning. He displayed it when he saw a chained dog. Hair raised, ears back, he would race at the chained dog as if to do battle. The dog on the chain would prepare himself for the fray—bark, snarl, growl. Blue, having gauged the length of the chain, would stop his mad rush and casually urinate on a post barely out of reach of the other dog. Inevitably the dog would almost strangle himself on the chain trying to get at our heroic animal who would casually strut on his way.

However, Blue got older and in his dotage restricted his activities to our garage. Here the resemblance comes in. He devoted himself to searching out and stalking an unseen enemy. Every hair on his body raised, tail straight out behind, ears pricked, he would silently steal up on a garage pile of rubbish. On the first occasion he did it there was great excitement.

'Jeez', they shouted. 'Snake in the garage!'

Shovels were produced and the particular pile of rubbish was dismantled piece by piece. No snake. I think we did this a few times before we realised Blue was hunting the spectres of his own mind.

I was young then and believed in appeals to reason. I'd always respected Blue's intelligence so I set out to prove to him he was deluded. I would take apart each pile of rubbish he crept up on and show him it was nought but a pile of rubbish. This would satisfy him about that pile, but he would immediately begin to stalk another. And so it went on and on, and, because he was only a dog, and a senile dog at that, he'd return to piles we'd already investigated and stalk them again. So I had to admit defeat. Blue wouldn't admit defeat. He stalked the rubbish piles of that garage until the day he died. It was obvious from his effort and concentration that he expected each pile to render up the object of his hunt.

I'm Blue. My memories—his rubbish heaps. I sneak up on an event in memory, senses alert, expecting it to give a clue as to my predicament and meaning. I examine it carefully, then start again with undiminished enthusiasm. Expectations inevitably high. I'm a little smarter than Blue; certain rubbish piles of my memory I do not intend to examine again.

I don't know if Blue ever really knew what he was hunting. I know I'm searching for the reason I'm an old dog stalking the rubbish piles of his memory—often on chilly nights, when all the other dogs except the occasional adolescent are curled up in bed fast asleep.

A RUSTY OLD BLOKE

Joan Jackson, Warwick, Queensland

We named him Rusty but later found that his name was Tex. He arrived at our property very footsore, rheumy eyed, thin and very bedraggled. He appreciated a good feed and slept for a long time under the tank stand. A very tired old red dog.

We put ads over the radio and in the paper. Within a few days we heard his story. Since he had become too old to work the sheep on his home property, he was tied up while the younger dogs went out barking and bounding around, happy to be useful and able to do a day of mustering and yarding sheep.

Tex watched them—miserably whining and pulling on his chain, wanting to join them. His master decided to take the dog to his brother, who had also been 'put out to grass' and had a cottage 150 miles away. Tex stayed there two days and then left.

He found us 50 miles from where he started and when we looked at the map and drew a line from the cottage to our property and then to his original home, we found he was walking in a line as straight 'as the crow flies'.

When his owner contacted us through the ads we told him that Tex was settled and we all decided he would stay with us.

Although he had a reputation as a first class working dog, he never again looked at a sheep. He just slept in happy retirement in the sun. He seemed happy with his new name of Rusty, too—that is, until he became too deaf to answer to anything.

SLOWLY BUT SURELY

Judith Ridgway, Wolseley, South Australia

Old Purdie, our brown kelpie, had been on her last legs for a couple of years. She was fifteen years old with her hearing going, arthritis in legs that have covered many miles of paddocks and sheep yards, and lungs and heart not a hundred per cent. Despite all this she still managed to chase and bark at the washing trolley or lawn mower.

One particular day, four rogue sheep defied all attempts of the boss and young dog in the ute to get them to the yards. Then along came old Purdie, stumbling down the paddock. Slowly but surely she rounded them up, bringing them over to the boss to catch and load up. With head high, she rode home on the back of the ute with her catch.

Sadly she has died. We sat with her, talked to her and held her until that huge heart stopped beating. She was a friend and companion for half our married life.

She is still with us in spirit—buried at the top of the drive.

TO SAY GOODBYE

Mattie Allman, Sale, Victoria

Thirteen years ago my husband was given a brown kelpie pup and he named him Sim. A wonderful sheepdog, he loved every minute of his work and was very obedient.

My husband John retired two years ago but of course we kept Sim. The dog really missed his farm work.

One Tuesday in February this year, we were in the kitchen having morning tea. Sim amazed us by walking right into the kitchen. He had never been in the house before. He didn't seem distressed in any way and we wondered why he had come in.

Next morning my husband went out to let him off the chain. He found old Sim unconscious and he died two hours later. We think he must have come into the house to say 'goodbye'.

RETURNING THE PIGLETS

Kathy Cooper, Forbes, New South Wales

I recall vividly the day when Red had to fetch a litter of piglets through the gate to the correct side of the fence. Nothing unusual in that, perhaps, except Red was at that stage in the autumn of his life and almost totally blind.

He was a typical kidney-coloured kelpie who had worked in shearing sheds in western Queensland where my brother was shearing.

As he worked the piglets along the fence, it was difficult to tell that he had almost no sight. He would stop, cock his head, wait for a squeal or grunt from the main group of piglets, or a soft whistle from my father, then slowly advance on the squealing mob. Any breakaways from the main group were waited upon in silence until they returned, and then Red and Dad would recommence their job together.

Finally, when all the piglets were through the gate and relocated with the sow, Red just wagged his tail after a few rewarding words from Dad, who during the whole exercise had not moved one step from his spot near the gate, and had communicated his instructions to Red with soft whistles throughout the entire performance.

ENJOYING A LIFE OF INERTIA

Jennifer Hetherington, Grenfell, New South Wales

When our neighbour sold his farm to retire to the coast, he faced the dilemma of what to do with his faithful but blind old sheepdog Tim.

We offered Tim a home and the company of our deaf old sheepdog Bully. The veterans of paddock and sheep yard shared the house yard with a mutual indifference. Bully, a silent dog, did not intend abdicating or even sharing his role as boss and would deliberately ignore the newcomer. Tim in turn chose not to acknowledge Bully's position and constantly muttered to himself as he wobbled from one resting place to another.

Both enjoyed a life of inertia in selected spots of winter sunshine or in the reliable shade of the tank stand or vine-covered pergola in summer, living out their gentle retirement.

WORKING
DOGS

HISTORY OF THE
BORDER COLLIE

Stephen Bilson, Orange, New South Wales

On the border of England and Scotland in September 1893, almost exactly 100 years ago, a pup was born that has changed the way sheepdogs work right around the world. It was a 'Working Colley' pup called Old Hemp—an exceptional dog, recognised as the father of all modern Border Collies.

Old Hemp himself resulted from an amalgamation of bloodlines from many different sources, for the history of the Border Collie goes right back to the Roman invasion of Britain in 55 BC. The Romans brought with them their own breed of sheepdog, described as large and heavy-boned, and carrying either a long or a short coat. They were usually black with tan and white markings. These dogs spent most of their time fending off wolves and foxes and guarding the shepherd's possessions and sheep from other humans. It is thought that these dogs resembled the large Bernese Mountain Dog that is still popular today.

In AD 794, Britain was invaded by the Vikings, who brought with them a small Spitz-type breed of dog. Over the centuries the Romans' sheepdog and the Spitz-type dog were crossed and various strains of Working Colley were bred to suit the conditions in each locality. Many of these strains specialised in particular jobs. For instance, Welsh Greys were good for feral goats. The Welsh Hillman was a breed that evolved and was then crossbred with dogs coming from North Africa. We also know that in 1514 Polish Lowland sheepdogs were introduced into some of the working strains in Britain. Another Working Colley strain was the Highland Collie, which was left unchanged until Queen Victoria took an interest in the breed in the late 1800s. The Queen was even reported to have attended sheepdog trials. With its new popularity, this breed, too, was crossed.

During the long period from the Roman invasion to the 1800s, people in Britain did not travel much and dogs in various districts generally remained mostly unchanged for centuries. When nationwide trade began to have an effect on British farmers, it also had an effect on their sheepdogs. Many of these dogs were cross-mated to produce better dogs. This also meant that over the years some of the Working Colley strains disappeared in favour of more efficient breeds. The Working Colley in Britain still had many different strains and these, with various cross-matings, produced the Bearded Collie, the Smithfield, Shetland sheepdog, Australian Kelpie, American McNab, Old English Sheepdog, Rough and Smooth collies, English shepherd—and very likely played a strong part in the development of other breeds such as the Australian shepherd, the Corgi and the German coolie (or German Colley, as it is sometimes called.)

The Australian Kelpie was bred up from crossbreedings of different strains and imports to this country. In 1869 John Rutherford of Yarrawonga, Victoria, used a pair of imported Scottish dogs as a foundation for the Kelpie breed, intermingling their blood with dogs imported by other breeders such as Messrs Elliot and Allen of Geraldra station and George Robertson of Warrock station. Another influential breeder was G S Kempe of South Australia.

Without doubt, though, Border Collies are the British Working Colley's most noted sheepdog ancestors in the world. As the name suggests, the Border Collie was found in the region of the Scottish and English border. All Border Collies trace back to that single dog, Old Hemp. He was bred by Adam Telfler and was described as being jet black with a very small amount of white on him. His coat was long and similar to a lot of Border Collies today.

Old Hemp began to compete in sheepdog trials at twelve months of age, and in his entire life remained unbeaten. It has been reported that he didn't excite the sheep but instead held them with complete control by his intense gaze. No-one had ever seen a dog work sheep so well. It was also reported that he was a good-tempered dog but with a tendency to be excitable—in fact it was noted that he sometimes trembled as he worked.

As a result of his talents, his services as a sire were widely sought after and soon everyone wanted a pup by Old Hemp. It is estimated that he sired more than 200 male pups in his lifetime before he died in May 1901. His importance is further enhanced by the fact that his offspring also showed many of his outstanding characteristics and the line continued holding many of these traits that we now take for granted in the modern Border Collie.

Hemp's sire was a black, tan and white dog called Roy. He was described as being a plain working but easily handled dog. Hemp's dam, Meg, however, was described as being very sensitive, intelligent and showing style and eye when working. She was an all-black bitch. Both were from old, solid lines of Northumberland Colleys.

In Britain the first sheepdog trial was held at Bala in Wales on 9 October 1873. It was reported that most of the dogs used a lot of barking while working on the course, but the dog called Sam, who scored third place, was said to have shown eye when working. This characteristic is what we now know to be a typical trait of the modern Border Collie. The term 'eye' refers to the way a dog can persuade the sheep to move by looking intensely at them instead of rushing about. This trial was won by Mr James Thompson with his black and tan Working Colley called Tweed. She was a small black and tan dog with a white forefoot, compactly built with an intelligent, foxy head and a fairly thick coat. There were ten competitors and up to 300 spectators. For many years this was thought to be the first sheepdog trial in the world, but we now know there were trials as early as 1866 in New Zealand and a few years later in Australia.

In 1906 the International Sheepdog Society was formed. Scotland, Wales and England each had their own National Trial, which was the highest award for each country. A little later Ireland also joined. The best sheepdogs in each country then competed for the highest award in the combined countries, which was called the Supreme Championship. Many of the Supreme Champions were exported to New Zealand, which indicates how high the standard was of early Border Collies in New Zealand. The imported dogs included Moss 22 (1907 champion, later known in New Zealand as Border Boss); Sweep 21 (1910, 1912 champion); Don 17 (1911, 1914 champion); Lad 19 (1913 champion); and Glen 698 (1926 champion).

The first Border Collie to come to Australia was Hindhope Jed in 1901. She was first imported into New Zealand by James Lilico and had already won three trials in Scotland. At the time, she was in pup to another of the 'new' border strain called Captain. She was also the first of the Border Collies in New Zealand. She was purchased soon after her arrival for 25 pounds by Alec McLeod of the famous King and McLeod Kelpie Stud in Australia. Hindhope Jed was placed fourth at the Sydney Sheepdog Trials in 1902. She then won the event in 1903 against a field of thirty-two. Jed was later mated to some pure-bred Kelpies by McLeod.

The next Border Collie imported into Australia also came through New Zealand. This was Maudie, a daughter of the famous Old Hemp. Later the King and McLeod partnership also imported Moss of Ancrum, Ness and Old Bob from Britain.

The name Border Collie was used as early as 1905 by King and McLeod in an advertisement for their dogs in Australia, but the name did not become official for the new breed until much later. The Border Collie today plays a large part in Australian sheepdog trials and on farms across the country. Even though Border Collies have been bred here very successfully, some breeders still import new dogs from Britain, and to some extent from New Zealand, to add to their bloodlines.

A BLACK AND WHITE CASE
FOR A QUIET WORKER:
A PROFILE OF BYN DINNING
Angela Goode

When champion sheepdog trialler Byn Dinning was a lad of ten he remembers riding through scrub with his father on their block at Border-town, South Australia. With them were always a few dogs whose job it was to flush sheep out of the scrub. This was in the early 1930s, before much clearing or fencing of the land had been done in those parts. Their block consisted of one paddock of 16,000 acres. Mustering had to be done with great skill and care to ensure that all the sheep were brought out of the scrub for shearing.

Byn maintains that was when he first learnt the value of a good dog— a quiet, gentle, but forceful dog that wouldn't push the sheep too hard, was able to probe them out of the undergrowth and was tough enough to walk them the twenty miles they sometimes had to travel to get to the shearing shed. Those dogs were always border collies.

Sixty-two years on and Byn Dinning's respect for the black and whites is as strong as ever. Hardly surprising. He and his team over the past 45 years have won most major sheepdog trials in the nation, as well as run several farms without much outside labour.

To emphasise what it is about border collies that he loves, he tells a story about something that happened when he was a boy. Byn's father was out mustering in some rough country when his horse fell and rolled on him. His father broke his pelvis. His dog, Bot, one of a string of particularly good dogs on the place, went after the horse, grabbed the rein which was hanging down and brought the horse back to him. Byn's father was able somehow to climb aboard and get home. Byn maintains his father wouldn't have survived if the horse had left him. After that, no other breed of dog ever got much of a look-in, although Byn has had the odd kelpie on the place from time to time.

'It's a popular misconception that the border collie can't take hard work,' is his answer to the common belief among kelpie owners that the black and whites are soft. 'It's all in the strain. Some are soft, some are tough. I have only ever had tough dogs.'

In his 45 years of trialling Byn has had success right from the start: 'At the first trial I went to, I got in the prize money. And I won the next one with a seven-month-old pup.' (That pup that gave him his first win carried the bloodlines of the Homeleigh stud in Victoria where Arthur Kemp, one of the very early serious border collie breeders, turned out many champions. That bloodline is still pulsing through Byn's dogs today.)

But it's not Byn's own prowess this solid rock of a man is boasting about—it's the dogs he's proud of. He squirms a bit in his chair when the spotlight is put on him and his undoubted ability to breed and train extraordinary animals. However, while Byn is not given to boasting, there's an amazing array of ticking clocks, silver platters, silver cups and championship ribbons arranged all around the room we are sitting in to do his boasting for him. To ensure that everyone realises they're a result of the dogs, not him, there are large, hand-coloured, ornately framed photographs of his greatest champions hanging around the walls.

So it is only with quite a bit of effort that the truth can be excavated from the rock. After a bit of jackhammering, the big man with the gentle face walks off and returns with a pile of exercise books. But the books don't record Byn's wins—just the dates and names of dogs, the trials they entered and where they were placed, all methodically tabled in a neat hand.

This man with the big kindly face needs more prompting to talk about his achievements, so I start reminding him: in 1992 there was 'A Dog's

Life', the television series on the ABC in which he competed as South Australia's representative with Old Mill Laddie. He didn't win that trial—a minor lapse—but he helped put dog trialling on the television map. And what about the Canberra National?

From there Byn starts talking. Yes, he won the National in 1992—regarded as the supreme test for working sheepdogs. It was his first win out of only three attempts. But he regards his major triumphs that year as winning the Commonwealth Championship at Koroit, Victoria, rated as one of the biggest trials in Australia and the South Australian championship at Roseworthy Agricultural College.

In 1991 and 1992 he represented Australia against New Zealand with three other team members. Warming to the theme, he brought out the green blazer: embroidered in gold on the pocket are the words 'Australian Sheepdog Workers' Association—Test Team'. In 1991, the New Zealanders won, but only by a few points despite the Australians having had no time to acclimatise or loosen up before the tussles in Palmerston North and Christchurch got underway. You get the feeling, though, that he was sorrier for the dogs that tried their hardest in difficult conditions than for the handlers. In 1992, in Bendigo, the Australians evened the score.

He gets rid of further talk on the subject of his successes by waving his hand dismissively: 'I won open trials all over the place.' And that's the end of it. So we focus on the dogs, and the going is easier.

Old Mill Laddie, he volunteers, the dog bred by Damien Wilson of Littlehampton, has been in the prize money 28 times since July 1990, and has won more than $5500. Although he is a well-known dog because of the television trials and the Canberra National win, Byn doesn't reckon he is the greatest dog he's had. 'He'd be in the top ten,' Byn says, leafing through his exercise books.

At the top of his list is Glenromian Judy, a bitch he bred, who reached the finals twelve times in fifteen competitions between 1949 and 1960. Glenromian, Byn's stud prefix, is made up of the names of his three offspring: Glenice, Roma and Ian. Then there was Glenromian Jack, followed by Kenton Hope, with whom he won his first South Australian State Championship in 1963.

He lingers over the names of Navarre Wally and Penmore Bradman, a dog who won nineteen opens. Then Kynoona Deane (a Queensland-bred

337

dog), Glenromian Tamie (named after Tamie Fraser), Kelton Tom and Glenromian Cindy. The last two dogs became famous as a breeding pair, with progeny sold in five Australian states. One pup of the same strain was exported to Montana in the United States to work sheep in the mountains.

When I caught up with him, Byn was reluctantly taking a bit of a forced break from farming and trialling because of some 'nonsense' with his heart which he didn't want to go into. The doctors were ordering him to town for tests and making him rest. However, his Naracoorte house backs onto a lake and some scrub, and he's got room in the back yard for a small mob of quiet wethers. Tied up in the yard was a young bitch he had bred who was just starting to work. All his other dogs had been farmed out amongst his friends while the heart was getting attention. But the bitch was giving him something to do—and she was coming on well.

He was a bit dark that he wasn't in Canberra that week to defend his national title, and that he wouldn't be taking on the New Zealanders in the Test Team: 'It's good to give some of the young ones a go coming on up,' he says. But it's blatantly obvious he'd rather his wretched heart hadn't got in the way.

Despite the trophies, ribbons and clocks, Byn maintains that trialling has never been anything more than a hobby, one he took up in 1948. 'It's the people I've met, that's been the thing for me,' Byn says. The weekends away at trials with other farming people pitting their dogs against each other for a bit of sport have made him friends all over Australia—people he feels comfortable enough to drop in on and sling a swag on their floor. 'They're a great bunch of people, the three-sheep triallers,' he says.

Not that he's got anything in particular against the yard dog triallers—though he does reckon many of their dogs are a bit too pushy, too noisy and waste an awful lot of energy rushing about to achieve their ends. 'And yard dog triallers are a lot more commercial than we are. They're in it to sell pups and make a living.

'There's a lot more finesse in what we do. Sure, the yard dog has a place. But I know what I like and, really, you don't see the same level of skill. The test that we get our dogs to do means that if they can do that, they can do the other—and usually without all the yapping.

'I've got to have quiet dogs. I hate these yap, yap type of dogs that hustle and push the sheep around, making them bash themselves on the side of the yards. You don't get the job done any faster stirring the stock up—it's probably slower.'

It runs deep, this love of the border collie. While he admits there are good kelpies around, Byn's love of careful dogs, ones that are biddable— he calls them 'press button' dogs—makes him, he admits, a bit one-eyed. 'I've never bred dogs commercially,' Byn points out. 'I breed dogs when I'm looking for a better one for myself and just sell off the surplus.'

On the properties he's run since 1945 near Bordertown, Lucindale, and others near Naracoorte and Edenhope, he says he's only employed labour spasmodically. His good dogs, he reckons, are worth up to three men: 'I was the lazy one. I could sit in the ute and let the dogs do all the work. And these have always been the same dogs I've won trials with.

'My best farm dogs have also been my best trials dogs. They are always the first dogs I let off when I've got hard work to do—and sheep or cattle, it doesn't matter to them.

'No, there's nothing soft about a border collie. They might be quiet workers, but they're tough.'*

---

* Byn Dinning was selected to represent South Australia in the Supreme Australian Working Sheepdog Championship held between 27 September and 4 October, 1993 on the lawns in front of Old Parliament House, Canberra. The photograph below shows Byn with Old Mill Laddie and Glenromian Flag.

PART 1
WHERE THE BIG GUMS GROW

In dappled shade mobs of sheep sit out the heat of the day. Cattle chew their cud contentedly. Big gums with peeling bark reveal smooth new skin beneath, and gum oozes from unhealed wounds where branches have snapped off in wind or still heat. Creeks and dams mirror tangled branches, red and white coloured bark and glossy leaves. Grasses wave. In the air hangs eucalypt scent. Blue seedlings erupt after flooding and big rains. Under thick brown bark, small lizards and ants live, while hollows shelter noisy corellas and galahs.

A huge gum—dense canopy against bright blue sky making grey purple shadows underneath—epitomises grandeur and stateliness. This is the country where the topsoils are deep, water is plentiful and the seasons relatively pre-dictable. There are vineyards, pine forests and irrigated crops, and predators like foxes, rabbits, bushfires . . . and tourists. There are also neighbours close by and pubs.

The dogs of big gum country have a particular tale to tell.

MESSIAH OF THE LAMBS
Garth Dutfield, Wellington, New South Wales

We rim about 4,000 sheep on 'Stockyard Creek', our property on the shores of Burrendong dam. The views of its waters from most of our paddocks are great but it's in winter, when the hills are cloaked in fog, that I find myself overawed by the beauty around me. On cold crisp mornings, shrouded in mist, I ride through mobs of lambing ewes to ensure that all are safe and to retrieve any lambs rejected by their mothers. Many a cold wet orphan lamb has been revived with a warm bottle of milk by the open fire in the homestead. And so to my dog tale . . .

As a young man I saw many funny incidents involving dogs, but I reckon that Sam, the whippet-beagle cross, one of the members of the rabbit pack, gave me the biggest laugh. Sam's position in the pack was semi-fast rank outsider in any chase, with very little chance of ever coming up with the prize money. He was a likeable dog, pure white with black patches stretching up over each eye to cover his large floppy ears. This description is important.

Mustering and lamb marking time had come around again—a time of year most of us sheep men don't much like. This particular year we were a bit late and the lambs were wild and large. As the bellowing ewes hung back, all trying to find their lost lambs in the mob, the lambs started to ring the edge of the mob, with more and more joining in the 'frisky' run. I knew we were in trouble. I had turned the surging tide back into the centre three times. Sheepdogs and motorcyclists were becoming frantic when strolling across the hill fair bang in front of the mob came Sam.

You can't imagine what I called him. Sam knew he was in trouble and turned for home. At the same time, however, the lambs broke and, seeing a pure white comrade (albeit with black floppy ears) making a beeline away from the mob, they followed. Sam glanced back but was not impressed to find upward of 300 charging lambs bearing down on him and a further 400 screaming ewes coming after them. Sam changed into a higher gear and headed for home.

I was thinking murderous, unprintable, blasphemous thoughts about 'white rabbit dogs'. But being dimwitted as sometimes I am, I hadn't recognised heaven-sent assistance when I saw it.

Sam bolted for home. The lambs followed as though he was the annointed Messiah of all sheepdom. The faster Sam went, the faster the lambs went. He tried to lose them at the creek, but the leaders cleared it like Olympic long-jumpers. Sam stuck to the road like glue except for a smart circular move through a patch of scrub which he had learnt from chasing foxes. But, because the lambs were strung out through it, he ran into them wherever he turned. He soon dodged back to the road at even greater speed.

The gates had all been left open and Sam made full use of them—but still the lambs followed their leader, propping and bucking with glee. As we watched in astonishment from the rise where it all started, we could see Sam approaching the yards. The lambs were gaining on him. My mother looked up from the homestead garden and was aghast to see a line of 300 lambs heading for the yards with no ewes in sight. They were strung out far behind, all panting.

Finally, after being pursued for a mile, Sam hurdled the gate at the sheepyards and escaped to the safety of his kennel. All we had to do was pick up a few exhausted ewes along the way. When we finally reached the yards, my mother had already closed the gate.

344

This event happened about twenty years ago, but I can still see the tears of laughter rolling down my dad's cheeks. Sam probably had recurring nightmares.

EXPOSING DAD'S HABITS
Anthony Honner, Brentwood, South Australia

Dad's home property was at Brentwood and he had a scrub block, called Paling Hut, 22 miles away. Once a week Dad and Spike, his kelpie–collie cross dog, would check the water and stock at Paling Hut.

In 1949 Dad left for a trip to England. Mum kept an eye on the farm at Brentwood and a sharefarmer checked the scrub block. After about three weeks the dog went missing, and while Mum was on the phone to the sharefarmer she mentioned this. He said that when he had checked the sheep the previous day a friendly dog had been circling them. The dog then went over and lay down by the trough. As it had done no harm, he thought no more of it, except that in hindsight the dog did indeed look like Spike.

Mum then rang a few Warooka people and a local identity said he had seen Spike hanging around the Warooka Hotel all day two days earlier. He'd been there again that day—lying on the mat at the hotel front door.

Next morning the dog was home again.

Mum put two and two together, and realised the dog must have thought that no-one was checking the sheep in Dad's absence. Spike had therefore set off on foot on the usual trip—which rather exposed Dad's habits. First he went to Warooka and had a long wait at the hotel. Then he went twelve miles south to Paling Hut to check the sheep and water, before returning to Warooka for another long session. He then returned home.

And we had thought Dad's long day was all to do with sheep.

THE DUCK HUNTER
Peter Chantler, Casterton, Victoria

Aron (pronounced A-Ron) was a sheepdog of great repute, known for feats of bravery while facing savage mobs of rampaging wethers, not to mention keeping packs of irate rams at bay. His most memorable feat, however, occurred one Saturday during the duck season.

A good mate of mine, 'Coop', came out to our place to go shooting on a large billabong which is usually chock-a-block with black duck. Coop had brought out his new duck dog, Heidi, to show off her skills. From what he'd been telling me, Heidi was going to do everything except shoot the ducks. I'd been taking in this drivel for several days by then and finally, thank God, the dog's day had come. I couldn't have handled too many more stories about the utterly amazing superdog Heidi.

So off we went to the billabong, Coop and me, with Heidi waddling along behind. As expected, there was a stack of ducks swimming around among the weeds, and we were able to bag a few. One duck, however, landed smack in the middle of the water.

'No problem,' said Coop. 'This is exactly what I brought Heidi along for.'

Well, I rolled my eyes and thought to myself: Lordy! Surely I don't have to listen to this all over again while Wonder Dog is freestyling out to bring the duck back to the bank, do I?'

My silent prayers were interrupted by the volume and tone of voice that Coop was using to command Wonder Dog to bring home the duck. After a couple of minutes, Heidi's parentage was being seriously questioned, and I don't think the dog was too impressed with the 25-kilometre walk home that Coop was generously promising her. Needless to say, Heidi was on the bank out of arm's reach from Coop, and the duck was still in the middle of the billabong.

As neither of us was too keen on giving Heidi a practical demonstration of how to do it, I said rather jokingly that perhaps Aron could show us how to do it. So I ran back to the house and brought the other wonder dog back to the scene. Coop had that 'don't be an idiot' look on his face, but I was becoming quite convinced that Aron was up to the job.

Luckily, he loved to fetch sticks and balls and return them to the thrower. So I grabbed a stone and threw it in the vicinity of the floating duck. Aron took a mighty leap into the water and made a beeline straight for the duck. As the only thing floating out there was the duck, he immediately assumed that I had thrown out a dead duck for him to fetch back. And he did just that, dropping it right at my feet.

I just looked up at Coop and smiled. I never did hear another Heidi story.

THE SHEEP AND HAT DOG

Graeme Bassett, Newstead, Victoria

I was bringing in some sheep one day for drenching. I was on a motorbike and had my dog helping out. As I approached the creek I noted another mob on the other side coming toward me. I did not want the two mobs to mix, so I left the mob I was following with my dog to bring them to the creek. I accelerated swiftly to cross the creek and head off the second mob. As I did so, my woollen beret fell from my head onto the ground.

I could not stop to pick up the beret. Instead I intended to leave it there until I returned to take the sheep to their paddock. I proceeded to escort the first mob to the shearing shed for drenching.

About half an hour later I came out of the shed to get on my motorbike. There, next to the bike, was my dog, looking quite proud of himself. At his feet was my beret. The dog had gone back over the creek, got my beret and brought it to the shed. It was wet from where he had swum the creek.

The breed of dog? A fox terrier.

RABBIT HABIT
Helen Sutherland, Scotsburn, Victoria

A rabbit pack consisting of ten or fifteen dogs of various descriptions—
greyhounds, whippets, fox terriers etc—was always to be found on
properties of any size in Victoria in the 1920s. Where my husband lived
on his parents' sheep farm, such a pack was kept to keep the rabbit population in check.

As a small boy he remembers the great interest aroused by Bruce,
one of the dogs. Bruce was a Russian collie and he had a most unusual
habit. When he caught a rabbit he would trot off to the nearest waterhole, hold the rabbit under the water until it drowned, and then return
in an unhurried manner to present it to the man in charge.

NO LAUGHING MATTER
Brian Kilford, Kersbrook, South Australia

This story was serious, dead serious, while it was happening, but when
I tell it, everyone laughs!

I was about to leave to do some wool classing up round Broken Hill
when I found the battery in the one-tonner truck had gone flat. I took the
battery from the car, put it alongside the truck and jump-started it. As
soon as the truck started, I hopped out to remove the jumper leads and
close the bonnet.

Jack, our border collie, thought, 'Here we go. It's time for work.' He
bounded into the cabin, knocking the handbrake off in his rush. I
couldn't get back inside because the truck was already moving down the
slight slope in front of the shed. Bracing my foot against a young pine tree
behind me so I could stop the truck, I yelled to Marj, who was down at
the house, to come and help.

'Jesus, I'm gunna lose it,' I thought as I struggled to hold the truck from
rolling into the dam. Then the pine tree snapped, my legs buckled and
I fell backwards just as the truck rolled on over me, its wheels going right
over my thighs. I thought that would be the end of the truck. But next

second, the engine was revving. Marj had seen the danger the *truck* was in, had jumped in, revved it up and reversed it back—*straight over my legs again*!

Luckily for me there was a ditch around where the pine tree had been standing and my legs went into it. Otherwise I would have had two broken legs for sure, and not just bad bruising. What's worse, while I'm rolling around in agony, Marj decided it was funny. And Jack, well he just loved all the shouting and swearing and revving—and jumped all over me with delight.

It was two months before we did any more work together. And I still can't understand why it is that everyone laughs.

HELLO, DINGO
Cavell Keevers, Sandgate, New South Wales

Having lived in a forest area on the north coast of New South Wales where dingoes were plentiful, I have developed great respect for the intelligence of our native dog. Its cunning is extraordinary.

Our family has had several half-bred dingoes, but one stands out in my memory. We called him Dingo. He was the result of a furtive mating of my father's blue heeler bitch by a big red dingo which had forced its way into a locked slab barn.

Dingo, who was red like his father, was a wonderful household pet and a very intelligent farm working dog who seldom left my father's side. Because of this he frequently used to hear my father shouting 'Hello-o-o' to the neighbours when a telephone call came in for them. This was in the early days of telephones, and the neighbours had not yet installed one. The dog would sit by my father's feet and echo this call.

One day a friend living on a heavily timbered property nearby came to me very distressed, saying, 'Something seems to be wrong across the road from me. I can hear someone calling out "Hello-o-o" repeatedly, as if he needs help. I have searched the scrub and called out, but got no answer.'

When I told him that it was probably Dingo, he was most indignant, but had a laugh about it later.

After my father's death I lived by myself in the forest area. This half-bred dingo became very protective of me and would snarl and bark savagely to prevent any stranger from entering the front gate. I well remember the look of disbelief on people's faces when I told them to say 'Hello-o-o, Dingo' to be allowed inside. As soon as they did, however, the snarl would be replaced by a smile and a wave of the red tail. I must admit, though, that they always kept a close eye on the dog as he followed them up the garden path.

The other member of that same litter was not like Dingo in any way. He had thrown back to his mother's looks but, although a blue heeler in appearance, he had all the ways of the wild dingo. He was a thieving devil and, if caught at any wrongdoing, would freeze and stare at you in such a manner as to be really frightening.

A LEANER CHRISTMAS WITHOUT LENA

Christine Stratton, Strathalbyn, South Australia

In September 1978 we bought two dozen day-old turkeys to fatten and sell to help bring in some cash for Christmas. It had been a lean year for us. We put our two working collies, Lena and Sonny, on guard over the turkeys to ensure their safety.

At 11.30 one late November night, about two weeks before the turkeys were ready to kill and dress, we heard a terrible squawking coming from the barn where they were kept. We had thought they would be safe in the well-protected cage we had made. The dogs had been asleep on the old settee outside the back door. They took off, barking. As they ran toward the turkey cage they were met by a large fox with one of the biggest turkeys in its mouth.

The fox raced through the fence and into the paddock, with the dogs in full pursuit. We could do nothing but listen to the dogs barking as they chased the fox toward the dam. In the moonlight we could see the dogs circling the top of the dam wall and the fox swimming for its life. The dogs refused to let it leave the water and we found next morning that it did eventually drown.

'Well, there goes our Christmas dinner,' I said to my husband. We had taken orders for all but one turkey which was to have been ours, so it looked like we would have to eat chicken.

Just then I felt something warm against my leg. There were the dogs looking very pleased with themselves, tails wagging like windmills, as Lena dropped the large white turkey at my feet.

That Christmas, no turkey ever tasted better. But I did swear the kids to secrecy until after the guests had eaten, even though I think the bird must have died of fright. There wasn't a mark on it when I dressed it.

'I'LL HIT HIM WITH THE SPADE'

Ian Ward, Keppoch, South Australia

My wife, Jenny, and my mother were going around the ewes and lambs when they came across a large foxhole. They had no spade, so decided to come back later and fill it in.

When they returned, Kiwi the sheepdog, unseen by them, jumped off the ute and disappeared down the hole. The women then started stuffing screwed-up newspaper down the hole with the spade handle. As they were about to start filling the hole with dirt, they heard a rustling and scratching noise.

'Quick,' shouted Jenny, 'call Kiwi. I think the fox is coming out. I'll hold him down with the spade until the dog gets here.'

She jammed the spade handle against the paper and they called and called to the dog, who of course didn't come. The more they called, the louder the scratching became.

Finally, Jenny gritted her teeth, stood back and said, 'I'll hit him with the spade as he comes out.'

Poor Kiwi suddenly shot out of the hole, narrowly avoiding a spade on the head—and terribly thankful not to have been buried alive.

COINCIDENCE?

Murray Staude, Naracoorte, South Australia

Some years ago it was our good fortune to have a thirteen-week overseas trip. Our son, whose property was five miles away, took Talbot, our working dog, to his place to care for him.

Not once during those thirteen weeks did Talbot attempt to come home. But on the morning after we arrived home, I walked out the back door and there he was, lying on the mat, delighted to see us.

I still wonder if it was a coincidence—or did he somehow know we had come home?

He is still with us, fourteen years old and still working sheep—although he's badly in need of a hearing aid.

A TOUCH OF TELEPATHY

Barry Field, Tilba, New South Wales

Chad wasn't born a sheepdog. He was a German shorthaired pointer—a hunting dog. He lived with us on a small property overlooking a lake in southern New South Wales. He had been a gift to us.

He was ever keen to please and performed all the tasks a good working dog should. He was my constant companion and possessed an uncanny ability to understand everything I asked him to do. For instance, I was working on a fence line one day and I told him to fetch my jumper, which I had left on a fence post a couple of hundred yards away up the hill. Chad returned a few minutes later holding the jumper gently in his mouth.

Another time my son and I were again working on the fence line, repairing broken wires, when we lost a pair of pliers. We searched for about fifteen minutes, then gave up and continued down the line using an old pair from the tractor tool box. Chad had been watching keenly while we searched. About half an hour later, to our great surprise, he turned up with the pliers in his mouth.

SUNDAY STOWAWAY
Beth Henke, Mumbannar, Victoria

It is extraordinary what lengths your best friend will go to so she, too, can go visiting on a Sunday afternoon—despite having been told to stay home. Wocky, our blue heeler cross, was as broad as she was tall and reckoned she knew as much as her boss. On this occasion, she outsmarted even him.

We set off in our old XR Falcon ute to journey across country to the parents-in-law for the afternoon. Wocky was determined to be part of the visit. She came with us to the first gate, but was growled at and told to stay home. We shut the gate and when we couldn't see her, didn't think much more of it. We thought she had slunk off through the rushes and swamp for home.

We travelled on, opening and closing seven gates. We stopped to change a flat tyre but then continued on across country and into a pine forest. We were stopped there by tourists who asked questions about the lie of the land. Suddenly the old XR died. We opened the bonnet to investigate the problem—and there was determined old Wocky, sitting between the engine and the mudguard.

The tourists looked a little stunned, but the boss just casually remarked, 'Oh, that's where we carry our dogs in this part of the bush.'

In her keenness to meet the tourists' labradors after her cramped and bumpy journey of twenty miles, she had wriggled the petrol pipe off the engine block.

KEEPING AN EYE ON THE JOB
John Bodey, Edenhope, Victoria

My wife and I run a sheep husbandry contracting business. We have a black and white shorthaired border collie named Bob. He is a forceful dog who helps move sheep into sheep handlers for teeth-trimming, crutching or foot-paring. When one of our staff nicknamed him

'Wonder Dog' I was quite pleased until I overheard the explanation: 'Bob is called Wonder Dog because we wonder what he's going to do wrong next!'

Bob has a habit of staring at any one sheep that has been separated from the mob. This frustrating trait reveals itself all too often. A client may remove a stray lamb from a mob of ewes or a frightened sheep can jump out of the forcing yard. Until that sheep is returned to the mob, Bob's attention, to our extreme annoyance, is fixed only on it.

One day on a property near Coleraine in western Victoria, Bob's bad habit turned to great advantage. Our client's sheep had footrot, so our team was employed to eradicate this highly contagious disease. This requires *every* sheep on the farm to be mustered, then thoroughly foot-pared, inspected and treated.

Bob was pushing sheep through the force into our sheep-handling machine for foot-paring. He had been doing a great job but, quite unexpectedly, completely lost interest in working on the four-year-old wethers. Instead, he was staring out into the paddock, the boundary of which we could not see as the land was hilly and dotted with huge red gums.

I thought that for Bob to have gone on strike there must have been one sheep that had jumped out of the forcing pen, escaping out of view. I mentioned this to my client and suggested that he check the paddock. Sure enough, ten minutes later he returned in his truck with one sheep, Bob's eyes still firmly glued to it.

Bob didn't know it, but he probably saved the entire footrot eradication program from ruin.

PART 2
HEAD WOLVES
AND UNDERDOGS

As in any effective organisation, someone has to be in charge—and it certainly can't be the dog, even though that's what most of them would like.

The secret to success, according to livewire dog trainer Neil McDonald, is to emulate the dynamics of a pack of wolves, close relatives of working dogs. In a pack, the head wolf takes authority and punishes insurrection amongst his underlings.

Getting to the stage, however, where the human is revered as head wolf by the working dogs is not always an easy path, particularly if the wolf is a mere woman. It's highly likely she'll be blatantly discriminated against by the working dogs if they're anything like Suzie, Sam or Ringer.

And while the aim might be to lift your dogs to a higher intellectual plane, there'll always be creatures like Boxer and Boots to drag you down to size. Indeed, the question of who is actually supposed to be doing the educating is worthy of deep consideration.

With a good mix of genes, character and training, theory has it that all you need to do is point your working dog in the direction of the quarry and issue commands. But as the bloke at Peter Murphy's trial discovered, boasting about a dog has its hazards.

If it weren't for dogs like Peter Mercer's, that demonstrate they can think as well as obey, many would wonder whether the agony of transforming a dog from freeloader to useful employee was worth it.

THE WORKING DOG'S JOHN CLEESE: A PROFILE OF NEIL McDONALD
Angela Goode

If you're ever way out in the backblocks and you see a bloke in a ute with about 50 kelpies on board, you've probably stumbled on Neil McDonald of the Sherwood stud on his way to another working dog training school. This South Australian dynamo with a John Cleese streak has for the past four years given schools all over Australia—about a hundred in total—plus numerous talks and working dog demonstrations. I caught up with him just before he loaded up and headed for central Queensland for schools at Julia Creek, Richmond, Hughenden and anywhere else on the way.

Out of his 33 years around dogs and the bush, Neil has stitched together a training philosophy that obviously makes sense to plenty of hardened dog handlers. In his three-day schools, the twenty or so participants get plenty of exposure to the colourful McDonald turn of phrase, coming out at the end of them, according to Neil, with a new approach that will make their dog's life happier, and save them money on their farms.

The fact that Sherwood dogs have earned glory no doubt gives the message some clout. Sherwood Ace, owned by Rob Macklin, has won South Australian Dog of the Year twice and Sherwood Macka has won three open yard dog titles. Sires Wabba Kelp and Capree Beau have produced numerous trial winners, among them the rising star Sherwood Adios.

McDonald sees his task as training the handlers, not necessarily the dogs. 'I observe in my travels that most people feel they're too big and tough to be affectionate to their dogs. The dog's the thing they laugh at. It's neglected the most.

'So when I go somewhere, I play their game and say, "Well, you've gotta get your dog, bash him round with a crowbar, smash him down with a shovel, put him around some sheep, then run over him with the ute a couple of times"—and you see them sit up and take notice and say, "Right, we'll start listening to this fella. He's on our wavelength."

'Then I suggest we crash-tackle a few beasts. So I call all the rough, yahoo dogs out and, unsurprisingly, they find they can't shift the stock because they apply too much force in the wrong area.

'So I come out with a couple of sneaking, pussyfooting dogs and, amazingly to them, my cattle or sheep flow. The good stockmen amongst the group quickly see that what I'm on about is a softer approach and that it produces more desirable results.'

At about that stage, Neil says he sees the tough guys slip to the back of the mob.

Basically the only thing wrong with most handlers, he says, is that they don't know how to play and be affectionate with their dogs and how to discipline them. 'The guts of the issue is—good dogs are bred, and champions are made. To get there you have to put them under your wing and make a companion of them. But if I bowl up into Proserpine and say,

"Look here, you fellows, grab yourselves a little puppy dog and we'll spend two to three hours patting it and talking to it", they'd laugh you out as a wimp.'

When he arrives at a school, Neil says the usual scene is of dogs fighting, piddling all over the place and straining on their chains.

'I usually tell them that if they think it's a dog training school, they've been tricked. It's a course on how to make more money through getting cooperative livestock, and you get them by having good dogs.'

According to an old stockman friend of Neil's, only about five per cent of the population is capable of working a dog. 'And I reckon that's generous,' says Neil.

The John Cleese streak finds expression in the McDonald impersonation of the 'normal farmer', the 95 or so per cent who don't get as much as they could out of their dogs. Standing at the back of the mob doing star jumps, model aeroplane-style manoeuvres and making insane whooping noises earns McDonald more than a few queer looks, but this bloke doesn't care what sort of galah he makes of himself so long as he gets his message across. For it's those Cleese-type antics that an awful lot of farmers perform unknowingly in their yards at home. However, if they stand in the right place in the yards, the dog will do the work for them, the stock will flow and everyone will feel more relaxed.

Although he is away from his farm at Keith in the south-east for months at a time, he finds teaching people how to work dogs suits him well. 'Even if I won a million dollars, I'd keep doing this just for the fun.'

So having tapped into the minds of the handlers, Neil takes the school off to remote central Africa in a story to help them plumb the minds of their dogs: 'If we were all wolves at the waterhole in central Africa 300 years ago and we spotted five antelope, we'd hardly jump in the air and say, "Oh! what a feeling, antelope!", because the noise would scare the antelope away.

'We would recognise the antelope are a bubble to be patted, just as livestock are a bubble to be patted—because they've got eyes in the side of their heads. If we make a heap of noise, the antelope run off. So the boss wolf is going to tell his team that if they make any more noise, he'll crush them. Naturally he gets a bit of order in court.

'In the pack there might be an enthusiastic young wolf called Caroline who spots the antelope and wants to impress the boss wolf by getting them. She launches herself straight at them, and when the antelope look up at her and see her coming flat-out, they show her a clean set of heels. So when she comes back, the boss wolf says, "Do that again and I'll cripple you. Instead, go out wide, past the tree and the dam, so they don't detect you coming. If you have to, go on your belly and make sure your scent will not blow onto them."

'So now, as the boss wolf, I'm putting a plan into action. It's not a matter of just hoping we get some antelope today, because this time the antelope see a semicircle of Carolines, and they run away from her. Antelope take the spot where there's no pressure. All Caroline has got to do is stay back and run the antelope into where the others are waiting to pounce.'

That understanding of the basic hunting instinct that propels or motivates a sheepdog to work, the desire to go and shepherd stock and bring them back, is what Neil believes all working dog handlers should absorb. 'What self-respecting young wolf would ever get a mob of antelope and chase them away. He'd get killed by the others in the pack, and they would all starve.'

All too often, the first thing many stockmen do is get a pup, get a mob of sheep, stand at the back of the mob and send the dog around to tuck the wing in. Of course the pup goes too far, so they call him back and punish him. They try to teach him to 'come behind' before he gets a chance to follow his instincts.

'Every time you tell a young dog to come behind, you dampen his enthusiasm. Blokes will say to me, "Geez, it was a real keen young pup. All he wanted to do was work sheep, and he's sort of gone off. He must have got bitten by a snake or it was too hot." What's happened is, he's stripped the wolf out of him by continually telling him to come behind. In doing so, he stripped the work out of him.'

For a young pup, you need to break in four or five sheep or cattle so that when the pup is introduced to them, he becomes a winner right from the start and can use his instinct to herd them back to you, the head wolf.

The head wolf, Neil says, is like a football coach. If he doesn't have respect, he's got no team players. 'A spongy old wolf that's friends with all his pack will cause them to die because he hasn't got enough authority over them to stop them running straight at the antelope.

'If you look around at the majority of the prominent trial people, they're egotistical, they've got to win at all costs and they're a bit schizophrenic. Those factors have a lot to do with their success. A dog's got to see a good side and a bad side of you. Someone that just mopes around and is the same all the time doesn't give their dog any up and down, any contrasts.

'A dog's got to see what happens if he doesn't perform. I'm pretty tough on my dogs for sniffing, for marking out their territory, spinning their wheels and flicking up clouds of dust, trotting past another dog arrogantly, snarling at another dog, ignoring me. I give them an open hander for any antisocial manners.

'Too many people let their dog get up to all the most horrible habits under the sun, like licking another dog, sticking its nose into its bottom, cocking on the side of the house. Then when they take them to the workplace, because they haven't set the environment right, it's inevitable the dog cuts off a sheep or does something a little bit wrong. Then they go and belt the dog so it ends up thinking he's getting pummelled for working.

'By the time I go near sheep, my dogs know full well I'm boss. If he goes in and cuts off a sheep or something, I ignore it for a while.'

People make a big mistake by not ensuring their dogs are civilised: 'I can tell when someone gets out of their car and walks over to the yard whether their dog will work properly. If the dog's giggling all over them, jumping and straining the chain and being a pinhead, then I know they've got very little chance of having success in the sheepyards.'

According to Neil there is no such thing as a dog trainer, only a 'situation creator'. He maintains that shepherding dogs such as kelpies, collies, some Smithfields and some coolies don't have to be trained. 'All you have to do is create a situation where they'll work just as they would in the wild. Then, if they look like going clockwise around their sheep or cattle, you give them an appropriate order like "get over", "go left", whatever. If you are consistent enough, they will correlate that command with that action. Therefore they won't treat the learning process as an imposition—and note I said learning, not training.

'For most of us, however, it's "get here", "go there", "do that". Too often, the workplace for a dog is like a bloody torture chamber.'

As for picking your future champion out of the litter, there is no formula. 'Just pick the one you like most,' says Neil. 'Then you'll be prepared to put the work into it.'

To be any good, though, it has to have instinct to go around stock and receptiveness to commands. It must be able to take orders, because eventually you'll break the dog from only going around stock to do other things that are against its natural instinct. 'Once we grasp that dogs need to be allowed to develop their natural instincts, then we are halfway home.'

A good dog also needs intelligence, as well as a good memory. There's basically no difference, Neil believes, between kelpies and border collies, and indeed both are crossbreds from the same basic source. The kelpie, however, seems not to have as good a memory as the collie. While a collie will remember a lesson from the day before, the kelpie needs to go through it again. However, collies tend to lack initiative and independence. 'It always will be a kelpie that does the legendary feat like retrieving five runaway cattle that escaped to the mountains,' says Neil.

But whatever the breed, your chances of getting a decent pup are increased, Neil says, if you go to an established breeder who also successfully trains and trials dogs. And yes, of those 50 dogs with him on the Queensland trip, about 36 pups and young dogs are for sale.

Basic care of the dog involves tying it up short so it doesn't fall off the ute or get snagged around objects. And he's particularly heavy on 'Gold Coasters': 'You try going to the Gold Coast with a couple of hundred thousand dollars and see if you want to work after that,' he says in explanation that a working dog should be tied up whenever it is not actually working.

But back to the school in progress in sheepyards in some far-off town. You might see Neil with his tight mob of quiet sheep running clockwise around them and a pup on the opposite side doing the same. When Neil switches direction, so does the pup. He corners the sheep and points to demonstrate that the pup will move opposite to the way pointed. It's all to reinforce that wolf instinct buried in the brain of every shepherding dog. He demonstrates how to link these natural characteristics in with commands which will eventually lead the mature dog to work counter to his instinct.

Then it's time for the psychology of livestock to be explored and, for this exercise, Neil paints up a quiet mob of sheep in different colours to demonstrate the role of the leader of the mob. By using gentle dogs, it can be seen that the leader through the gate is nearly always the same one.

'Then we put in a rough dog and immediately he'll chop up the order,

362

knock over the leader, and turn him into a tailender—totally changing the psychology of the mob. Because the tailenders then start going through the gate, they don't know how to lead, consequently they get half way through the gate, turn, and before long you get a row of bums in your gateway.'

People then try to shift them with tougher dogs: 'They try and shift them with force, but you don't untangle a ball of string by yanking at it, do you. So I let them make a great mess in the yard and everything goes wrong. Then I go in with my dogs and unravel them straightaway, simply because they are receptive to commands and they get into position. It's not the sheep that are wrong, it's because the dogs are not in position.'

After problem-solving sessions on matters like dogs being 'too fast'— 'That's rubbish. You want a dog that's fast. The problem is it's working too close'—they tackle a few other sacred cows. 'Teaching a dog to sit is the ruination of a dog,' says Neil. It eventually means they give up trying to head off the 'antelope' because they can never get to them.

There are lessons on backing, mustering a big mob, casting, and teaching how to push stock away. The final exercise involves people being paired up as 'dog' and 'handler', trying to work sheep. Besides being entertaining, it helps participants to understand things from the dog's point of view.

'Above all, the schools teach people where to stand and when to keep their mouths shut,' says Neil. It sounds like advice for more than just dog handlers.

ACCORDING TO DAD
Wendy Treloar, Cummins, South Australia

Boots was a barker, a biter and a marvellous watchdog—but not much good at anything else. He only *thought* he was a sheepdog. Our cats lived in trees. But he was loyal—he loved all our family and slept beneath his master's bedroom window. He would always be at the back door to greet us each morning with a smile. But he was not even half-decent as a sheepdog.

My father, a pioneer of the district, always had good dogs, so we always had to justify Boots's consumption of dog food and his sheer existence—especially as my Dad had Nicky, a dog who could do everything that was asked of him. Everything. Dad continually compared his dog with ours. He forgot how much training was required to achieve such perfection—and that it was all the actual shouting involved that taught his daughters how to swear.

Nicky knew, according to Dad, whether or not he was going to town (good clothes) or around the farm (old clothes). Our dog, Boots, leapt onto anything that moved, no matter what it was wearing. He *loved* barking all the way through towns, stirring up the town dogs. He thrived on going to footy practice too, on the back of the farm ute—plenty of noise and action. But everyone kept their distance.

Nicky, according to Dad, 'slept at my feet and knew a mile from home when it was time to sit up.' Boots *never* stayed 'down'. He hung over either side of the ute, around corners, and leaned, as far as was possible, into the driver's face, where he puffed and dribbled. His frantic galloping from side to side one day caused him to be sucked out by a passing road train. Neighbours recognised the wounded, snarling and mortified dog by his bristling neck hairs and quickly devised a foolproof 'dog retrieval' scheme whereby they grabbed, lifted and threw, then shut their car boot simultaneously.

Boots wasn't born fierce. He just was never friendly to strangers. After an illness and a visit to a vet when a pup, he reacted violently to anyone who appeared as though they may be aiming a thermometer at his rear end.

Dad's dog, according to Dad, *never* attacked chooks. Boots did. He loved chasing and playing with chickens if the chance arose. Boots was caught 'red-handed' one day with a dead chicken, so we tried an old remedy. 'Tie a dead chook around their necks and they'll never touch poultry again,' they had said. Ha! We did that and he ate the chook.

According to Dad, Nicky followed him around the paddock during seeding, only pausing to rest when the combine was filled at headlands. Boots, when weary, slowed to a walk right in front of the wheel, making us stop. He then rode on the wide old tractor seat, eyes closed, paws and head on the driver's lap. His breath and body odours were hard to take—but it was in the days before tractor-cabs and radios and air-conditioning, and it was better than no company at all during the long tractor hours.

According to Dad, Nicky obeyed his commands and knew what meant what. Boots didn't. 'Right back' to Boots meant get up on the back of the ute. 'Around' to Boots meant run around anywhere. 'Trough' meant a swim, never mind about showing the sheep where water was.

According to Dad, his dog mustered at just the right distance. Boots couldn't stand that. We called him 'ALB' (aggressive little bugger) as he worked so close to the mob the sheep thought he was one of them. We called Boots 'Smoko' too, as it was only at shearing time he was really good at anything—*food*. He loved hot toasties. He eyed the old shearer called Tog and, pressing close, begged him to part with some of his food.

Nicky, according to Dad, knew his place in the shearing shed: 'Never on the board and only in the shed at penning-up time.' Boots didn't. He roamed. It was *his* territory and if forced to defend it, he did. Whenever Boots was needed for penning up, he would be stalking the shearers' dogs and claiming and staking out his patch. And he never worked for the boss's missus.

Dad's dog never bit anyone. Boots did. Often. Never savagely, but as a warning. When it became unsafe for neighbours to get out of their car and conversations had to be shouted from half-wound-down windows, we had to consign Boots to the great salt patch.

When Dad retired, *his* dog was put to stud at the kennels where he was bred and lived in stately dignity to an old age. He couldn't have come to our place. He was always bashed up by our bitzers.

Dad still lives nearby. He reminds us frequently of how bad our dogs are. None of ours would have saved our lives as Nicky did his when the sugar gum fell and pinned him to the bulldozer. Nicky licked him and kept him conscious until Dad got free and found help.

The older the old farmers get, the better their dogs were!

ONLY ORNAMENTAL
Joyce Shiner, Albany, Western Australia

On a bleak July morning in 1940, we heard the convoy moving out under cover of darkness, just as they had come. For more than a week the white-gum ridge above the homestead had concealed a battalion of soldiers from the Northam Military Training camp.

It was said to be a survival exercise and all week long small parties of khaki-clad men had straggled around the district trying to live off the land. They were hungry and readily accepted what food donations we made. Garden vegetables were consumed on the spot. Fresh-laid eggs and Keep-eggs also failed to reach camp, judging by the piles of eggshells behind the trees outside the orchard fence. The rabbits were also temporarily eradicated, leaving paddocks looking as though a major battle had already taken place where the warrens had been ripped open with shovels and bare hands.

The last time I saw them, they'd come stumbling up the path like a bunch of weary schoolboys, khaki shirts and baggy shorts, their thick woollen socks hanging over heavy army boot-tops. They were following the little Scottish sergeant, who was being towed along at a rather undignified rate by a big yellow dog on a length of frayed binder twine. As they scuffled into a semicircle around the basket of wet clothes I was pegging on the line, Scotty said, 'We've come to say goodbye t'ya. An' me and the lads thought we'd like to show our appreciation of your generosity by offering you our mascot.'

I looked at the dog, a handsome, noble-looking creature, but I said, 'It's a sheepdog we need.'

'Tut, tut,' said Scotty. 'Not too loud, or he'll bring all the ruddy sheep in the district and we'll be had for sheep-stealing.'

'What's his name?' I asked, trying to ignore his tomfoolery.

'Teddy,' they chorused, but the dog was too absorbed in the activities of some hens scratching under a carob-bean tree to recognise his name.

'He doesn't look much like a sheepdog,' I observed. 'Looks more like a poultry retriever to me.'

'Well, lady,' said Scotty, 'ye could set the dog t'mind the bairn and bring in the sheep y'sel'.'

There was a shuffling of boots as Scotty went on: 'Well, chaps, it looks like the firing squad for our faithful friend.'

'You mean shoot him?' I asked, thinking to myself that he might be just what Bly needed to bring in the cow at milking time, as Peggy was one of those exasperating animals that seemed to have to graze all the way home. The clan was beginning to break up, so Scotty said, 'I'll tell y'what, lady—we'll leave the dog with y' until y' good man gets in and we'll come back tonight and see what *he* sez.'

I brought the collar and chain from our last beloved sheepdog and Scotty fastened the collar around Teddy's neck, leaving him chained to an old fig tree near the back door.

When Bly rode in that evening, I heard him snorting as he dismounted: 'What the devil is this! Who does it belong to.' he asked.

'He's supposed to be good with sheep,' I said lamely.

'Looks more like a blasted Alsatian to me,' he scoffed.

I recounted the story briefly as he handed the bridle reins to me and walked toward the dog. Teddy wrinkled his nose, showing strong, white teeth and looking very ugly. We offered him food and water but he ignored it. I told Bly that the soldiers were coming back that night to see whether or not we wanted the dog, but he scoffed: 'That's what *you* think.'

At the end of the second day, the dog still refused to eat and, as it seemed there was no getting near him, Bly said, 'We can't keep the poor brute chained up forever. We'll have to think of something.'

A little later he came from the house carrying the rifle. At first I thought he meant to shoot the dog, but he cocked the rifle and handed it to me, saying, 'Now I'm going to walk straight up to the hound and let him loose. He can go to Timbuktu as far as I'm concerned, but if he turns on me, let him have a bullet anywhere you can . . . I'll finish him off.'

It wasn't easy to keep the rifle steady, even though I rested it against the verandah post. Bly walked matter-of-factly to the dog, who had his eye on me. Bly dropped the chain from the collar and the dog bounded over to me! We fondled him and called him a good dog, then he went careering around in circles and back to us again and again. Bly emptied the bullet from the rifle saying, 'He's all right. It was only fear.'

He put the gun away and I continued with preparations for tea, while the dog went scampering around the orchard. When the dog returned a few minutes later, he dropped one of my best laying hens at Bly's feet, but before he could get angry, a handy hint came to mind—one we had been storing for just such an occasion. Taking the dead bird by the legs and the dog by the collar, Bly administered a token beating. Feathers went in all directions, while the dog yelped and writhed, then capitulated with his four feet in the air.

Teddy proved to be utterly useless with sheep and despite Bly's painstaking attempts at training him to bring home the cow, he would desert and make for the house.

Early one morning Bly came to the bedroom searching for bullets in the drawer. 'I'm going to give that mongrel hound a lesson in obedience,' he said. 'I'll shout "come behind" and if he doesn't, I'll fire a shot into the dirt just ahead of him. Don't look so worried, I couldn't hit a moving object if I tried.'

I must have dozed off, for presently there was a lot of scratching and scrambling on the polished lino in the passage, and the next instant the whimpering hundred pounds of dog landed on top of me, flapping his ears and spraying blood everywhere, trying to get under the covers. I was still trying to get him off the bed without waking the baby when Bly strode in demanding, 'Where's that fool of a dog?'

'I think you've killed him,' I wailed.

'Nonsense,' he declared. 'I merely did as I said I would.'

Then, when he took a look at the dog, lying as still as death at my back with his head on the pillow, he went quiet. We got the flaccid body onto the bedside mat and dragged him out into the daylight.

'He's still breathing,' Bly said. We started to search for the wound and found, to our surprise, that all that blood had come from a minute hole in the tip of one ear. Bly insisted it could only have been made by a grain of sand sprayed up by the bullet.

As soon as Bly's back was turned, Teddy came to life.

He wasn't even a good watchdog, but he certainly was loyal and very ornamental, and he never even looked sideways at another fowl. Bly reckoned the new roll of barbed wire, left where they had cut the fence, was the army's way of saying 'thank you'.

TRAINING THE OFFSPRING
Marjorie Noll, Ballina, New South Wales

When I was a small child in Victoria, we lived on a sheep property owned by my father. Our working dog, Sally, a beautiful sable kelpie, was also the mother of all our dogs.

She usually had two pups, and my father trained them by attaching them to Sally with straps when they were about six months old. Sally would walk along, moving the sheep. The pups on the straps would do the same as Sally, and every now and then she would lick the pups—I'm sure telling them they were doing well. After two weeks they would be out on their own and really worked well.

My father could always sell these pups if we did not want extra dogs, and was always complimented on their being well trained.

WASHAWAY WONDER
Peter Mercer, Euroa, Victoria

There is great benefit from breaking in a young dog by always using the same commands, the same signals and insisting that it does what it is told from the start.

In the late 1930s I was pleased to be given the job of jackeroo on a beautiful property in western Victoria. It was quite large and in a lovely red-gum area. Several permanent creeks ran through wide, deep valleys which had well-grassed, gently sloping sides.

The manager was a very experienced man and good with sheepdogs. As a young man he had worked with Mr Walter Field, a well-known breeder of good dogs and a successful trials man. We made inquiries in the district and soon heard of a chap who was breeding Field-type dogs. They were of medium size with quite long hair and prick ears, all black except for a little white bib on the chest. We decided on an alert and friendly young male pup and called him Rod.

When he got going and was under some control, I was instructed to see that he always came around behind me. When I held out my right arm and said 'go back', he was to go to the right hand side of the mob. If I held out my left arm and said 'get over', he was to go to the left side of the mob. He was always expected to turn the mob and then return to me the way he had gone out. If he 'crossed his cast'—that is, going from my right across in front of me to the left of the mob (or the other way about)—he would be spoken to severely. I stuck closely to these rules and he developed into a beautiful dog that I could use to bring home to the shed or yards any mob without the slightest worry.

One day we had mustered about 900 young ewes and were travelling home with them along one of the broad valleys when I stopped to block a rabbit in a hollow log. Looking up I saw that the mob had gone around the head of a small but steep-sided washaway and was heading back to cross the creek again down below to the right. I said to my dog, 'Go back', and off he went. However, he found he could not easily cross the washaway, so went up to the head of it and then worked his way down the right hand side of the mob, quickly shifting the ewes away from the steep edges as he went, turned them in the direction of home when he got to the head of the mob down near the creek and came slowly back to me.

Over the last 50 odd years I've seen many dogs at work and feel quite sure that a very large proportion of them would have taken the easy way—gone past the head of the gully, crossed their cast and raced down the left side of the mob, thereby pushing the sheep towards the creek and quite probably making them splash unnecessarily through it.

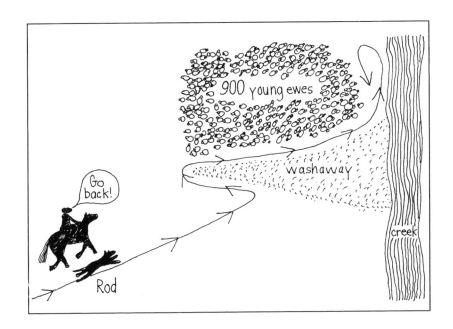

'WATCH AND LEARN'

Peter Murphy, Mildura, Victoria

During 1985 I was studying at a Victorian agricultural college where dogs played an integral part in the management of sheep and cattle.

One of the farm staff who was renowned for his dog breeding and training would often sell the progeny to students. In most cases they were students who had absolutely no use for a working dog, but fulfilment of the agricultural image required a dog to stand in the back of a ute. I knew a couple of blokes who had bought these dogs and witnessed the world of new interests owning a dog opened to them. Among these interests was the old favourite, sheepdog trials.

It was at one of these trials that two college lads, clad in the appropriate bush gear, dogs by side, were questioned by Ted, a so-called expert in the field.

'Are you blokes entering those dogs in the trials?' he queried.

'No, mate. We've just come to watch the event,' they replied.

'Probably just as well because those dogs look pretty useless to me. Take that one, his eyes are too close together, back legs are bowed, front legs

371

are too short,' and so he continued until he had exhausted every fault that could hinder the performance of the dogs.

With their pride shattered, the lads were convinced there was no future for their dogs. Through sheer embarrassment they hid them and returned to catch a glimpse of the master at work with his perfect dog. Patiently they waited until finally Ted stood forward with his dog. It was his turn. A flock of sheep was released in the distance as the judge explained the rules.

'Not a problem,' was the confident reply from Ted.

One mighty whistle and the dog was off. Seeing the young lads nearby, Ted turned to them, smiled and said, 'Watch and learn.'

The two *were* watching and couldn't believe what they were seeing. The dog was running straight for the middle of the flock, certain to cause absolute chaos. When Ted turned around, he too saw what was happening and quickly tried to remember the command that would rectify the situation and save face in front of the students. Ted cupped his hands around his mouth and, as loud as he could, yelled, 'Split them.'

There were roars of laughter from the crowd and then Ted's ultimate humiliation—disqualification.

The lads returned to the college, their pride restored, to gleefully tell the story of the great sheepdog expert. As the story floated around it was exaggerated to the extent that Ted's commands also included 'Leave those three' and 'Kill that one.'

NO, YOU GO FIRST

Charles and Moira Warburton, Lyndhurst, New South Wales

The usual procedure on a rice farm when checking the level of the water in the rice paddies was to send the sheepdog up ahead to scare off the snakes. These would be lying in the sun on the grassed rice banks, waiting to catch frogs.

Randy, our working kelpie, soon woke up to the system. Certainly he would start off in front of us, but then invariably he would leap into the paddy and kindly let us lead. We would always have to do his dirty work—scaring off snakes and disposing of any within reach of the irrigation shovel.

For seven or eight years we tried many times to correct the procedure but when Randy got that faraway look in his eyes, we knew our efforts were useless.

HEELING THE RUNAWAY
Daphne Bannerman, Macleay River, New South Wales

When my elder daughter was born, we had a blue heeler dog. While being a very good dog with the cows, he was also very good with her.

From the day she came home from the hospital, the minute she cried, he would bark and carry on. I always knew when she was crying if I was outside. He had a track worn around the house.

When she learned to walk, he followed her everywhere, but the minute I called her and she started to run away, he would knock her over and wait until I got to her.

SMUG SUZIE
Liz Bishop, Laggan, New South Wales

As soon as she saw me I knew we were not going to get along. It was obvious she thought I was intruding and should get no respect from her.

In the beginning I hoped I would overcome her attitude. I complimented her, gave her lots of affection and generally went out of my way to become her friend, but to no avail. She never overcame her contempt for me. I was from the city and she was of the country—and no way was she going to let me forget it.

We started to work together, along with Nippy and Lassie who had decided if the boss thought I was all right then I couldn't be too bad. On a typical day we might have to bring in a mob of sheep for drenching or crutching. We would pack lunch, put the dogs in the back of the Landrover and set off on a bumpy gate-opening trip.

Being in charge made me feel quite important, but Suzie just knew I had to be brought back to size. I'd open the door of the Landrover and send the dogs off. 'Go back—far back,' I'd say, and two streaks of enthusiasm would race away. Suzie would jump down and slowly make off at her own pace, giving me a withering glance over her shoulder. Eventually the mob would arrive with Suzie in charge. She would just gently hold them together, no mad dashing about and yapping. She knew her job and did it well—without any help from me.

One day when I had the mob to myself, the boss being away, I decided to drench them in the old race which was held together by bits of wire and several poles. I had put them through there before, so saw no problems. But I didn't take Suzie into account, did I? It was her moment of glory. I was totally at her mercy. I would get the mob into the race and she would promptly put them back out. I roared. I yelled. I told her to get in the Landrover, to go home—just get out of my day. The non-barking Suzie turned into a yapping, growling, snarling monster—not directed at me. She was just telling the mob that I wasn't the boss and not to be fooled—she would save them.

It wasn't long before bedlam reigned supreme—scattered sheep, shattered nerves. Then, feeling she had achieved what she had set out to do, Suzie went and put herself under the Landrover in the shade. I'll swear she laughed at me for the next hour, smug beyond words.

The boss had to shoot Suzie later because she had cancer. I wept to think that one of the personalities I loved in my life had gone.

MOVE OVER!
Shirley Low, Port Lincoln, South Australia

Ringer, that was his name—this large, sleek, black kangaroo dog. A top dog he was, when 'roos and emus were causing such devastation in crops. He was indeed the 'ringer'.

Years of hunting and tramping over the hills had built a very close rapport between him and his master. When I became the third party in this arrangement following our marriage, another side of Ringer emerged.

If we walked side by side, Ringer was never content to walk alongside his boss, but always pushed his way between us as if to say, 'He was mine first!'

Just a dog? Sometimes one wonders.

WHY BOTHER ABOUT HER?

Cheryl Lockhart, Wedderburn, Victoria

Sam, our kelpie–retriever cross, tends to be a very possessive dog. He usually lies on his mat beside the kitchen table, near Dad's chair. Once Dad finishes his second cup of tea, clanks the cup back on its saucer, slides his chair back and says, 'Righto, better do something,' Sam is promptly up on his feet and whining (we call it talking as it is a very loud 'Aaauurr-ar-ar' deep in his throat) for Dad to get going.

As soon as Dad stands up, Sam takes off into the lobby, ready to fly outside. Much to Sam's chagrin, though, Dad always gives Mum a goodbye kiss and hug. Talk about jealous—Sam comes rushing back in, barking and jumping all over Mum and Dad as if to say, 'Hey, come on, Boss! Why bother about her? Let's go!'

As always, Sam gets his own way, trotting out before Dad with his tail and head high in the air.

BOXER

Rod McIntyre, Pambula, New South Wales

An old cockie once told me
That he liked to pick the runt,
I had no better theory then
So I thought I'd take a punt.
He was the smallest of the litter
From Dad's kelpie bitch called Jen,
By old Cobber who was really
Working at his prime back then.

Well he grew into a useful dog
In a funny sort of way,
Although he had this tendency
To muck around and stray.
He'd go off chasing rabbits,
Lead me almost to despair,
Yet when I really needed him
He was always there.

And he seldom did the wrong thing,
Like split the mob in half
Or push them too hard up the hills,
And he often made us laugh
How he'd take his share of credit
When the job was finally done,
Although Cobber had done all the work
While he'd had all the fun.

Yet . . . he had one tasteless habit.
He used to mount the lambs
And other creatures, if they'd stay still,
Though he wouldn't take on the rams.
And oh—how he'd embarrass me
When the ladies were about,
I used to have to lock him up
And hope he wouldn't get out.

I became a bloody laughing stock,
I could see the people snigger,
And although I tried to hush it up,
I found it hard to figure.
Till this sheila up and asked me
As I went walking past her,
Was it true what they were saying
That dogs take off their master?

Now he's not the type of dog
That you'd take to any show,
The distractions there would be too great,
If you ever let him go—
And if I put him in a sheepdog trial
I'm scared that we would find
He'd give a whole new meaning to the phrase
'Push up', from behind.

PART 3
CROPPING
COUNTRY

Where paddocks wave and rustle like green-gold taffeta, a dog can have a heap of fun. When the machines move in to cut and tie the fabric into knots, comb it into windrows, and to extract the grain, a dog with time on its paws can run down a fox, deliver a message or even 'drive' the ute.

With the humans safely tucked up in their air-conditioned tractors or headers, or delivering grain to the silos, dogs can enjoy unfettered bliss. They lie around in the shade watching everyone else work, or peel away to visit an obliging friend or two.

Because their farms are multi-enterprise operations, these dogs have to be versatile too. They can sniff out a lost hat, move pigs, or do some pretty fancy mustering in difficult conditions.

There are dangers, though—big, unforgiving machines, snakes, baits, argumentative farmers and even . . . low-flying aircraft. The dogs in cropping country are a gallant lot indeed.

MIND YOUR MANNERS
Denis Adams, Apsley, Victoria

Dad's Uncle Ralph has become a legend in our family. He was a drover in the 1920s and we always delighted in hearing his stories.

His most popular route was up along the Coorong with 'coasty' sheep collected from the south-east which he would take to the districts further north. After feeding them gently along the grassiest roads for a while, they'd make a splendid recovery. Then he'd take them back to their homes. Once it was discovered that Coast Disease was simply a deficiency of trace elements, Ralph's favourite job ceased to exist. He'd loved travelling along the Coorong. It was teeming with fish and wildlife then, and Ralph was a campfire connoisseur long before the Bush Tucker Man got it on the act.

Sometimes he hired sidekicks. Few were satisfactory, though, and none was half as loyal and dependable as his sheepdogs. Ralph loved his dogs. They never got on the grog, never demanded money, never argued or shirked their duty, no matter how tired and hungry they were. They also had better manners than some of the people Ralph met.

You hear of drovers cutting fences or opening farm gates to sneak extra feed for their stock. It was not Ralph's way, however. He got on well with most landowners. Sometimes he took farm dogs with him to train. He was able to help farmers out in many ways and usually they were appreciative. Better being asked in for a yarn and a cuppa than being hounded out of the district.

There was always the odd person, though, that no-one could get along with. One of the nastiest specimens Ralph ever encountered was a newcomer to one of his favourite wheat-farming districts. He was a man so lacking in bush etiquette that he didn't even say, 'G'day.' He came charging into Ralph's camp in his buggy, scattering dogs to the four winds and almost skittling Ralph. Then he began maligning all sheep and all drovers, concluding his attack with threats of physical violence and legal action if just one of Ralph's sheep got into his wheat. Not only was he concerned for his wheat crop, he warned Ralph in no uncertain terms to keep his sheep moving past his farm. Apparently all the roadside grass was his too.

Ralph was too flabbergasted to make a suitable reply before the aggressive cocky had whipped his horse up and headed back to his farm. 'That fellow could do with a lesson in manners,' Ralph spluttered at last to his dogs. They were just as offended as their boss and were looking disdainfully at the vanishing buggy.

There is a close, almost psychic bond between most drovers and their dogs. Not many farmers have their dogs with them night and day, seven days a week. Ralph's dogs were a sort of extension of his personality. They knew almost by instinct exactly what he required of them without a word or gesture from him.

That morning the dogs got the sheep moving with more vim and vigour than usual. The sheep hardly had time for a bite of grass on their way to the forbidden wheat crop. By the time they arrived, the wheat cocky had his large family drawn up in battle formation, armed with sticks and stones and backed up by a motley mob of dogs. 'Keep them sheep moving!' the farmer shouted as he and his small army of kids and dogs moved along just inside their boundary.

The fence was in a shocking state. Fair enough to be on hand lest any sheep push through. Not knowing Ralph or his dogs, the farmer was not to know that normally some of the dogs would have stayed between the sheep and such a rickety fence. There was no excuse for his verbal attack, however, or for his possessive attitude to the roadside grass. Pointedly ignoring all the fuss, Ralph let the horses pulling his little wagon stop for a spell while, with studied nonchalance, he leaned back in the seat. His dogs, taking their cue from him, also decided to take a rest.

Sheep are only stupid when it suits them. Within seconds they had summed up the situation. Soon they were pushing through the fence in a hundred different places, skipping and bucking light-heartedly as they ran rings around the opposition, grabbing great mouthfuls of the young crop. There was pandemonium from the farmer, his wife, and all their kids. They yelled and screamed, ran this way and that, waving their sticks, throwing their stones, jumping up and down and thrashing their arms about, vainly trying to turn the invasion of the woolly monsters. Their dogs had cleared out for home, thinking the sticks and stones were meant for them.

Before long the farmer and his family had all collapsed exhausted, leaving their crop to the mercy of the sheep. All the farmer could do was glower his hatred at Ralph, who shook his head sadly, like a parent forced to punish a naughty child. It had all been so unnecessary. Not that any damage had been done. If anything, the crop would stool out better now.

Ralph gave his dogs the nod. Soon all the sheep were back where they belonged, feeding along well clear of the fence—exactly where they would have been all the time, had the farmer not antagonised Ralph.

There was neither physical violence nor legal action from the farmer. It had all been hot air. Ralph's only problem was living with his dogs for the next day or so. They were a bit swollen-headed for a while after they'd shown off in front of the farmer.

NO TROUBLE FOR PATCH
Prue Boswell, St George, Queensland

This is a true story about my brother's dog Patch. She was a black and white kelpie bitch and one of the best. My story goes back twenty years or more to when I was about seventeen years old. My father had asked me to go and bring in the killers. In those days it was all stock horses, no bikes, and of course no day's mustering was complete without half a dozen or more accompanying dogs.

I caught the old night horse and whistled Patch. She was the only dog who would work for me. The other dogs would only work for their owners. We had to ride about half a mile to the paddock where the killers were and it just so happened that this particular paddock had recently been pulled. For those of you who may not know what I am talking about, this simply means that two large bulldozers with a monstrously heavy chain attached between them had driven through the scrub pulling the timber down in their wake. Later the timber would be raked into rows and burnt, leaving a clear piece of land for crop planting.

Well, it was a really hot afternoon in the middle of summer and all the timber was lying on the ground. After about an hour and a half of sheer exasperation, I rode home without the killers, nearly in tears. The sheep just went everywhere—over logs, under logs, through logs, you name it, there they went. Dad, of course, wasn't very pleased when I turned up minus the sheep and, as it turned out, minus the dog.

It must have been about dusk a good two hours later when Dad called out to me, 'Come and have a look at this.' The sheep were in the yard and Patch was lying in the gateway, waiting for somebody to come and close the gate.

BUMPY LEAP TO STARDOM
Wendy Treloar, Cummins, South Australia

There can't be too many dogs in the world that have been hit on the head by an aircraft flying by. When our eldest son Peter bartered a box of seedling trees he had raised for a kelpie pup from a neighbour, we were not to know that Baldric, as he became known, would achieve such unusual fame.

Baldric is one of those hyperactive types that loves footy practice, flying over fences and jumping onto anything. Consequently he scores more rides on trucks than the other dogs in the family, simply because he can leap so high. He soars up from paddocks, chasing after birds which he races for miles.

Baldric was all set to compete against my other sons' dogs in a home-style obedience and sheepdog trial, but the event was totally upstaged when Baldric became too famous to compete in anything. Before this terribly important test of the worth of the various dogs—and accompanying ego-boost to the successful owner—took place, the sons had a job to do in the paddock.

The aerial sprayer had been called in and Peter and the two other boys, John and Michael, had to act as markers for the plane. As the plane zoomed in, Baldric did his usual leaping, nipping act as it went overhead. Suddenly, the pilot was heard to mutter over the two-way radio: 'I think I've hit your bloody dog.'

Peter had heard a thump and when he looked across, there was Baldric, prone—out cold in the crop. John couldn't leave his mark but yelled out to Peter, 'Pick up the gun. We'd better put him out of his misery', not believing for a minute that the dog could have survived the thump they had heard.

Feeling miserable and wondering how on earth he would manage without his now special mate and good working sheepdog, Peter also kept marking the runs until the plane had completed the paddock. Then they both raced back to try to find the dog.

Baldric had already come around and was staggering, with a definite sideways tilt, toward the ute for which he aimed, leapt at and missed, getting another thump in the process. Peter lifted him up onto the back where, apart from his eyes sticking out quite noticeably, he appeared unharmed. He must have leapt and been hit by a wheel, but not hard enough to kill him.

Apart from short-term memory loss, he is back to leaping for birds, but absolutely hates the sound of planes. He barks frantically when one comes too close, but he now stays right next to Peter's legs when marking for agricultural spray planes. The pilot, by the way, was very pleased to know the dog was alive.

So, after a cartoon in the local paper depicting Baldric as the Red Baron, as well as a photograph and story, the planned farm dog trial seemed a bit tame and the other competitors slunk off miffed. No-one, it seemed, could compete with such a performance.

IN A STATE OF SHOCK

Malcolm Seymour, Miling, Western Australia

My black and tan kelpie was eleven months old at the time of this story and was spending a lot of time with me as part of his training. During the day, between spells on the header and trips to the silo with the wheat trucks, he would sleep on the passenger-side floor of the utility.

Harvesting a long, narrow, sand-plain paddock next to a shire road one day, I noticed as I came around the top corner that the header steering was not normal. One of the back tyres was half flat due to straw stuck in the valve. Since it was too flat to carry on with, I had to walk about one kilometre to the other end of the paddock where the truck and ute were parked next to a gate leading onto the road. I drove the utility, which had the compressor on the tray, back to the header to blow the tyre up again.

That being done, I was then faced with the problem of returning the ute to the other end of the paddock and another long walk. Because the paddock was clear, I decided to point the ute straight at the truck, put it in low-range first gear, and let it get there on its own. I tied the steering wheel to the seat springs and started it off slowly back down the paddock.

Carrying on with the header, I kept one eye on the progress of the ute to ensure I was near the truck when it arrived. As I went past I saw that the dog, who had been asleep on the floor, had woken and jumped up onto the driver's seat to see what was happening. I was getting close to the truck with a header bin nearly full of wheat when I noticed that a car had pulled in off the road and a salesman was standing waiting for the ute to arrive so he could tell the driver all about his product.

I stopped at the truck and left the header unloading to walk over to the ute which was just arriving. The dog was sitting in the driver's seat, front paws on the steering wheel, being watched by the salesman, who had just realised the dog was apparently in full control. Opening the door, I pushed the gears out and turned the engine off. I casually remarked to the surprised onlooker that, although the dog drove quite well, he wasn't heavy enough to work the clutch, so I had to start and stop the ute for him. Conscious of the header unloading, I quickly found out what product the salesman was selling, decided we didn't need any, hopped back on the header and carried on harvesting.

The salesman, who was a stranger to the district, appeared to be suffering from mild shock as he slowly drove off. I have often wondered since whether he ever mentioned to anyone about the smart dogs in our district, or if he wakes up in the early hours and lies awake worrying if he really did see a dog driving the ute that day.

A NOSE FOR FLOPPY HATS

Joan Judd, Wycheproof, Victoria

We were in the middle of haymaking, so I decided to take lunch out to my husband, who was on the rake. While he ate his lunch, I offered to do a round or two. It had been a few years since I had raked hay, so he gave me a quick refresher course. 'There's nothing to it,' he said. 'Just keep the front wheel of the tractor beside the windrow.'

It was hot and sunny so he offered me his green floppy hat as there is no cabin on the old Fordson. It felt a bit big, but as it was a still day, I thought it would do the job. However, I had hardly got started properly when a sudden gust of wind whipped the hat off—only for it to disappear into the newly raked windrow. It took some time to pull up as the hat blew off right on a corner and I was concentrating on keeping the front wheel on the inside of the windrow, as instructed, while getting the rake around the corner.

My husband and I spend ages walking up and down the few chains of windrow,' peering, throwing and kicking the hay, but to no avail. 'Not to worry—surely it's not that valuable,' said I nonchalantly. My husband replied that some poor cow might choke on it. He then hopped onto the tractor and went up and down, again and again, slowly raking and turning over the hay with me peering intently—only to eventually give up.

'Why don't you go home and bring Mitch back,' my husband suggested. 'He's always sniffing out birds and rabbits. He might find it.'

I thought it was a pretty remote chance but as I had nothing urgent to do, thought I would give it a go. I duly returned to the paddock with Mitch and another of my husband's hats. I shoved the second hat at the startled dog's nose and told him to 'fetch'.

I think he thought it was a good game, running up and down after me along this line of hay. On our third trip down, he suddenly stopped, jumped over the hay to the left, jumped back to the right, sniffed the top of the windrow and started scratching at it. I enthusiastically helped him and a few inches down from the top was the old, green, floppy hat.

I was amazed and my husband was suitably impressed when the dog and I drove over to the tractor to show him.

EARNING HER KEEP

Joyce Chandler, Ceduna, South Australia

We picked her up from the neighbours down the road. She was a small brown kelpie pup and we named her Brownie, for obvious reasons. She was a good all-round farm dog—travelling on the front of the motorbike for sheep work when needed.

What was unusual about Brownie, and it is a story we remember with humour, occurred back in the days when harvesting involved the bagging of wheat. It was then loaded onto trucks to be driven the long miles to the port where it was stacked ready for shipping to overseas markets.

Brownie would always insist on riding on top of the load, wind whistling through her hair as she enjoyed the view perched high on top of the bags. When we arrived at the weighbridge, no amount of calling would get Brownie off the load and she would inevitably be weighed in with the bagged wheat.

However, when weighing out after the wheat had been lumped off the truck, she could never be found—thereby always giving us a higher net weight and a few more shillings for our load. When we were ready to leave the port, the perverse creature would hop up into the cabin of the truck and sleep all the way home on the floor. It would be interesting to know how much extra she earned for us over the years.

BUSH REMEDY

Joyce Shiner, Albany, Western Australia

In 1940 my husband Bly bought a little red cloud kelpie pup at a sheep sale in Northam. He carried her fifteen miles home in his greatcoat pocket after having missed the train. We named her Greta and she became a great worker and family pet. She was one of those dogs that would bring the sheep along behind a horse, or a slow-moving vehicle of any kind, and she would never leave an animal behind.

When I contracted German measles my brother-in-law's niece, Rita Neve, came to Bakers Hill to help keep house and care for the baby. It was shearing time and our lovely little kelpie suddenly began to take fits. We thought she may have been poisoned, and all kinds of remedies were suggested such as cutting the tip off an ear to make her bleed, giving her a bit more strychnine, large quantities of warm milk, salt water and so on—but still she suffered paralysing convulsions.

Rita asked if she might try a remedy she had read about in the *Western Mail* which had worked when they had tried it on their own sheepdog. Rita was a big, strong young woman and she found it no trouble to pick up the dog and swing it around and around by the hind legs. This caused the dog to vomit up what looked like a poison bait—and after a few minutes the fits ceased.

Greta was back to her old self by the next morning and anxious to be back at work among the sheep. She continued to serve us faithfully until her death at nine years of age.

CUT OFF AT THE BLOODLINE

Frank Bawden, Tumby Bay, South Australia

My father, who had been a farmer all his life and a bit of a wag, became fascinated by the working dogs at the Tumby Bay sheepdog trials.

He decided that he would like to buy a dog and go into breeding good dogs. He had it all worked out. He told us—a family of six boys and a girl—that he thought he would charge a $5 service fee and take his choice of the pups for allowing outside bitches to come to his dog.

He eventually made his purchase of a fine border collie dog at the trials that year. The owner said that Dad could collect Spot in a few weeks. When he was finally collected, Spot proved to be a good sheepdog, but a better playmate for the boys. After a wrestling game with Spot one day, young brother James came rushing in to inform the old man, 'Dad, Dad, your dog's got no nuts.'

Dad didn't miss a beat and calmly informed us that he'd still take the service fee but would have to overlook his choice of the pups! It seems that gelding a dog was common to stop people obtaining the bloodline.

WORKING OVERTIME
Irene Arnold, Tambellup, Western Australia

Our family was watching the television program 'Countrywide'. Skipper, our red kelpie, was lying at our feet.

A close-up of a dog working sheep appeared on the screen and immediately caught his attention. Then, as some sheep went to break away, Skipper rushed forward to head them off.

You should have witnessed the look on his face as he came from behind the television set wondering where the sheep had gone.

META THE MESSENGER
Jean Ferres, Macclesfield, Victoria

My father used to walk lambs five miles from Kallista to Emerald to put them on the Puffing Billy train to market. His kelpie, Meta, always helped him. They used to pass my father's brother's farm in Emerald and on the way home would always drop in for a chat. The dog got very used to this routine.

One day my father was sowing oats on his farm at Kallista. Huge flocks of crows kept flying in to eat the seed. He shot at them to deter them, but then ran out of ammunition.

He decided to write a note to his brother in Emerald asking him to send him more. He attached it to Meta's collar and sent her off. It was a good five miles there, but in due course she returned with the ammunition. Luckily it had been rolled in a waterproof cover as Meta had crossed a creek on the way.

NO WAY DO WE PART!
Elsie Dunn, Macgregor, Australian Capital Territory

My father was a farmer at Majura in New South Wales, but we had to move when Dad's land was taken up by the government in 1900 to help form Canberra.

I was five when we bought land near Boorowa, between Canberra and Binalong, to re-establish our mixed farm. We grew wheat, oats, barley and lucerne. Dad also ran a lot of sheep, a few cattle, 32 bullocks for his team which were changed about each day, and Clydesdale horses for the wagon and farm work. We each had a saddle or stock horse and there were several for sulky and buggy work. We also bred pigs.

At the age of fourteen, I was asked by Dad to drive 52 pigs about two and a half miles across our paddock, then across the end of the wheat paddock, across a grazing field, through a gate, across the main road and through the gate of the man who had bought them.

I set off early, riding my pony and taking my ever-faithful fox hound, Patch. He was a tall, sturdy and strong dog who was always with me. It was a difficult task keeping the pigs along the track. Without Patch I would never have managed. It took a couple of hours to get to our gate on the main road. Nearby was a huge dam and the hot, tired pigs immediately headed for this and wallowed in it blissfully.

I saw with dismay that along the road a drover was bringing a large flock of sheep. I rode along the fence and asked if he could hold his sheep until I had got my mob of pigs across the road. He called a couple of kelpies to his aid and soon had the sheep stopped. I rode back to the dam, which by now was full of wet and muddy pigs over which Patch was standing watch. I told him to get around them, so in he dived. He swam back and forward around the pigs, snapping and barking, while I swung a stockwhip and rode close to the dam's edge. Between us we got them out.

I opened the boundary gate while Patch stopped the pigs from returning to the dam. I then opened the gate on the other side of the road and we rushed them across and into the other field where the new owner was waiting—although he never offered to help.

The drover came along when the road was free. He must have been impressed by our performance as he offered to buy both my dog and horse.

'No way do we ever part!' I told him, nevertheless feeling quite elated.

Later that night he dropped in to see my father and told him how well I had done a very difficult task. He again offered a good price for the dog and horse, which was very flattering, but we took great delight in rejecting it.

GRINNING FROM
EAR TO EAR
Val Pate, Renmark, South Australia

When we were first married my husband owned a nondescript red kelpie called Sailor. He was a constant companion as well as a workmate on our partly developed property at Mingenew in Western Australia, some miles from the nearest neighbour. He was also somewhat of a lady-killer.

In mid-January one year, we were doing some contract harvesting about five miles from our home for a neighbour. Just after lunch during the hottest part of the day, we took a load of grain into the local siding, leaving Sailor with the tractor and header. We considered it would be kinder and cooler than taking him in the hot truck with us.

On our return Sailor was missing. We thought he had taken umbrage at being left and had returned home. When we discovered he wasn't at home, we tracked him for about eight miles along the road heading north into town until nightfall prevented us going further.

Next morning we headed into town 22 miles away and asked around if anyone had seen him. No luck. We proceeded on to visit my parents, nineteen miles north of town, to be greeted by a furious father and a very contented Sailor grinning from ear to ear.

The night before, Father had locked, so he thought, his bitch in the shearing shed in solitary confinement for the duration of her heat—only to be greeted in the morning by two happy dogs lying peacefully side by side.

Sailor had been with us three weeks earlier when we had all had Christmas with my parents. He had not seen the young 'lady' in the interim, but had been quite prepared to walk 48 miles in the heat, somehow knowing the timing would be right. And to think we had been feeling sorry for him.

EVENTFUL ENCOUNTERS
Jeff Eime, Port Lincoln, South Australia

I am a retired wheat and wool grower. In my many years in the industry, both in the lower north and on Eyre Peninsula, I bred border collies. I found them very intelligent and faithful. One of these was Rip, who, in his working life with me, had several eventful encounters with wildlife.

During harvest one year I went out reaping early to finish off a small area that took between ten and fifteen minutes for each lap. Rip was following the header out to one side, putting his nose under heaps of straw and chaff left the day before from the machine. I was just about around for the first time when up jumped a big fox. I saw the fight begin and, as the header moved past, thought the fox, like many before it, had no chance.

When I returned about ten or so minutes later, I came over a slight rise around a corner of the paddock. I could not believe my eyes. There was the fox, mounted on Rip, with his front paws clasped tightly around Rip's hindquarters in the mating position. Both the dog and the fox had their tongues hanging well out and were puffing. There was some blood over them: When I called out, 'Get him, Rip!', he spun around. The fox, still gripping him, came around as well.

They were both near exhaustion, so I stopped the header and took a shovel off the machine to go and strike the fox. I hadn't quite reached them when the fox let go and tried to run off. It stumbled and Rip grabbed his throat and finished him off. I have often wondered if others have seen similar acts of cunning by foxes trying to overpower dogs.

Foxes weren't the only wildlife in our paddocks. One morning I sent Rip to round up the rams and ration sheep that grazed in a small paddock near the homestead. He went in the right direction but could not jump through the cyclone fence like he usually did, so I helped him. He went a few yards and looked back at me. I sensed something was wrong so I went to him and noticed he was having trouble walking. I took him back to the house where he just lay down—obviously he was a very sick dog.

I rang the vet and went into town with Rip lying motionless on the seat. By the time the vet saw him, Rip was completely paralysed. The vet suggested putting him down.

'Not on your life,' I protested. 'Not my Rip.'

The vet gave him little hope, but gave him an injection of antivenene and handed me some pills to give him every so often. I had a heavy heart as I took him home and put him in a stone shed that had doors. I made a bed for him out of bags and lay him out flat. He couldn't move any part of his body, not even his tail or ears. We could look into his eyes and see life, but that was all. His jaws and tongue wouldn't move, so we had to lift his head up to pour liquids down his throat with his vitamin tablets and a bit of mashed-up food. We kept a good eye on him, talking and patting him whenever we could spare time from farm duties. This went on for about three weeks.

One evening when covering him for the night, I noticed his heart was beating very unevenly. I went to bed thinking Rip would die overnight, but next morning he was still with us. His heart was beating more evenly. Then one morning when I went in and spoke to him, the tip of his tail moved a little. It was the first sign of life in three weeks. Every morning after, I noticed small improvements. First his tail started to wag, then his ears moved. Then the jaws started moving, and he could drink. We had won, but there was still a long way to go.

Eventually he started dragging himself around the floor, so we made a portable sling for him. It was a frame on castors that we hooked a bag into, then put him in it. His legs could just reach the ground. After the first five minutes in it he was exhausted, so we just did a little at a time. Later he pushed it outside. He seemed to be getting stronger and was now looking more like a healthy dog even though he still could not walk.

Sometimes we used to carry him to other sheds where we were working. One day my son, who was filling the ute with petrol, yelled out to me, 'Look at Rip!' There he was, standing up alongside my son. That was after ten weeks of tender care and encouragement. Before he was ill he had always seemed to understand what we were saying, so perhaps all the talking we had done, telling him to hang on, had helped.

He was once again able to come along with us mustering sheep, and he seemed to be looking forward to working again. Some weeks later he seemed very much alive and as I had a flock of 400 sheep needing to be moved to a back paddock, I thought I would give him a go. The sheep were about 500 yards away, around a dam near home, so I sent Rip around them, keeping my other two dogs with me. The tail wagged, the eyes shone and off he went. He couldn't get there fast enough. He rounded the flock and brought them up to me—but the exertion had made him very tired.

I praised his effort, which seemed to please him, and then I told him to sit where he was until the ute came to pick him up later. The other dogs and I were going to take the mob out the back. We moved off, looking back when we got to a rise and there, about 900 yards away, Rip was still sitting. It took us an hour to travel the mile and a half to the paddock and my son arrived soon after with Rip in the back of his ute. Rip jumped out and gave me a lick. My son had picked him up right where he had been told to sit an hour earlier.

As I said before, Rip always seemed to know what we were saying to him. I'll finish by telling you of an incident that always makes us laugh. If perhaps one of us had to go away for a few hours, he would greet us on our return and we would ask him where everyone was, mentioning a name or two. He would promptly turn around and lead us to whoever it was we wanted to see.

One day I was on the long-drop toilet near the shearing shed with the door shut. All of a sudden—bang, it flew back against my leg, giving me a hell of a shock. There was Rip with, I think, the biggest smile on his face I have ever seen, and my son behind him was having a good laugh too. One of my sons had asked Rip where I was . . .

PART 4
BLIGHT'S BLOCK

When the call went out nationally for tributes to working dogs, numerous large packets of wonderful stories started arriving from a place called Narrogin in Western Australia. When I subsequently discovered that Narrogin, on the edge of the wheatbelt, south-east of Perth, had been officially dubbed Sheepdog Country by its citizens, it seemed imperative to pay a visit and meet Geoffrey Blight, the person responsible for that avalanche of dog stories.

Just in case I was under any misapprehension about this being the land of the sheepdog, I was met at my lodgings by the ebullient Blight at 6.30 am in a ute loaded down with twelve working dogs of all shapes and sizes, including one that looked very much like a dingo. So began a most informative and entertaining visit . . .

THE STORYTELLER OF SHEEPDOG COUNTRY: A PROFILE OF GEOFFREY BLIGHT

Angela Goode

Geoffrey Blight, 53, is round, jolly and whiskered, a farmer, mulesing contractor, philanthropist, entertainer and writer. He is the driving force in the Narrogin shire to publicise the contributions of working dogs far and wide. It is a task he tackles with almost envangelistic zeal. He wants to see signs and a large sculpture in the town proclaiming to all that this is indeed Sheepdog Country.

Pride in the achievements of the district's dogs is certainly justified. From a tiny local working sheepdog club founded in 1983, two of its seven members have hit the heights. Last year Doug Connup won the Australian Sheepdog Challenge Series, which was broadcast on ABC television on 'A Dog's Life', with Glenromin Dinny, a dog bred by Byn Dinning. This year, Phil Slade won the second Challenge of 'A Dog's Life'.

Geoffrey Blight's own dog, Broc, first alerted him to the extraordinary abilities of dogs. Broc, who lived to the age of nineteen, was half-dingo, the result of a mating with an obliging kelpie at the famous Haddon Rig property in New South Wales: 'He became a legend on the hundreds of farms we worked on,' says Blight. 'He had a way of coping with everything. He was the most popular animal I have ever known.' Broc became so famous on Blight's mulesing rounds that even today people bow their heads in respect.

Blight had the body stuffed and mounted. While most sheep farmers usually hate dingoes with a vengeance, Blight is different. The dingo, he says, is able to be trained, is highly intelligent and also has a greater ability than most dogs to read a human mind. One of his stories—'A Northern Territory Kelpie'—reveals some of the talents he has observed. These talents are shared by many kelpies, a fact that, according to Blight, is hardly surprising since many have a dose of dingo in their genes.

So, in Narrogin on the morning of my visit, I climbed into the ute and embarked on a day of total 'indogtrination'. First we visited Old Bill, whose story—'Not the Best Dog in Highbury'—as told to Geoff Blight, appeared in *More Great Working Dog Stories*. It was a story of great poignancy about the night 50 years earlier when Bill returned home unannounced during war leave to find his dog was there to meet him at the railway station when the train pulled in at midnight.

The existence of a telepathic bond between dogs and humans is something that Geoff Blight is convinced about. He has seen evidence of it countless times during his voluntary work with handicapped children, when one of the team of dogs he takes to entertain the children befriends the loneliest and most afflicted child and makes it respond. 'Look at Sam there. He spends his whole life just telling people he likes them,' says Blight. 'Where in technology can you find a machine that tells people it likes them? Dogs will sit for hours with crippled children that other people are frightened of.'

To further demonstrate his dogs' talents Geoff Blight has, on a number of festive occasions, driven sheep and a variety of other animals through the main streets of Perth. The parades were ostensibly to publicise the Royal Show or help impart the true meaning of Christmas, but leading the merry throng of ducks, geese, goats and sheep and wearing a pet chook on his hat, Geoffrey Blight had a heart bursting with pride that his dogs were able to keep their concentration amid a noisy lunchtime crowd of 20,000 people.

On our travels that day we also visited Ken Atherton, president of the working sheepdog club. Ken had some young pups he wanted to put around a mob of sheep so Geoff could take his pick. There in the watery morning light, the five little workers and their mother loped around the sheep. Before long we were enclosed in the mob with no way of escape since the pups had obeyed their instinct to return the prey to the head wolf.

After cups of tea inside the house, we departed with a little blue kelpie bitch added to the load on the ute. She had an interesting free-flowing style and showed potential as a trial dog, so Geoff Blight was going to start her on her way. Although he hasn't had the same success as fellow club members, Geoff Blight still enjoys the challenge of training and working dogs to a high level.

His great pleasure at present, however, comes from working in the feedlots where wethers are held before being shipped to the Middle East. While a dog trial hinges on a dog's finesse with three sheep, loading trucks and moving 40,000 headstrong wethers through the yards takes not only finesse but also extraordinary stamina and courage—for dogs and handler.

Blight leaves Narrogin on ship-loading days at 2 am for a 4.30 start. He and his three rotating teams of four dogs don't knock off until about 8.30 at night, and sometimes ten-thirty. 'It's just another challenge,' says Blight. 'Up until I went to the shipping job, the biggest mob I'd moved with one dog was 5,000 sheep. The job is teaching me how far I can test the bond with my dogs. But I can tell you, the more I see of men, the more I like dogs.'

We finished our day in Sheepdog Country by driving over to Geoff's farm where the eight or so dogs he hadn't been able to fit onto the ute that morning rattled their chains with ecstasy. It was time for their run. If you have never seen twenty or more dogs taken for exercise at once, I can tell you it is a stirring sight. A seething mass of bodies, which included two yellow dogs a bit like Broc, rushed from tree to tree before taking off across a paddock.

One may indeed wonder when this man—who has also been a shearer, a racehorse trainer, stud sheep breeder and is the father of five sons—ever gets time to produce even one dog story, let alone the hundreds in his folders produced since only 1986. Suffice it to say, if Geoffrey Blight does not wake up until 3.30 am, he considers he has 'slept in'. He writes in the quiet of pre-dawn the stories he has heard the day before in the yards, at a trial, in the street, or around the mulesing cradles. Many of these he tells at schools and community groups. He has also released a cassette tape, *Broc Sheepdog Country*, of his stories and poems to raise money for cancer research.

Geoffrey Blight remembers with affection the storytelling tradition he grew up with. As a small boy, he stayed up all one night listening to the old men of the district yarning as they kept vigil over a bushfire, watching for outbreaks. In the main street of Narrogin, there would always be knots of people standing around talking. They are not there any more. People now rush past in cars and are too busy even for a chat. He regrets that technology and television in particular have interfered with that storytelling art. Geoffrey Blight is doing what he can to keep the tradition alive.

I SEE ROVER

Geoffrey Blight, Narrogin, Western Australia

'I see Rover, Rover sees me.' As a five-year-old boy these were the first words I learnt to read and understand, as any child would have done if they'd attended a state school in Western Australia in 1944. To me they had a special meaning. I knew Rover. He was part of our family, a cattle dog and pet. A massive brown and black kelpie-type dog with a white chest and blaze, he had been a member of the family since my parents' marriage in 1937.

Many things made the dog I knew special—his gentle handling of the milkers, his dedication to keeping the garden free of cheeky hens, his babysitting my little sister. Everyone seemed to know Rover but, above all, he was said to have saved my life. Following the birth of my older sister and myself, Mum made a practice of leaving us, either in the pram or on a rug on the grass outside, in the company of Rover. Should either of us cry or move, he could be counted on to bark or attract my mother's attention. Many early photographs that go beyond my memory bear witness to this, showing us sitting with, or embracing, the big dog.

It was when I was able to walk and really get around that one day Mum made the frightening discovery that I was missing and could not be found anywhere. Our small dairy farm was on a winding little road on the north side of Mt Shadforth, near Denmark. We were only chains from all manner of dangers—forests of impregnable thickets, running creeks, pigs and horses, Guernsey bulls.

The alarm was raised and neighbours were summoned to help but, as time passed, I was not found on the farm. A creek ran to the north of the house and it was believed I may have fallen in. Nobody had thought I might have crossed it by following the road. I hadn't been seen on the road.

The search of the creek proved fruitless, several more hours passed and I still couldn't be found. By now everyone was nervous. The only bright spot was that Rover was missing also. This was important—with Rover I had a chance, without him the outlook was very grim.

The day was drawing on with more and more help being called. It was by sheer luck that a young lad, riding his bike a long way from the search area, saw something move in the bracken adjoining a forest reserve. He stopped, but it had vanished. Then he saw it again—it was a dog's tail moving slowly through the bracken away from the road and into the thick forest. He whistled and there came a bark. It wasn't his dog. He whistled again, but still it didn't come. He hadn't been told about Rover but he knew I was missing, so he decided he'd take a look.

It was a very excited young man who pushed his bike feverishly into my parents' farm bearing a toddler under his arm, followed by a big dog. The lad told how he had found me carrying a billy only yards from the wattle thicket, where vision was down to only inches, and there were numerous creeks and swamps. My mother offered thanks to the Almighty for our safe return. I showed no ill-effects from my adventure whatsoever.

It was this incident, more than any other, which made Dad very proud of Rover. As the dog grew old and his time was near, Dad decided he could only replace him with the best dog that money could buy. He answered an advertisement for a guaranteed, Queensland blood, champion stock, trained blue heeler. A supreme cattle dog which was to cost a month's wages and replace the reliable old mongrel who had been part of the first twelve years of marriage and family. Dad knew the value of a good dog. I was living proof of that. He was going to have the best.

Arriving home from school one day, I found we had our new dog. Up until then, my after-school chores were to bring in the milkers and help with the milking. Our small farm boasted several little paddocks both sides of the narrow, winding road. To get the milkers, I would call the dog, go with him and open and close the gates and follow them home. When I opened the gate old Rover would take three steps into the paddock, bark loudly and sit himself down. The cows would immediately stop grazing or rise from where they sat and amble quietly past the sitting dog toward home. To keep control of the situation and to prevent loitering, the old dog usually made a habit of nipping the heels of the last cow or heifer through the gate.

Being a bit of an adventurer, I used to like to get a ride home. I would make haste and beat the slow-moving old dog to open the gate and try and get seated on the nearest quiet cow before he barked. There were only six in the herd I was not prepared to mount and I always made sure I didn't get the one that was going to be last out of the gate. The practice came to an abrupt end one day when Dad caught my sister and me sitting astride the same cow, Old Lady—strolling up the road, oblivious to the danger we faced if a vehicle should come along. With a solid slap on the butt, we were told it was not permitted.

Back to the day of the new dog: Dad told me he would get the cows in so he could try out his new acquisition. He was all excited with this dog. He had dreamed of an aristocrat, a true blue blood, bred from centuries of champions. He had spent as much on him as he had on any animal he had ever owned.

With me standing behind the gate, old Rover confined to the house yard, Dad gave the order and the young dog flew into action. Straight onto the heel of the nearest cow, then to the next and the next. Before Dad could stop him, the cows—with startled bellows, tails straight up in the air, the air full of flying wet dung—had rushed straight through the back fence, over the creek and into the swamp. My father's roar of outrage seemed only to spur the dog on as he flew from heel to heel or swung on any tail within reach. No matter how we tried, the cows would not leave the swamp and risk the dog, who Dad was persisting with—he was also trying to save face with Mum, who had not been at all happy with the price that Dad had paid.

Dark closed in. I was sent to bring the lantern so we could see. The dog continued his chasing while Dad bellowed and cursed the jungle of bog, scrub and reeds. I arrived with the lantern just as a number of very loud 'Come here' commands brought to heel the devilish-looking young dog, tail wagging and bearing a dead fox nearly as big as himself in his jaws. This proved just too much. The pure rage of my father as he kicked the air and cursed the 'dirty rotten BBB' was alarming. But he was totally unable to either catch or humiliate the energetic blue dog, who seemed to be enjoying the whole charade immensely.

We didn't get many cows out that night. Things were pretty strained in the house when we ate tea, everyone being careful not to talk about the new dog. I think Dad was having second thoughts about his would-be champion.

We did get the cows milked next morning but things warmed up again when the heeler almost caught the neighbour's daughter as she pedalled her bike frantically past the front gate. She wasn't so lucky that afternoon when the heeler, who by now had had some practice, caught her and tipped her upside down in the thick scrub on the road's edge, with her bike landing on top of her.

Dad's humiliation was complete when he went to put a rope on the old gelding to run the upset girl home. The now over-excited and uncatchable dog flew in and locked his jaw on the cart horse's heel, sending the horse galloping round and round the paddock with the champion, the blue blood, the best dog that money could buy, yap-yapping at his heels.

I was surprised when the school bus stopped to drop my sister and me off. Rover was there to meet us, as was his usual habit, when he should have been shut in the house yard away from the new dog—who wasn't to be seen.

I don't know what happened to our new dog, but I know when I was told to use Rover to get the milkers in that night, four of Dad's top pedigree Guernseys had the end of their tail bitten off. I think the bloke who sold Dad the dog probably thought he would be safer if he took it back.

Dad was always to have a dog, mostly good ones but nothing spectacular. He was content to settle for just ordinary, inexpensive pups that reminded him of Rover and who could be forgiven if things didn't always turn out right.

I remember best old Rover on a Saturday night when Dad and Mum, rug over their knees, sat tightly together on a cart seat. We children, on a mattress beneath them, would be cuddled up to the big warm bulk of Rover as the old gelding plodded through the cold, dark air to a dance or the pictures.

I remember him as together we travelled the creek's favourite gilgie holes, and his joyous bark and high-tailed carriage as he raced with me up and down the long lines of vegetables in our market garden. I remember his protective snarl if danger threatened, or beast trespassed on our path.

Strong, too, among the memories are those of my mother crying as we arrived home from school and Rover wasn't there. The words 'I see Rover' were no longer a reality, just a memory of a wonderful childhood with a dog. As time dragged me forward into youth and manhood, to other dogs and other places, I would often repeat these words to myself— 'I see Rover, Rover sees me'—as I sought the dog of my dreams among the adverts for champions, the expensive blue bloods and the unwanted mongrels. But never did I find one that could wear that coveted title among dogs of 'Rover'.

TRIALLING SHEEPDOGS
Geoffrey Blight, Narrogin, Western Australia

So often I have heard the comment, 'Trialling sheepdogs is far removed from the realities of sheep farming.' Unfortunately, after several years of trialling, I must agree.

Trialling sheepdogs is a good sport and very educational in teaching communication between dog and master, but it falls short by miles in demonstrating what support a top sheepdog can give in the real sheep world, where labour is very expensive, time is precious, hours are long, climate varied and sheep are most unpredictable.

Probably the major difference between a trial dog and one that is used to earn a living is the fact that in a trial the master does nothing to support the dog. In sheep farming and handling the master is continually working and the dog is supporting, quite often uncommanded and out of sight of the master. In a trial the dog is supposedly told everything it should do, which makes the trial a test of the master's sheep sense. But farm work needs a dog with initiative and commonsense, anticipation, endurance, strength and patience. It must also be able to cope with unpredictable situations and interference.

Not that a trial dog can't be a good farm dog, but I now believe the very best farm dogs are actually hindered by the restrictions on their movements and instincts that the discipline of trialling places on them. Heading sheep probably comprises five per cent of farm sheep work, yet is 75 per cent of trialling. Cover and cast are very important to both, but in farming a vehicle is used to help dogs gather sheep and check the paddock. Barking is frowned on in trialling but is essential to farm work. Most farm work consists of *driving* sheep. Most trialling consists of *drawing* sheep. A trial requires only fifteen minutes of concentration and fitness. Many farm jobs can last hours, if not days. A dog that over-concentrates tires quickly and will eventually quit.

No doubt the skill, or lack of it, of a dog is highlighted in trialling. His biddability becomes obvious, but not necessarily his loyalty, endurance and adaptability.

Every farmer knows there is a time in sheep handling when a dog might have to bite, even to save his life. (You can't bluff *all* sheep *all* of the time). A dog must be able to convey his superiority over sheep when tested. If he doesn't he will soon become a weak dog in a tight spot. But biting as a habit is undesirable and damaging, so a dog who only does it when he *has* to is the ultimate. How dogs work in the company of other dogs and men is a major factor in farming but not evident in trialling. Cunning is an important part of a farm dog's make-up.

No doubt the sheep trialling sport is a testing ground for sheepdog breeds in the same way car-racing might test the rubber used on a truck tyre. Ninety per cent of sheepdog triallers are old shearers and most know the difference between the sport and the job. Most of them have a favourite dog, but it's *always* the one that does the best farm work.

A SHOT OF WHISKEY

Geoffrey Blight, Narrogin, Western Australia

Back in the 1960s when I was much younger, I was working at an almost insane pace mulesing lambs seven days a week and well into the nights, because in those days no-one else would do it. I suddenly found I'd lost my sheepdog. To get by, I had been using my father's, but that was causing friction.

We had been mulesing for a Scotsman at Williams and he had a dog that was a biter. It actually killed four lambs the first day we were there. He was far too rough for me, but that doesn't mean he wasn't still there twelve years later. After he'd had some of his teeth kicked out, he actually worked sheep pretty well.

On that farm one day, I happened to be asked to shoot a dog that was blamed for much of the rough stuff and therefore had to be left tied up. I could see it was a yellow collie, a very pretty young dog, that had cut a channel round and round at the end of his chain, till he had nearly buried himself. What they had to say about him didn't impress me—he wasn't the sort of dog I wanted—so I agreed to get rid of him for them as he was said to be hopeless with sheep.

Shooting a dog is a job that sometimes has to be done and is often kinder than seeing an animal ill-treated. But I didn't have the gun with me so I ended up taking the dog all the way home, hooking it to the tank-stand until I could get around to the task.

Somehow, being tired, I forgot about him, and he was still there next morning. Being so pretty he had attracted the attention of my wife and my mother, who immediately suggested that, as I needed a dog, I should give him a try. I told them how bad and useless he was supposed to be, but that apparently wasn't sufficient excuse, so to please them all I actually took him down to the yards and let him go.

Well, I could spend all day telling you what farmers get wrong about their sheepdogs, and with Whiskey, as he was named, the Scotsman certainly was way out. He was what you call a good heading dog with a lot of cover and a fair amount of eye. He appeared to have none of the faults I was led to believe he had. No doubt an older dog had been influencing him and probably getting him into trouble. Very few farmers draw sheep toward themselves or go in front of the mob– most prefer to drive from behind, usually in a vehicle, tooting the horn every few yards and revving the motor to keep them going—so Whiskey's skills had probably not been recognised. I was quite taken with the dog and decided he was worth a try—anyway, I had nothing to lose.

He was probably the easiest dog I have ever trained. I went working at the farm he'd come from about a week later and he was already working far better than his former mate, who was still intent on chewing lambs to pieces. It was there I soon found out why Whiskey had not done well for his former owner. Every time he made a move, the other dog would attack him in jealousy. Whiskey, being no coward, would make a fight of it. This eventually led to 'the ripper' dog getting put on the chain and his owners, who were very good people, coming to realise why they had been so unsuccessful with Whiskey.

But I had one problem with Whiskey—he was too easy to make friends with. However, I was delighted that he got on with two Aboriginal workers I had with me and helped restore their confidence with dogs after their experience with 'the ripper', who'd bitten them too often. Everywhere I went people wanted to play with him because he was so attractive, and it started to ruin him at work. He started looking for pats. I wanted a dog no-one would be able to take again, so I started to teach Whiskey to bare his teeth and growl every time somebody stroked him. It wasn't hard to do and he did it to a T—and we were back in business, with him improving every outing.

I suppose I must have bragged about how clever I was, teaching him to growl and bare his teeth when stroked, because my young son soon woke up to it and used to show people, even though I scolded him. I soon found that every time there were people around, all the little ones would get Whiskey and cart him around to some unsuspecting mum and ask her if she would like to pat the dog. On touching him, only to have him bare his teeth and growl, the mums would usually go into orbit. On landing, they'd demand that their child, who by then was usually cuddling the dog, 'get away from it'. The kids would just laugh and demonstrate all over again what I had taught the dog, usually with Whiskey furiously wagging his tail.

Whiskey was a very useful sheepdog, particularly in the mustering of ewes and lambs where indeed he had some wonderful tricks. When faced with a bunch of breakaway lambs, he would head the front runaway and stop it, even by making it fall over. Then he would stand perfectly still for several seconds until the bunch halted, which it usually did. At this point, rather than try to cover the lambs, he would walk casually back toward the main flock and the runaway lambs invariably followed, walking all around him.

He was also a master at yarding lambs. Near the portable yards, when they would start to circle the flock rapidly threatening a break, he would go to the head and, rather than stop them, he would increase their speed as they neared the opening into the yards. He would then deviate, straight into the yards, with the lambs hot on his heels. By jumping the back fence before circling rapidly to the tail of the pursuing flock, he'd trap them neatly in the yards. This is a trick light-coloured dogs seem to do very well. I regret it was before the advent of the video.

Unfortunately, Whiskey's career came to a sudden halt in the early 1970s. He went mowing hay with one of my sons and when a rabbit appeared suddenly, he pursued it straight into the path of the mower. His hamstring was injured and as he was unable to run again, he lived on as a housedog.

His injury was a blow, but it was the day after Whiskey's accident that I was forced to take a gangling, ugly red kelpie with an undershot jaw from the pen where he had spent his first nine months, and use him to muster sheep. Little did I know, at the time, that this would be the beginning of a nineteen-year association with a dog that I later named Broc. Together we worked more sheep than most others would in Australia's sheep history. This dog is still regarded with awe in and around our district, which many have dubbed Broc's Sheepdog Country.

SHOWING THE ARISTOCRATS
HOW IT'S DONE
Geoffrey Blight, Narrogin, Western Australia

Many are the men who have been brought down to earth by skiting about their great sheepdogs. In half a century on farms in Western Australia

I've seen plenty come a cropper. When it comes to dogs, we're all in a class of our own.

One of the most memorable occasions was in the early seventies, out in 'wild west' Williams. I was a mulesing contractor and we had the job of doing about 3,000 lambs for a recently arrived English squire who came from generations of best British stock and knew the value of a good sheepdog. This had led him to buy the best (said to be state champion, in fact) sheepdog money could buy at the time. He was a beautiful border collie, trained to the whistle. The dog was about as obedient as I've ever seen.

His new owner was very proud of him. So much so that on our second day of mulesing, we were told by the English gentleman that a friend was bringing some British aristocracy, in Australia on holidays, to see the dog work. To this end, he had left a mob of 1,400 ewes and lambs to be mustered when the visitors arrived. He asked us to keep our kelpie, Broc, out of the way in case he interfered. Broc was locked in the car even though it was unnecessary. We did it to please the boss.

My crew for that day was a very strong eighteen-year-old girl named Judy, who was catching the lambs, and three of my sons, aged from twelve years down to six, doing the earmarking, castration, tagging, etc. The little six-year-old was dressed in a plastic urea bag and had to stand on half a 44-gallon drum. He was vaccinating and releasing the lambs. We were averaging about 1,200 a day, although our best day was nearly double that. By the time the four black cars, including two Mercs, drove in we were well and truly covered in the usual mess.

The visitors included a Lord and his Lady who farmed 6,000 acres just out of London, and also one of Western Australia's biggest sheep farmers, who was their host—all coming to see the best sheepdog in Western Australia. They never came near us, much to my boys' disappointment. We were well used to doing the tourist special (castration with our teeth), which usually left the visitors with a very gruesome picture of the Aussie sheep farmer.

Even though we didn't stop, the whole crew was all eyes as the boss, with his dandy little cap and whistle, was followed by a washed and, I'm sure, scented border collie. His guided his visitors out into the adjoining paddock and, after all the pleasantries, sat down, then cast his very obedient sheepdog. He guided him with well-rehearsed blasts on the

411

whistle, stopping and starting him to perfection. For a while it was all admiration. The big mob bunched and came up close to the yards where twenty people were standing admiring his skill and effort.

But these were ewes in 'wild west' Williams and the dog was new. They weren't about to make it easy for him. As the boss waved, whistled and sat the dog, first one lamb made a bolt, then another, then swoosh— they were gone. The dog was still rising and sitting to his orders, totally unable to hold the mob. They did it all again, and again, and again . . . each time losing them faster than the time before.

The whistle was now forgotten and the bellowing had begun. The guests were even asked to spread out around the sheep and help. Alas, all in vain. The sheep completely had their measure. Nearly an hour was wasted with the sheep not one bit closer. It was a very frustrated boss who had to give it away. I guess to save face, he brought his visitors over to see us since we were very nearly finished the flock we had been working on.

With a twinkle in their eyes, my sons went straight into turning the well-dressed visitors off tailing lambs. While I made certain I had the odd testicle still hanging from my chin, the boys were pumping out five lambs a minute with red bottoms, tags, earmarks, vaccination and drench.

The ladies weren't keen on watching and a couple of them had found Broc in the car and were talking to him. We broke our routine to refill the pen. My six-year-old, who was letting the lambs go and was covered in blood, jumped down, strutted over to the car and opened the door to let Broc out. He turned, pointed in the direction of the flock and, imitating his 'betters', shouted 'Way back, Dingo, you old bastard,' making the ladies flinch with his gusto. Broc, who had been watching the whole episode, strutted off at his usual gait towards the flock. We went on working, forgetting about him.

It was about ten minutes later when the guests were about to leave, having heard many excuses as to why the Champion had been unable to pen the sheep, that the two ladies who had been far more interested in watching Broc than lambs getting cut about suddenly became very excited and pointed at the flock coming in. It isn't hard to know why a dog who musters ewes and lambs every day might know something that a dog who is told how to muster three wethers in a trial might not. In his casual manner, Broc had ambled out around the big flock. Using his voice with great skill, he had the flock pushing up to the yards where now there were no people in the way. An open gate led to a few remaining lambs. The bolters of the flock, sensing escape, charged straight into the pens.

The twenty visitors just stood gaping in awe at the ridiculous ease with which Broc put in those sheep. He then sat in the gateway waiting for a very proud, six-year-old, blood-covered Australian boy to go and close the gate. The boy patted the 'old bastard' he was intent on calling 'Dingo' that day.

When one of the visitors said something to one of the older boys about how 'the dog could do anything', the lad replied that he still wasn't very good with the drenching gun, but they were working on it.

That was a long day and we had a lot of laughs about the look on the boss's face and his excuses. I also clearly remember reaching home well after dark that night and untangling a sleeping ball of dirty six-year-old boy, curled up in the lap of a big yellow dog on the back seat of the car, and having a great sense of pride in that hairy brute the boys occasionally called 'Dingo'.

DUDS
Geoffrey Blight, Narrogin, Western Australia

Anyone who breeds stock for sale has unsaleable culls or 'duds'. They have to be got rid of in the best and most humane way possible to make room for fresh stock. I had been breeding sheepdogs for a few years and selling about forty dogs a year. A week before Christmas is a time you often take stock of things. Wanting to cut down work in the holiday season, you don't want any unwanted stock to look after.

I had two dogs that were over a year old that nobody wanted. One was a kelpie runt and too small, the other a very rough-coated border collie and very ugly. They hadn't attracted any interest whatsoever and were costing money to feed—so they had to go. But when I went to get bullets I found my sons had taken the two packets I'd had, not even leaving me a single round.

When I tackled Mike, my eldest son, he wanted to know what I wanted them for so urgently. After I told him, he said if I looked in his ute I might find a couple of bullets to get me out of trouble, and get rid of the unwanted dogs. Sure enough, I found two, lying among the rubbish of the glove box. I decided I'd dispose of the dogs immediately while I knew where the ammunition was. It didn't happen, though, as neither bullet would fire. I pointed the single shot .22 and only heard . . . click.

That night I had a call from a chap wanting a dog. His dog had been killed accidentally, so he was impatient to replace him. A woman rang next day wanting a dog as a Christmas present for her husband: could he come by and pick one out? I had several very nice pups and didn't think I would have trouble supplying something suitable.

However, when the first chap arrived, he wanted an older dog that he could start immediately. I tried to tell him the eighteen-week-old pups would work but he wasn't convinced. I mentioned I only had a couple of one-year-old dogs that probably weren't what he wanted, but he insisted on having a look. It's crazy how some people select a dog, but this chap wanted the ugly dud the minute he saw him. He was just so much like a good dog he used to have, he had to be a good dog too. I suddenly found I had a cheque for two hundred dollars in my hand and only one dog to shoot.

I had to wait for the second chap to arrive the next morning before I could go to town and get supplies, including bullets. The chap turned out to be really fussy, and it didn't look like I had a dog to suit him. Pups from an Australian champion weren't quite it: too much eye. Brothers to a state yard champion weren't it either: too much bite. A top New Zealand Huntaway pup: too boisterous, too much bark. Then he spotted the runt. 'What's that one?' he asked.

'One that didn't grow,' I told him. 'He's too small.'

'Too small be damned. The best dog I ever had was smaller than that. Will he work?' the chap asked.

I wasn't sure but there didn't seem to be any reason he shouldn't. So I let him out onto the small flock we had been testing the dogs on.

The dog hadn't even reached the sheep when the bloke decided that was 'his dog'. Even I was surprised at how keen the little fellow was. I wondered later if it had anything to do with me trying to shoot him two days earlier with a dud bullet.

So it was Christmas Eve and. I had another two hundred dollars in my hand and no dogs to shoot. I had even suggested to the bloke a hundred and fifty for the runt was enough. He decided, seeing I'd kept him over a year, that two hundred was a very cheap dog. Blimey, I wish it was always that easy.

But that's not the end of the story. On Christmas Day I was bragging to my sons about the sheer luck of the dud bullets and being able to sell the two culls that the other forty customers hadn't wanted. I even had the dud bullets still in my pocket, so I put one in the old single shot to show Mike, pointed at the sky and . . . BANG.

PUTTING A STINK
ON SOCIALISING
Geoffrey Blight, Narrogin, Western Australia

Simon is an ordinary farm lad on a dairy in south-west Western Australia. To help get the cows in, he got himself a lovely blue heeler. He was very careful to get one with a really kind nature as he felt little would be gained by having a savage pet—although he did have friends who took delight in owning such dogs.

Cloudy was, as his name suggests, almost a crimson blue, and very lovable. As Simon gradually got him interested in the cows he found he was often distracted by visitors—they always made such a fuss of him that Simon soon realised it was spoiling him completely.

At the shed one day, Cloudy was working away exceptionally well when Simon spotted some children coming to play with the dog. It really annoyed him. They had been doing this far too often and he was getting nowhere. Suddenly he had a thought. Grabbing Cloudy, he deliberately dunked him in the large pile of fresh cow manure that always built up at the end of the dairy. He made sure Cloudy was well covered with it.

It must have been very confusing for Cloudy when suddenly the children rejected him and didn't allow him to jump up. They left quite quickly. A very disappointed Cloudy went back to work, much to Simon's delight. From then on, as soon as Simon saw anyone coming, he would make every effort to find some fresh manure and dunk Cloudy's front feet in it.

It took Cloudy a while to get the idea, but with visitors it worked immediately. Now if you go and see Simon, you'll spot the very quiet heeler just sitting and waiting his boss's pleasure. He no longer needs 'to put his foot in it' to make himself unpopular with visitors.

A 'NORTHERN
TERRITORY KELPIE'
Geoffrey Blight, Narrogin, Western Australia

Annie was the first dingo I owned. She came from Central Australia via a truck driver who dropped her off at a friend's wildlife park.

As she crossed the Western Australian border she had to become a 'Northern Territory kelpie' in order to get around state laws which attempt to prevent ownership of a dingo or dingo cross dog. Bureaucracy ignores the fact that a large percentage of working dogs in Australia are already dingo crosses. However, this was a fact about which I was not confident when I was younger. After an association of over nineteen years with my big ginger kelpie, Broc, I decided I owed it to him to investigate his heritage.

I had tried to find books or information that could tell me more about dingoes, but nowhere was there anything about the possibility of dingoes making working sheepdogs. I had heard stories and spoken to men who said they had owned dingoes or dingo crosses. In the end I decided to get myself a dingo and test out my own theories.

It wasn't easy and I waited a long time before Annie turned up. Many people had tried to own dingoes as pets but most had difficulties with the Agricultural Protection Board. Someone usually made a complaint about the dingo getting into a neighbour's chooks or the like, and they were confiscated or destroyed.

I noticed immediately that there were many clear similarities between my kelpies and Annie. So I started training her as a sheepdog. She was friendly, very attractive and intelligent.

The first big shock I got was when I released her into an open paddock to see if she would cast. After sending two border collies around the flock, I let her go. She took off in hot pursuit but the collies got around the sheep first. She didn't waste time. Instead she cut straight across the backs of the running flock to reach the collies. It was the best bit of high-speed backing I have ever witnessed.

She proved all my suspicions—especially with her ability to read my thoughts. She wasn't as good as the sheepdogs I had—no doubt because they came from 400 years of rigorous selection—but to me there was no question that these dogs were very much a part of the kelpie history.

She often gave me heart attacks when she took things into her own hands. I became very wary of using her in public. Although she worked sheep, she did bite sometimes and I would have to discipline her. She was also very good at climbing out of her pen.

There were some incidents that I remember well. On one occasion a government stock inspector was looking at our sheep when Annie got out. I wasn't around and the farm hands panicked that she might get into trouble. They saw her trot past the yards where the stock inspector was. As she disappeared over the road, the workman set out to find me or my son Mike. He realised the department would love to have evidence of stock damage. It would solve their problems of dealing with my dingo venture and the publicity it had gained when I displayed her at the Perth Royal Show.

When the workman found me I rushed down to where Annie had last been seen. There, standing near the gate, was the inspector. In the paddock were over a thousand weaners moving slowly up to the yards with Annie trotting along behind. I soon got her out of sight.

Some months later she climbed out again. On that day I had to attend my mother's funeral some 250 kilometres away. I was upset and impatient to leave when I noticed her standing in the paddock over the road from my house. When I tried calling her, she wouldn't come. I got angry and went after her, only to find she kept retreating across the paddock.

I couldn't get near her. I went back home and released some of her sheepdog mates for a run, thinking she would join them. The little rotter didn't. She just stayed over the road and continued to retreat if I approached, or came back toward me if I turned to walk home. I was getting very annoyed. I had to leave and no way was I going to leave her loose with no-one around for two days.

417

So I got the ute and went after her but she even outran that. Halfway across the paddock I realised she was going to beat me to the next paddock. This wasn't mine, so I stopped and returned home ... for the rifle. It seemed the stories I had heard about dingoes going wild might indeed be true. I had never had this kind of trouble with her before. I certainly didn't want to shoot her, but I was running late and out of ideas. When I came out with the rifle she was back near the ute. As I approached she seemed to read me and took off down the exact same line she'd followed each time before.

I jumped in the ute and pursued as fast as the paddock's rough surface would allow, noticing that she was occasionally looking back to see where I was. There was a small group of trees right in the far corner and she was heading for it, flat-out. I thought she would just jump through the fence and keep going, and I tried to get the rifle ready to get a shot.

Suddenly, without warning, as she reached the trees she stopped, turned and sat. I couldn't believe it. As I drove right up to her, I could see her lip curling, which was her way of talking to me.

What was even more surprising, right beside her, jammed between two small trees, was a woolly hogget. It couldn't get out. I don't know whether Annie had chased it in there or what had happened, but it was unharmed and I let it go. Meanwhile Annie had jumped up on the ute and was ready for a lift home. I suddenly realised how close I had come to shooting her, believing she had gone wild.

I have seen several films and read the stories of dogs that wanted to tell their owners something important. Even after 40 years of working nearly every day with dogs, I had thought many such stories were probably mostly fictional. However, on that day, a very sad one due to the loss of Mum, I was confronted with evidence I can never dismiss. A plain ordinary desert dingo went to quite a deal of trouble—and risk—to attract me to something it felt I should know about.

SEEING-EWE DOG

Geoffrey Blight, Narrogin, Western Australia

People often ask me what is the cleverest thing I've ever seen a dog do. No doubt some of the dog acts in circuses are extraordinary, but they are taught to the dog. I have also seen some very good working dogs doing great things under command. However, my soft spot was always for the intelligent dog working out the solution to a problem on its own. Very few dogs get such an opportunity and very few people believe a dog has that ability.

The most intelligent dog—although not necessarily the hardest worker—I ever encountered was Elbon Park Gus AA259, a Scottish merle shorthaired border collie. The incident that brought me to that conclusion occurred on a property just east of Narrogin in the late eighties. We had mustered a flock of ewes and lambs into portable yards but one ewe, totally blind, had separated from the flock and was left half a mile away, continually walking in a tight circle.

The only way to shift such sheep is to catch them and return them to the flock where they survive by following sound and smell. When a flock becomes infected with pink eye, temporary blindness can cause trouble and even make sheep work dangerous if a big wether takes fright and charges into you. I have known a farmer to be hospitalised through such an encounter.

Anyway, Gus spotted this sheep and as he was never happy leaving a sheep anywhere, off he went. The men and I watched with interest, believing he would certainly fail since the sheep couldn't see him. But we underestimated old Gus.

After he realised that normal tactics weren't going to steer the sheep, Gus gradually got in closer and closer. He moved first to one side and then the other, letting the sheep bump into him so it would turn. Gus never gave up. We had to go on with the mulesing and tailing, so for some time we forgot about Gus—until one of the men drew our attention to the fact that Gus was still at it and had halved the distance into the yards.

So for the next half hour we watched as we worked, and to this day how I wished I could have filmed old Gus. Realising that to make

419

progress he had to keep touching the sheep, he continually put himself in a position where the blind ewe walked into him before he could eventually walk it into the yards. The ewe followed in the same way it obviously did to survive in the flock. It took him a while but he did it without any commands or assistance whatsoever.

I have never seen another dog move a sheep in such a fashion. I doubt that many believe a dog capable of solving such a problem, part of which was understanding the sheep was not like normal sheep and couldn't see him.

ENDURANCE
Geoffrey Blight, Narrogin, Western Australia

I know there are many stories about the endurance of a good working dog, but often it is hard to measure these feats in concrete terms. However, in 1964 we got a good indication of the endurance of one of my kelpies when I did some contract ploughing for a chap in the north-eastern wheatbelt.

Using an International A554 tractor we drove in transport gear (I guess about 16 mph) for 22 miles and ploughed for a straight 36½ hours at 6½ mph before returning home. It was over 39 unbroken hours, except for refuelling, nature stops and meals. It was approximately 240 miles or 380 kilometres. Throughout this whole time the sheepdog, Sally, never dropped behind the tractor. She arrived home looking exactly as she had left.

I must point out that the kelpie, who might have had some labrador in her, had made a habit for two years of running with the working tractors. Catching field mice, she was probably as fit as a dog could be. I don't recall her being anything but lean, and she was none too great at working stock. Her demise came in 1965, when she was following a bulldozer in virgin bush and picked up a dingo bait laid by the Agricultural Protection Board.

TUCKERBAG TAILS
Geoffrey Blight, Narrogin, Western Australia

The most common way of counting lambs at tailing time is to count the pile of severed tails. Frequently there is a bit of argument about how many tails the dogs ate. Farmers have strange rules. If their sheepdog pinches a tail, that's fine. But if you're the contractor and your dog has one, he's at best likely to score a broken rib.

Yet the most successful working dog food I have ever used is unskinned lambs' tails. Dogs need to get used to them, but they certainly thrive on them. I now regularly feed over twenty dogs every day during tailing season on them.

The best dog I ever had on the job in the early years of mulesing was Broc. He lived on lambs' tails from May till November for sixteen years. On average he ate about nineteen as we started the day and another twenty at about 4.30 in the afternoon.

We had a lot of years of watching and counting his eating habits. Although there was always an open bag of pellets left for him in the garage, he rarely touched them while the tails were coming off.

In the early years I used to worry about the wool blocking him up but now, with the luxury of hindsight and experience, I realise that the wool was probably the secret to his long working life. Bowel cancer is a common killer of dogs and nature has a way of combating it. Modern pet foods ignore the fact that in their native state dogs were meant to consume prey with either wool, fur or feathers still attached to it. I have never had a dog suffer damage from the consumption of wool.

The dogs that eat the tails straight out are not a problem—let them have their fill. The ones that want to suck on the juicy end are a damned nuisance. They will spread hundreds around all over the place if you don't watch them. So will the dogs that think it's a good idea to bury some. In order to see how many a dog would remove if left unhindered, we sometimes did a count, and noted that they're capable of disappearing with well over a hundred before tiring of the novelty.

That would be a hundred I don't get paid for, so I ensure the dogs don't get stuck into the tails until after they have been counted!

THE BEST SEATS FOR
THE BEST WORKERS

Geoffrey Blight, Narrogin, Western Australia

In all my years of going contracting on sheep properties in the southern part of Western Australia, I have always made a habit of giving the best seats to the best workers. In other words, the dogs rode in the front and the men on the back of the ute.

For many years I only had one dog and we usually travelled in a car pulling a trailer. This generally allowed the three human workers ample room in the car with the dog.

In later years I started using a one-ton ute with dog boxes on the back so a team of dogs could go with us. The dog boxes were extremely well built and comfortable. There were four compartments on each side of the tray and their doors could only be opened when the drop sides of the tray were down, which was good insurance against a door rattling open.

Fitting up to four people in the cab was a very tight squeeze indeed. When we did try it we would arrive at our destination with all sorts of cramps. One of the lads working for us at the time decided that, as there were only four dogs on board, he'd throw an old mattress in one compartment and get in the dog box.

This certainly helped the space problems a lot. However, the lad was so comfortable—he was even able to sleep for the one and a half hours it took to get to the job—that the workers started fighting over whose turn it was to get in the dog box. In next to no time I had two workers stretched out in the box, which often led to one dog having to sit on the front seat.

When I arrived at the job, farmers never really got used to seeing me alight from the cab with a dog or two, then walk around and drop the sides of the dog box to let out the men.

A WORDLESS LESSON

Geoffrey Blight, Narrogin, Western Australia

Some years ago, I was asked to give the Children's Talk during the Sunday morning service at the local Narrogin Uniting Church. Our church is well attended with a considerable number of small children who participate until the Children's Talk, after which they branch off to their Sunday School. The time allocated for such talks is three minutes, although we have had some lasting many times as long, which weren't popular. As it was my first time, I was told to be sure and keep it short.

Being near Easter, I was informed that the thought for the day was the need for affection, loyalty and sacrifice in life. These are things I have often claimed I have learnt more about from a sheepdog than from some human beings. Therefore I decided I would take Broc, my sixteen-year-old kelpie, along as a prop, since kids are a tough audience.

Immaculately dressed in collar and tie, Broc walked into church close behind my wife and me and sat himself on the pew facing forward, with all the dignity of any other member of the congregation. Already he had the attention of every child in church. Half an hour later I was asked to come forward and give the children's address.

Old Broc followed me to the front where the Pastor had invited the children to come and sit. The dog sat on the carpet immediately in front of me. The children, immediately very curious, came forward and eyed off the well-dressed dog. While I began a deliberate search in all my pockets for notes I didn't really have, I relied on my intuition for what might happen next. Sure enough, I wasn't wrong.

A very small child, too young to have any inhibitions, suddenly wobbled forward and embraced the old dog, who responded quietly. Within seconds, every child in front of me became part of a tangled mass of patting, affectionate children, responding to a very near deaf sheepdog, who welcomed each in his own manner.

Needless to say, all the children were oblivious to my continuing search for the speech notes. The congregation was amused at the turn of events. My three minutes ran out very quickly. I quietly apologised for having forgotten my notes and explained that I'd intended to tell the children of the wonderful rewards of loving one another—though on this occasion, I would have to leave that message to my dog to deliver.

As the children untangled themselves and filed off to Sunday School, the Minister said he doubted if anyone present would ever forget the 'wordless lesson' which had been delivered that morning, given in affection by an old sheepdog.

BOB THE UNBEATABLE
Geoffrey Blight, Narrogin, Western Australia

Bob was a border collie that was said to be well bred. I paid $400 for him when he was about nine months old. I badly needed a dog to replace Broc and thought Bob was a quick solution, but he fell a long way short of the mark.

A big dog, he was supposed to have been trained, but whatever training he'd had was very limited. He had a bit of a cast at a speed that usually left a third of the sheep behind, and he loved to jump fences in the yards. That was about all there was to Bob. Compared to Broc he was as 'thick as a brick'.

Far too much eye made him very hard to get to respond to commands as he would stand and stare and stare . . . usually until you tossed something at him, at which point he would go flat-out at what he thought you wanted. He had two speeds—stop and flat-out. It was irritating, but in those days I believed a good trainer could change such things. I had as much to learn as Bob. Having owned only four dogs in 40 years had not given me much dog training experience.

I was told I shouldn't have bought him by someone who'd had him on trial. He called him a gutless wonder as he had showed a tendency to run off and crawl under the ute for this fellow. What he didn't tell me was that he had accidently hit him with a large stick he had thrown, cutting his eye as a result, an injury still visible at close inspection.

I tried to teach Bob to trial, and ended up with sheep going around and around and around until we were all exhausted, but finally one day I penned. It was the first time I ever had and I got a score of one. Meanwhile we had sorted Bob out in yard work and he had a couple of useful moves. He'd bark and he'd push or crawl through anywhere, no matter how the sheep might belt him around. I soon realised Bob was not going to be anything marvellous, though, so I started to get other pups, some even more useless, hoping for another Broc.

My trialling career was going well if making my mates laugh had anything to do with it. I often used to wonder how, after working so many sheep in my day, I could not seem to come to terms with the three-sheep trial, never seeming to get steady enough to look in control. I became known for my shouting at the dog in exasperation, something I rarely ever did away from the trial ground. I would get disqualified for everything in the book: walking backwards, patting my dog. Even if they didn't disqualify me, I'd end up running the sheep ragged by trying to get a dog up close, just as I had always worked them in the pressure of contracting.

I soon started to wonder whether I had any talent at all and whether I could make a dog do anything other than by accident. The thing that bugged me most was that several of the triallers became friends and I worked contract for them on their farms. My dogs would have guts and moves that made their trial dogs look weak. Many times they couldn't even yard a flock of ewes and lambs and my 'mad bastards' would do it with style, even with them being in the way. This had gone unnoticed and had led to me being given every conceivable bit of advice, much of which just frustrated me and made me even more impatient and hopeless.

Bob was always my masterpiece. I'd enter him in all three sections: novice, improvers and open. Strangely enough, he was usually so exhausted by the time the open came around that this was usually his best run, nearly always lasting fifteen minutes—of not quite catching up with three wethers.

We didn't have many utility trials in those days, where a dog has to work yards, but they held a big one at Muresk College to coincide with the Americas Cup Challenge in Fremantle. We were even lucky enough to have some American participants. It was held at night because it was January and very hot. I only had one dog I could enter: Bob. He wasn't much, but I really wanted to have a go against what could be argued as many of the best yard and field dogs in the world.

My run was on the third night and there had been some brilliant trialling. I'd been brushing up Bob as much as I could, and during the day he had been doing all the work of bringing in and taking away sheep for the trial—strangely, being as good or better at this than most of the dogs. Off the trial ground, neither he nor I were hyped up. We were just working and nothing ever went wrong. I'd had 40 years of this and I guess I did it well. But in trialling, you wouldn't believe what I could make happen.

The sheep were very big wethers. Many were stags that had horns due to late or faulty castration. They were also half-woolled, which sometimes makes them very hard to trial in smaller numbers as they tend not to be able to see the dog and panic when he is behind them. They are very apt to stand up and fight the dog, as I was to find out.

When my time came I started off well. Bob was behaving beautifully (for Bob). Blimey, I was in with a chance even. As we made the cast, the draw, the yards and so on, everything was on track. My excitement was rising . . . then disaster.

I was clearing the very tightly packed race and a big stag with long curly horns suddenly decided he was going to have Bob. The race was very narrow and didn't allow a dog to jump clear. Bob tried to duck under the charging stag as was his habit, but the long curly horns gathered Bob's hind legs, not only turning him up but dragging him heavily along the entire fence of the race. It was sickening and I made a jump at the sheep in the hope of helping Bob get clear. The sheep stopped and Bob fell clear, yelping.

I stood there looking down at Bob, wondering what to do. He stood up and, without looking at me, charged straight back down the race at the horny predator. Not giving it time to turn, he was under it and, with a snap, had it and the race cleared. I realised that the crowd had spontaneously applauded the dog's effort.

I could see Bob's back leg was up high from the ground. He could be hurt, I thought. To touch him meant disqualification—and we were being applauded for the first time in our career. Maybe I was just thick too, but I kept going with Bob, who was still working keenly on three legs. Out in the field we didn't do too badly but Bob was battling. Our final score left us one place out of the final, but I was happy as I left the ground with a badly limping dog. Men were heard to comment on the guts of the dog, never having seen a dog take such a bad knock and get up and go on. Not bad for a gutless wonder, I thought.

When we got to the vet and had Bob X-rayed, I felt sick. His leg was broken in two places and his hip ball broken off . . . and I'd kept going. I felt terrible. They fixed Bob up. It cost a fortune, and I gave him away to a chap who had light work and asked for him.

Bob was the most expensive dog I ever owned. He was as thick as a brick, yet in a few short seconds on that ground that night, he showed the world something that is the envy of all dog men: guts and loyalty. And he did it for me. When half the dogs in the final failed by being forced to retreat from fighting sheep, I was not surprised to hear people recalling Bob's effort. Whether I learnt something I needed to know from that, or whether it impressed my mates, I was given some rather brilliant old dogs that had finished their trialling days. They became very popular with children in hospitals and schools where we shared our bond in all sorts of displays.

Bob was not the best dog I've ever had—far from it—but when the chips were down he gave his all. I remember that 'thick bastard' with much affection.

A DRIVE THROUGH PERTH

Geoffrey Blight, Narrogin, Western Australia

Farmers are always trying to find ways of describing the brilliance of their sheepdogs and I am no better. When the yarns are being told, you've got to come up with something!

It was a boast I must have made a thousand times that finally got me into trouble. As a contractor handling sheep practically every day I always had a dog—for most of the time only one, although that has changed in recent years. When talking Dogs I would often say that mine were 'good enough to drive sheep down Perth's main street'. This was always a convincing boast, but in the mid-eighties a reporter from the *Sunday Times* asked me if I'd ever tried it. I said I hadn't, but as I was doing some sheepdog publicity for the Royal Agricultural Society, I made the statement that I was giving it some thought. This statement appeared in the *Times* and everyone seemed to get interested.

427

The Agricultural Society and Perth City Council asked me if I could. My best mate, who is one of Australia's best sheepdog triallers, told me how a top trialler had done it seventeen years earlier. So what the hell! Why not? I was always trying to show off my dogs, but as a new worker in the sport of sheepdog trialling, I wasn't doing too well. I was far more acquainted with the pressure of angry farmers, stupid dogs and mean sheep on the farms where I worked.

Saying I would was a mistake. The first thing that happened was the animal libbers went mad and wrote to the Society and the Council urging them not to let this 'idiot' with 'marauding' dogs and 'disorientated sheep' onto their streets. They claimed that sheep would be killed running under the feet of the public. I thought this would be the end of the idea, however the instigators urged me on and I decided to let people judge for themselves.

Commonsense had it that if I was to drive sheep through Perth, I would have to walk in front and show the way. As the time drew nearer I decided I'd use five dogs and about 25 sheep so that I could cover most situations, especially as at one part of the trip I would be walking within ten feet of oncoming traffic doing 70 kph. I had found out that the earlier drive I had been told about had involved only seven wethers and one dog, and that the sheep had escaped soon after the press shot had been taken. My mate told me this only two days before the event, which really took the wind out of my sails. But I believed that I had dogs that I could rely on—they'd had plenty of experience coping when things went wrong, as they often did on the farm.

On the day the first thing that had me in a panic was the crowd. Blimey, I hadn't thought too much about the people side of the thing. Then there were the TV crews ducking and diving in and out of the sheep like my neighbours' mongrel sheepdogs. The streets were to be cleared by the police, but that amounted to only a couple of officers on bikes who weren't always able to prevent cars coming from carparks and side streets and turning up in the middle of things. As I hadn't been keen to be on my own, my daughter-in-law and two grandchildren came along to help.

When the policeman waved me on my way, I can remember wishing then that I had old Broc—the four border collies and one kelpie I had were showing obvious nervousness. But with Regal working backwards in the front, Merle on the left, Nigger on the right, Steve pushing the rear and Gus troubleshooting, we were off on the most anxious two and a half kilometres I have ever walked. But those mongrel dogs didn't let me down as very quickly they realised their jobs—despite considerable starting, stopping and attempted breakaways early, they rose to the occasion far better than I did.

Even though Merle swiped an unsuspecting little girl's ice-cream from off the cone as she stared at the sheep, and Gus stuck his head in the occasional bin, we made it in front of some 20,000 onlookers, but not without a price. Being warm, the bitumen road played havoc with the dogs' feet and Nigger, who had had to do most of the covering, was bleeding from all four feet, but was still giving it his best shot.

It was well into the drive when my nerves settled and I thought again of that boast I had made a thousand times—'good enough to drive sheep through Perth'—and old Broc, about whom the boast had usually been made. He was still alive at the time, in his nineteenth year, so I bought him a paper and let him see it on television.

PLEASE, LADY, THERE'S NOBODY ELSE

Geoffrey Blight, Narrogin, Western Australia

Jenny lay quietly in the dark, her husband Phillip sleeping peacefully at her side. An eerie silence surrounded everything. Faint beams of moonlight stretched gently across the room. The small red digits read 2 am.

Rolling over, Jenny stared into a dark corner, unable to dismiss from her mind the events of the last four days. Her thoughts wandered to the old, near-white collie dog sitting outside. For four days it had refused to eat. Its sad eyes haunted her. She had tried so hard to make friends and have it eat, but to no avail. What would become of Sally-Anne? How the dog missed the man who had brought her here.

It had all started four days earlier, with that 9 am phone call, after Phillip had gone seeding. She had answered the phone with her usual 'Hello', and was shocked at the violent coughing which assailed her ears. The heavy breathing and gasping made her wonder if anyone was going to talk. Finally, a very weak and strained voice mumbled a series of disjointed statements: 'Dog . . . back . . . bought.'

Trying to make sense of the call, Jenny asked who she was speaking to, but the man's voice immediately broke into another violent coughing fit, which seemed to go on forever. Then she heard the faint voice again: 'Jim . . . sorry . . . sick . . . hospital.' Then, 'back' and 'dog'.

By now Jenny was totally confused and said she didn't understand, could he ring back later? Then came the five words that now haunted her: 'Please, lady, there's nobody else.' The sentence she could never forget, from a man called Jim.

It was these words that sent a shock through her. Initially she had thought the man might be drunk, but now she wasn't sure. In a daze, she mumbled, 'All right', not knowing what it meant, but Phillip could sort it out later.

After replacing the phone, she made herself a cuppa and thought about the call. Perhaps it was a bloke who'd bought a sheepdog off Phillip, messed it up, and now wanted his money back. Probably for booze by the sound of it, but it wasn't worth worrying about. She wasn't a great dog lover like Phillip. They always seemed to be the centre of attention around the farm. She felt jealous of the way Phillip always seemed to idolise them. He should try getting them to clean his house and sit here, miles from anywhere.

At times she was so lonely she would cry. The children were all away at boarding school—a farmer's wife, the great life! Well, you can have it, thought Jenny.

The noise of an approaching vehicle, mid-afternoon, cheered her up after a very dismal morning. Perhaps Phillip was home early, was her first thought, or maybe Gwen had popped over from next door . . . but the unmuffled spluttering and jerking of the motor told her it was neither. As it stopped in front of the house, it brought back memories of the dreadful sound of coughing on the phone some six hours earlier, which, till now, she'd forgotten. Peeping out the window, she saw a twenty-year-old rusty ute. The grey paint was all but gone and the rust holes gaped in the guards. She could not see who was driving and felt a twinge of fear. It was probably someone wanting petrol—better keep out of sight.

She sat quietly, hoping to hear the vehicle start up and leave, but there was not a sound, nothing happened. After nervously waiting nearly fifteen minutes, she decided to take another peep. Whoever it was may have been stealing something.

Just as she was about to open the door, someone knocked on it, weak and low. She jumped then stood paralysed as she heard that sound again, the coughing and spluttering. It sent shudders through her. Slowly stepping forward, she gingerly opened the door. 'Yes?' she asked—then gagged. It was the smell that hit her first, a dreadful, decaying smell. He sagged down by the door in another fit of coughing, unshaven and utterly filthy. Horrified, she stepped back, almost tripping over the dog that had quietly moved up behind her and was sniffing her dress.

The gasping body called, 'Sit, Sally-Anne.' It cringed.

At first Jenny thought it was Sally, but Sally had died ten years earlier. Sally was one dog she had liked. My God, it did look like Sally. 'Sorry,' she whispered, and put out her hand to the frightened old dog.

Looking again at the figure trying to rise, Jenny could now see his face. She'd never seen anything so ravaged and tormented. The eyes were glazed and staring at her, just like the dog's. Good God! What on earth . . . the man's nearly dead, she thought as he tried to speak. Help, her mind screamed, then she put both hands forward as the man slid further down the wall in a gasping fit. The phone, she had to phone for help.

The sergeant's quiet voice came through to her. 'Jenny, just sit down, I'm on my way. We'll handle it. Do you know who he is?'

The waiting seemed to go on for hours. She tried to give the man a sip of water and sit him more comfortably, but he was so filthy. There was blood and spittle all down his front. He kept trying to talk. 'Dog . . . back . . . hospital,' which only confused her more.

The dog was not one Phillip had sold recently. It was far too old. Yet the man had called it Sally-Anne. It looked so sad and frightened. She hadn't moved an inch since being told to 'sit'.

Finally Jenny heard the sirens, then saw the police car followed by the ambulance. The problem was no longer hers.

She tried to place the dog in the ambulance, which brought a weak protest from the man, so she kept a firm hold on the frightened dog. The ambulance sped away. Jenny told the sergeant everything she knew about the man, which wasn't much.

That had all happened four days earlier. They now knew Jim was a hermit who had a caravan in the coastal bush 200 kilometres away. He'd rarely been seen for years. Phillip also recognised the similarity between the dog and their first dog, Sally. He said it must be her pup as he'd sold a litter thirteen odd years ago. A shearer called Jim had taken one, but they hadn't seen him since.

The police found his caravan in poor shape. Four chooks were the only sign of life. It appeared Jim had had a family break-up some twelve years earlier. She wondered if they would find his family, for he was very sick. The doctors said that he had no will to live.

In a coma, he'd called for Sally-Anne, but they hadn't been able to locate anyone by that name. Jenny realised she had not told the police she had heard him call the dog Sally-Anne. She must tell the sergeant . . .

The moonlight looked so soft and gentle. She felt the wet warmth of her tears as she remembered his words, 'Please, lady, there's nobody else.'

It began so low, so sad, she almost missed it. Then she heard it again. The howl of a dog, a very lonely, old dog. A dog who had not eaten in four days. A dog in mourning.

Jenny rolled over, her sobs coming freely. She buried her face deep in the pillow and began the wait for the call that she now knew, with morning, would come.

PART 5
HIGH COUNTRY

Where the earth heaves up in stony surges leaving behind valleys streaked with silver, the call is for dogs and people with tough bodies, iron stamina and strong character.

In the high country human contact is sparse, so livestock are touchy. Scrub is dense and there are plenty of places to hide. Terrain is rough. The weather is unpredictable—quiet days with limpid sunshine turn vicious, with driving, freezing winds and fog and snow and rain.

Dogs and handlers need all their guile, for the potential for tragedy is great.

A MOUNTAIN MAN AND HIS SHAGGY DOGS: A PROFILE OF RUSTY CONNELLY

Angela Goode

Above the Beloka Valley in the Benambra district of the Victorian high country, Rusty Connelly lives the life that has made a legend of mountain cattlemen. Every year before the snows arrive, he has to bring his cattle down off leasehold country 4,500 feet up in the Alpine National Park. His leasehold adjoins Tom Groggin station, that sacred site of folklore immortalised by Banjo Paterson in *The Man from Snowy River* in 1895. This was where Jack Riley did his epic ride up Leatherbarrel Creek, which feeds into the River Murray.

With his home-bred Australian stock horses and four dogs, 55-year-old Rusty, who has been in the high country all his life, heads off up the mountains for three or four days at a time. High up in the Great Dividing Range among the snow gums, running streams, rocks and fallen logs, Rusty Connelly couldn't muster his cattle unless he had a team of good dogs. 'You've got to use dogs in the mountains,' he says. 'It's scrubby, rough and steep. Some of it is one-in-one gradient. In fact, good dogs are even more essential up here than good horses.'

The dogs which accompany him belie their looks. They are, in Rusty's words, 'not a pretty sight and they make terrible pets'. They are as shaggy as the shedding bark on the eucalypts and as tough as the terrain. They are Smithfield–kelpie cross dogs that Rusty specially breeds for his alpine cattle run. These whiskery, hairy dogs have brownish black, tan and greyish coats extending from their ears to their paws and to their naturally stumped tails. On the run they look like a moving shagpile carpet with beady black eyes—anything but a super-efficient mustering machine.

'They are hard-working dogs,' says Rusty. 'Great at finding cattle in this rough country. And they are faithful, hardy and tireless. They are so tough, they sleep quite happily out in the snow. But they are not sociable dogs. They don't like being petted or fussed over.'

So off they go—Rusty, with his Akubra on the red head that gave him his name, oilskin, chaps, warm sweater and thick socks, sitting deeply in his stock saddle, with pack horses and dogs—picking their way over wombat holes and rocks to scour 10,000 acres for his Herefords. When he gets to the hut where he'll camp, he spells his team, checks his holding yards and prepares for the following day's muster.

At dawn he takes two dogs and leaves two behind. As he searches for cattle tracks in the dense scrub, he also keeps a close eye on his dogs. They'll tell him when there are cattle nearby. Their noses, poking through that shaggy mat, sniff the air and if the scent is promising, the dogs walk in its direction.

They cast wide and flush out animals toward the horseman. Some Smithfield cross dogs, Rusty says, are forceful and give the beasts a quick nip, but mostly they work quietly. If they do bark, it is with a relatively soft voice.

Rusty remembers with fondness many great dogs over the years, but especially Biff, who could track and scent cattle and handle up to 100 head on his own.

In the old days, before times got tough, Rusty had his two sons to help with the muster. These days one works at the copper mine at Benambra and the other is a mechanic in the town. He does 90 per cent of the stock-work on his own, just bringing in casual workers at branding and weaning time.

Rusty and the others who graze the alpine runs are not just battling a failing rural economy, they are struggling to retain their alpine lease-holds. Claims that the cattle are damaging the mountains are nonsense, say Rusty and other members of the Mountain Cattlemen's Association.

'Log trucks and four-wheel-drive vehicles do far more damage and bring in weeds. Cattle don't do damage, and they help with fire control by keeping the grasses down. If anything, the mountains are under-stocked.'

He rides away among the broad-leaf peppermint, the black sally in the creeks and the snow gums twisting on the slopes. The shaggy dogs that will help move about 200 cattle into the lower country in the next few weeks lope behind him, sniffing the leaf-scented air for work waiting to be done.

UP ON THE SEAGULL BEAT
Peter Chillwell, Harvey, Western Australia

Having been a shepherd in the high country of New Zealand's South Island, I reckon mustering sheep in Australia is easy. Being at 7,500 feet on the 'seagull' beat in the Awatere Valley with no motorbikes or four-wheel-drives really tests out your shepherding skills. I was one of a team of four or five shepherds on Middle Hurst station to 'bark up' the side of the mountain in the tussock country. We had to get up at 2.30 am, have breakfast, collect our teams of dogs and be climbing by 4.00 am.

It's a long way up to the seagull beat and damn steep too. Some of New Zealand's most popular tourist lookouts nestle in the land the shepherd walks daily. Although sheep rarely get up above the 6,000 feet mark, I sometimes had to go up to nearly 9,000 feet looking for strays. So you certainly need a good head for heights. Often a helicopter is used to take men and dogs up to a high plateau where they will be dropped off to start their mustering, way up in the clouds.

I was new to the game and like many in that position, I was keen to impress my older and wiser workmates. We were mustering a station on a day of immensely thick fog. We flew in above the incredibly thick murk that lay like a custard over the mountains, leaving only the peaks above 6,000 feet jutting out in all their magnificent rugged glory.

The pilot put us down on a wide ledge which was actually level with the fog's upper surface. It was so thick you couldn't see more than a few feet into it, so it was apparent we would have to wait until it lifted before we could get our bearings and start work.

With nothing to sit on, my mustering mate just squatted uncomfortably. I decided it would be much more comfortable to sit on the ledge and dangle my feet over the edge just above the impregnable fog—despite advice that it would be wise to keep away from the edge. I had already worked a few weeks in the high country so felt very confident—even cocky. I wasn't scared of slipping a few feet down a shingle slide. However, I hadn't been up on a seagull beat before. My bloody dogs wouldn't come near me as I sat there waiting—kicking stones off the edge to fall into the blanket below my feet.

When mountain fog lifts, it can do so very quickly. I can still feel my stomach heaving as I sat there in my foolhardiness, showing off, and looking down . . . and down . . . and down. I became paralysed with fear as I suddenly realised that there I was perched, wriggling around on my bottom, on a very unstable ledge a thousand feet above absolutely nothing.

I remember now with sweaty palms the incredible fear that overtook me as I lay back and ever so carefully brought my feet onto more solid rock—slowly retreating to where my dogs sat with sombre, know-all looks on their faces.

Another day I was the man high on the slope. This time there was no fog, but because it was so steep I could hardly see the next bloke below me. There weren't many sheep right up at the top—there never are, just small bunches here and there.

I had a team of four dogs, all Huntaways—Chum, Nell, Bruce and Ruff. Some days you needed even more dogs if you wanted to get off the hill by mid-afternoon. I sent a few little lots down to the next man and was checking out the crags, bluffs and knolls. Crikey, it's beautiful up there—it was worth doing the job just for the view. In one particularly steep part I was looking out over one of the many sheer drops. Right below me, between 70 and 100 feet down, I spotted a small bunch of sheep crowded on a ledge.

All four dogs were looking over the edge. They'd seen the sheep and were waiting to see which one I would give the word to. It looked safe enough. There was quite a wide track leading down to the ledge and on down the slope, so I thought I would let Chum go. He was the keenest and liked to get the nod. However, when I said, 'Chum, come out,' I thought he'd cast out down the track to them, but the silly idiot went straight over the top before I could stop him.

I'm sure I could see him looking up at me as if to say, 'Blimy, Boss, you ask a bit of us poor dogs,' as he floated down, legs spread-eagled, ears flapping like a parachute. I was sure he was a dead dog.

But he got it right. He landed slap-bang in the middle of those big woolly wethers, sending them scattering after breaking his fall. Completely undaunted, Chum soon had them back together, off the ledge and on their way down the mountain.

On the mountains, like in the Australian outback, there's not much between you and the stars. I didn't work in the high country long, but long enough to learn its ways. I witnessed the human effort, the beauty, the skills of the dogs—and the tragedies. It took just one tragedy, the death of Chum, for me to decide to give the mountains away and try my hand where the land was a bit flatter.

Churn was just an ordinary Huntaway. He was no national champion, but he was my best dog. We spent a lot of time together up there in that mountainous country and he never let me down. He was always keen as mustard and the dog in my team that had to do the tricky work. Up there, you sometimes don't get the chance to do things twice. You do it right the first time—or you're dead. The mountains have claimed a long list of men and dogs who didn't get a second shot at the job.

I was shepherding up the Growler Creek near Mesopotamia station. Things were not going too badly. I'd 'barked out' several small bunches of merino wethers, but there were half a dozen stuck on a very narrow ledge overlooking a sheer drop.

With the ledge narrowing to as little as six inches in places, there wasn't room to get past them. Besides, the ledge had no exit path, so I decided it was far too dangerous. I'd leave them there and move on. A well-known New Zealand high country proverb was in my mind: 'It's better to have a live straggler than catch a dead sheep.'

Just then the boss flew past me in his Cessna and circled to let me know he'd seen the sheep that I had supposedly missed. Shepherds aren't supposed to leave sheep—only bad shepherds do, and they get known. I had a good name and since I wanted to keep it, I went back.

The job was tricky, so I had to pick Chum. I couldn't even get across to the ledge, but even if I could have, it was only going to put me in the path of the wethers when they came out. It was simply too narrow, so I stayed where I thought I would be able to see what was going on. When I sent Chum, it took a while to steer him over onto the opposite slope and bluff. Finally he spotted the sheep. The only hope he had was to drive them along the ledge to where he could pass and then push them back out. His approach was stealthy but the sheep moved quickly along the ledge and out of my sight. Chum followed and then he was on his own.

For five minutes I waited, hoping to see the sheep reappear with Chum behind them. As the minutes passed I knew Chum was in trouble.

Suddenly they came into view much further around the bluff on a much narrower ledge—a thousand feet over pure nothing. Chum was past the sheep but they had turned on him and were coming at him. There were six big woolly mongrels, all of them four times Chum's weight. Chum obviously wasn't the first dog they'd seen. That's why they had retreated onto that inaccessible ledge—I bet they had escaped a dog before.

Chum had nowhere to go. The sheep knew that and I guess Chum did too. There wasn't a thing I could do but watch. He did his best. He barked and stood his ground. But a big merino rig knew he had him cornered and charged. Chum met the charge as best he could but it wasn't good enough. The rig belted him that hard, he went straight over the edge.

I went down a shingle slide I normally wouldn't have dared tackle, hopelessly calling to Chum as if some miracle could save him. I cursed the sheep, the mountains, even God—but I was wasting my time. Chum hadn't a chance.

I just sat there for a long time, hours, dampening the shingle, remembering. Finally, when I knew I had to think of getting in off the mountain, I built a mound of stones over the mutilated body of my Chum.

I got back to camp hours after the others, but no-one said a word. No-one said, 'Where have you been?' or 'What happened to you?' They could count. They had counted a mate's dogs before. They knew. They let me be. The story would be told in good time.

It wasn't the last day I shepherded sheep on the mountains, but I knew, everyone knew, that I'd be moving on.

Station bosses in New Zealand can be pretty fussy about the men they employ to shepherd their flocks. I found this out when I applied for a job at Gray's Hills in McKenzie country.

In order to ensure that one weak, lazy or gutless shepherd doesn't blow a whole muster by leaving sheep behind or knocking them up, they have a novel job specification. They insist that all their shepherds are smokers who 'roll their own'. Gray's Hills is a 70,000-acre dead-flat spread and these unconventional rules have evolved over the years to protect the flock.

Because the country is so flat, shepherds are always tempted to push the sheep too hard. This makes a lot of extra work collecting the sheep that can't take the pace. If he's on 'rollies', a bloke has to stop or dismount from his horse and search his pockets for the 'makings'. While his dogs take a quick camp under the nearest tussock, he has to go through the whole ritual of gauging the right amount of tobacco, getting the paper right and completing the task with an experienced lick. And don't underestimate how much longer it takes to light a rollie, especially in New Zealand's climate. Even the weakest of sheep has a fair chance of keeping up with the mob.

I was told to be sure to be seen rolling my smokes if I wanted the job, and to keep it. It was the only time in my life I had to resort to such primitive satisfaction for my addiction. Exasperation with my DIY fags meant I probably gave the sheep on that station the easiest walk home—and my dogs the slackest time in their working lives.

LEFT IN THE DARK
Les Brooks, Barraba, New South Wales

After spending 60 years in Sydney, I came to Barraba to become a wool grower and cattle breeder. One day I had to do repairs along the boundary fence, so set off with my motorbike and border collie, Sonnee. I found a large hole in the fence in the south-east corner of the property and set to work on the necessary repairs.

The repairs took me ages. It was only when I had finished that I realised how late in the day it was. It was so dark that I had to feel for my tools on the ground. I couldn't even see my hand out in front of me. I turned around and started to walk back to my motorbike but found, to my horror, that it was so dark, I had no idea where it was.

Realising the seriousness of the situation—I had never been to that part of the property before—I felt that my only hope of getting out of there was to call Sonnee. It was one of those dense black nights—no moon, cloudy sky—and bitterly cold for we were at 2,000 feet in the New England area in the month of August.

I called out to Sonnee but nothing happened. Then I called a little louder. Nothing. Then, feeling the panic rising, I called at the top of my voice. I was relieved to hear a rustle in the bushes and feel him brush my legs. I knelt down, put my arm around his neck and said, 'Sonnee, I'm lost.' I then asked him to take me back to the motorbike.

He immediately set off and I followed the sound of him rustling the bushes. Sure enough, he led me straight back to the bike. I knew we were there by the smell of petrol which had been leaking from the carburettor.

I patted Sonnee, thanked him for leading me back to the bike and said, 'Now, my boy, you'll have to take me back to the homestead.' For that was my next problem. When I started the bike the headlights immediately came on, but although the track through the heavily timbered ironbark could be found easily in daylight, it was impossible to recognise at night. Everything looked the same. So once again I was totally lost.

Sonnee had already taken off, so again I had to call out to him but, as before, I had to call out three times and at the top of my voice. Then came the familiar rustle of the bushes and the brushing against my legs. Once again I got down on my knees, but this time I put both arms around his neck and said, 'Sonnee, I'm really lost. Take me back to the homestead.'

So off he went, but this time he only went a few yards before he stopped, turned around and looked back to see if I was still following. He did this all the way back to the homestead—even at the public roadway where normally, during the day, he would try to beat me back to the homestead over the last 1.5 kilometres. This time he kept stopping, looking back and ensuring I was still following.

I got home, cold but safe and eternally thankful to Sonnee. I quite forgive him for not being the world's greatest worker.

A GUTSY LITTLE AUSSIE

Stuart Leigh, Heyfield, Victoria

We need to go back to the late fifties and into the mountain country of eastern Victoria for the story of Rupert. Those were the post-myxomatosis years. Myxo went through the district in the summer of 1951–52, spreading by contact. As there were no mosquitoes to carry the virus, the build-up of rabbits had begun again.

The country was rough and the paddocks were covered with fallen, ringbarked snow gums, a haven for rabbits. The prime method of eradication was fumigation of the burrows. The fumigant was larvicide, and a pack of dogs was required to flush rabbits out of logs and scrub and into their burrows.

The pack consisted of dogs other people did not want and ranged in number from four or five up to as many as ten. Over the years it contained a multitude of differing breeds, mainly hunting dogs—Irish wolf hounds, whippets, greyhounds, deer hounds and many others. Then along came Rupert, an Australian terrier weighing no more than a couple of kilos, hairy, with Bob Menzies eyebrows, docked tail and bristles around his mouth. His gait was offset—that is, his back legs tracked to one side, similar to a truck with a broken rear spring centre bolt. This gave the impression that he never quite went in the direction he was aiming for. He was definitely no beauty, but was most certainly the leader of the pack.

The pack was housed in a half-acre enclosure, surrounded by six-foot wire netting slung between black sallee trees, with a post here and there for support. The kennels consisted of several square, riveted steel water tanks of 1920s vintage seen around many farms. Sleeping arrangements were strictly regimented, with the same clique sharing a kennel and not going outside their allotted place. Except for Rupert. He was accepted by any clique at any time and spent his nights in the kennel of his choice.

A working day for Rupert would begin with him being first out of the enclosure when the gate was opened, but never participating in the general free-for-all created by the yelping, barking mass of dogs celebrating their freedom. Instead, he came dutifully to heel, ready for action. The mode of transport was tractor and trailer, the latter loaded with shovels, mattocks, fumigant and lunch. There was no room for dogs. With the first turn of the tractor engine there would be a wild forward scrambling of dogs—but not Rupert. He would follow closely behind the rear wheels of the trailer, trotting along with his offset rear legs.

Once in the paddock he was in his element, running to a log or a squat and yelping to the others that here was a rabbit. He was everywhere—into hollow logs, burrows, stumps—tail wagging, barking furiously and always looking to the others for support. A fully grown buck rabbit was almost bigger than Rupert, and the few times he was able to catch one, he had great difficulty in subduing his quarry. Mostly, of course, he would flush out the rabbits and the pack would tear off after the victim with Rupert a long, long way in the rear.

If one of the other dogs caught the rabbit, Rupert would pester the captor until he gave up his kill and Rupert would proudly bear the victim back to the camp as if it was his own achievement.

If things were a bit quiet with nothing much to chase, Rupert would suddenly jump up and dash off, yelping and carrying on, and the rest of the pack would follow with great excitement. After covering 100 yards or so, he would stop short, turn around and trot back, very pleased with himself for having organised a successful wild goose chase.

Rupert had somehow acquired a cat's 'nine lives' survival facility and over the years had many escapes. The technique of fumigating was to cut back the mouth of the burrow with a mattock or a shovel, squirt the fumigant into the burrow, then seal the entrance with soil, stamping it firmly with the boot. On one occasion during smoko, the crew was sitting around the fire when Rupert was noted as missing. A hurried search located some muffled barking and, after a few quick shovelsful of dirt were removed, out came Rupert. He was a very sick little dog, gasping for breath, eyes watering, but still grinning. He flopped under the trailer for half an hour then was off again, right as rain.

Another time the entrance of a burrow was being cut back. Rupert, who had gone unseen down the burrow, decided to resurface. The descending mattock caught him flush on his head and opened up a big wound from ear to ear across his scalp. Back to base, out with needles, catgut and disinfectant, and we sewed him up. Within 24 hours, an unbowed and 'ready for anything' Rupert was back on the job.

One October there was a very big flood in the river which bisected the property. An early morning inspection revealed twenty or more sheep marooned on a nearby island with the water levels still rising. Poor Rupert, who happened to be with us, was thrown into the torrent upstream of the island—it seemed to be a good idea at the time. We thought he would swim to the island and chase the sheep into shallow water on the other side.

Unfortunately, we had misjudged the strength of the current. He missed the island and was last seen disappearing downstream very quickly, his head bobbing up and down in the pressure waves created by the torrent. An unsuccessful search on horseback followed for several miles until the river fell away through a chasm and down some 50 feet.

During the long six- or seven-mile ride home, there was time to contemplate the situation, and that 'good idea' suddenly seemed cruel and unnecessary. However, each day brings a new dawn, and next morning, there on the back doorstep, never a place he would ordinarily be seen, was a very hungry and bedraggled small dog.

The story of Rupert would not be complete without mention of his love-life. It took some time to discover the full extent of this other world of his. As the pack was strictly a 'male only' society, he had to take advantage of every opportunity that presented itself to guarantee his genes for posterity.

He made several attempts with the cattle bitches from time to time, but these were unsuccessful because of the height disparity. It was not until several reports were received from neighbours describing litters of pups with bristly hair and short legs that Rupert's lustful activities were revealed. It was discovered that, when especially tempted, he could scramble up the wire netting of the enclosure and tumble down the other side to be off to his latest flame. He would roam far and wide on these sojourns, making one regular excursion of sixteen miles there and back to satisfy his passion. The neighbours even used him as an early warning system because he would arrive, ready for action, before they realised their bitch was due on heat.

All good things must come to an end and even in his last chase, he showed courage and tenacity. One of his very bad habits eventually led to his demise. He took great delight in chasing the horses whenever he was free and especially if there was an audience. His final horse chase went unnoticed until a whimpering was heard and observation revealed Rupert crawling up the driveway to the homestead. His injuries were massive—a broken leg, broken ribs and a split in the skull revealing his brain.

He had dragged himself 300 yards in that condition and had to be put down. But after all these years and dozens of working dogs later, the most memorable of them all is still Rupert, a gutsy little Aussie.

AT YOUR SERVICE
John Harland, Mount Hope, New South Wales

A few years ago our neighbour, who lived ten miles to the south of us, had a good red kelpie named Digger.

This particular day the neighbour and Digger had been out all day mustering. They arrived home after a hard day's work just before sundown. After feeding Digger, the neighbour went inside. Digger went to bed on his favourite mat.

Next morning bright and early Digger was still on his mat and eager to go to work. Unknown to the neighbour at the time, this is what had happened that night. After the neighbour went inside, Digger must have sniffed the night air and headed out, because just after sundown Digger was noticed at our dog yard. I went out to tie him up, but he was gone.

Another neighbour rang later that night to see if I knew who owned a big red kelpie dog because this dog was over there with his bitch. This neighbour lives another fives miles to the north of us. When he went outside to tie him up, Digger was gone.

Overall Digger must have covered at least 30 miles that night to find his lady love. But he was back home in time for work next morning.

LOOK, UP IN THE SKY

Mavis Summerell, Bega, New South Wales

In the early 1930s during the Depression, we owned a small black and white cattle dog, Flop, who was almost human. We spoke to him like a person.

We were lucky to have a job paying 30 pounds a month which we could have lived on if we had actually got the money. Because the boss was feeling it hard too, we only got five pounds each month and two sheep for meat. We supplemented this income by trapping rabbits for their skins and often we had to eat them to survive. Lots of families had no other meat source.

We often lost traps but the dogs all learnt to scent the rabbit or fox or whatever it was that had taken off with them. Flop became adept at finding anything. If a possum had taken it, he'd scent it to a tree. One day it was a huge goanna with a trap on up a tree.

We were very puzzled, however, when he started scenting down the hill and then looked up in the air whinging and whining. My husband said he thought Flop was going mad.

About a week later one of our neighbours asked if we had lost a trap: 'There is an eagle flying around here with a trap on it,' he said. We realised then what Flop had been trying to tell us.

BRIGHT AMBER

Lesley Klan, Rathdowney, Queensland

We were mustering cattle in the foothills of the McPherson Ranges. It is very hilly country with quite a bit of lantana growing. At the time of mustering, the grass was high due to an overabundant rainfall season.

I had driven some cattle down a ridge alongside Amber, my four-year-old kelpie with a dash of border collie. We left them and went on further in search of more. On our return, the cattle were nowhere to be seen. I didn't know whether they had gone down into the gully for a drink or continued along the ridge.

447

As Amber was looking hot due to the high humidity, I sent her down into the gully for a swim. Having done this she came back up to me. I continued along the ridge but Amber disappeared. I called but she didn't come.

On reaching the end of the ridge, about a quarter of a mile along, I looked down onto clear country where the cattle congregate before being pushed into the yards. There was Amber with the missing cattle. She must have seen them while she was swimming and therefore decided she would go back and take them down.

This is but one example of her mustering expertise.

CLAWS LIKE A WOMBAT

Bruce Rodgers, Merriwa, New South Wales

Our son picked Max up as a pup while he was a jackeroo on Gunbar station in the Riverina. When he went off to work in the US, Max was left with us along with a brown mare that had not long been broken in.

As a working dog Max, who was jet black with mad, staring eyes, got about three points out of a hundred; but he was a hell of a character. Energy abounded—you couldn't wear him down, but his energies were all at the wrong time and place.

One of the things our son had taught Max when he was a pup was to hop up on the pommel of the saddle. He became clever at it. You only had to look at Max and he would be up on the saddle with you.

Although we didn't get much work out of Max, we had the brown mare going quite well at this stage, although she was still pretty touchy. She had just learnt to stand at a gate while you leaned over and opened it.

And that was when Max performed his most woeful deed. The mare was stationary—Max thought he was a little tired, so he decided to jump onboard. I saw that look in his eye all too late.

'No, Max! No! Get away you black animal!'

There was no stopping him. He didn't quite make the saddle and had to claw his way up the mare's shoulder. The mare took off. Through the gate—head down, ears back, me yelling and Max clawing on for dear life. He had claws like a wombat. No amount of pushing and swiping would free him. Half a mile we went like this—a terrified mare, a more terrified rider, and a black dog enjoying the whole business.

Max was at last despatched from the saddle at 30 miles an hour. He was not only exuberant, but also very tough. He bounced three times and got up running—and barked at the horse's heels for good measure.

'If I live, I'm going to kill you, Max,' I said between gasps for air and through clenched teeth while we galloped on flat-out.

Well, I didn't kill him and a relationship persisted with that dog for a long time. Whenever you felt like throttling him, he would come up and look at you lovingly with those starey eyes and offer you his paw to shake hands. That always broke me right up. So Max would save himself from a hiding and everyone would go away in stitches.

MOUNTAIN SAVIOUR
Margaret Weston, Nimmitabel, New South Wales

A good working dog is a wonderful asset, but if he also happens to be your best mate and saviour, then he's priceless.

My story is set back in the 1950s, high in the Snowy Mountains above Jindabyne. Our neighbours used to lease land in the mountains where they grazed sheep during summer, a practice not allowed these days—which still raises the hackles of many mountain people.

At the time my brother Jimmy was a boy of twelve, and so proud when our parents agreed that he could go to the mountains and help with the muster. He felt really grown-up being part of such an assignment. My father's best dog, Ring, was to be his helpmate as Ring was reputed to have more brains than Jimmy and knew twice as much about everything.

Our mother, a descendant of the Pendergasts who were pioneers of the mountain, had prepared Jimmy for the trip and warned him of the dangers that he might encounter, and how to overcome them. However, during a heavy fog Jimmy lost his bearings, became completely disoriented and failed to rendezvous with the other musterers. Ring stayed by his side and Jimmy said his presence gave him confidence and subdued his immediate panic.

At nightfall they sought out a hollow log and both crawled in. Although the temperature dropped dramatically that night, Ring's body kept Jimmy warm. Jimmy said his short life flashed before him. He could imagine his father wailing, 'Mary, I've got ten more kids, but only one dog as good as that one.' Jimmy was my twin brother and one of eleven children in the family.

Next morning the majestic mountains were bathed in sunshine and Jimmy was rescued after an all-night search on foot and horseback.

Ring was revered in our family after this incident and was assured of a pampered retirement. My mother always believed he saved Jimmy's life by providing body warmth throughout that freezing night in the mountains.

PART 6
BACK OF BEYOND

Far from the bitumen and streetlights lives a breed of dogs and people who share the qualities of our pioneers. They survive without mollycoddling, without doctors or vets, without shops and theatres.

Some, like Gundars Simsons, find the transition to the blackblocks a startling culture shock—but a dog helped strip away his naivety. Others, like Aboriginal jilleroo Jannial Thunguttie Kamilaroi, reveal the close relationship formed between dogs and people when human company is scarce.

Through such close bonds, a dog will risk its life to save its master, as did the Arnolds' pig dog in Queensland. They'll also run miles to get help for a stricken friend, like Old Don of St Kilda. They learn to work in an equal partnership, like Copper the rabbit dog. And Jim Stephens's dog seems to have spent a lot of time acutely observing its master.

Trucks and two-way radios are vital links to the outside world. Travelling dog Mate understands technology, while Linda was transported far from home. Frank, however, with his light-hearted approach to work, found a truck dog's life his only means of survival—but for how long?

DOG'S-EYE VIEW

Jim Stephens, Northampton, Western Australia

He's pathetic. Absolutely pathetic. Without me he would never survive.

He has no fur, or at least very little. He has to put some on before going out of the house. His feet are so big he cannot avoid a blob of sheep manure. He is so slow at running, and no wonder—he tries it on his back legs. I've tried it and it's hopeless.

He seems defenceless. His teeth are so blunt, and another thing—his teeth aren't even real. I saw him one night when we chased a fox: no upper teeth—just like a sheep!

His ears are useless. They are small, round and can't swivel to pick up a sound. His nose is always dry—no wonder he can't smell. Sometimes he gets a moist nose, but then he doesn't seem well.

His eyes are poor, even with those bits of glass in front of them. He's also very fussy—he won't eat rotting sheep. He nearly chucks up from the smell of my breath after I've had a good feast. Then when I roll for a bit of extra perfume, he does a strange sort of dance and bans me from the ute. Still on smells—his female even has to buy the scent to let him know she's on heat. They've really lost the plot those two.

It's quite obvious he completely lacks ability to express his affection. In the ute I often lick his face and hands, but he has never once licked my face. And as for having any pride of ownership—he's a wimp. He'll let anyone into his territory, and no wonder—he's got no idea about marking out his plot, and is totally lazy even about ute wheels.

He's too scared to fight, doesn't understand the pleasures of a good scratch and has no appreciation of my attempts to beautify his garden with bones. So, I do the best I can to brighten this poor creature's life a little. I smile at him and laugh at his jokes, and when he's sad I try to be sympathetic. If I didn't stay with him, who would?

OLD DON OF ST KILDA

Beryl Thomas, Toowoomba, Queensland

My childhood was spent on St Kilda, my parents' property twenty miles north of Roma in western Queensland. Sheepdogs were part of our life. They lived in kennels under the pepper trees, chained up when they weren't working in the paddocks or the sheepyards. They were kelpie-collie crosses mostly, some red, some black and white, some a mixture, with names like Snip and Don and Treacle, Lassie and Laddie. The dogs changed but the names were recycled.

Old Don was one of the red ones. At that time, in the early 1940s, my father rode a horse called Derry, a big chestnut. Don always trotted alongside. The three of them were very much a team. If Don was very tired or the burrs bad, he would be taken up on the pommel of the saddle, for there were no motorbikes then.

On this particular day, my father went off in the morning with Derry and Don to check the dams. He rode past the windmill and the wool-shed and my mother waved to him from the verandah of the house. We children were all away then—one brother in the RAAF and my other two brothers and I were at boarding schools near the coast. It was a lonely life for my mother and a busy time for my father because of course during wartime there was little extra help available.

Mother used to write all the news from home in letters describing everything in detail for us. The events of this day—a day we still discuss at family reunions—were recorded with special care and have been repeated often, because this is the day Old Don became a hero.

Dad always came home for a hot dinner in the middle of the day, but he was sometimes held up, so my mother was not unduly concerned by his lateness that day. She was surprised, though, when Old Don came home by himself and barked at the bottom of the back steps. An occasional dog was sent home in disgrace, but never Old Don. He stayed close by my mother, whimpering and barking.

Clearly, all was not well. Although my mother had driven a sulky as a country schoolteacher and as a young wife, in all her 90 years she never did learn to drive a car. She called the nearest neighbour on the phone, a party line with five families connected. The neighbour was over in half an hour with his widowed mother, who had been a nurse. They drove out across the paddocks following Don, who led them to my father, lying injured and in great pain in a steep gully.

Derry had tripped and fallen forward as he was going up the side of the gully and Dad's foot had been caught between the stirrup and the bank. Many bones in his foot and leg had been broken when the horse had struggled free and scrambled out of the gully. Derry was lame, but he set out for home and arrived very late that day. Don was determined to stay with my father. Apparently it had taken some persuading by my father to convince Don to leave him and go home, but persuade him he did and off Don had gone, as fast as he could, straight to my mother. Had he not done this, a search party would have had enormous difficulty locating my father—it may have taken days.

My father recovered after first aid from the neighbour and a bumpy ride home, followed by many weeks in hospital. He went on riding horses and working sheepdogs for a very long time after that. He lived to be ninety-one.

My nephew lives on St Kilda now and the sheep have long been replaced by cattle. There are no sheepdogs under the pepper trees now. No more rattling chains and wagging tails. Just the ghosts of the Snips and Treacles, Lassies and Laddies and fond memories of Old Don.

THE GETTING OF WISDOM

Gundars Simsons, Devoit, Tasmania

Charlie was a weather-beaten farmer of indeterminate age who was instrumental in my development from being a soft, young, city-bred schoolteacher to a human being with the first glimmerings of wisdom.

I had been posted to Australia's southernmost school, on Bruny Island to the south of Hobart. It was a community which time had passed by, and I felt somewhat dislocated. There I was, newly graduated from college, thinking I was pretty clever. I was also well used to the comforts and excitement of city life—but here I was appointed to this extraordinarily remote rural region.

Charlie and his family took me under their wing. He had twelve children and many of them were associated with my school. From Charlie and his sons I learnt how to farm, use a chainsaw, split fence posts, slaughter, butcher, build fences and drive farm machinery. These rough diamonds exposed me to many important human values which were quite new to me.

I associate the time I first began to understand these tight-knit locals with the day I borrowed Charlie's sheepdog Patch to drive a small flock of 33 Polwarth ewes to a nearby farm. I was accompanied by the farmer who had purchased the flock from me and assured him that, with a good dog, the task would be simple.

Patch was an extremely well-behaved working border collie. However, as we got started it seemed to be me who was running from side to side in a lather, barking commands at Patch, who simply cocked his head to look calmly into my eyes as he walked quietly along behind the flock. It was as if he were saying, with that wise dog look, 'What *are* you doing, city boy?'

I knew he could and would work and I knew from previous observation that I was using the correct commands. As I stopped a moment to catch my breath and look into the dog's disbelieving eyes, I contemplated the problem. Could it be that my tone of voice and lack of colourful adjectives were confusing the poor animal, who was more used to rougher treatment?

In desperation and frustration, I yelled in my gruffest impersonation of

456

Charlie's hoarse tones, 'Get back, you bloody mongrel bitch,' at which Patch sprang into immediate action. I kept up this voice impersonation and relieved Patch from his schizophrenic confusion. The sheep sprang into immediate action, recognising at last some real and purposeful authority.

FROM THE LAB TO THE LAND
Bill Clissold, Maryborough, Queensland

The first time I set eyes on him, he was a half-starved, half-grown dog which had been collected from a pound in a Sydney suburb. He had been picked up as a stray running the streets and had been brought to the veterinary research farm where I was employed as a stockman. He was to be used in an experiment to develop a tick serum.

I took an instant liking to this miserable-looking black kelpie with a white chest—a trait from a border collie somewhere back in his breeding—and couldn't bear the thought of him being stuck in the laboratory and then being killed when the experiment was finished. When I asked the vets if I could have him to make a working dog out of him, they laughed so much. I thought they would all have a fit.

A few months later, though, I was the one laughing. Sam, which was what I called him, grew into the best dog I have ever owned—the most intelligent dog ever to look through a collar. The vets watched in awe as his talents revealed themselves.

Although at first he was terrified of sheep and cattle, he became a strong and fearless workmate, unafraid of any beast on four legs, no matter how wild it was. With sheep he was gentle, working equally well in yard and paddock. But let a steer break from the mob or turn on him and he could bring it to its knees by grabbing hold of its nostrils.

He would block a lane while I opened the gate and after the stock were through he would push the gate shut by standing on his back feet and pushing with his front ones. I could leave a mob of sheep with him while I rode home for lunch and when I returned, perhaps an hour later, he would still be shepherding them. He would allow them to spread out a little in order to feed and then turn them back into the bunch. I could go on for ages about his exploits, both during our time at the vet station and in the years we worked at other places.

He did his last job for me when I was on a stud farm. One afternoon I sent him to bring up the milking cow and calf, which he promptly did. But then he came up to me, looked into my face and lay down by my feet. He was clearly unwell and I took him to town that afternoon to a vet. He was operated on that evening and it was found that he had a large growth in his stomach. Although he must have been in a lot of pain and aching like hell, not once did he show any sign of discomfort until that last day. He didn't survive the operation and died that night.

Although I no longer work with stock, I'm sure I could never be lucky enough to find another dog like Sam. He certainly would have been wasting his talents in that laboratory.

WELCOME HOME!
Ethel Batten, Dubbo East, New South Wales

Bonnie is a black kelpie with a loving nature—and she thinks she is almost human.

When she was about ten months old I was away from home for two weeks in hospital. Upon my return her joy was ecstatic. She showed her loving welcome and her pleasure at seeing me by racing around me and about the gardens and trees, tail tucked under, ears up, eyes bright, tongue lolling from a big toothy grin.

On her last lap under the grapevines she paused to snatch off a bunch of grapes and placed them on my foot. It was truly a marvellous welcome home from a loving friend. It made me cry!

LITTLE GIRL OF THE BUSH

Jannial Thunguttie Kamilaroi, Ashford, New South Wales

Since my old cat had mothered a variety of baby animals, I presented her with the two pups my friend and I had been promised. Their mother had been killed when they were one week old.

Beershee (meaning 'wild cat'—all my animals and birds get Aboriginal names), a grey, white and black tabby, sniffed around the tiny puppies, licked them and then pushed them towards her teats. They became hers to raise with her odd assortment of other babies. She had three kittens, the two pups, two rabbit babies and one baby guinea pig. She was an amazing old cat.

My pup, Bami (meaning 'little girl'), was a little Australian silky/ Sydney silky/wirehaired terrier. When she was six months old we moved out onto a farm called Yurialawa, which was about 21 kilometres out of town. I went there to work as a jilleroo/caretaker/gardener.

From time to time when I was not needed to work, I would find Bami missing. I would call and call and look everywhere but I could never find her. Finally the manager's wife came over and told me not to worry about her. She was with her husband. 'He loves your little dog,' she said. 'Have a look when he comes back and see where she is.'

She obviously did enjoy his company too, because there she was in his saddlebag on the horse. Other times she would be up front on the saddle or at the back on the rump. Or sitting on the seat of the tractor. Or up alongside him in his truck. I soon learnt that whenever Bami was missing, she was always with him.

I also had a little orphaned goat brought to me to hand rear. He had kicked up a terrible stink when my boss took Bami with him—so my boss took Daryal the goat with him too. I had been looking everywhere that day for the little goat so I could give him his bottle, but could not find him.

I went to the manager's home thinking he may somehow have got out of the gate and gone down there, as he often used to follow me there when I went to do gardening. But the manager's wife said she had not seen him. We were both puzzling over it when her husband came toward us on his horse. To our surprise he had the goat kid over the saddle in front and Bami sitting at the back on the horse's rump. His wife and I were laughing so loudly we nearly split our sides. Bami and Daryal used to team up with working dogs when they rounded up sheep and cattle. They were quite a sight. During a bad drought later on, I had to find Daryal another home. That farm was sold when the owner got very ill and I moved on.

Three farms later I was rounding up the sheep on foot and a Suffolk ram knocked me to the ground and would not let me up. I called the working dogs to help me but they did not come. But Bami did, and she ran between his legs and grabbed hold of his testicles with her teeth and hung on for dear life. He turned around and around trying to shake her off him. He jumped and pushed back onto the rails of the sheepyards. No way could he get rid of her. I got up off the ground and laughed until I cried. Shaking with laughter, I shut the gate of the yards on the ram and called Bami. She let go and came to me. The ram never gave me trouble again.

About three months later the boss sold some old ewes and the stock truck came to pick them up. We had drafted off what we had wanted but then this same Suffolk ram somehow got into the yards and no way could we get him out. Not even the stock truck driver and his dogs could budge him. We tried the other dogs too, with no success.

'I know how to fix that ram,' I said, and called Bami. Well, you should have seen the look on his face—and did he move!

Jim, my boss, was amazed. 'Have you ever seen anything like it?' he said. 'That little dog is the only one that can manage that ram.'

The truck driver said he had seen all sorts of dogs work but nothing like Bami. He wanted to buy her, but not for anything was she for sale. Bami could work goats, cattle, sheep, horses, pigs, poultry, wild ducks on the dams—and even children!

She lived until she was fourteen years old. I think she fretted for me when I unexpectedly had to go into hospital for nine weeks with a leg ulcer. I was a bit upset when I found out the boss at that time did not bury her but just threw her body out into the bush. When I came back I found it and buried her where she could see the sun going down over the hills.

THE FORTUNES OF
FESTIVAL FRANK

Pauline Smart, Port Augusta, South Australia

I used to suspect that it was only the good dogs that met an early death. Since knowing Frank I am convinced this is so.

Frank was given to my husband at ten weeks of age as a replacement for a dog that had died from snakebite—a *good* dog, of course. Frank was pure black, had an undershot jaw and an unquenchable spirit. As time went by he developed a light-hearted approach to life and work that no amount of discipline could discourage. It wasn't that he was idle—it was just that he didn't feel as though he should take things too seriously. However, he had also developed an uncanny ability to realise when to display just enough talent to keep him from that celestial paddock where all sheep have wings.

One day my husband was trying to draft some ewes ready to truck and was running late, largely because Frank was his offsider. Ears pricked, snout pointed skyward and tail up jauntily, Frank would rush about barking at the birds, showing no interest in the sheep. It was looking as though he had, finally Gold Coasted it once too often.

The heat, the dust and the tempers were all rising as the truck pulled up and the driver got out. He jumped the fence to lend a hand, but from somewhere up behind the sheep he could hear a continuous yapping and catch glimpses of a very enthusiastic black dog. A thick haze of dust obscured the total picture. Once the sheep were loaded, the truckie commented, 'Not a bad dog you've got there.'

A whistle brought Frank, expecting praise, bouncing up into my husband's arms—and greatly appreciating the weight being taken off his feet.

Without a word my husband walked over to the truck, opened the door and put Frank in. 'He's yours,' he said, throwing in Frank's chain for good measure.

The truckie was a bit suspicious of the haste with which Frank was being given away, but my husband muttered something about needing a paddock dog rather than a yard dog—and that the jackeroo also needed a bit of exercise. The last I saw of Frank, he had his paws on the dashboard, ears pricked, eyes bright, tail wagging, and he was grinning widely at his new associate, happily unaware of the consequences had he not opted for a career change.

A few years later we were helping in the yards at my in-laws' property a couple of hundred kilometres away when a truck pulled up to load some weaners. I recognised the driver, and there was absolutely no mistaking the black dog with the pointed snout and the festival attitude. He was still barking at birds and didn't seem to have developed a more thoughtful outlook on life at all.

We asked the truckie how Frank was progressing and he said, not suprisingly, that he nearly hadn't kept him. But it seemed that every time he had serious doubts about his continued association with Frank, the dog would miraculously deliver a performance worthy of survival at least.

The time to pay up registration fees had come and Frank's future was hanging in the balance. His output had lately been very ordinary and it looked as though his apprenticeship would be terminated. But while the truckie was away on a trip his wife had gone ahead and paid the fee.

Maybe one day Frank will turn out to be a good working dog, or maybe one day his luck will just run out. In the meantime Frank is sporting a shiny new registration disc and can continue to pursue his life of pleasure with just the right amount of shrewd judgment thrown in.

COUNTING THE SHOTS
Paul Holst, Ravenshoe, Queensland

Pete was a rabbit shooter camped out in the never-never about 80 miles north-west of Bourke. I met him when I was out that way doing a bit of fencing in the early 1960s. Pete's spotlight was mounted on a frame on the dashboard of a bashed-up Landrover with no doors, no windscreen and no roof. It had a rack made from old water pipes and bush saplings on which the rabbits hung. His rifle with 'scope stood in a rack handy to his left hand.

I conned him into taking me with him one night. It was very uncomfortable. I had to sit in the back, but there were two very good reasons for this. The first was that when I went to sit in the passenger's seat, Copper, who was big and black, was already there. The huge bared fangs and the warning growl convinced me that it would he unwise to insist. Secondly, Pete said the dog had to sit up front to be able to work properly. I thought he was having me on, but I clambered into the back with my hurt feelings and we drove off.

We followed a vague track for a few miles before turning off and going bush. Pete turned on the spotlight, which he operated with one hand while steering with the other. We came to a small flat surrounded by tea-trees and dotted with rabbits. Eight shots rang out in quick succession and eight rabbits died.

Copper, who seemed to he part Doberman and part ridgeback, sat upright and alert, watching the scene intently. Pete switched off the spot and turned on a small work-light hanging from the rack. He then turned to the dog. 'Okay, Copper, go get 'em,' he said.

The dog disappeared into the darkness and Pete reloaded the rifle. Copper returned with a rabbit held gently by the loose belly skin and dropped it at Pete's feet. Eight times he did this without another word of command. He then jumped back on his seat.

Pete gutted the rabbits and paired them by slitting the leg of one and threading the leg of another through the slit. He then hung them on the rack. We set off again and Pete was mumbling something that I couldn't quite hear. It turned out he was talking to his 'dawg'—in fact he did most of his talking to the dog.

We worked on until about midnight, then stopped to boil the billy and have a feed of cold mutton and spuds washed down with black tea. Pete rolled a smoke and cleaned the lens of his 'scope. It seemed an appropriate time to ask how Copper knew exactly how many rabbits to collect when he stopped shooting.

The look I got would have withered a crowbar. 'He counts the bloody shots of course. He's not stoopid!'

'But what if you miss one?' I asked.

'I tell 'im.'

'Oh right, sure,' I said, mindful that he was a big man and it was a long walk back to camp.

We set off again and at the next stop Pete shot seven rabbits, then fired an extra shot into the butt of a tree. He turned to Copper. 'I missed one, mate. Go get 'em.'

Seven times that dog returned with a rabbit. He didn't hesitate at six and he didn't go looking for eight.

At sunrise we were back at the camp and Pete stacked the rabbits in the freezer which stood about 100 yards away because of the noise from the diesel motor. I fried some eggs and bacon and we were having breakfast when the fortnightly truck arrived from Bourke to pick up Pete's rabbits. The truckie joined us for a cuppa.

I was yarning to the driver and telling him about Copper. 'He's the smartest dog I've ever seen. If I hadn't seen it with my own eyes, I'd never have believed it,' I said.

'Yeah, well I never seen it, and I reckon no dog can count,' he said.

'But you're only a bloody truckie and that dawg is smarter than any truckie I ever met,' rasped Pete. 'Would ya believe me if I told ya that there dawg can tell the time by the clock?'

'I wouldn't believe no rabbit shooter unless I seen it with me own eyes,' the truckie said.

'Righto then, I'll give ya a demo. It's time someone put ya tail between ya legs. If Copper can't tell the time I'll load that truck by meself. If he can, you load it. Now watcha got to say?'

The truckie grinned. 'You're on!'

Pete disappeared into his tent and came out with a battered old alarm clock. He wound it up and set it by his watch. Copper was asleep under Pete's vehicle and Pete called him over. The dog sat up in front of him.

'Now, Copper,' he said, 'I want you to *lie down* here and keep your eye on the clock. I have to go over to the freezer and count the rabbits because this bloke is going to be loading them by himself and ya can't trust a bloody truckie. You *stay* here until exactly twenty past eight, then come on over.'

The clock showed five past eight. Pete put it on the ground in front of Copper and walked, off over to the freezer. The dog stared at the clock with pricked ears as it ticked away.

The truckie looked at me and scratched his head. 'I reckon Pete's been out in the scrub with the rabbits for too long. He's slipped a cog for sure.'

I said nothing. We poured ourselves another mug of tea, rolled a smoke and watched the minutes tick by. Copper lay on his belly, head on paws, in front of the clock. He was tired and seemed to be dozing with eyes half closed. The clock showed nineteen minutes past eight.

The truckie was feeling relaxed. 'By Gawd, I'm gonna enjoy watching while that silly bugger loads them bunnies,' he said with a laugh. 'Serves 'im right for skitin' an' bullshittin' about his bloody dawg.'

The big hand reached the twenty-minute mark. Copper jumped to his feet and bounded across the flat to the freezer like a bloke running late for his bus.

The truckie gaped and gasped—'Gawd! I don't believe it!'

'You'd better believe it,' I said. 'You've seen it, haven't you?'

The truckie got to his feet and moved off to the truck, muttering to himself and shaking his head. He drove over to the freezer. Pete and Copper were walking back and Pete gave a cheery smile and raised his hat as they passed. He got a puzzled look in reply.

Pete went into his tent and came out with a bottle of Bundy rum. 'I reckon that's worth a drink,' he said with eyes that laughed.

The rum helped revive me after the long night, so I got the courage to ask whether Copper really could tell the time—or was he pulling a swiftie somewhere, which was what I suspected.

Pete looked at me really hard and then grinned. 'You're not stupid, are ya?' And he paused.

'All right, young fella, if ya promise not to let on to that truckie, I'll let ya in on it.

'Remember all that spiel I gave 'im when I got the clock? He really only got the "lie down" and the "stay" outa all that.'

Then Pete took a whistle from his pocket and blew it. Not a sound came from it but Copper, who had been asleep under the vehicle, jumped to his feet and came running. The penny slowly dropped.

'You bloody old fraud! That's one of those high-frequency whistles that are inaudible to our ears but dogs can hear like a bugle blast. That truckie will shoot you if he finds out!

'But what about that counting act—how do you rig that?'

Pete turned serious again. 'That's the Gawd's truth, young fella,' he said earnestly. 'He really does count and he is the smartest dog in the country.'

LOVELY LINDA

Emmie Cripps, Northampton, Western Australia

Years ago, in the late 1940s, we bought a pure-bred border collie pup from a breeder in Northam in Western Australia. Her grandmother, The Horwood's Linda, was a champion sheepdog at the Royal Agricultural Show of Western Australia and was the winner of the annual sheepdog trials on more than one occasion. Like her grandmother she was a sable colour, not the usual black and white type. Her ancestors were from Scotland.

This very intelligent wee pup arrived by train at Northampton after being some two days in transit. She had been transferred no less than three times before arriving here, shut in a small box with slats and a tin inside for water. My husband and our young son went to pick her up. Once home, having been removed from the box and nursed by son Geoffrey, we gave her a good drink of water and later milk on and off for the first day as we felt giving hard food such as meat may be too much after so many hours of starvation.

Once she had recovered, she was put on a leash and taken for walks around the house and the paddock close to the house so she could see around her and look at some sheep nearby. Although so small, she was very interested in the animals. This was a good sign. We called her Linda and she learnt immediately to sit and come to us. She quickly grew and before long was able to accompany my husband when he inspected sheep in the paddocks further away.

He was quite surprised by her intelligence as she picked up the commands to sit and come back and so on. In no time Linda could round up a small number of sheep successfully. She always stood her ground if some stubborn animal stamped its feet—Linda always won. We had always had a good sheepdog but Linda was something special, and so obedient at all times. Before long we could trust her to go out of sight and bring a small mob of sheep without leaving any behind.

We had a small sheep stud and that meant the sheep were handled more than ordinary flocks. The rams were never far from the homestead and if we wanted to check them over at any time, my husband could tell Linda to bring them to the homestead gate by pointing to where they were. While she was away he would have a quick cup of tea before walking out to see how she was coping. She would always have the sheep at the gate and would be lying down facing the mob so she could watch any sheep likely to try to escape. If they did they were soon brought back to the fold again.

When autumn came, the showery days meant the stud rams and ewes had to be shedded. There was only a small mob of ewes so they went into a small shed a short distance from the shearing shed where the rams were put. The usual procedure was to put the ewes in first, then go down the hill and bring in the rams. We would call Linda and point to the ewes and off she would go to put them into their shed. By the time we had caught up to her she would have them on their way, bound for the shed, and we just had to help them run up the ramp into the shed. She would instantly set off for the rams and, although they always protested, Linda got the upper hand and sent them to the sheepyards, up a race and into their shed. The only time she queried our orders was if the rams were closer to the shed than the ewes were. She would still want to put the ewes in first, but would reluctantly obey when we insisted.

In the north-west corner of the property we had a yard made from old branches off the trees nearby. The gate was also made from a couple of branches of jam tree. Once the sheep were inside, we pulled the branches across the gate and the sheep were secure.

One day I walked up over the hill to this makeshift yard to give my husband a phone message about a sheep sale. I waited until the sheep work had been completed, then pulled the branches back so the sheep could go out quietly. We set out for home, stopping to look at the only old quandong tree still alive on the property. I put the kettle on for morning tea and my husband had a good wash. Suddenly he looked through the flyscreen door and outside the house but he couldn't see Linda. He called her as this was unusual, but she wasn't there.

Then the penny dropped. He remembered that he hadn't told her we were finished and that she could come home with us. Although the brush gate was open, Linda had apparently remained there, guarding the sheep in the yards. When my husband arrived back at the yards, he felt so sorry for his lovely dog. He gave her a great pat and set back home.

Another example of Linda's devotion to duty was when my husband and son Geoffrey rounded up a fair-sized mob of sheep in the middle of a paddock near the house. They examined the animals and dressed the lightly blown ones, then decided to go back to the house to have a cup of tea. Again, because they were talking about farm doings, my husband overlooked telling Linda that the job had been completed. When they got back after remembering the error, there she was, busily keeping the animals all in a circle. Poor soul, she would have been very occupied as the sheep would have seen the men leave and would have tried repeatedly to break away.

By request from the local show society my husband taught Linda to yard three sheep in a pen in the middle of a paddock. She did this perfectly, so he gave a couple of exhibitions at our local show but refused to take her to Perth because he was worried about loud noises from the sideshows that might frighten her.

In time we purchased an early Landrover with a canvas hood which was often removed. One day on the highway to Carnarvon my husband passed a large transport in a cutting six or seven miles from home. It was crawling very slowly up the hill but he quickly left it behind as he went down across the sand plain, where he met another large transport going south in a great hurry. The road was narrow so he suddenly had to pull right over onto the edge of the highway.

A few miles after this incident my husband glanced back to find, with horror, that Linda was no longer in the back. He thought she must have overbalanced when he'd swerved to the side of the road. He turned back and stopped and whistled in the spot where he had veered sharply. There was no answer. He checked the short shrubs bordering the road to see if she was lying there unconscious.

The slow-moving transport which he had passed earlier came by and my husband tried to stop it, but the driver ignored him. He didn't know what to do, so he returned home and rang the police. The policeman informed him that Linda hadn't been picked up, but he added that another farmer's sheepdog had recently been stolen by a truck driver. He believed sometimes these dogs were sold to station hands for stock work. What a horrible thought!

We wondered if the transport that passed going north, which wouldn't stop, had picked up Linda. The police in Carnarvon said they would stop the truck south of the town around midnight, when the transports usually got there, and see if they had a dog that looked like Linda. Next day we did another search of the area where Linda must have fallen off, but no luck. The whole household was feeling so sad. The Carnarvon police hadn't had any luck either.

A couple of days passed and then early one morning when one of us opened the back door, there was poor Linda, looking drawn and covered in bright red mud which was caked on her long fur. She was lying down on the step. Her feet were raw from walking on stones. We had no idea how far she had travelled.

The police were pleased to hear our news and said that she must have come from near what we called the Half-Way roadhouse, now called The Overlander. It's between Northampton and Carnarvon and was the only area that had had a thunderstorm in the past couple of days. Otherwise she could not possibly have had a bath in a puddle, which clearly she had done. The roadhouse was nearly 100 miles away.

Linda could hardly hobble. I bathed her feet with warm water and put some ointment on them but, as with most dogs, it was soon licked off. We fed her a light diet for a few days, wrapped her up in a blanket and put a covered hot brick with her at night.

She was back on deck in about a fortnight, ready to help with the sheep, but we did not use her for a while longer. What a wonderful, faithful animal she was, and how lucky no-one else picked her up. Perhaps she kept herself hidden in the scrub at the side of the road until the way was clear. We would never know.

When my husband died suddenly she mourned her loss by lying sadly at the back door. She did not live many years after that and died in her sleep. Linda—a valuable, loving animal missed by all who knew her.

SALUTE TO A HERO
Barbara Arnold, Goolwa, South Australia

When we lived in far north Queensland, we kept three Rhodesian ridgeback/red heeler dogs for culling wild pig numbers for station owners. Pigs were a terrible menace up there. They would tear down fences, eat the cows' feed, kill calves and savage people if they got a chance.

My husband was a truck driver at a wolfram mine 50 miles from Mareeba and 100 miles north of Cairns. Most weekends we would head off along the river banks where the rubber vines grew so densely that they created hollows where pigs would hide.

My husband would drive and the children, Shayne and Deanne, and I would keep a lookout. The three dogs would lean out, sniffing the air for pigs. As soon as they picked up a scent they would jump off the vehicle and run it its direction. We would follow on foot until the dogs had located the pigs and bailed them up in a rubber tree hollow. They would then distract the pigs to prevent them charging at my husband as he came in close with his gun.

Some people taught their dogs to bite the ankles of pigs, but my husband taught ours to stand back and distract them, so he could aim and shoot without having the pigs turn on him. The biting type of dogs, because they came in close, often got gored and killed. Since our dogs were also our friends, we didn't like to make them take too many risks.

One weekend when we had just shot a mountain dingo, we spotted a huge boar disappearing into the scrub. My husband grabbed the .222 we keep in the Toyota all the time and went after him on foot, followed by Shayne, who was then twelve.

We lost the trail in the dense rubber vine. Just as my husband was bending down in the river bed, looking into the scrub at a level with the bank, the boar came charging at him. He didn't have time to fire before he was knocked over backwards, smashing the gun barrel on Shayne's head. A hole was gouged in my husband's elbow and he grazed his knee. Before he knew what had happened the pig was standing over him, ready to rip open his stomach. I was watching all this from a distance and was frozen with terror.

Suddenly, in a flash of red, Sam, the big male dog, appeared from nowhere, grabbed the pig's flank, turned him away from my husband and distracted the pig. My husband was then able to quickly find his gun. He fired all the bullets remaining in it and killed the pig.

We regrouped after that close call, checked all the injuries and bound up Shayne's head with my shirt. He later had to have stitches. Very shaken by the experience we made our way back to the Toyota, and when we got home we gave Sam an extra serve of dinner to reward him for his loyalty. Without doubt my husband would have been killed had the dog not charged in when he did. The feat was all the more remarkable since the dogs had been trained not to bite, yet Sam had recognised a time when he should.

AS POPULAR AS A NEW GOVERNESS

John Hawkes, Yaraka, Queensland

In 1985 at Mt Marlow station near Yaraka, Queensland, I was walking a mob of about 2,000 sheep down the Barcoo River when the overseer, Steven Gray, brought down a pup he had just got from Arno, the neighbouring property.

He dropped it on the ground to see if it would show any interest in the sheep. An hour later, four of us eventually caught it. In that time he had circumnavigated the mob a dozen times in an orderly fashion, never pursuing too hard or once cutting off a sheep.

Although some tempers were rising, I was very impressed and next week went over to Arno. After a carton of home brew, I eventually persuaded Billy Morton to part with the last of the litter, a black and tan kelpie dog. I named him Jess after Jessie Owens, the athlete.

As a contract musterer, I travel extensively with Jess. He is as popular as a new governess at every place we go. He is a natural backer, will unload trucks and swims rivers to get to sheep in a tight spot.

One day I was mustering at Diamond Downs for John Parkinson. I was in my Cessna 150 and my wife, Neen, was on the ground with Jess, John Parkinson, his daughter Kerry, and Tony Morley. They were all on motorbikes. We were mustering four paddocks as though they were one—20,000 acres in all—as the fences were shot. As it turned out, the main mob (about 1,500) ended up on one side of the fence, and little mobs of a dozen or more were scattered through the scrub all over the other paddocks.

One by one people were directed to other mobs until four stockmen were in one paddock putting together 500 stubborn sheep while Jess was in a paddock by himself with 1,500. He was, I could see from the air, also

471

going through the broken-down fence at every sweep of the tail of the mob and working into the mob any that were getting through. With about two kilometres to go to the corner, everything looked pretty well under control, so I radioed the boss and told him I'd fly home.

He said, 'Well, I've only got a hundred or so here, and I can see Tony hasn't many. Who's with the main mob?'

'Jess has them in the next paddock,' I replied. 'He'll block them in the corner and wait for you there.'

And sure as eggs, that's what he did.

Someone later volunteered to give Jess his headset, so I could tell him what to do from the air.

'You hang onto your headset,' I said. 'Jess knows what to do.'

THIRD TIME UNLUCKY
Marjorie Atkins, Bayswater, Western Australia

Many years ago my father had a sheepdog named Bluey. He was a good dog and as well as working the sheep, he would also lead my father's horse back to the house after it had been saddled.

One day the dog went missing for rather a long time. When he came home, he had a fit. He had eaten a poisoned bait. The remedy which my father had recently learned from the Aborigines he worked with was to cut off the tips of his ears and tail. Unfortunately, it was the third fit the dog had suffered, so he died. Apparently this remedy would have worked if it had been the first fit the dog had had.

YOU TELL 'EM, MATE

Jule Nancarrow, Broken Hill, New South Wales

When former station owner Wreford Whitehair befriended Mate, she was on an outback station property out from Tibooburra in the far north of New South Wales.

She was suffering from malnutrition, had infected sores around her neck which had been rubbed bare of hair by a chain, sores on her body, and was timid and frightened when approached. She could not stand the sound of a whip and cowered at the sound of a shouted voice. Somehow she knew that Wreford was different. He healed her wounds, he fed her and gave her love. Today she is known as The Wonder Dog.

Wreford now works as a station consultant, and on his travels Mate sits up front in the passenger seat to observe the road ahead. Whenever she sees kangaroos, cows, sheep or emus, she barks to warn them to get off the road.

She is a remarkable sheepdog and will work in the shed, in the yards or in the paddocks. When the sheep have to be hurried along, Wreford says, 'You tell 'em,' and she starts to bark. If he wants her to cease barking, he says, 'Take five.'

When they are travelling together in the outback, Wreford contacts station properties on his UHF radio to advise them of his impending arrival. But once he's found the right channel, he leaves the communication to Mate.

'You tell 'em,' he tells her, and she does. She barks into the mike, and from the other end gets the same customary, cheery response from station properties all around the region: 'Hello, Mate! How are you?'

Both Wreford Whitehair and Mate are very well-known and respected identities in the Broken Hill area.

PART 7
FLEECE COUNTRY

The horizon shimmers in the hazy, dusty distance. It's hot. The trees are sparse. From the wooden verandah and its low, overhanging roof, you hear a windmill creak and gates clank.

In far-off runs measured in square miles rather than acres, hardy merinos graze saltbush and bluebush, Muster them, and they'll run like stags. They'll split, they'll sit down, they'll hide. Station dogs need to be cunning and tough and fast. Their feet get prickles and are cut by rocks. Troughs and dams are far apart. The shade is thin.

In the yards where the mobs are drafted at shearing time, urgent yaps of the yard dogs pierce through the indignant complaints of ewes and falsetto-voiced lambs. On the big stations, shearing will go for months—eight shearers working flat-out, rouseabouts sweeping the board, tossing fleeces and keeping pens full for each shearer.

Dogs get little rest in the shed and yards, and it helps if they use their initiative—although they sometimes go overboard. There are dangers and diseases. And some dogs, like Soda, end up looking 'like a hard-boiled egg'.

Dog and owner work as a unit and think as one. They know each other well . . . or, like Karla and Rover, they think they do. You also find unexpected gems like Midget and Kate—and humour as dry as a creekbed in drought to keep a sheepman hanging on.

And then there are the one-man dogs that don't recognise wives and jilleroos as part of the plan . . . dogs like Pudden. Fred and Jinny. The returns from wool are bad enough—but to have the dog on strike because its treasured boss is away can really strain the friendship.

CELEBRITY ON THE ROOF

Blanche Niemann, Mildura, Victoria

Growing up on a south-western Riverina wool property called Mindook station provided me with many, many wonderful memories—the country, the river, the lifestyle and especially the animals.

Looking back on my childhood, no memory is stronger or more vivid than that of our gallant sheepdog, Pudden—a legend, a friend and an outstanding working dog. He had been a soft, wriggly, licky puppy, coloured grey, black and many other earthy colours all mixed together, with one blue and one brown eye. He learnt fast, displaying the intelligence of the German coolie breed and the timid demeanour of his kelpie cross. He watched the other dogs and copied—but a raised voice was enough to send him scurrying away, tail tucked between his legs, not to be seen again until the heat had passed.

He was my father's shadow, never to be found far from him. As he grew older, his personality also began to develop. He took up the unusual habit of travelling on the roof of the farm ute. He would leap into the back of the ute, then bounce up onto the roof, legs braced against the rough country roads. He wasn't even discouraged by the highway travel—nose pointed straight ahead, flop ears flapping in the wind. He became quite a celebrity in the district. Truckies tooted as they passed and described his antics to their mates over their CBs.

His endless movement began to take its toll on the tin roof of the Suzuki ute. Cracks began to appear which let the cold July rain cascade into the cabin. Something had to be done. Fortunately the local garage owner had heard of Pudden's exploits, so he designed and built a cover for the cabin which solved the problem.

Pud always had the ability to worm his way into people's hearts and avoid their wrath. I can see him still, returning home after a rendezvous with the neighbour's friendly bitch, standing calmly and proudly on the roof of Mr Murphy's new Commodore. The scratches in the royal blue duco hardly showed at all, but the tension on Murphy's face, although carefully veiled, was evident.

As older dogs died, Pud stood alone as 'the only dog worth his salt on the place', according to Dad. Mustering for shearing on one of those late March days that make you think that summer won't ever dissolve into autumn, Mum and Dad paused to discuss the best way to get the 'woolly brutes' home. They had 1,000 wethers in full wool to drive home, five miles in flaming heat. Mum was in the ute with Pud. Dad was on the bike. He decided to do one final check that they had got all the sheep, but told Mum to start pushing the mob homeward. 'Send Pud,' he told her.

Dad headed off, calm in the knowledge that the mob would be halfway home by the time he rode around for a final look. Unfortunately, like all good working dogs, Pud wasn't about to let the mob move until the boss returned. This is where, he left them, and this is where they'd stay.

478

'Come behind, Pud,' came the casual instruction from the ute. Pud stayed put.

"Hind, Pud,' Mum yelled. No response. The door of the ute creaked open as Mum stepped out.

'Pud! Come behind,' was the command, this time the frustration evident in her voice. Mum had never been renowned for her patience, or her gentle temper—and the heat and flies, combined with a hard morning's bumping around the rough paddock after 'maggoty sheep' had done little to improve her mood.

'Come behind, you bloody useless mongrel.' Mum started to stride around the mob. Like the fine example of a working sheepdog that he was, Pud loped around the mob to cover the opposite side.

Mum changed her tack. 'Here, Pud, come here. Good boy, jump up, come on.'

For the ensuing hour, Mum shouted, screamed, ran, swore, cursed and wheedled her way after Pudden, with no result.

After the hour of eternity, Dad returned looking for the mob, finding his wife beside herself with rage, and Pud, cool as a cucumber, tail wagging and smiling at his master. The sheep had not moved an inch. Mum maintains to this day if she had had a rifle, Pud would have been an ex-working dog.

As the seasons passed, Pud's limbs grew stiff and his sight dull. He was still master of the younger dogs and still a fine, proud sheepdog with a calm intensity and dignity in his soft eyes. There was a void in all our lives when he was gone.

THE STORY OF KATE
Alex Haley, Berrigan, New South Wales

I was travelling from my sheep farm at Tocumwal to Melbourne on a business trip, when I stopped off at Wahring Cottage Service Station for fuel. John, the owner, came out to serve at the bowser, followed by his faithful corgi dog. But this morning there was an addition, a black and tan kelpie female about ten months old. She sat down just a couple of feet from my door to wait for the petrol to be served.

I looked at her and she looked at me and I guess she knew she had found her destiny. 'Who owns the kelpie, John?' I asked.

He said a bloke had dropped her off three weeks ago and was supposed to come back and pick her up. He hadn't shown up.

'I'll buy her off you,' I said. 'What's the price?'

'I'll ask the wife,' he said. 'And if she agrees, you can have her providing you bring her back if the owner turns up. Call back on your way back from Melbourne and if you promise a good home, I think you can have her.'

Seldom has the day taken so long to pass in Melbourne. I am usually short of time rushing from one venue to another and cursing because the day is going too quickly. My mind was with the little black and tan at Wahring. I conjured up in my imagination how, in my absence, the owner had returned to take her back—or worse, a truck had come in too fast and run over her.

I left Melbourne at 6 pm in the dark, and drove non-stop at the maximum speed the law would allow to cover the 130 kilometres as quickly as possible back to Wahring and the dog. Twenty kilometres before my destination, I eased back because I knew she had been killed or taken by someone else. I even felt anger that John hadn't given me the dog for safekeeping when I went to Melbourne that morning. I drove into the service station and couldn't believe my eyes. There, sitting out waiting for me it seemed, was the dog.

'Yes, she's yours, but a good home now.' John was all smiles as he knew that I wanted her. I opened the door of the car and, believe me or not, that dog knew she was going with me and jumped straight into the car.

'I'll be blowed,' John said. 'She hasn't accepted an offer to get into a car before, and she has been sitting at the end of the driveway entrance all day, as if she was waiting for you.'

'She's no good with sheep, you know,' John went on. 'The other bloke has a stock crate and she wouldn't work for him. Although he did say she was only ten months old.'

John's words had about the same effect as a bucket of cold water thrown over you unexpectedly on a hot day. 'She'll be right,' I muttered, a little flattened, and I drove away without a thank-you to John.

Kate sat next to me. I told her her name was Kate and she rode like a lady in the car. When we reached home she walked inside.

At the sheep farm the next day, I did my immediate tasks quickly as I wanted to start Kate's training. About 60 weaners were ravaging the lucerne paddock, so there was a genuine job for Kate. Woody, my faithful friend, had no idea what to do with sheep but liked to come along and try. Woody accepted Kate into the household without fuss. The three of us went to the lucerne paddock and I pointed at the sheep and told Kate to 'go away back'.

Kate looked concerned but stood there. I said 'go away back' again, and then, with Kate and Woody watching, I ran around the sheep. The neighbour yelled over the fence, 'The other way around, mate. You stand there and the dogs run around the sheep.'

Very bloody funny . . . the world's full of comedians. But foremost in my mind were John's parting words—'She's no good with sheep'. No good with sheep—hell, it doesn't matter. I like the dog anyway and I've managed without a dog this long—so what?

The sheep going out of the lucerne paddock turned left instead of right and ran the wrong way down the lane. 'Way back,' I shouted, and ran after the sheep to head them off. The sheep were fast and I was slowing and puffing and thinking I'd have to get the ute. A black and tan flash went past me to the front of the sheep and turned them, and then she stood there looking back, sending the message, 'What the hell do I do now?'

'Bring 'em up,' I coaxed. She stood there. 'Push 'em up,' I pleaded. She stood there. 'Bark!' I yelled. 'Ruff, ruff.'

Woody rushed to the sheep as she knew about barking, and barked. Kate barked too, and the sheep ran. Kate began running from side to side, and I realised that I now had myself a sheepdog.

Times are tough. The economy of the farm is on a sharp downhill slide with no bottom in sight. Every day things go up, fuel costs rise, wool prices drop, and every other person who can only survive by increasing his charges is doing so. The only way I was going to save this farm was to go contracting, foot-paring sheep. I advertised for work, and everyone who had sheep too rough to handle or too difficult to treat rang up. The established foot-paring foot-rotters wouldn't handle these sheep and the owners couldn't, so I accepted these jobs as I didn't have much choice.

I employed a couple of strong young men, set up my sheep-handler, and with Kate and a new pup, Bedee, onboard, we left for our first job.

Kate had shown much improvement and an immediate grasp of her duty only three weeks after that first-day lesson. Kate and I drafted 300 sheep without any assistance from any human. A neighbour and friend who sometimes lent me his good dog saw Kate in action and was quite put out that Kate was turning out so well so quickly.

Bedee was a mistreated and cringing black bitch that I had rescued. After Kate, Bedee was a disaster. She wouldn't come when you called her and she just ran straight at the sheep, scattering them in all directions. But after sleeping inside for a couple of weeks and eating regular meals, she began to come when called and do simple things like sit down, come behind, get off the chair, and things like that. I let her out with the sheep to see what would happen and she killed the first of three sheep by chasing a crazy weaner into a strainer post. She killed two more in similar fashion before she became Kate's well-behaved apprentice.

So, with two young, inexperienced men, two inexperienced dogs and being a bloke who is getting a bit old for this sort of caper, we arrived at our first foot-paring job. Shock one was, they weren't sheep but long-horn goats, big and tough, moving restlessly around this high-fenced sheep pen. We discussed the situation and decided we needed the work, so we set up our handling machine.

One of the workers provided shock number two. These were feral goats captured at Wilcannia, and they had never been handled. Our special race would have been useless, so we set up the machine against the permanent pen. The worker said his job was to keep them up into the handler for us all day. We were ready to go.

I took Kate and went to help the workers move the goats forward. 'Get over,' I said to Kate.

'Stop!' the worker yelled. 'They killed the boss's good dog this morning.'

I yelled to Kate but she was already around them. One goat charged her but somehow she got out of the way. I got in the pen and a goat charged me. I ducked. The worker wasn't so quick and the goat crashed into his shoulder and broke his collarbone. I dragged him to the side of the pen as goats charged and leapt high all around us.

'Get me out before we're killed,' he yelled as we dragged him over the fence and put him in the car. The boss arrived.

'Haven't you bastards handled goats before?' he said.

'Not wild ones like these,' we said.

482

He asked us who was going to pen them up because the injured worker was the only one who would do it. Then he looked into the pen and asked what was going on.

Kate hadn't got out of the pen as we thought but had gone around and around and had the goats circling in the big pen. I was surprised but pretended I knew she could do it. Trying to impress the boss to gain future work, I said I'd pen them up.

Kate worked all day and the boys cursed and swore, and the boss worked all day in my place on the machine, so pleased that at last he had found someone that could handle wild goats. When the goats got their wide horns stuck in the machine another worker ran in with a saw and cut the horns off, and as they tried to pull away Kate nipped-them on the legs to keep them up. The day was hot and dust swirled continually. At afternoon smoko Kate couldn't jump the fence out of the pen to have a break because she was so tired. She lay in the shade for the 20-minute break and I lifted her back in for the last two-hour run.

Kate had handled the goats, wild as they were, so well at her first attempt that I eventually told the boss she hadn't seen goats before. He replied that I wasn't a bad worker but it was a pity I talked so much rubbish. Kate was lifted out of the pen and lay down in the most privileged position possible—in the twin cab ute—for the trip home. Despite the two boys' bruising and aches, they patted and wiped Kate down with a damp cloth for the duration of the 30-kilometre trip home.

Next day the word had got around the goat farm's neighbours that a bloke had a pretty good dog that could handle goats, so a few people wandered in during the day to see her work. From that job, people started to ring more frequently with offers of work.

The next job was a relief for everyone—1,500 head of Suffolk ewes needing a manicure. We set up the machine with our specially designed twin race so that sheep walked up to the machine side by side. They went into a single race at the end as they climbed up into the handling machine. The trick is to keep both sides of the race full all the time and if this is done efficiently, the sheep will run and enter the race a lot more easily, causing less stress on the sheep and the workers.

Bedee was about to get her first turn as she hadn't been allowed near the goats, or there would have been a substantial grave for dead goats if not some persons as well.

Kate, I must point out, had never seen the twin race system work before, nor had Bedee. So two boys worked on the machine as I was going to work with the dogs to teach them what to do. We filled the race and work started. As each race emptied I would walk up the side, push the stragglers up the front and then fill the race with more sheep. Soon Kate and Bedee both started pushing the sheep up the race on one side and I would get the other. I decided to make Kate stay on one side and get Bedee to work the other.

By 11.00 am on the first morning, the dogs knew what they had to do. Bedee would come around Kate's side and Kate would snap at her, nipping her to send her back. If they were filling the pen and Bedee stood in the wrong spot Kate would go up and snap at her, biting her sometimes, until she stood in the right position. After several jobs and two weeks, the dogs had become as professional as one could believe.

We started work at 7.30 am and stopped for 30 minutes at 9.30 am, and then worked through until noon, breaking up the afternoon in the same manner. We were working in 40 degree temperatures in the Riverina, and the only way to survive was to pace yourself correctly. The dogs learned the work schedule fast. If we called 'smoko', the dogs would stop work halfway through a bark to go and have a cold drink and lie in the shade, until time was up to start work again. We carried iced water for the dogs to drink and we always put it out for them. It turned out they wouldn't drink water, no matter how thirsty, unless we put it down for them.

Some time passed and the reputation of the dogs seemed always to proceed us.

For one job, we arrived at the property of a very big sheep dealer, a noted dog trainer, animal lover and, in general, a great bloke. Coincidentally, the person that gave me Bedee was shearing on the property with his four-man crew, so the place was a hive of activity. Since the shearers worked the same times as we did, the bloke that gave me Bedee didn't get a chance to see her work, but listened with increasing interest as the owner of the property related some of the skills of the two dogs.

On the first day we were there, the owner told me I would ruin the dogs as I used to pick them up and pat them and make a big fuss of them after any particular job they did. The boys also patted the dogs and made a fuss of them. The dog-trainer owner explained that dogs that work

484

hard can't be handled like this as they become too spoilt and soft and won't work. However, after working on this property for two weeks we noticed he was putting his young dog in the front of the ute instead of the back, and he was also picking it up and patting it.

The owner's father had a champion dog that people talked about. He came over quietly one day and said he had to move some very valuable stud ewes and lambs. He wondered if I could lend him Kate. I said I had to come too as Kate would not work for anyone else, not even for the boys with me on the machine. He was very happy with Kate's effort and said if I was taking orders for pups, could I put his name down and he would pay me immediately.

All the sheep had been shorn and only the wild rams remained unpenned. The owner's dog had been run over six months previously by a car, and his young dog was too inexperienced for the job, so the shearers and other helpers came out to pen up the rams. The father's dog and one of the shearers' dogs wouldn't go in the pen, so I told my dogs to hop over. Kate got in the pen and got behind a gate as a ram charged her. Bedee went after the ram and they started to turn the rams around and around like the goats until they eventually went up the race. The chap who gave me Bedee called out that he had only been joking when he said I could have the dog. The shearers stopped for fifteen minutes just to watch them work.

The job was finished after almost three weeks, and the owner came down with a cheque and paid me for the job. I thanked him and then he handed me a cheque for $2,000 to cash at the bank in the local town. I was a bit confused because he had paid full price plus a bit extra for the job. He said, 'Cash that cheque on your way through town and leave Kate with me. She will have a good home.' No way, but thanks anyway.

Another time, we went to a place near Oaklands to do a job, one of the worst ever. We had to remove the dags, dried and large and copious enough to fill a plastic bucket, from every sheep. We battled along for days, with one of the boys quitting the job. However, a highlight was the farmer who had a dog that no-one could better. Talk about smart, this one was super-smart. He was so good he only went to work when he believed no-one else could do the job. He was big, same colour as Kate, black and tan, but heavier and about three-quarters the size of an Alsatian.

One of the many clever things he did was to run up alongside an escaping sheep, grab it by the wool on its shoulder and hold it until a human walked up and took the sheep from him. Bedee watched this with interest and ran out from her duties to inspect the technique more closely.

At the very next job we were doing, a sheep jumped the race and ran away. Bedee went after the sheep, grabbed it by the wool on its shoulder and held it until one of us came to take the sheep. From then on I called 'catch' to Bedee if I wanted a sheep caught in the paddock. Kate looked on each time. One day I was moving ewes and lambs with Kate on her own. I called out 'catch', forgetting Bedee was not there. Kate ran up behind the sheep I'd singled out, grabbed it by the back leg, flipped it over and held it until I came up.

When fly time was prevalent we took the gear to the paddock, circled the sheep, and I would point out a suspect fly-strike, call out 'catch', and one or two dogs would catch the sheep. They caught on so fast that, after we'd done this a couple of times, they didn't need to be told—as soon as we put the fly-strike equipment in the ute to drive to the paddock, the dogs would round up the sheep into a circle, find any fly-struck sheep themselves, and catch and hold them until we were ready.

They had become so skilled at every aspect of sheep handling that I took them for granted, talked to them like humans, always let them ride in the front of the ute—and they even slept inside the house—without ever a blemish to their great record.

People came and stood and looked in awe as the dogs continued to perform their duties with ever increasing skills. Once I had to move 3,000 head back home—a trek of about five miles. We set the sheep on the way, left the dogs with them, and I went home to do some other jobs.

The neighbour who'd laughed at Kate the day she came home called in and told me to keep an eye on my sheep because a big mob was coming down the road and no-one was with them.

'Hell, what happened to my dogs?' I said in panic. But the dogs were there and the neighbour couldn't believe his eyes that the young dog, who only a year or so earlier didn't know the meaning of 'way back', could move 3,000 sheep down the road efficiently.

The battle to keep the farm was eventually lost, and I now drive a truck for a living. Kate and Bedee take turn about to ride with me in the truck. No more sheep to work, no more applause from the crowd, no more

486

excitement and challenge to do the impossible, but somehow the dogs seem to be happy to be with me—although sometimes I think they look at me and feel sorry for me because I no longer have the sheep to work nor do the jobs we loved doing.

AN ORIGINAL BILL

Bob Batchelor, Claremont, Western Australia

A drover gave me a big black dog,
He had a lot of white round his chest,
A friendly bloke, with an undershot jaw,
Always underfoot like a pest.

Living on me own at the shearing shed,
The Todds were both away.
Had all me dogs including this one,
And was working both night and day.

I tried him out—he had no idea,
I stuck with him day after day.
But in the end I'd had enough,
A 'twenty-two' would put him away.

I looked for a bullet, not one to be found,
It wasn't the day to be parted.
He began to work and never looked back,
This character's life had started.

I called him Bill, an original name.
He'd look up and smile at your face,
Then sneak up and piss on Jock Watson's leg
At orders—then step back a pace.

Jock never caught him, he was much too smart,
But he caught himself a bit later.
Fell out of a buggy and under the wheel,
I was sure he had gone to his maker.

But no—he woke up and gave me a lick,
Got into the box on the back.
He'd made up his mind he wanted to live,
And surviving's a bit of a knack.

I had him tied as a 'peg dog' one day
At a bridge high above water.
He went over the side and hung by his neck,
Archie saw him an hour or two later.

He looked quite dead. Archie left him there.
I didn't return until seven.
Took him back home to dig a grave,
You guessed it—he lived again.

He came on a train all the way to the West,
Settled into a different life.
Spent most of his time just sitting about,
It was hard to get into strife.

But he managed—was hit by a bullet.
Went walking, was shot in the chest.
Staggered home all bloody and helpless
And survived after treatment and rest.

I'm not sure I should tell this story
About Bill having ESP,
But he had it for certain in my mind.
It happened so often, you see.

I'd be out back driving a tractor
And see a sheep that had need to be done.
I'd think about Bill coming up the track,
And half an hour later he'd come!

We'd catch the sheep, fix up its flies.
Bill would lie around for a while.
Tractors were boring so he'd go home.
Does his story make you smile?

A HARD-BOILED EGG SODA

Garth Fragar, Little Hartley, New South Wales

In north Queensland's Longreach-Winton area during 1951, I had a black and tan sheepdog named Soda. He was a kelpie-collie cross with a lovely thick coat of not very long hair.

Following the advice of a local man, I treated Soda with mutton fat and kerosene for small brown dog ticks. Although I followed the recipe carefully, the treatment was far too severe and removed all the hair from his body, leaving him totally devoid of any covering. Soda was a pathetic sight but nothing could keep the smile from his face. He was a very happy, hard-working dog with plenty of spirit. As I wanted to work him at shearing time I made him a little sugar-bag coat to keep the sun from burning his bald back.

One morning we brought sheep to the yards at the shearing shed and I removed his little coat and tied him under a shady tree at the shed. After lunch I rode out in the 110 degree heat to get a small mob of sheep that had been missed about two miles from the shed. I left Soda tied up in the shade and took another dog to work the sheep.

Soda slipped out of his collar and followed me. He reached me just after I got to the sheep. This meant I had a problem—how to get Soda to the shed without him getting burnt and blistered by the sun.

It was a good season and there was water in a nearby creek, so I coated his back with brown-black mud and covered the mud with dry grass and we made it back OK. By this time, though, the mud had dried and it cracked off his back leaving him looking like a hard-boiled egg fresh from the shell, with every vestige of dried skin removed.

One of the shearers said his hair would not grow properly again, but in about two weeks he had a lovely new coat of crisp hair.

UNBROKEN BONES
Alison Chandler, Semaphore Park, South Australia

My son was helping to unload sheep from a four-tier semitrailer and was being assisted by his young kelpie, Boney.

They were working on the top tier and Boney was told to 'Get up front'. However, the dog had had enough, jumped overboard and crashed to the ground. There was consternation all around the yards.

Boney, fittingly short for Bonehead, lay still for half an hour. After being checked for broken bones, he went straight back to work, which kept the men talking for days.

ROVER'S ROPE
C C Cooper, Jamestown, South Australia

Many years ago my father was killing a sheep for the home table with, as usual, his dog Rover watching his every move.

When Dad reached the stage where he was ready to pull the carcase up off the ground, the rope which he always used was just not there. For a moment he hesitated, then walked off to get a rope.

He had not walked many steps when he met Rover coming to him dragging a rope in his mouth. It wasn't the right one, but Rover had realised what was needed.

A MEMORABLE PARTNERSHIP
Don Dufty, Albany, Western Australia

Alf Dufty, my late uncle, was a happy but firm boss and always had exceptional dogs. His best dog, Jeff, he had through the 1930s till about 1943.

Alf looked after the sheep on Hope Glen, which was about seventeen miles north of Nhill. The property was the estate of J C Dufty and extended almost to the southern boundary of the Big Desert. Most of the times I was with him he drove a 1939/40 Chev ute that had a wide parcel shelf at the back of the seat. This is where Jeff used to lie, with his head near the open driver's side window.

Going round a mob, Alf would just say in a conversational way, 'Looks like a blown sheep there, fella.' Jeff would jump out the window and catch the sheep out of the mob, almost always without any further direction. It seemed as though there was telepathy between them. When, now and then, Jeff caught a very daggy one that was not blown, Alf would say, 'No, not that one', and Jeff would let it go and find the one Alf wanted. I never heard my uncle yell or scold Jeff harshly. On the rare occasion that Jeff did the wrong thing, Alf would say, 'Hey, come back, you mad sod. You can do better than that.' And he invariably did.

It was more than six miles from the back paddock to the homestead, but it was no problem for Jeff to move a mob this distance on his own. Alf would let the sheep onto the road, say, 'Bring them home, boy', and a few hours later they would be in the yards, with Jeff sitting in the gateway waiting for Alf to shut it. The pat and few words he got were a quite sufficient reward from his point of view.

One day Alf drove down the road and was halfway home when he saw a sheep that looked flyblown. Leaving the wide wire gate open, he drove into the paddock only to find about fifteen or so blown sheep. With his young dog he pushed them into the yards in a patch of mallee about half a mile from the road. He was still working on the sheep when he saw Jeff's mob nearing the open gate. Jeff was slowly trotting from one side to the other, keeping the stragglers up with the mob. Suddenly he stopped, went through the fence into the paddock and made a wide circle around to the open gateway. He sat watching the gate about a chain back from the roadway until the last sheep had passed by.

Alf was amazed. How could he have known the gate had been left open? He went later to the spot where Jeff had left the mob and gone through the fence. It was impossible for him to see a wire gate lying on the ground—even less so from a dog's height. Alf swore that as he passed Jeff and the mob on the way home, Jeff gave him a look that said, 'Why did you leave that b . . . gate open?'

TOO CLEVER BY HALF

Bruce Mills, Tumby Bay, South Australia

In the first book of *Great Working Dog Stories* there is a story about Karla, a blue and tan kelpie and how I came to own her. She was a dog of exceptional intelligence, loyalty and natural ability.

One afternoon, however, her talent rather overextended itself. My wife had advised me when I got home that we were having relations for a barbecue lunch the next day and we had no meat left. Not having any killers handy, I called Karla and went in the ute to the bottom dam, thinking there would be wethers in for a drink. There were none at the dam, but a few hundred metres further on, there were about twenty just moving away.

I held Karla up above the bluebushes and pointed in the direction of the sheep and bid her to bring them back. Away she went and I waited. And waited. I then decided to climb the windmill to see what was going on. There, at least two kilometres away, was a pall of dust. The main mob of sheep no doubt had left the dam much earlier and was spread out over that distance. Karla had kept breaking out until she had reached the lead.

By the time the sheep were returned to the dam and I had caught a suitable killer, the sun had set. I called to Karla to let the rest go, and as she jumped into the front of the ute, as she always did when she thought she had done well, I cursed her for being such a stupid old bastard and that I would now have to kill and dress the sheep in the dark.

Karla wriggled her ears and thumped the seat of the ute with her tail. She knew by the tone of my voice that my blasphemous words were really praise and my heart was filled with pride at owning a dog that displayed the attributes of a true mustering, self-motivated, working kelpie.

MIDGET THE MIGHTY

Alan Masman, Lake Cathie, New South Wales

The working dogs most spoken of in the Australian bush are the kelpies, the cattle dogs, the border collies. However, the working dog in this story is a miniature black and white fox terrier, the runt of a litter with such small legs that her height when fully grown was only about seven inches. Her name was Midget.

She was born in Mudgee, New South Wales, and when she was old enough she was taken to Wamerawa, our 8,000-acre sheep property at Carinda in the north-west. She was to be a house pet for my wife and teenage children. This was the case for only a very short time, however, because she became very attached to me and my motorbike. She was soon riding with me, her front legs hanging onto the handlebars. She exuded an air of supreme confidence and an impression that she, not me, was overseer of the entire operation.

The sight of sheep sent her into a frenzy of continuous yapping, which became her hallmark. She became a brainy and very game paddock and yard worker, but because she was so small, she tired quickly. Ten minutes of frantic work at a time was about her limit, but she would put it to good use. She ran from one side of the sheep to the other, yapping constantly to give them a good hurry-up. When she needed a rest, she would come and nip my boot to tell me she needed to be picked up. In the sheep yards, she worked continuously and could even jump up onto the sheep's backs, yapping the whole time. She really got some action from the sheep.

On those occasions when I had to lift a sheep into another yard, I would often feel a small weight in addition to that of the sheep. Looking down I would find Midget fastened onto the wool. She would stay latched on until I was about to drop the sheep on the other side, and then she'd sit and look up at me for a pat. I think she believed she was actually helping me to lift the sheep!

Midget's skills impressed a drover passing by so much that he inquired if she was for sale. He liked her ability to yap and wanted her as a 'peg' dog to block off a laneway or gateway when the stock were camped at night. I refused the offer, of course.

Soon after this, though, Midget went missing. I had been running in the horses with Midget's help. As was the usual practice, when the bike reached the bridge near the house yard, Midget jumped off to return to the house. This time, however, the horses raced past the horse yard and took off to the far end of the paddock, so I wheeled round and took off after them. I didn't realise it at the time, but Midget must have followed and run among the trees where a wedge-tailed eagle was sitting on eggs.

Twelve months later I found her jawbone, with its double fangs in the bottom jaw, under a tree bearing the nest. There was no doubt that this was Midget's jaw as we recognised her teeth.

The household was never quite the same again and many a tear was shed for a quaint little dog who was not only a loyal and trusted buddy but an outstanding little worker as well.

SONNY AND THE ESCAPEE
Jennifer Coathupe, Kingston, South Australia

Our working dog Sonny is a big black and tan kelpie with a waggy tail that contorts his whole body when he's excited and happy. He wouldn't win any beauty contest, though, as he looks a little like a Doberman and he's a bit forbidding except when he knows you.

One time we were shearing our rams, and it had been a long day for my husband and the station hand. On the very last pen one of the rams decided he didn't want to be shorn. He shot out of the pen while the station hand was getting another ram out.

Bob, my husband, was busy shearing, so this renegade was able to canter out across the board. I saw it coming out and attempted to corner it with my broom, but he turned to face me, took one look at me and the broom, and decided I didn't present too much opposition—he charged right through, leaving me sitting upside down on the board wondering what had happened and where the ram had gone.

Sonny had been lying under the wool table having a kip, but he got up and sauntered out of the shed after the escapee.

We finished the rams in the shed and were cleaning up when our stock and station agent called in to have a talk about what was going on in the

494

markets. Bob and the agent were leaning against the wool table talking. The station hand was tidying up around the wool bins, and I had almost finished sweeping the board.

Suddenly there was a clatter from behind us and, on turning around, we saw that Sonny had done his job well. He had gone after that ram, cornered it, overpowered it and brought it all the way back into the shed. While we watched him, he hunted it across the board to where the station hand grabbed it and proceeded to shear it.

Needless to say, we were all stunned. We knew he was a good dog but hadn't realised quite how good till that day.

ORDERS FROM ON HIGH
Natalie Broad, Cue, Western Australia

Fred was a little, red, rough-coated kelpie dog belonging to Eric, my brother-in-law. He was top dog of the seven we had at the time, but very definitely a one-man dog who worshipped the ground Eric walked on.

I have a funny little story to tell about Fred during mustering time five years ago. Eric was flying the plane, so Jenny, the jilleroo who was working with us at the time, decided to take Fred because she had seen how useful he was. She thought he would be able to help out. We have an 800,000-acre sheep station in the Murchison, so we travel a lot of miles, especially at mustering time.

Eric directed Jenny onto a large mob of toey sheep. They started to go in about ten different directions at once, so she screamed and signalled to Fred, 'get back there.' All he would do was run along next to the motor-bike, waiting to jump on for a free ride. He wasn't going to work for her! According to Fred, he only had one master—and it definitely was not Jenny.

Eric flew over again and saw that Jenny was still in difficulty trying to control her mob. Over the mustering radio attached to the front of the bike, he asked her what the matter was. She tried to explain her plight. The other musterers were too far away to come and assist, plus they had mobs of their own to control. The only option was for Fred to lift his game.

Jenny called Fred back to the bike and Eric whistled into his radio and told Fred to 'get back round there'. Fred shot off the back of the bike like a bullet and did what he knows best. Jenny stared in amazement at this extraordinary little dog who, after taking his orders from his boss in the air, had the mob under control in no time at all.

WINNING OVER THE RIVAL
Betty Thompson, Bylong, New South Wales

When I married 43 years ago and came to live with my husband, I felt everything was perfect and the love we had for each other was sublime. Alas, I never dreamt I would have to fight for that love with a dog for two years and be treated with such dislike.

Jinny was my rival right from the very first day I took up my position as a loving wife. She was my husband's shadow and obedient servant, following at his heels wherever he went. There was some doubt about her breeding but she showed a mixture of cattle and sheepdog in her appearance and in her ability to work both cattle and sheep. She was really good to watch, biting as directed by my husband—either just a nip or a really good bite, first one heel and then the other—but she never bit the sheep and was quite handy in the yards as well.

Several months after I married she still eyed me off with suspicion and would have nothing to do with me. Even when it came to her feed-time she would not accept it from me and would wait until I was out of sight before she very gingerly ate it with distaste. If my husband put his arms around me she would slink off and refuse to follow us another step.

Having lived on the land all my life, I was accustomed to animals and the work associated with them. Naturally I helped with all the outside work when needed, which was often and especially with the stock. One day I went to help with the muster and, as my own horse was lame, my husband caught one of his horses for me to ride. Normally it was Jinny's habit to spin and bark with excitement, then rush off ahead of us as we mounted. This day, however, as I was about halfway onto the horse, Jinny unwound and, as quick as a flash, darted in and with all her pent-up hatred bit my horse on the front foot. Well, you can just imagine the result. My poor horse let out a wild snort, leapt in the air and at the same time spun sideways. How I managed to land in the saddle remains a mystery to this very day. When I finally quietened my horse and abused the dog, she smirked back at me as if to say, 'I got you that time.'

Her jealousy went on for almost two years and I had given up trying to win her over.

On one occasion we had a bad outbreak of bushfires, and my husband and all the available men had to be on the job both day and night while I was left at home to cope with the chores. We had just begun shearing and had just started into a mob of ewes and lambs and could not stop. As we only had a small two-stand shed, we did the rouseabouting ourselves and, in the absence of my husband and workmen at the fires, I had to turn my talents to being the shed hand.

Jinny was left at home with me and her spirits reached rock-bottom. She went into deep mourning for her master and true love, staying put in her kennel. About the third day, though, she actually followed me to the shed and watched me pick up the fleeces and throw them on the table and sweep the board. Now and again I gave her a pat and said, 'Cheer up, old girl, he will be home soon.'

Each time there was a small response from her—just a slight wag of the tail—but it was the first ever, and I began to wonder what would happen next.

On the fourth day, she began following me and when I picked up a fleece, she would pick up a piece of wool, bring it back to the table and drop it at my feet as if to say, 'There, I am helping too.' I would tell her she was a good dog, and get a big tail-wag.

By the end of the week she was keeping close tabs on my every move. She came to help me start the engine to run the generator for our lights at night. As I cranked the motor she would rush in and bark at the handle until it started. Then she would sit down and look at me with her head on one side as if to say, 'There, that helped you get it going, didn't it?'

The final capitulation came when she followed me to bed and slept outside the door all night. I knew at last I was accepted, but I did wonder if she would change when my husband returned.

It was a great surprise that when he finally arrived—exhausted and

497

smelling of smoke and gum leaves—and took me in his arms, she barked her approval and jumped up and licked, first him, then me.

I had at last won the day and she was willing to share her master with me for ever.

TO OUR TRIXIE
Maureen Turner, Old Junee, New South Wales

She was only a little red kelpie bitch,
Only a dog, that's true.
The kind that was bred for working sheep,
She was loyal through and through.
She came as a hungry, gangly pup,
And didn't grow very large,
But the stubborn old ewes in the mob would move
When that little dog took charge.
Clever and cunning and competent,
Working all day in the sun,
Till the lengthening shadows and cooling breeze
Would tell her that work was done.
And only then would she come to my side
And tongue at her master's feet,
Knowing the jobs of the day were done,
Her tasks were all complete.

A HUGE VOCABULARY
Greg Walcott, Horsham, Victoria

I am one of the fortunate sheepdog owners to have been lucky enough to have owned the 'freak' dog whose intelligence was simply outstanding and quite unbelievable. I have owned several good or very good sheep-dogs, but Whisky was extraordinary.

He was largely a self-taught dog. I trained him with the basics as a pup but rarely had to teach much else as he simply picked up things or worked things out for himself. His powers of reasoning and comprehension often amazed me.

His vocabulary was huge. I once read in a national daily newspaper that dogs could not learn more than twenty words, but simply reacted to tone of voice. As a result I wrote down in excess of 400 words in Whisky's vocabulary and quite often tested the tone of voice theory by including, in a conversation with someone, a simple order to Whisky in the same tone that I was using. He would invariably stir from his half sleep and do as suggested.

I was able to teach him many names—of people, pets, sheds, vehicles and so on. This was often very handy as I quite often used him to run messages to people. I would tie a note in a rag to his collar and send him off in search of a particular person—and he always found them.

One day I was having trouble drafting ewes. Whisky and I always drafted by ourselves with little or no trouble. This day, however, was very hot—the sheep were not running, the dog had his tongue out and I was getting hot under the collar. In desperation I decided to change the pens around to try to make things easier. In the meantime I told Whisky to 'Go and get a drink. Go to the dam and have a drink'—which he was only too pleased to do.

When I had sorted things out in the shed I called Whisky to start drafting again. There was no sign of him. I was really starting to get annoyed. I looked out of the shed to see Dad driving up from the house, which was about one kilometre away. He arrived looking very concerned and with Whisky on the front seat.

Whisky had knocked on the kitchen door demanding entry. When Mum opened it he marched straight past and up to the kitchen table. No sign of Dad so back past Mum, out through the lounge and up through the front room to where Dad was working at his desk. With a demanding couple of barks and an anxious look he about-turned and marched out with Mum and Dad watching in utter surprise and bewilderment. Thinking the worst, Dad followed him out to the car and promptly drove up to the shed to see what was wrong.

To this day I do not know if Whisky mistook 'dam' for 'Dad' or simply took it on himself to go and seek Dad's assistance with the drafting. Mum and Dad couldn't believe the assertive way he got his message across.

WHERE'S THE 'OFF' SWITCH?

B E Madden, Girilambone, New South Wales

Some years ago, for some mysterious reason quite beyond me, the station was experiencing a shortage of dogs. It's usually the other way around—an abundance of half-starved dogs that drove me crazy trying to fatten them.

The boss always maintained a good dog was infinitely better than two ordinary station hands—but they were in short supply also. Therefore my husband was instructed to keep his eyes and ears open for a good dog to *buy*! A few weeks later the sheepdog trials were on in town. What better place to find a dog suitable not only for sheep work but with good breeding potential? My bloke not only found the kind of dog needed, he paid real money for him—his first ever cash purchase for a dog—$100 no less.

On their arrival home, we all admired this sharp, alert-looking dog. He certainly looked the part and we could hardly wait to see him perform. On the weekend our daughter and family arrived, providing the perfect excuse to try the dog—they needed some killers.

Daughter, son-in-law and kids all climbed aboard the truck, hoping to see some fancy dog work, and after the dog had been tied up on the back, I jumped in the front determined not to miss the display. We got to the paddock and quickly spotted a likely looking mob of sheep. When the truck stopped we were all warned to stay still and quiet while my bloke let the dog go and sent him off to round up the sheep.

With ears pricked and a swift look around, the dog set off in a rush for the sheep. We were all very impressed with the way he rapidly had the sheep rounded up and brought back to the master. We were even more impressed with how he held them in a tight little bunch while the three killers were caught and tied up.

The master then whistled the dog to come behind and started off to bring the truck over and load up the sheep. Looking around as he got to the truck, he was a bit astonished to see the dog was bringing the sheep along too.

For the next half hour kids, daughter, son-in-law and my husband himself ran themselves ragged and yelled themselves hoarse trying to get the rotten dog to 'come behind' and let the sheep go. In utter frustration, my husband finally roared, 'The boss had better pay another $100 to stop this bloody dog!'

I have completely forgotten what the name of that dog was—but I do remember he didn't last here very long.

BACKING THE BLOCKAGE
Frank Bawden, Tumby Bay, South Australia

Friend, sharefarmer and shearer Andrew Mills comes from a family of noted kelpie breeders, owners and trainers. Accordingly, he has a particularly good dog called Boy.

During shearing we were filling the shed from outside when the sheep baulked in one of the catching pens. Andrew sent Boy up onto the backs of the wethers, up the ramp and into the shed to look for the blockage.

My brother Bernie, who is big and hairy, was the shed hand. Unbeknown to us, he was bending down, nailing the grating in the catching pen into place.

Boy, true to form, darted over the backs of the sheep and landed with a big 'woof' right on Bernie's broad back. It's still debatable today who got the bigger shock. Bernie leapt into the air with shouted obscenities, while Boy must have suffered a good deal from shock also.

We spectators had considerable difficulty controlling our mirth. Needless to say, Bernie was at a loss to see what was so funny.

PART 8
CATTLE COUNTRY

Swirling dust, beasts roaring like an angry football crowd, yards with fortress fences, the crack of stockwhips and the drumbeat of hooves—these are the essence of cattle country. Shiny-coated cattle, herded by helicopter, horse and dog, jostle and bellow and always await that moment to revolt. Dogs with jaws like rabbit traps eye them, alert to the slightest hint of insurrection.

Bred to cope with droughts and long distances between waterholes, Australian cattle are some of the world's toughest. To tackle a cow fiercely protecting her calf, or a wild scrub bull, takes guts. The dogs of cattle country, if they are going to survive, also have to be fit, intelligent and agile.

It's not all grime and sweat though. Out of the dust come the unexpected hilarious moments such as the time emus ruined the muster, as described by young Kathy Boyden of Charters Towers. And Errol Munt says he nearly fell off his horse laughing so much at his dog Gundy standing on top of an angry bull in a dam.

The ringers in Fred's team, though, might not have been laughing when the horse-biter gave them a bit of a nudge along.

For Rags, however, who was seriously injured while saving his owner, there is deep gratitude.

THE DAYS OF NO DOGS:
SHIRLEY JOLIFFE'S STORY
Angela Goode

More Great Working Dog Stories included a story called 'I Had Got Myself a Beauty' by Shirley Joliffe who, after she had got her children off her hands, went mustering. She left a comfortable job in a town to return to the bush, swapping pens for mobs of cattle and a desk for a horse and dog.

In the course of putting together this book, I heard from Shirley's cousin Beryl Thomas (whose story 'Old Don of St Kilda' appears in Part 6 'Back of Beyond' in this book) that Shirley, 59, was one of very few female contract musterers in the land. So I gave Shirley a call at her home in Mitchell, in south-eastern Queensland, and caught her in the middle of cooking a meal for some of her six grandchildren.

She told me that when she got Ned, the cream and tan bitzer of her story, in 1975, she had in fact headed straight out to Forest Vale station with a contract to muster 60,000 acres of wild cattle. That's some change from working in a newsagency and raising three daughters in a town. She employed three or four men and took over the cooking and the running of the stock camp as well as spending her days in the saddle running down wild cattle and quietening them in small mobs of coachers.

Shirley was no stranger to the bush, however. She had been brought up on her parents' 30,000-acre beef cattle property not far from Mitchell. She broke in her own horses, rode in camp-draft events, won a few and took out a Queensland championship.

She moved to another cattle property when she married. After the stint in the town, she and Ned took off and worked together until Ned was put down in her old age. As well as continuing to regularly muster cattle for Forest Vale, where she keeps her plant of twelve stock horses, Shirley takes on casual jobs as a musterer all round the Mitchell area.

This gentle-sounding woman, who admits to a love of fashion and who has no plans for retirement, not only runs down wild and stirry cattle, but in her early days at Forest Vale, even used to throw them. 'It's fairly rugged work,' she says in an understated way. 'The boys do it very well. I never had quite enough power to pull them over quickly.' Nevertheless, she did throw about six on her own.

These days Shirley and her men have the Forest Vale cattle under control, so there's no longer much need for such heroics. They spend a lot of time riding around the mobs and domesticating them. From August each year she spends twelve weeks mustering the station so the calves can be weaned. In January, another 12-week cycle begins, doing the branding muster.

On her own 1,500-acre place at Roma—which, like everywhere else in the region, is devastated by drought—she is handfeeding the few cattle that remain on the place. Her 45 breeding cows have been sent away on agistment.

Shirley knows of no other woman in charge of a mustering team, although she is sure there must be some. Many women these days have been forced to take up mustering to help their husbands out because of the financial disaster caused by interest rates, drought and the wool crash. But few opt to take up mustering as a full-time occupation.

Shirley admits she does get some strange looks from time to time when she's out on a horse . . . not so much because she's a woman, though. It's more because she wears the biggest felt cowboy hat she can find—with the brim turned down right over her eyes. Then, like some wild west outlaw, she ties a bandana over her nose and mouth, so all that's visible is a pair of eyes. 'It's not for looks. I just like to be protected from the sun,' says Shirley, who also wears gloves and long sleeves out on the job for the same reason.

Sadly, the days of dogs out in the mustering camps seem to have passed. Although Shirley has a blue stumpy-tailed cattle dog that would love to work, she doesn't dare risk it: 'Most people put out 1080 these days for dingoes, and I just couldn't bear to see my dogs poisoned,' Shirley says. 'It's getting very hard to use dogs out in this country because there is so much bait around—not that I blame them. It's good that they're trying to control dingoes, but I'd certainly use heelers in my work if I could.'

It's a pity indeed. The sight of a heeler retrieving a cow and then, as Shirley wrote in Ned's story, 'floating through the air like a trapeze artist on the brush of a cow's tail' is no doubt missed by many.

DANCES WITH EMUS
Kathy Boyden, Charters Towers, Queensland

I live about two hours out of Charters Towers in north Queensland on Moonlight Creek station. I am eleven and do correspondence lessons through the Charters Towers Distance Education Centre.

On one of those typical Aussie working days in the bush, my sister Jody, twelve, and I were allowed to take time off school to join in a muster for mickey bulls. It took a while for Dad to get all the kids and workers saddled up. The men were really looking forward to getting stuck into chasing the bulls and everyone was impatient. Probably keenest of the lot, though, were our nine eager blue heelers, led by Dad's dog Ned. Even though they were often called 'the useless mongrels', no mustering gang would be complete without them.

Finally everyone was settled and ready, so off we went on a hard day's work. It was a day we were always to look back on and have a really good laugh about—although at the time, Grandad and the other men didn't see the funny side of things. We had finally mustered a herd of scrub cattle together and all the troublemaking micks had settled down to a make-believe peacefulness when suddenly we had visitors.

The first we knew of this was when our working dogs, who had been taking a breather under the shady trees, sat up with a start and pricked up their ears. Of course Ned, the boss dog, couldn't resist the fun of a chase on a hot day. So off he dashed with bristles sticking up a mile high and that awful bark of his that always sets Dad in a bad mood. All the commotion was over just a few inquisitive emus who had seen the mob of cattle and the ringers, and had decided to join them. Of course Ned had other ideas that unfortunately didn't come true.

The poor emus, who had almost reached the cattle, were suddenly being mustered up by Ned and the mates in his clan. But you all know that emus can't be made to do what they don't consider dignified, so instead of running away so that Ned could have his bit of sport, the frightened emus turned in a semicircle and headed straight for the mob, with Ned and his team hot on their tails.

For the next ten minutes there was one mighty commotion, what with emus flat-out through the mob of cattle and 'the useless mongrels' right behind them. The dogs were letting out such a howl and whine that you can imagine what happened to that mob of cattle. I can tell you—those micks didn't hang around to see the fun!

By this time the emus had had enough and decided to give the dogs a bit of a fright, so they screeched to a halt, did a tight circle and darted straight for the dogs. Ned, despite being such a brainy dog, couldn't even guess what was in store for him. With a snarl and a brave bark he stood his ground but, honking as loud as thunder, the emus advanced with deadly intent. You should have seen those dogs with tails between their legs head straight for the horses. Ned, however, was the oldest and slowest of the lot and he wasn't quick enough to escape the kick of the leading emu's powerful legs or the cruel peck of his beak. The rest of the dogs found sanctuary under the horses' bellies.

Until this time, the men on their horses had enjoyed the spectacle of the dogs and emus and had been laughing their heads off. But all of a sudden they found themselves caught up in the turmoil too. What with dogs and emus running around the horses and the horses starting to have a good buck, there wasn't much peace and quiet. The men were yelling at the dogs to shoot through way out yonder, while the emus were stomping their feet to the beat of a drum. The dogs, meanwhile, were cringing on the ground like cowards. Just when the chaos was at its height, the emus turned and strutted away with necks held high, never to be seen again.

When the men had finally controlled their horses and discovered that their mob of cattle had disappeared completely, their tempers were up pretty high. Dad needed something to take his fury out on, so his keen eye roved around for the instigator of all the mischief. But Ned, the trusty, hardworking packleader was nowhere in sight and he stayed invisible for quite a few hours. No-one had ever said he was brainless.

PUTTING A BITE ON
THE RINGERS
Graydon Hutchinson, Alpha, Queensland

Chris was in his forties, single and semi-retired. He always had a few horses and cattle on his small block and did an odd day's outside work, but he spent most of his time sitting in a deck chair on his front verandah, or down town talking to someone.

He paid big money for a well-bred cattle dog to help him with his stock work but the mutt wouldn't look at cattle, let alone bite one. He would bite horses though—he was always chasing and biting them. He would even bite the saddle horse when Chris was riding him. Despite numerous beltings with sticks and whips, the dog persisted in his terrible habit. Chris had threatened to shoot him a few times but never got around to it.

One day Chris's best friend Fred arrived for a short visit. He was about ten years younger and led a much harder life. He ran wild cattle on a large property and for his efforts he received half the proceeds of the sale of the cattle. From these he had to pay wages to several men and maintain horses, dogs, saddlery and so on. Even with these expenses, he still made big money.

One of his biggest problems was finding suitable men and dogs. The men had to be able to ride fast in rugged country when running cattle into the coachers and be able to tie up a cleanskin cow or bull. The dogs were needed to bite a beast that had broken from the coachers hard enough to frighten it back into the mob, or to hang onto the nose of a bull while someone got onto his tail to pull him down. Fred went through a lot of dogs—and men.

Fred spotted the horse-biter tied up near the empty 44-gallon drum with the end cut out. 'Hell, that's a good sort of a dog you've got there,' exclaimed Fred.

'Yeah, mate, he's good but I haven't got the work for him,' Chris said. 'Take him with you.'

It was about a month later that Fred dropped in again. Chris was hardly game to mention the dog but eventually got around to asking how it was performing.

'Bloody beauty, mate—best dog I've ever had,' came the unexpected reply.

'Fair dinkum?' muttered the unbelieving Chris. 'Will he bite cattle?'

'Hell, no,' laughed the cheerful Fred. 'He won't even look at a beast, but by hell he can bite horses. That couple of slow riding ringers that were always hanging back on the tail are up in the lead on every run now.'

HEELING INSTINCT ON HOLD
Les Evans, Borden, Western Australia

Many give credit to dogs that is not strictly justified—dogs work after training and repetition. However, there are some who seem to have a brain.

When I was a boy we had a little red kelpie bitch. She was the only heeler, with horses and cattle, we ever owned. On this occasion my father was doing some fence repairs along a little-used road. He had two horses standing unattended on the road hitched to a wagon. Normally they would remain like this indefinitely, but on this day a limb broke off a tree and startled them. Away they went. When Dad saw Lassie take off after them he thought, 'Oh well, that's that. I won't see the horses for a while.

The wagon could break up and I'll have to walk home.'

However, instead of heeling the horses as she had always done previously, Lassie went to one horse's head and bit and barked till she had them jammed against the fence. When Dad finally got to them, Lassie was jumping up and down and her tail was thrashing happily. She had caught them and she was very pleased with herself.

It really was quite an extraordinary act since it was such a significant departure from her normal method of working. She had overruled her natural instinct to heel the horses in order to stop them. That seems to me to be using brainpower.

SHY AND WHITE
Enid Clark, Singleton, New South Wales

Shy was so named because she would whimper and squirm when I picked her up. She is almost completely white and has two blue eyes. I hadn't wanted a white dog but she turned out to be better than I had ever hoped—a tough, intelligent worker, a gentle and loving friend. She worked for five years at Singleton saleyards in between mustering wild cattle in the mountains.

Not having wanted a white dog initially, I have found they have great advantages over red or black dogs. Cattle can see them better and can therefore be stopped more easily. In scrubby country a white dog is very easy to see in the distance and I have noticed that they don't feel the heat as much as a dark-coloured dog. Some of these factors may account for Shy's talent with cattle.

We have a small place and work casually for other graziers. On one property we mustered there were some very steep and dirty gullies and if the cattle broke we sometimes had to spend half a day getting them together again. As we approached some of these gullies, Shy would leave the mob and go ahead to wait for the breakaways. She would meet them face to face with force, rushing and jumping up and barking in their faces—which would alter 99 per cent of their minds.

Once, on another property, a breakaway heifer about eighteen months old all but knocked my husband's horse over and made for the scrub. The dogs were sent to block it, but when we noticed that it was useless, we called them back as they were needed to take the mob to the yards a couple of miles away. We usually work two dogs each in bad country and one each in average country. This was bad country but only three dogs came back and Shy wasn't one of them. We put the mob in the yard and had lunch, then went on drafting—and still Shy hadn't shown up.

After about three and a half hours we noticed a beast coming around the mountain about half a mile away, just a few feet at a time. Then, as it got closer, we could see Shy rushing in at its head. It would charge and stop. She brought it all the way into the yards. It was the wild heifer and it hadn't gotten any quieter. It had taken her approximately four hours to bring it the two miles.

Shy is ten years old now and only does the little jobs around the house. It makes her feel important to still be needed. She gets the house cow and educates our weaner cattle in and out of the yards. She keeps our calves and our neighbours' calves sorted out if they get through the creek block when it rains. If we truck a new house cow from our other place, and she hasn't come along to help, she makes sure the neighbours end up with it the next day. She thinks it is a stray and that it must be sent back. If she helps us bring it home, then she'll leave it here.

A couple of months ago we bought three small black calves to rear. We put them in the calf yard under Shy's supervision. Next morning, one was gone. When we let Shy off her chain, we didn't notice where she went until we heard a cow roaring and saw her coming 300–400 yards away, bringing a little black calf with the mother in hot pursuit from our neighbour's paddock. She worked the calf through the fence and brought it right to our calf pen. We didn't like to disappoint her, so we put it onto the truck to take it back to the neighbour's place.

When we arrived we were surprised to discover they had our calf tied up at their yards and were wondering who owned it. Shy must have seen it get out of the yard and head off into the night, so was determined to retrieve it as soon as she was free.

SWAM HER IN

Jean Richards, Upper Lansdowne, New South Wales

The men were working in very hilly and heavily timbered country and they were mustering the top paddock. After getting all 150 head of cattle to the top of the hill, a heifer broke away. Nigger, the black kelpie, went after her.

The boss said not to worry about the heifer as they would first take the mob to the yard, then go and get her after lunch. Just as they finished lunch, they heard Nigger barking. The men followed the sound to the river and were astonished to see Nigger swimming along in the middle of the river with the heifer right in front of him. When the dog and heifer got to the shallow water at the crossing, the heifer left the river and Nigger drove her up the bank and put her in the small paddock near the yard.

Nigger must have swum her about two miles down the river, because there was nowhere else they could have entered the water because of high banks, fences, rocks and trees along that distance.

THE BULL-RIDER'S DEBUT

Errol Munt, Toowoomba, Queensland

This story happened some fifteen years ago and involved Gundy, a cattle dog I had been given as a pup by my uncle, Mr Norm Ehrlich.

I was on horseback and Gundy and I were trying to shift a Droughtmaster bull across the highway to the yards on the other side. We almost had him enclosed in the yard when he decided to break away and head back across the highway, which was about 250 metres away. The determined bull gathered speed and took no notice of either the horse or Gundy as we tried to block him.

When he reached the first road fence he leapt across the grid and over the highway and then smashed through a piping gate on the other side. By then I suppose he thought he was home and safe. This was not the case as Gundy and I were in hot pursuit. The language from me was 'blue' with rage, and Gundy was heeling him every step he took. By the time I opened the gate at the first fence and got across the highway, I could see the bull heading for the supposed safety of a dam. After a brisk gallop to catch Gundy and the bull, I arrived to see the bull make a leap into the dam. Gundy duly followed.

In the next twenty seconds I changed from being extremely angry to laughing so much that I couldn't sit straight on the horse. Imagine seeing your dog swim up alongside a bull, climb upon his shoulders, stand there on all fours, and bite the bull on the back of the neck. A bull-riding dog—I hadn't seen that before.

Deciding the water was no longer the best place to be, the bull swam to the edge of the dam, with the dog still aboard. Then he climbed up the bank and stopped some three metres away from the water. At this stage, Gundy jumped off. He had ridden his eight seconds and got top points from the judge!

If only dogs could talk—in between eyeing off the bull, he would occasionally look back across the dam at me with a pleased look upon his face that seemed to say, 'I got him for you.' After a minute or two's rest so we could all regain our composure, the bull was willing to be driven anywhere without resentment.

DREAM LOVER
Doug Allison, St George, Queensland

Lover was named after Rain Lover, who won the Melbourne Cup, but he was also a good lover by nature and produced many smart sons and daughters. He was a working freak capable of working big and small mobs, ewes and lambs, or lambs only, and with limited instructions. As a yard dog he had no superior. However, my story is of cattle mustering.

My horse-racing partner, Jack Dyball of St George, had a property called Peppercorn which was divided by Buckenbah channel. It had a 4,000-acre back paddock mostly consisting of thick mulga scrub in which eight head of grown, branded cattle plus four young calves had twice eluded two experienced stockmen. They had tried to muster them on horses but gave up, saying they couldn't be coaxed out of the mulga.

Following an overnight inch of rain I asked Jack to give me the four fresh sheepdogs and his utility so Lover and I could go out to retrieve his scrubber cattle. He replied that I was stone crazy. 'How are you going to get cattle out on foot that two good men can't get on horses?' he said.

The cattle were easily tracked, and with the burrs on the ground softened from the rain, Lover and the four sheepdogs were sooled onto the cattle as they took off. With Lover in the lead and the station sheep-dogs barking and the calves bellowing, the mob soon bailed up.

Armed with a stockwhip, I followed, and after half a dozen times of bailing the mob up, I had manoeuvred them onto the road. With Lover controlling the lead and the station dogs helping when necessary, I walked behind the cattle for six miles through three gates and eventually put them across a single-lane bridge 50 yards long. Jack Dyball was amazed. He couldn't believe a man on foot with five dogs could have achieved what we did with such stirry cattle.

Lover was a genius or a dream dog. He always helped me in my job as sheep and wool officer for the Department of Primary Industry in St George. Several times I classed and drafted mobs of up to 1,400 sheep with only the dog to help. Once, with the owner helping, we classed 3,600 sheep in one day. The owner voluntarily paid for 4,000 sheep, suggesting I should shout Lover a rum that night with the extra pay.

YOU LITTLE TRIMMER
Geoff Hamilton, Legume, New South Wales

In 1950 I was fortunate enough to be given a part-kelpie black pup from Mr Whaley Funnell of Jackerbulbyn. I called the pup Trimmer. His father, a fantastic dog named Spud, together with his master would muster the property of some 20,000 acres of coastal forest country.

When Trimmer started work, he was so hyperactive it took sixteen days straight mustering in the mountains and then a droving trip to settle him down. Among some of the amazing things he did was the time he

515

took a mob of cattle along a road, not collecting any other cattle on the way providing I was in front—although I might have been ahead by as much as two miles. I would canter along and enjoy a cup of tea with the neighbours until the cattle caught up, and then I would let them through the gate and go on again.

Another time I had 68 Hereford weaners on the road to Tabulam, just the second day weaned from the mothers. By 8 am I had them settled down and descending the ridge towards Rocky River when the lead, about a mile away, went through a gate to visit some Jersey cows. I sent Trimmer after the calves and he proceeded to bring them out steadily, but it seemed he'd left one behind. I cursed him profusely and got the Hereford calf—same shape, size and colour as my own mob—out of the paddock. I then realised from the earmark it was not one of mine.

In 1951 my cousin Jim Apps and I mustered 96 Hereford three-year-old heifers on Bungawalbyn Creek. We had considerable trouble separating them from other cattle in the same paddock where they had been on agistment. It was 3 pm before we set off to drive the heifers ten miles along an unfenced forest road. Jim took the lead and I kept the tail moving. I had two dogs with me, Trimmer and his mother, Smuttie.

Once we had lost our daylight, it was a hard, slow trip, travelling through thick scrub in the dark, especially as there were two calves with blight who would wander from the mob. I had to rely on my ears to work out where the cattle were, listening for movement in the leaves. To tell which dog was which, I'd call and get them to jump up on my foot in the stirrup so that I could feel their collars. I would then send one dog to each side of the mob. It was a real battle, especially as half misty rain was falling and added to the confusion and frustration. We yarded the cattle at eleven o'clock that night.

It was a great relief next morning to find all the heifers were accounted for, and without doubt credit for that was almost entirely due to the skill of the dogs.

SPOILSPORT

Ron Cherry, Armidale, New South Wales

I had a blue cattle dog named Ned. His favourite job was to bring up the rear of the mob. If they slowed a little, he'd rush in with his mouth wide open and bite hard and fast—and always seemed to enjoy the result.

We were droving a mob of sheep one time and I decided to let him have a run. Every now and then he'd open that great big mouth of his and rush at the sheep.

'No, Ned!' I'd yell, and you would hear his mouth suddenly snap shut and he'd crash right into the back of the surprised sheep and fall in a heap.

He'd pick himself up looking very annoyed, then glare at me as if to say, 'Bloody spoilsport.' Before long he'd be off for another try.

RICH GIFTS FROM RAGS

Carolyn McConnel, Esk, Queensland

Rags was a black and white, speckled, mostly cattle dog, but with a dash of border collie. She was given to me when I was first married and had just moved in from sheep country to the Brisbane Valley in southern Queensland where we ran all cattle. She was just a tiny pup then and quickly became a great mate and a fair cattle dog.

The only other dog on the place was a golden labrador, but together these two could outwit any bull that ever bailed up. Sandy the labrador grabbed the tail and Rags would go for the nose and, with an almighty crash, the bull would be down on the ground and these two would sit back and wait until he got up. If he headed in the wrong direction, they'd throw him again.

Rags was also very useful when we were repairing flood fences. One of us would go to the other side of the creek and she'd swim the creek as many times as you wanted her to with a cord attached to her collar. Whenever we needed such things as wire or a hammer, we tied them onto the cord and hauled them over. It saved us hours of wading through flood water and mud, and she thought it was great fun. She would lie on the bank just waiting to be called across.

Rags earned my deep gratitude when she saved me from serious injury when she was an old dog. We were working with touchy heifers, and the dogs accordingly were all sent out of the yards since the presence of dogs can make them even touchier.

Without warning a heifer suddenly rushed out of the mob and knocked me over. I hurt my hip and was unable to get away, which meant I was very vulnerable to another charge. However, Rags ran straight into the yard from wherever she had been lying and attacked the heifer, which forced it away from me. I was then able to get to the fence and safety.

Unfortunately, one of the heifer's charges broke Rags's hip. Despite the pain and the fact that she was able to use only three legs, and had disobeyed orders about being in the yards, Rags was determined to protect me. However, even with all the best care our vet could give her, she changed from being a carefree, happy-go-lucky dog to a very snappy dog with everyone but me. It was obvious she would always be in pain, so with great sadness we had her put down.

PART 9
KERR'S TERRITORY

Up near the Gulf of Carpentaria, at hot and steamy Borroloola in the Northern Territory, I spent a few days yarning with Ron Kerr about dogs, his days of mustering wild cattle, of droving, of horses and the crocodiles he once hunted.

Drinking strong tea made by the gallon, we sat in a kitchen where a baby brolga squawked for food, a galah and a sulphur-crested cockatoo perched on chairs and a few dogs walked through. It was not hard to imagine we were sitting in Ron's camp out bush, yarning around the fire.

You might remember from More Great Working Dog Stories that Ron's evocative story of Sandsoap was judged winner from almost 2,000 stories received. I wanted to know more about this man who has lived out bush all his life . . .

THE LAST OF THE OLD-STYLE STOCKMEN: A PROFILE OF RON KERR

Angela Goode

Born under a wilga tree alongside the Namoi River near Gunnedah, Ron Kerr spent all his childhood on the track, listening to stories around campfires and following mobs of sheep or cattle with his drover parents and six brothers and sisters. He was a useful stockman by the age of four, left school at twelve, had his own horse plant at fifteen and went off droving on his own at sixteen. He married Mavis, the daughter of another droving family, when she was fifteen.

He's walked cattle from Collarenebri to Coonamble, and he trapped rabbits in the 1950s for 30 pounds a week. In 1952 he took cattle from Dirranbandi to Bourke, broke in horses when there wasn't much droving work around, then picked up mobs of sheep which he shifted around between Bourke and Cunnamulla, Hungerford and anywhere a dollar could be made. He took sheep from Broken Hill to Tibooburra, and took cattle from White Cliffs to Fowlers Gap. He started on wild cattle in 1959 as a contract musterer, being paid a half-share of what he caught. He's seen the land from a saddle, and stock routes from Swan Hill to Quilpie and Borroloola.

It's been a spartan and independent life of rolling a swag out under the stars and cooking on an open fire, and following the mobs. He makes his own pack saddles and repairs his saddles. Dogs and horses have been his life.

'If you don't have horses, you don't have money. But if I don't have money for something, then I don't need it,' says this man with the tanned, wiry body, bushy beard and thick explosion of hair on his head. 'I don't need a wage,' he says, adding that he has never been beholden to governments or banks. 'I can always eat from the bush, things like berries, turtles, kangaroos, goanna, fish. One time, when we were really hungry, we even had a brumby.'

Droving, despite the romance of it all, is an unforgiving game where only the best stockmen will survive. Ron, Mavis and his team had a near disaster in 1960 in desert country when he was droving down the Cooper and he missed a bore during three days of dust storms. Instead of travelling 30 miles between bores, they went sixty. The stock were two and a half days without water and 'I nearly killed my horses,' he says. He made the decision then to never again be anywhere near drought, and in 1962 he headed for the Territory. When he crossed the border, he and his team had a pound between them.

He soon got work at Balbirini station to muster wild cattle and from then on he was in demand. Those were the days when the station country was being cut up and the sale of feral cattle was the only source of income the new settlers had in their early years. In the late 1970s, during the government-sponsored eradication of feral cattle to control brucellosis, blue tongue and tuberculosis, Ron and his team of mainly Aboriginal stockmen, horses and bull terriers were in demand: 'I've mustered just about every property from here to Roper River,' he says in a drawl honed after 57 years on the track.

These days Ron is the last of the old-style musterers. No-one else still works with dogs and horses on wild cattle. They use helicopters and four-wheel-drives for speed and efficiency. Ron is critical of these fast and noisy methods, but in a quiet bushman's way: 'The helicopters are making cattle wild again and they run all the fat off them. You have to keep them twelve months longer to put the fat on again before you get your money.'

On top of that he reckons mustering with horses and dogs is at least

50 per cent cheaper and sees a continuing role for him and his two sons who work with him. He also thinks that the days of the drovers could come back because of the high costs of transport. He says he could take cattle 100 miles for $2 a head, get them fat on the way and handle them gently. The 'ball-bearing drovers,' as he calls the truckies, can't compete with those prices but they are, of course, quick. 'It's a hell of a lot cheaper with a horse that runs on grass,' he says. 'Everyone's got to come back a peg or two.'

Ron still throws the occasional wild bull out on Lorella Springs station, 300 kilometres west of Borroloola, where he has a mustering contract. About 2,000 wild cattle still roam there among rocky creeks and thick scrub where, in places, only dogs can go and vehicles certainly cannot.

For about six months of the year, Ron, with a team of men and a plant of about 90 horses, ties up bulls and quietens them down in coaching mobs before yarding and trucking them away for sale. In this, the toughest job in the cattle game, injuries and accidents are frequent.

'There are plenty of falls from horses, and horses that fall on people. I'd average one a week of those,' he says with a laugh. He's been stabbed by sharp horns, trampled by bulls, skidded on his face 'and come up with no skin on it. Jumping off your horse has got to be timed right—you mustn't leave too early,' he says about the knack of grabbing a beast's tail and throwing the animal before tying its hind legs with straps.

The risks for the bull terriers, whose instinct it is to grab onto nostrils and hamstrings, are even greater. At the end of each bull-catching season, Ron has to start breeding and training more dogs. Not all the hazards, though, come from cattle. One of his newest dogs died before he even got out to Lorella Springs. A cane toad, part of the recent invasion from Queensland, got into his bowl and poisoned the drinking water.

Ron has recorded much of his life from his earliest memories right through to the present in a series of old exercise books that travel with him out to his stock camps. Following are just a few stories lifted from those memoirs. They give not only an insight into the role of dogs in the Territory, but also into an increasingly rare breed of stockmen.

MORNING MUSTER AT
BALBIRINI

Ron Kerr, Borroloola, Northern Territory

I had the men bring the seventeen head of quiet cattle and put them in the yards overnight so we could get an early start. We would be back late for our midday dinner after a short muster.

Because we were short of horses, I told Dimond, the oldest fellow in the team, that he looked like he knew how to fix a yard so cattle couldn't get out. It would be no good knocking our horses about getting cattle if they were going to get out of the yard again. He readily agreed to stay behind and make the yard strong, saying how 'those younger blokes don't know much about making good yards'.

The evening before I had talked to Pludo, the head Aboriginal stockman, about doing a short muster. I quizzed him about the rough cattle we'd seen along the river, where they would leave the river and where they would run into the cane grass. It helped to have a plan in your mind.

Next morning we set off. I went to within two miles of some flat ground with the coaching mob, then sent them on with four men to set themselves up between two hills on that flat site. Three others of us and three dogs waited until the coachers were in place, then we went into the river. Ten minutes later we found between eight and ten head in the water. They went up the bank and into the cane grass. I sent one of the boys up the creek and cut around through the cane grass.

He came back saying he couldn't see or hear anything, but thought they were planted where they went into the grass. So I sent in the dogs. Within minutes there was a bellow and the cane grass came alive. There could have been 40 head in the grass, which was six feet high. Heads bobbed and because the cattle were panicking they didn't bother looking for their walking pads through the grass.

For 300 yards they ploughed through the grass, chased by the one dog that wasn't already hanging onto a beast. Our little brumby horses were flat-strap to keep in hearing distance. They ran about a mile before we caught sight of them, but by then they had dropped back to a trot. Pludo came up alongside to tell me that the open country was just ahead and that the cattle would pull up and try to turn back. We eased up to a trot too, and waited for the dogs to catch up.

They caught up in about two minutes. The three weeks that they had been on near-starvation diets had obviously done them good. They still had their tongues in their jaws and looked like they could run another mile if they had to, but we were only 100 yards away from the cattle. When I sent the dogs, they took off like they knew there would be reinforcements to help them out at the end of the run. They hit a big spotted bull on the tail and I swear the bull 'dozed' a half-dozen cows and weaners ahead of him.

The cattle didn't have time to turn back—besides, they were bunched so tightly they couldn't turn. They came out about 300 yards from the coachers. It was hopeless to try and bend them into the coachers. It's not easy trying to manoeuvre 40 head of cattle in a tight bunch, especially when they're all in overdrive to get away from the snapping ivory behind them. To head them at the coachers meant that they would pick up the coachers and take them with the mob. If the boys didn't have horses any faster than the ones we were riding, then the cattle would take the coachers with them too, especially as the mob of scrubbers was much larger than the coachers.

The boys with the coachers could see that we were making no attempt to wheel the mob their way. They moved between the coachers and the galloping scrubbers, which by now the little run-out brumbies were up on the tail of. Their legs were working like pistons. One of the boys started dropping back even though he was throwing everything at the horse to get a bit more out of him. I yelled out to him to hold the coachers, as we were getting close and the fellows holding them had fresh horses under them. The idea was for us to blow the wind out of the scrubbers as much as possible. I could see that the four fellas holding the coachers had cottoned on to what we were about.

There was nothing to stop us throwing at least one beast each as everyone was carrying two straps around their waists. The fellows stayed behind the coachers, leaning low over their saddles out of sight of the galloping mob while waiting for them to go past. Then they, too, could join the fray of the throwing spree. The blokes with the failing horses had turned toward home, knowing their horses wouldn't be much good for throwing.

With six of us now in behind the scrubbers, it was every man for himself. Already Punch, one of the boys on fresh horses, was right up on the tail of a young bull, one hand flat on the pommel of the saddle on the offside, foot clear of the iron. It was only a matter of yards now and he would leave the horse. With any sort of luck he would get two head of this mob so long as his horse stood still when he jumped off.

My horse was still holding on, not getting any faster but not losing any ground. The scrubbers were dropping back fast. Punch was off his horse and in three or four strides he had the bull's tail. The brush of the tail was wrapped around his hand, and the heels of his riding boots were going in for brakes as he sat back. The bull stopped his forward movement as Punch stepped out to one side. The bull had woken up to why he couldn't keep going and his head came around to get rid of the load on his tail. When his nearside front foot suddenly left the ground to spin around for the man on his tail, Punch pulled the tail towards the head. The now completely off-balance bull only had one place to go—flat on his side. When the hind leg came up stiff from the fall, Punch had the leg in his hand. With his knees over the short ribs, Punch used one hand to tuck the tail between the hind legs and over the flank, to hold the bull flat on his side, while the other hand took the strap from around the waist.

The strap—or the bull strap, as they are called—is a double-buckled strap one and a half inches wide and around three feet long. Once you've got it properly in place around the two hind legs, you can stand up and walk away from a tied bull, and he'll still be there when you bring the coachers around to pick him up. After you have left a bull tied up for ten minutes, he'll get his wind back and sit up. In a short time, he works out how to stand up with two hind legs strapped together. He may hop a little way, but he won't be far gone when you come back several hours later, unless the strap has been left too loose.

Looking around to see what was available for me, I found, right in front of my horse's nose, a big old bottle-tit cow with big curled horns, like a speedwheel racing bike. She was going to be mine. As I grabbed the tail, I had a name for her—Bikehandle Bertha. By the look of the horns, I would say Bertha had been doing the disappearing act for ten years or more and had served her time as a school mama to the younger cattle in how to dodge the stock camp.

I ran back to my horse in the hope of getting another one out of the mob. A quick look around indicated there were cattle in straps all about. Some of the boys were on their horses again. Pludo and Punch were well up in the lead, both on foot, going for a tail 100 yards away. Most of the cattle were now climbing the rocks up the hill in front. It was little use throwing anything up in the rocks as they would only knock themselves about too much in the straps. I waved to the boys to pull out and it was then that I realised that everything had gone like clockwork. No more than half a dozen words had been spoken. Eight head had been tied up by one hour after sunrise.

The boys were all talk about the dogs getting the cattle out of the long grass, each one giving his version of what the dogs had done. It was only then that I missed the dogs, and the boys said that they weren't still chasing the cattle. As we drew nearer to the coachers we could see the dogs sitting behind Norman's horse.

As we got closer I noticed that a fresh cow had joined the coachers. Norman said that she had come out of the long grass behind us and had trotted into the coachers. When she saw him she had taken off again. When the dogs that were following us saw her, the big white dog had grabbed her by the nose, then another dog had got her by the ear, and a third had caught her on the back leg. That cow just stood there singing out, so Norman had brought up the coachers and the dogs let go of the cow. She ran into the mob and only came out once. A bite on her nose made her quickly retreat.

We sat around there for another half an hour and the boys reran the whole episode in their own lingo. Each one had his own story. As we now had nine head and eight to pick up, I told the boys that we had better get started, and that the big scrubber cow would only keep her horns if she stayed with the coachers. The ones on the ground had no choice—to get one of our horses horned now would mean a man on foot. Three of us were carrying horn saws under our saddle flaps. There would be eight more homemade polled cattle on Balbirini that night. The scrubber cow made one more desperate attempt for freedom, but within ten steps she had one dog hanging off her jaw and in five more steps another hanging off her flank. She made it back into the coachers before the third dog arrived.

We eventually stood up all the bulls we had caught, after giving them a bit of a horn trim, and joined them in with the coachers. We walked them around the little sandy flat to get the fresh ones used to what was going on.

The station yard was no more than three and a half miles and it wasn't yet midday. I thought I should have another look in the cane grass not far from my own camp. Beyond the cane grass there was a creek and a sheer wall of sandstone rising some 600 feet and quite inaccessible to cattle. At the base of this wall was a cattle pad going down towards the McArthur River. I felt sure there were more cattle along the river, plus I was curious to find out more about this part of the station.

With seven of us spread out around with two riders in the lead, plus three dogs, we headed back. The young bulls tried to make a half-hearted break for the long grass but didn't want to have too much to do with a man on horseback, and even less to do with the dogs. After two miles there was little difference between the coachers and the nine fresh cattle, so I left four men with the coachers and took Pludo and Punch and two dogs. The third dog was older and never liked leaving the cattle that were being driven.

We crossed the river and rode along the back of the wall as quietly as we could in order to see cattle before they heard or saw us. At the bottom of the rock wall it was like a tropical rainforest—big paperbark trees, four to five feet through their butts, and water trickling out of the rock walls. The temperature was about ten degrees cooler and there wasn't much humidity as the high sandstone wall seemed to funnel a light breeze along the river.

We had struck fresh tracks indicating a few bulls were around and we found where they had been eating the bark off the trees. The bark tastes salty and most times that you find paperbark, you find bulls. The bark has a lot of uses for Aboriginal people and they can light fires with it very quickly.

About a mile down the river we found four bulls chewing hunks of paperbark. The boys assured me that when the bulls spotted us they would charge across the river, which was only six inches deep, and then go into the cane grass on the other side, and most likely hide in it. A few minutes later, they did exactly as predicted.

We didn't go charging after them as a bull in hiding likes to draw first blood. If you come on to them quickly, they charge first and retreat second. Then they go for the belly of the horse. We could hear them in the cane grass. How many there were, no-one knew, so I sent the two dogs in. Seconds later, the cane grass erupted. None of the dogs was a barker and the cattle didn't know they were coming until they latched on to the hamstring. All we could do was follow the sound of the cane grass being trampled and hope that all the bulls were ahead of the dogs, and that we didn't meet any stragglers head-on. The bulls were heading across the cane grass, which was about 100 yards wide, making for open country to get away from the dogs.

On the other side of the cane grass there were bulls going everywhere. We saw four going in the long grass and there must have been fifteen others which came out in fifteen different directions. The dogs had three going close together, so we went after them. After a bit we had them running in one direction. There were some clumps of cane grass to go through before we could get them out into the open ground.

On the last patch of cane grass before the open ground, the two dogs had the bulls really wound up. We were cutting to the left to meet them on the other side when we struck a washaway with steep sides and had to go further down to a pad going across. On the other side, there were only two bulls in front of the dogs. We never did work out how the third one gave us the slip.

Meanwhile the two bulls were out on open country and I thought they wouldn't be too far from where the coachers were. Riding up to the bulls we put them into top gear for 50 yards until they were showing signs of tiring. One bull stumbled and ploughed along on his nose with his front legs buckled under him. By the time he regained his feet the dogs were gaining on him. The bull saw this and decided to stand and fight. His first lunge at the dogs was his first mistake. The old white dog, Bull by name, had him by the nose and Boofhead, the other dog, had him by the hamstring. I could see by the faces of Pludo and Punch that they were a little confused about what to do, so I waved them both on after the lead bull before he got his second wind.

I took my horse away from where the two dogs and the bull were dancing around. I left my horse behind some bushes to give the dogs plenty of time to educate the bull, who was by now just standing still and bellowing. Taking my leg strap, I walked up behind the bull. I intended to tie the bull's hind legs while he was standing up. I had done this many times before with these two dogs and I knew they wouldn't let go until I did.

Boof had a neat way of holding a bull by the hamstring. He grabbed it on one side then worked his body around to the other side. Then he leaned against the other leg, keeping his front feet pointed outwards to stop his toes from getting stomped on. When he got into position, both hind legs of the bull came together and it was simple to wrap the strap around them and pull tight. Then I took the tail of the bull and pulled so the hindquarters came over and the bull overbalanced and flopped on his side. Then I called the dogs off.

Bull terriers have interlocking fangs, with two large teeth on the top jaw and a single one on the bottom that close up together. When they get them locked up they cannot let go while the beast is pulling against them. Sometimes they don't want to let go, and teaching young dogs to hold on and then let go again has its problems,

Anyway, after tying up the bull the two dogs had caught, I went to see if Pludo and Punch had caught the other one. I found their horses not far up in the open country, but there was no sign of the boys or the bull. A bit further on I found a hat and, a little further, a shirt. I could see their tracks and also the bull's tracks. There was a little stony knob not far away and from there I could hear them singing out to one another.

I knew that if they were foot-walking the bull, he must have bailed up on them. They would have had one bloke on horseback and the other on foot in an effort to make the bull chase him. The one on the horse would then have had time to get off, run in and grab the bull's tail. The shirt and hat with the smell of 'man' would have been thrown under the bull's nose to make the bull charge. If one bloke has a chance to go for the tail, it can be very dangerous at times when a bull is in a fighting mood.

Just over the ridge, Pludo was on the tail. I pulled up and kept the dogs back while Pludo and the bull were having it out. Pludo was crouched fairly low to the ground and the bull must have got some of his wind back, for now both were spinning fast. If he could hold the weight of the bull long enough, sooner or later he would get the bull off balance. If he couldn't he would have to pick his time to let go so he could get a head start to the nearest leaning tree. Anyone coming to help right at that moment could do more damage than good. Pludo and Punch's horses were 100 yards away and there was no hope of taking the bull away.

I waited to see if the bull would come down or Pludo would let go. It seemed like minutes, but it was probably only a few seconds before I saw the bull's horn go into the ground and over he went. Pludo twisted his tail between the hind legs and Punch came racing in with a strap. The look on their faces showed how happy they were with the win. It was as good a catch as you would see anywhere.

Half a mile out we found the other boys waiting with the coachers, which we then drove back to the two bulls tied up. We tipped their horns and let them up into the coachers. We were within three-quarters of a mile of my camp and a mile from the station, and it was still only just after lunchtime.

Dimond had done a good job on the yards, so when we had all had food, we worked the mob around, settling down all the freshly caught beasts. Just before sundown I told the boys we would start yarding, in case we had trouble. Pludo rode across and asked if I was going to bring the dogs which I had tied up at dinnertime. I told him to start the cattle off and that I would let three fresh dogs go. I had three specially for yarding. One was a stumpy-tailed dog, called Stumpy, and the others were young dogs with a bit of pace.

All went well until we got to the gateway, then back they came. We turned the lead back to the gate the first time. The next time around, the cock-horn cow and two bulls went between the horses. The cock-horn cow made the mistake of trying to jump over the little dog, Stumpy. As she went in the air, he went for her bottom jaw. He was between her front legs and when they touched the ground, her nose and horns hit the ground together and her hindquarters kept on going. She landed with four feet in the air and she was about 30 feet in front of the gate. Stumpy held her bottom jaw. Both horns were buried in the dirt and he wasn't about to let her go. One of the boys had a strap on her before she knew what was happening.

Punch and I were on the shoulder-blade of a bull each and had a dog as a rear gunner, picking up one leg then the other, and their bellows were fairly flying out of them. I think they were glad to have a horse alongside to guide them. We pointed them at the gate and took them right into the coachers at a hand gallop. The whole mob went straight through the gate. Only the cock-horn cow lay outside in a strap.

Don Rory wanted to know if we would be able to drag the cow through the gate, but I said that we should get the horns off her and that Butch, the big red and white dog, would lead her in. I tied Stumpy to the fence as Butch wouldn't go on the nose while another dog was free. When they had dehorned the cow, we turned her around so she would be facing the gate. Taking her tail, I asked one of the boys to take off the strap. As she came to her feet, I held her facing the gate and called in Butch. He went straight for her nose and when I knew he had a good grip, I let go. The little white dog was wailing her tune as the cow tried to bunt Butch. He jumped back, still hanging on.

The white dog, Jill, was a heeler and when she bit, they really knew they had been bitten. Forward motion was started. Butch was on his hind legs letting the cow carry him along and Jill was making her keep in step through the gate and into the coachers, where they dropped off.

I think that if you had asked the boys to share their supper with the dogs that night, they would have let the dogs have first pick. They reckoned they hadn't seen dogs work cattle like that before.

Likewise, Laurie Morgan hadn't seen dogs working like that. A few weeks later we had an almost identical problem with another cow. Laurie was standing outside the yard when we put Butch on the cow and he came dancing through the gate, leading her. Laurie then started screaming about getting the dog off the cow. When no-one took any notice of him, he jumped into the yard and ran up, trying to kick the dog off the nose. The dog let go and the only thing in front of the cow was Laurie.

Just as well she had no horns, as she would have driven them clean through him. You could hear the wind come out of him when the cow butted him right in the solar plexus. Laurie held his stomach and crawled through the yard, heading for the homestead, without saying a word.

UNDERSTANDING THE WORKING BULL TERRIER
Ron Kerr, Borroloola, Northern Territory

Bull terriers have powerful tools of destruction in their big boof heads. They should only be used for the job they were bred for, which is biting.

They can be very docile, but they can also change to be the opposite. If they're tormented or someone has upset them, a bull terrier can lock on.

While the person is trying to get away, the bull terrier can't leg go. His teeth are locked in there and they can really do a lot of damage on a human leg. As well as that, nine out of ten bull terriers close their eyes once they grab hold. They just shut their eyes and hang there.

A good working bull terrier is a valuable dog and it takes a long time to get a dog working properly. Because they are doing such dangerous work, many of them get injured and killed, so I try to have new dogs coming on continuously. The older a dog gets, the slower his reflexes, and he's more inclined to hang on a bit longer than necessary. If a bull can get him out in front while he's hanging on the nose, the bull's got a chance of ramming him into the dirt or swinging him against a tree. If you get a good dog, you really miss him if he gets killed.

Pure-bred bull terriers are only used on one side to start off a working breed. The other side can be pure blue heeler. I also like a second cross blue heeler as a foundation bitch to breed a bit of colour into the dogs. White pups often get sunburnt. With five-eighths on both sides, you get a good type of working dog— a lighter build for speed and travelling long distances, while retaining the jaw strength of the bull terrier.

If you have quiet cattle, you won't need to use bull terriers. Blue heelers will do. Wild cattle need heavy biters as they have to go through a crash course of education. Bull terriers also help take a lot of work off the horses.

The breeding pair should be the non-barking type. Pups should be taught to follow a horse at about ten or twelve weeks of age. I take them far enough away from home to ensure they follow me and don't try to return home.

If the breeder owns the bitch, she can play a major part in training the pups to follow a horse. She can also help get the pups used to cattle, which initially should always be without calves. Otherwise the cows charge at the dogs and can destroy a pup's confidence. Children should not be allowed to play with any of the pups undergoing training.

During training a few things must always be in the trainer's mind. Firstly, a pup should never be allowed to run in front of a horse and, secondly, it must always be under control. The first is simple to teach. I just ride through timber country and if a pup runs in front of the horse, without saying anything I just break off a small stick and throw it at him. If he does it again, I use a heavier stick or improve my aim. You may find it easier to teach him if you take him out on his own. You'll know you are making progress when the pup gets back behind the horse as soon as he hears the stick being broken off the tree.

The importance of training pups to stay behind a horse cannot be overemphasised. Usually riders have to get off the mark fast, but if a dog is running in front, it could bring down a horse and rider, or the dog could be injured. Dogs have to know their place. The right sized stick and aim will give you control without saying a word. A fellow bellowing at his dog is worse than a barking dog.

Never force a young dog to go in on cattle. He will go onto them when he is ready. You may make the mistake of encouraging a pup to get in the way of a dog that is working, leaving the older dog no leg room and no way of escape from the horns. Alternatively, you could make the pup start barking before he gets a chance to latch on.

You should never hit a dog to get it off a beast. If you do, you could end up defeating the purpose you bred the dog for, by making it scared of latching on. I like to put the beast on the ground and have someone hold it down. I then take a strap and put it around the dog's neck. With the other hand, I push the buckle down tight and cut off the dog's wind. When the dog gulps for air, I pull the dog's jaws clear of the beast and hold him away. When the dog realises the beast is going nowhere, he is prepared to stand there and watch. It is important to keep him out of reach of the beast and call the dog behind. By now, with the beast quiet and restrained, he is able to hear you if he wants to. Breeders and trainers should be aware that bull terriers have a hearing problem—or they are just headless. Avoiding the pure breed solves some of the problems.

I also teach dogs from a young age to be aware of the stockwhip. I crack this over their heads to break up any fights among them around the camp. A whip is the safest way, as it is hopeless trying to pull them apart. When there is a mob of dogs, you could finish up with a dog hanging off the seat of your trousers.

We are also careful to tie up the dogs before feeding ourselves. Dogs are a problem in any camp when you are cooking over a fire. With open pots and pans around, it's easy to end up with a mob of pan-licking dogs.

Mavis devised a quick method of training dogs not to do this. It might sound tough, but you can't have dogs eating your tucker when you've got no spare supplies, and the men have to be fed. She used to have a billy of hot water on the fire all the time and, right from when they were pups, she would flick a spoonful of hot water on them if they got too close. It worked all right. If the dogs were loose, you would see them lined up twenty paces from the fire or food table, and they wouldn't come any closer. There were also very few fights over any scraps of food thrown to them.

When they're not working, you should tie your dogs to a tree to ensure they get a good rest after working all day and don't spend their time fighting. And leave them tied up until you've settled your horse next day. I've seen fellows let their dogs off the chain before catching their horses in the morning. When they've climbed on their horse, which might be stiff or bad-tempered and not going well for the rider, the last thing they want is a bull terrier hanging off the horse's flank.

Working bull terrier cross dogs have been taught to grab hold of anything madder than themselves. No-one has yet taught them that a bucking horse with a rider on top should be excluded.

STUMPY

Ron Kerr, Borroloola, Northern Territory

We always preferred storms to come in late afternoon as it would give us time to be dry again by the time the sun went down. Night storms coming in on strong winds meant you would have to get up and roll up your swags and wait out the storm, which could last two hours. After a hard day's riding and throwing bulls, we needed our sleep. Plus during daytime storms, every man was already mounted and able to hold the cattle in the open—far safer than trying to rely on a yard holding them, which would be the case at night.

Late in 1966 we were mustering wild cattle on Balbirini station not far from the McArthur River. I had started the season with a pack of thirteen bull terriers that I used to pull down bulls so I could catch them, tip their horns and force them to join up with our special quiet mob of cattle, the coachers. I only worked two bull terriers at a time and spelled the rest back at the camp. It was tough work for the dogs and very dangerous. By

December, at the end of the bull-catching season, I often didn't have any catching dogs left because they were all injured or had been killed.

The first storm for the season hit us at about 2.30 one afternoon and lasted for an hour. It couldn't have been a better time as we had just thrown about six head and they were still tied up in the leg straps. The weather had been hot and sticky and we still had to manhandle the cattle in straps. As the storm broke we were able to get the cattle up and into the coachers in the rain without the danger of overheating them. If this was going to be the pattern of the storms, it would suit us.

It was one of those six bulls we were letting up that rushed Stumpy, the stumpy-tailed dog who was looking for shelter from the rain. He didn't hear or see the bull coming before it tossed him higher than a man on horseback. He landed on his side and I could see blood, but before I could get to him he was up and going back at the bull. This just happened to be the only bull we had ever let up with his horns on as we had broken the horn saw on the previous bull and the spare was back in the packs at the camp.

The dog had the bull by the nose and I sang out to the boy that the dog was hurt and to get the bull tied up again so we could get the dog away. He now had part of his stomach sticking out and as soon as the boy pulled down the bull I grabbed the dog, turned him upside down and carried him away from the cattle. Holding him down I could see the running gut, the small intestine, wasn't busted. The horn had pierced the skin, which had rolled with the thrust of the horn, then had gone into the stomach. I poked the gut back in and the skin rolled over the hole in the stomach wall. The two holes were not in line with each other, which meant the wound would stay relatively clean and secure. As it was still pouring rain, it was also fairly well washed.

The dog was now cold, so he was feeling the stiffness that comes with injury. He went into the long grass and lay down to lick his stomach. I left him there after making sure the bleeding had stopped. I intended to come back later, when I was sure the boys weren't going to have any more trouble with the cattle, and carry him on the horse. After moving on about two miles, and judging the cattle were under control, I rode back to Stumpy—but he was gone.

After singing out to him and riding through the grass, I couldn't find him. I thought he must have headed off towards the camp at the yards, about two miles the other way. I went back to the cattle thinking he would be better making it back to camp at his own pace. Sometimes when the dogs were hot, I would leave them and they would come into camp after dark. The only thing that worried me was that the smell of the tracks was washed out by then, but it wasn't far to where we were now camped compared with where we had come from that day with the horses. He would know where he was once he came onto the pad going to the waterhole. It was 30 miles back to the main camp.

That night the dog didn't turn up, nor the next morning. So I rode back to where he'd got horned and searched again. There was still no sign of him. We camped another day and the dog never came, so we moved camp toward the station as we had had another storm about the same time of the day and there would be cattle walking towards where the storms had come from, straight into the wind.

We came onto the edge of some country we had previously burnt, and already there was green feed about two inches high and plenty of cattle tracks. Just short of where we had built a yard we found probably the biggest mob we had struck at one time. There were 60 to 70 head of cattle—about the same sized mob as the coachers. They were just coming off water when we topped a ridge that had a sandy depression on top where we blocked the coachers. We left three boys with the coachers and went back down over the ridge we had just come up and rode downwind of the cattle.

Using the cover of the timber along the creek we were able to come up behind the cattle, which we started towards the coachers. Being full of water they were completely out of wind getting the half-mile up to the coachers. In the mob there were six big bullocks we thought we would have trouble with. All were about ten years old and still fat. Holding them in the coachers we could see the BAT brand standing out and knew that they were Tarwallah bullocks that Fred Ellis had owned a few years back. We had picked up odd bullocks of his before. If these six handled as quietly as the others had, they would give us no trouble.

True to form, as we moved them off to see how they would go, the six bullocks moved as one, coming out into the lead and walking right up behind my horse, following every move the horse made around logs or trees. As they were only three feet behind my horse, I let them walk a bit faster, then stopped to make sure that they knew I was there. All six would stop, only moving again when I moved. When I rode around a fallen tree they never lost a step turning after the horse. When a beast from behind looked like passing them, they threw their heads sideways and gave the beast a bump with those long sharp horns. Even the young bulls gave the bullocks room. The size of those bullocks attracted respect from the other cattle as if they were some sort of armoured tank.

Reaching the yard I rode through the gate and the bullocks never slackened their pace. They came straight through and right across the yard. I think all the fresh cattle were in the yard before they even knew a yard was there. We cut the mob back to 40 head of coachers, including the bullocks, and started back up the McArthur River to Bessie Springs. It was three days of mustering before we got to our camp and again the bullocks proved their worth—we got back to Bessie Springs with 60 head, an increase of twenty, plus two more brumbies joined the horse plant.

When we reached the new camp about twelve miles north of where he had got hooked, Stumpy met us. He was as lively as a cricket, with only a small lump to show where the bull had got him. He had returned to the camp a few days after he had been injured, and Mavis and the kids had looked after him. I was pretty pleased to see him as he was a particularly good 'noser'. I had never seen him get flipped off a nose. He could even drop a bull to the ground by pulling the bull's head down between its front legs to throw him off balance. That dog could hold them down long enough for me to put a strap on their back legs. I thought so much of the dog that he was my main breeder.

The following year I went up to Nathan River station on the Limmon Bight River, very rough creek country. To get there we had to swim stock horses, pack horses and dogs over nine creeks and rivers. Among the dogs were two of my best, Stumpy and one we called Blue Bitch.

Within about six miles of our destination two brumbies came out of the scrub. They were good types and we decided to run these in as they'd be a couple more breakers and could join the horse plant. I was on a good horse and was able to head them off all right. Stumpy and Blue Bitch came too, but they couldn't keep up. I lost sight of them when they dropped back. That night we put all the horses, including the two brumbies, in a holding paddock, and settled down to wait for the dogs to show up—but they never did. Next day I went back as far as Rosie

Creek, thinking that they could have gone back to where we had our last camp. Since it had been raining each night, there were no tracks for them to follow and I didn't find them back there.

Six weeks later the local copper sent a message that my two dogs had turned up at the police station—160 miles back at Borroloola. They had gone back through all those creeks and over that tough, stony country. The message came through on a two-way radio at Nathan River station, so I told them to hang on to the dogs and look after them until I returned.

It was quite a few weeks before we got back. It was then that I found out that both dogs had eaten a poisoned goat carcase. It had been put out for the dingoes which had been killing goats kept to provide milk for the Aboriginal people around the town. The stumpy-tailed dog died, but Blue Bitch survived.

The death of Stumpy meant the last of that good strain I had been breeding from. But I got hold of more good dogs, trained them up and started over again for the next season. It's a story that just repeats itself.

LADY AND RED
Ron Kerr, Borroloola, Northern Territory

In 1949, when I was thirteen, my father, my brother Colin and I were returning to Scone after taking a mob of cows and calves from Aberdeen in the Hunter Valley to Quirindi, up over the Dividing Range. I was chief cook and bottle washer. Colin was horse-tailer, responsible for getting the horses unhobbled and brought to the camp by daylight.

When the cows and calves came off camp just after daylight, and after the wagon horse was caught and tied up, Colin would have breakfast. The rest of the horses would be put into the mob with the cattle and driven along with them, and Colin and Dad would leave camp. I would be left to wash up, pack the wagonette, top up the water keg and harness up the wagonette horse to follow the cattle to the dinner camp.

Dad had a red kelpie sheepdog that never missed a droving trip, whether he was needed or not. His name matched his colour—Red— and he worked either sheep or cattle. Red had taken a holiday on this trip

539

because Dad wouldn't let him near the cattle. There were a lot of old cows who hated dogs. They really gave him a rally around the flats, protecting their calves. So instead, Red trotted along under the wagonette, taking in the sights.

Dad reckoned that every time Red came near the cattle he lost about an hour of travelling time. The old cows would chase Red then go back into the mob in a panic searching for their calves, which would be halfway into the middle of the mob. The cows would then have to sniff every calf to get the right smell.

Along with us in the horse plant we had Mum's pride and joy, a brown mare called Lady which she drove in the sulky. She was also Red's best mate. They both used to take us to the pictures on any Saturday night when we were at home—a place a bit of a way out of Scone. On those nights out, we would unhitch Lady from the sulky and tie her to a tree with a nosebag of chaff and oats slipped over her ears. Red always sat down alongside Lady and we knew they would be there for the trip home.

So after this droving job, we came back over the range past Murrundi. We camped just short of the Burning Mountain, about one good day's travel from Scone.

Next morning Colin brought the horses into camp with the news that Lady was missing. Dad had already eaten so he saddled a horse, telling us she couldn't be far and for us to pack the wagonette while he searched. Horses often feed off on their own, so we weren't too worried, just annoyed that we had to waste time looking for her.

As the foothill of the range was fairly stony, even a full plant of horses didn't leave many tracks. One horse would therefore be really hard to pick up, so Dad arrived back at camp about dinnertime without Lady. We then informed him that Red was also missing and that it seemed highly likely to us that Lady and Red were together and had headed towards Scone.

We arrived home just before dark and the first question we asked Mum was whether Lady and Red had turned up, but she hadn't seen them. We searched for them for two weeks and couldn't understand what could have happened to them.

Three weeks after they had gone missing from the camp, a car pulled up at home and a bloke asked Dad if he had lost a brown mare and a red dog. They had been up at his place for the past two weeks, where the mare had found some pretty good feed. The dog wouldn't leave the mare's side, so this man had taken food out to him.

Next day Colin and I rode 40 or 50 miles to the foot of the range to collect them. They were both in good shape. The dog was pleased to see us, but he still wouldn't leave the mare's side. It is unusual for a dog to attach itself so closely to a horse, but we've had it happen more than once.

Another dog, Emmie, was so fond of the wagonette horses that she always used to trot in the small space between them, right under the centre pole. We couldn't understand why she never got trodden on. She seemed to be tuned into their minds and to know when they were turning.

PART 10
OUT ON THE TRACK

The big sheep and cattle droves are a thing of the past, but that doesn't mean that the dogs of the bush don't keep travelling. They hit the track to search for their masters. They cross rivers to meet their heart's desire. They keep a weary truckie, the modern drover, company in the front seat as the miles roll by. And they also ride pillion on a motorbike like the best of the Hell's Angels, even in defiance of the law, and sometimes without permission—like Jet and the postie.

Those epic droving trips, however, from which the legends grow, are when a dog comes into his own. Lionel Hewitt tells of taking sheep on the road in the drought of 1958, and how Rusty averted tragedy only to suffer agonies of his own.

Then there was Peter Richardson's trip in the 1940s with sheep destined for a ship at Onslow. When the droving cart broke down his dog—also called Rusty—was left behind, too footsore to continue and not expected to find his way home. Life can be terribly unforgiving for dogs and people out on the track.

DROVING UP TO ONSLOW
Peter Richardson, Toodyay, Western Australia

I was in the pastoral game in the Gascoyne for a good number of years and owned and saw many dogs. This story is about a red cloud dog of mine called Rusty.

In the late 1940s, when I was 23, four of us were contracted by Elders to take a mob of sheep from Carnarvon to Onslow. It was a distance of more than 400 miles on back tracks to collect wethers from properties along the way, to be shipped to the Middle East. We collected the first mob from a property called Wandagee. From there we went up the track to Midialia, Williambury and Lyndon to end up with about 2,000 head. We followed the Lyndon River most of the way, and as it was winter we had plenty of water for the trip, which took in total about five weeks. For most of the way, the going was terribly rough.

Each man had a dog and of the four, Rusty was the best. As well as our stock horses, we had two pack horses and a cart pulled by two other horses and a mule. On the cart we carried all the swags, cooking gear and food, as well as big rolls of hessian with which we made temporary night yards for the sheep using steel droppers to keep it in place.

About twenty miles out of Lyndon, the track was so rocky and rough that our cart broke an axle and fell apart. We had no choice but to load all the gear from the cart onto the two cart horses and the mule. Since we had no spare pack saddles, we had to use the most extraordinary improvisations imaginable. We folded the hessian over each animal and bundled droppers each side and tied the rest of the gear on top. In this fashion, we continued on with the sheep to Onslow.

Once we'd delivered the sheep and rested up, we set out on our long trip back to Carnarvon to return the plant. Normally the dogs would have travelled home on the cart after their weeks of work, but because we had no cart, they had to walk. About halfway between Onslow and Lyndon, the dogs were so tired and footsore, they could not travel any further. We couldn't carry them on the horses because of all the extra gear we had to carry, so we had no choice but to leave them there on the track—much to my sorrow. Some weeks later we reached Carnarvon and I returned to Wooramel, where I was the overseer.

About two or three weeks later, I got a phone call from Tim D'Arcy, the manager at Lyndon, to say my dog Rusty had turned up there. I felt this was remarkable as he had obviously pushed on after me as best he could. He must have come the best part of 100 miles.

Tim D'Arcy put him on the mail truck and I picked him up in Carnarvon. We enjoyed many a good year together after I thought I had lost him. None of the other dogs made it back.

A CHORD OF
UNDERSTANDING

H H Cay, Coonabarabran, New South Wales

First appearances were not promising, but I was desperate. Next day I was starting work as boss musterer at Portland Downs on the Barcoo. It was a place of 250,000 acres and I had no dog. What was worse, I had sandy blight and couldn't see more than 150 yards.

The dog, called Binky, was slate grey in colour, dejected in appearance and his ears were blocked and swollen by a massive infestation of blood-sucking ticks. Nevertheless, he greeted me gamely, wagging his tail if not with enthusiasm then at least with courtesy.

'Yeah,' I said. 'I'll take him.' I thought we might just make a team: he could hardly hear and I could hardly see.

That was the inauspicious start to a friendship that lasted for eight years. It stretched from the gibber plains of central Queensland to the high hills of the Hunter Valley and beyond. And what a team we made! I never had a better mate, four-legged or two, while Binky had a boss who knew and loved him for what he was—the best, gamest kelpie ever bred on the western plains.

Once well-cared for, his coat was shiny. And go . . . that dog could outwork the rest of the dogs in camp and leave them belly-deep in the bore drains. By the time Binky was two years old, I was the envy of the stock camp. Some dogs can be taught, some have to be bullied, but Binky, well, he was a natural. He knew when to stop, what to do, and could out-think the crankiest ewe. Binky was always a bit deaf but that didn't worry either of us. We were linked by an umbilical cord of understanding that surpassed words, whistles or signals.

Years passed. I left central Queensland and crossed the border into the south-west of New South Wales. Binky and I hitched a ride in a cattle truck down to the Hunter Valley. Barsham, a steep property on the mountain slopes of the Hunter, was a massive contrast with the plains of Queensland. What a challenge for the poor dog. But I needn't have worried. Once he had mastered the art of lifting his leg on a slippery slope, he had no problems. Instinctively he worked wider, always blocking the cunning, paddock-wide wethers, never panicking the ewes and lambs.

Again the years passed and we were still inseparable. Only the scenery was different. Now the cliffs and rugged ranges of Arizona on Upper Mauls creek in the Manilla district replaced the green Hunter hills. In dog terms, Binky was getting on in years. He was worn by the hot Queensland sun and frozen by the cold nights of the mountains. But what a mate. He was always waiting as I tightened the girth straps, though now he trotted an inch behind the heels of my horse and left the younger dogs to cast ahead.

One morning Binky didn't answer my whistle. I found him stiff as a board under the saddle rack. Thirty years have passed, and I still dream about the dog that shared my mustering years.

THANKS A LOT, MICK
Neil Macpherson, Tamworth, New South Wales

There is no doubt in my mind that a dog is surely man's best friend, but not just any dog—a kelpie, a working sheepdog. In my life on the land I have had control of numerous sheepdogs—some good, some not so good—but I am going to try to relate a story about one of my highlights of the sheepdog world.

I had got myself a new truck in 1965 and went stock carrying, something I had always wanted to do. A chap from Bendemeer gave me a small red kelpie pup. I liked the small breed of kelpie because, as truck dogs, they could manoeuvre around the pens and run in under the sheep easily. This pup's brother and sister had been sold for high prices and finished up in New Zealand. So I had high hopes for Sandy, as I called him. As time went on, I was proved correct.

Sandy was put in that new truck when he was six weeks old. He sat or lay on the floor and later, when he got a bit older, he sat on the passenger's side which I had covered with a blanket. In those days heating wasn't considered necessary in a truck, but one dog was as good as a heater. Sandy travelled in that truck for five and half years and was never sick or smelly. Mind you, every time I got out, so did my dog.

I needed to spend every Monday at the Tamworth saleyards where about 10,000 sheep and lambs went through each time. Among other jobs, I would cart about six or seven loads of sheep to the abattoirs. Sandy and I could load these with the minimum of work and trouble. He was an outstanding truck dog. I would leave the side window down when I arrived at the saleyards and Sandy would stay in the truck until I gave him his special whistle. Although there would be 100 trucks and about 200 dogs and all the noise of the sheep, gates banging and men shouting, he would somehow find me.

One day Sandy didn't answer my call, so I asked around: 'Have you seen my little red dog?' Everyone knew him but nobody had seen him that day.

After some time, maybe two hours, I was convinced he had jumped into some other red truck and that I wouldn't see him again. The next thing, along came Sandy, full of apologies and very wet and tonguing. He had just had a cool-off in the trough. Mick Pullman, one of Jack Smyth's right-hand men, came hobbling after the dog and said to me, 'Thanks for the loan of your dog, Mac. He is a real little beauty. He and I have just drafted 2,000 sheep on our own.' That was high praise indeed, because Jack Smyth was second only to Sir Sid Kidman as a cattle dealer and dealt in hundreds of thousands of sheep, so Mick would have seen a lot of dogs in his time.

But thanks a lot, indeed, Mick. Despite the flattery, my dog had done a day's work for someone else and I still had six or seven loads of sheep to put on my own truck. Nevertheless, I was proud of my dog, but he was pretty tired that night.

Sandy was never tied up in later life. He always slept near that truck and everywhere the truck went, so did Sandy—even carting wheat from local farms into the silos in Tamworth.

When eventually I sold the truck and business, the buyer turned to me after he had given me the cheque. 'Righto, Mac,' he said, 'how much do you want for the little red dog?'

I was moving to town and town life is no life for a dog, let alone a working sheepdog, so I informed the new truck owner that he didn't have enough money in the bank to buy Sandy. But if he promised to give him a good life and let him ride in his truck, then he could have him for nothing.

I saw that dog ten years later when he was very old. He answered me when I called him and we had a bit of a cuddle-up. He was happy.

SITTING PILLION WITH THE POSTIE

Helen Firth, Nambour, Queensland

Jet was a highly strung black kelpie of ours that spent many an hour running beside a horse or riding pillion on a bike. She was an excellent working dog and devoted to her master.

Many years ago my husband and I went on a working holiday. We took Jet and her daughter Scubie, whose father had been a bull terrier. We decided to work in Brisbane for a couple of months, so we moved into a caravan park in Hawthorne, on the banks of the Brisbane River. The caravan park wouldn't allow the dogs to stay there even though we promised faithfully that they would not be a problem and would stay tied up whenever we weren't there.

Next door to the caravan park was a shipbuilding yard, so we approached the people there and asked if it would be OK to tie the dogs there. They would be in easy reach of us for feeding and regular exercise. They agreed to the arrangement, so we took the dogs over and tied them up where they wouldn't be in the way. We stressed to them that the dogs should not be let off under any circumstances.

The next afternoon, when we went to take them for a run, we heard the following story. City people, being what they are, couldn't resist feeling sorry for the dogs, so while the men were sitting about at smoko break, they decided to let them have a run and some scraps. Scubie didn't leave their side because of the attraction of the food, but Jet, being the highly strung type, decided to have a sniff about the yards.

She then heard the sound of a motorbike—actually it was the postie, delivering mail. Something must have twigged in her mind and made her think that it was her master. So off she went, running after him. A few of the employees started after her on foot.

It must have looked like classic comedy with the motorbike tootling along, followed by a black dog with several men running behind her in frantic pursuit. She led them a merry chase through the streets of Hawthorne before she managed to spring up on the bike with the postie—who hadn't been aware he was being chased. Imagine his amazement to be going along, quietly delivering mail, and suddenly to find a strange dog sitting pillion on his bike.

She finally disembarked and managed to find her way back to the ship-yards with the men hot on her heels. Meanwhile, Scubie was still having smoko with the rest of the employees. They didn't let the dogs off again, but thoroughly enjoyed telling us all about Jet's ride.

IN CONTEMPT OF COURT
George Stewart, Toowoomba, Queensland

I was acting as Presbyterian minister in Mt Isa in July and August of 1991. While I was there I met Bill Hartley, who had formerly been self-employed as a bore-drain cleaner in the Goondiwindi district during the late 1960s and 1970s. As I had been a minister in Goondiwindi from 1956 to 1960, I knew the district well. Accordingly, Bill Hartley and I found we had a great deal in common regarding the district and its people. Bill, now retired, told me of an incident that took place while he was bore-drain cleaning on the New South Wales side of the Macintyre River west of Goondiwindi.

Bore drains run out at long distances from artesian bore heads which are, in most cases, never turned off. The water coming up from the artesian basin is extremely hot as it emerges above ground. Bore drains serve two purposes—to take the water considerable distances to stock for drinking, and to allow time and distance for the water to cool sufficiently so stock are able to drink it.

Naturally, over a period of time the drains tend to clog up with vegetation and silt and require attention to keep the water flowing. Bill Hartley's job was to maintain the drains. To save time and money commuting from where he was working to where he was living, he purchased a small motorcycle. Because of his age, he was given a restricted licence which prevented him from carrying a passenger. However, Bill was devoted to his kelpie dog Booker, who Bill found invaluable for clearing stock, especially sheep, away from the drains when he was cleaning them. Accordingly, Booker soon became Bill's pillion passenger.

At the time there was a somewhat officious police officer aptly

551

nicknamed Radar by the locals. One day on the Mungindi road, Radar stopped Bill riding his motorcycle with his dog sitting behind as a pillion passenger. He checked Bill's licence and pointed out the nature of the restriction and informed him that he was not qualified to carry any passenger and that included his dog. Then and there the dog was removed from the pillion seat and Bill continued on his way at a speed slow enough for the dog to run along beside the bike.

When Bill had gone a mile or so further and was out of sight of official-dom, he stopped and Booker once more resumed his customary seat. However, the zealous officer of the law, suspecting such an event would occur, had followed Bill. Coming up quickly behind the bike, he pulled Bill over and promptly issued a ticket for a traffic offence.

Bill decided to contest the indictment and on the day set down for the hearing at the Boggabilla Court House, he came armed with Booker. As Bill ascended the steps of the court house, an attendant stopped him and told him the dog was not allowed into the court. When Bill informed him that the dog was the chief figure in the case, he was somewhat grudgingly allowed to proceed. Booker immediately showed his contempt for the court by lifting his leg against the doorpost as he entered the building.

Bill's appeal was disallowed and he duly paid the fine. However, the law was seen by the locals for the ass which it so often is and Radar's reputation was further dented.

STOPPED IN HIS TRACKS
Dorothy Harrison, Geraldton, Western Australia

My son owned a very good black shorthaired collie–kelpie dog called Pedro. He was never far from his heels in crowded places like sheep sales, bars or on beaches. He could handle a single sheep or a thousand, and would run along the backs of sheep to force the lead when drafting, filling the shearing pens or loading trucks. He would grab the front leg and toss a sheep that needed treatment when the animal was pointed out to him.

Throughout the district he was well known and when he mysteriously disappeared one day, my son spent weeks phoning and visiting farms for miles around, hoping for a lead. Advertisements placed in papers brought no answers.

Eighteen months later fencers on a large property 50 kilometres away were having lunch in an out-camp when a strange dog, hungry and thirsty and with a piece of rope around his neck, walked in. They took him home, fed him and, after testing him out, the manager took him on as his new working dog.

I sighted the dog with others on this manager's utility one day when he was in town. I was sure it was Pedro for he had ruptured a salivary gland under his jaw when he was younger, and the dog I saw had the same affliction.

On hearing this my son travelled to the manager's property early next morning and waited in his car for him to arrive and give out instructions for the day to his men. The manager whistled and half a dozen dogs raced for his vehicle. My son gave his particular whistle, which caused Pedro to stop in his tracks. On hearing the same whistle a second time, he raced back and jumped through the open window of the car onto my son's lap for a joyous reunion.

All who witnessed this were satisfied that it was the dog stolen eighteen months earlier. It was deduced that he was trying to find his way home when he met the fencers in their remote camp.

ABSENCE MAKES THE DOG WORK BETTER

Margaret Bell, Taralga, New South Wales

In the early days of the last war, my husband Joe left our property to join the Light Horse and start military training.

Joe had a particularly good and faithful sheepdog called Tong. He was a cheeky little fellow, a dedicated worker and one who knew every gate and paddock of the family properties. One place was ten miles from Goulburn and another, newly acquired place was about 50 miles to the north.

Tong always thought he knew more about mustering, droving and working sheep than any man, and often he was right about that. But when he was wrong it took an awful lot of whistling and shouting before he would bow to his master's commands. He also would always rather work sheep than have a meal any day!

When Joe joined up, Tong could not comprehend the absence of his working mate. Any opportunity he got, he would head off to the other property to find him. He would wait by the front gate of one or the other property until someone found him and tied him up again. The two old retainers on the newly acquired property were amazed when Tong first turned up obviously looking for Joe. In those days there were no telephones and mail only once a week, so there was very little contact between properties.

When Joe returned, Tong seemed to be transformed into an absolutely new dog in his sheep work. Instead of always thinking he knew best, he became a devout follower of Joe, only too ready to do as he was asked.

QUEENS OF THE ROAD
Fred Eldering, Crookwell, New South Wales

I was returning home after a sheep show around midnight, towing the canvas-covered trailer behind my ute. Beside me, stretched out on the seat with her head resting on my leg, was my old border collie bitch, Stardy—still travelling after eighteen years, mother of many champions and veteran of many sheepdog exhibitions and trials.

Since 1947, a Stardy had always been on the front seat of the truck or ute with me, keeping me company during the long, lonely hours on the road trucking cattle and sheep. They all carried the stud names of Greyleigh Stardust, but the Stardy on my seat that night was the last of the original strain that had formed the basis of my stud, the oldest registered working border collie stud in Australia, founded in 1947.

The lights of the ute shone down the highway and I fondled the old girl's ear and smiled. Coming up behind me, I could see in the side mirror the fairyland lights of a big rig. I pulled down the mike of the CB: 'You're clear, mate,' I told him. The rig passed and pulled over to the left and back came the words of thanks from the driver.

The CB crackled again. 'That you, old Freddie?' the driver said. It was an old mate, Mac. So as the kilometres rolled by, the two of us, whose paths had not crossed for a few years, chatted on.

'I don't suppose old Stardy is still on the seat beside you, Freddy?' he said. 'She would have passed on by now. I would sure like a quid for every mile she's shared in the cab with you.'

Back went my reply that she was indeed sleeping in her usual place. We both swung off the highway and drew up in the parking area of a truck stop. The rig driver came over and we greeted each other warmly, then he gently lifted the old dog from the seat and hugged her before placing her on the ground for her wee break.

Inside the truck stop, the woman on duty insisted on taking 'the offsider', old Stardy, her usual two sausages—before she even got our black coffees. We settled down for a bit of a chat and, seeing the fuss that everyone had made over my old dog, I told Mac the story about how I had got a replacement for old Stardy, for the time when she would no longer be with me in the cabin.

About eight months earlier, Stardy had picked up a virus and was very sick. The vet had advised putting her down, but I took her home, treated her and nursed her through her illness. One day when she looked like she was never going to get back on her feet, I whispered to her to hang on. 'I don't want to lose you yet, old girl,' I told her. 'Who will be my truck dog? I've got no-one to take your place.'

Extraordinarily, some weeks later my top breeding bitch, who was then twelve years old and had not been in season for over three years, came on heat and mated with a young dog I had. She never looked pregnant at any time, yet presented me with two beautiful pups and reared them well. In all my years of breeding dogs, I had never seen an old bitch come on heat after such a break.

When the pups were ten days old, I was looking at them when the old girl walked in. 'Mac, you know how the old girl is with pups that are not hers once they are three weeks old?' I said. 'She savages them.'

'Well, I picked up the bitch pup, showed it to her and told her to look after her as she was my next truck dog. She nuzzled the pup, put her head under my arm and looked up as if to say, "I understand boss".

555

'From the time the pup was a month old, she shared the old girl's mattress, sleeping between her legs and sharing her feed. Old Stardy never once snapped or snarled at the pup, the way she does with all the other youngsters. When the pup was old enough, Stardy allowed her the privilege of sharing her rug on the front seat of the ute—a thing that was taboo to all other dogs. She had never let another dog into the front of the ute or truck before.

'The pup is now four months old. The old girl has taught her how to behave in the cab—a quick snarl usually pulls her into line. The only reason the pup is not with Stardy and me tonight is that I have been away for a few days and my grand-daughter insisted the pup stayed with her.

'So, Mac, although I thought I knew animals, I cannot explain how it is that both bitches seemed to work together to produce a new truck dog for me. It was as if they knew of the big hole there would be in my life with the loss, eventually, of the old girl.'

We parted after we had finished our meal, but not before Mac had opened the door of the ute and fondled the old dog's head. 'See you, old girl. If not, thanks for the memories.'

Stardy lived on for another year and was nineteen when she died. The new truck dog carries the name of Little Stardy, but we also know her as The Miracle, because that's what we reckon she is.

I am nearly 70 now, but I still do sheepdog exhibitions in Sydney at the Castle Hill Show, and Little Stardy is one of my stars. I also give overseas visitors at conferences a look at how our dogs work. One of my recent escapades was to drive some sheep into the Regent Hotel in Sydney, put them into the lift, then shepherd them among the tables in the dining room where the delegates were enjoying dinner. That went down really well!

In 1979 and 1981 I won the Australian Championships at Mudgee with Greyleigh Mist and Greyleigh Snoopy—but I still reckon the way my old dogs produced a truck dog for me was one of the really special things that has happened in my life.

WHY GET WET?
Jack Rossiter, Bellbrook, New South Wales

We live on the wrong side of the river in flood time, and on one occasion we had a power failure. It was necessary for a couple of county council men to be transported by boat to attend to repairs.

On arriving at the river bank, the two men and a dog waited for us to pick them up. The dog was the first in the boat. When we reached our side, the dog was first out.

That afternoon when we arrived at the river to transport the men back, there was the dog, sitting on the bank waiting to get across. He was first into the boat again.

As the men left the boat we mentioned their dog. They assured us it was not theirs and that they had never seen it before. When talking about the incident some days later, we found that the dog had come from about three miles away and had been visiting a lady friend on our side of the river.

Now a dog would be just too silly if he swam a flooded river twice when there was a boat service running to a suitable timetable, wouldn't he? So there he was, home and dry, after a pleasant day's dalliance—and he went back to doing his cattle work the next day.

The strange part about it was that the dog, from all accounts, had never been in a boat before.

SERVED ON A PLATE
Marjorie Noll, Ballina, New South Wales

As soon as the working dog's pups were ready for solid food, my father trained them never to take a bait.

The food and bones were always placed on a dish. After three or four days of getting the pups to eat from the dish, my father would then wrap some tobacco in the meat and throw it to the pups on the ground. This would make them very sick. Sometimes he would have to do this two or

557

three times, but eventually the pups would learn never to take food unless it was on a plate. This meant he could take the dogs away droving for many days at a time without their ever taking a bait.

When I lived in Caringbah with my husband, I trained our house dog the same way. Even though there might have been bones and food on the ground and he was hungry, he would never touch them unless they were on a plate.

THE 'BLUE BLOOD' OF
THE BORE DRAIN
Lionel Hewitt, Kapunda, South Australia

I was travelling by car to Sr George in Queensland from Southampton station, where I was a jackeroo in 1952. By the 17-mile bore drain out of St George was the poorest long-legged brindle pup one would ever expect to see in a lifetime. The drain was dry so I gave him a drink from my waterbag and left him there.

On my way home that night, I found him sitting in the middle of the road. He was so weak that as his tail wagged, his whole body wagged too. So I picked him up and took him home with me. The boss, George Watson, came out on my arrival and immediately told me, 'Take that Alsatian and shoot the thing before it starts killing.'

It took a lot of explaining that I thought he was a kelpie-German collie cross, but I convinced the boss and so began an association that lasted for fifteen years. After a month of good feed, Rusty, the name I gave him to suit his colour, was fit enough to start work. I took him and another dog to muster the big back paddock. As happy as Larry he was to follow the horse.

I found the first mob of sheep at about 7 am, and they promptly headed for the mulga. My other dog went to the lead to head them off and Rusty went in behind them, barking wildly. He scattered them for miles. I ran him down on the horse, whistling and yelling, but to no avail. So I left him and mustered with just the one dog—and got home in the dark as usual. It wasn't a good beginning.

At about 9 pm the station dogs all started barking, so I went out and quietened them. It was, of course, Rusty returning home. I took him, by the ear, shook him and carried him to the chain.

Next morning I had to go and get the sheep we had lost because of his actions. I took Rusty again, plus my .22 rifle. I found a mob and sent the good dog to the lead. This time, Rusty went with him, straight to the lead, stopped when I whistled—and brought the mob back. He never ever gave any more trouble or bit a sheep for the rest of his life.

Rusty worked with me on stations until 1958, when we had to take mobs of sheep on the road because of drought. We were heading towards St George on one trip and I made a habit of going on ahead to cut scrub for the mob. Rusty would take care of the lead. Not far from the bore drain where I had found him back in 1952, the dog started barking furiously, as though he had found a wild pig. When I investigated, I found the corpse of a man which had been in the sun for a week. After reporting our find, we went on to St George, Nindigully and Talwood, then to Boomi and Garah in New South Wales, travelling six miles a day or less.

The Macintyre River had flooded a lot of country and we saw the first grass in the six months we had been on the road. We agisted the sheep on the stock route and camped in one spot for three months. Rusty would go to the lead every evening and bring the sheep back to camp.

One evening a violent storm with thunder, lightning and sheets of rain hit us. At about 4 pm I took a horse and went to help Rusty turn the sheep back. When I got to the lead, I couldn't find him. I thought he must have returned to camp as the storm was getting worse. I turned the sheep back into the wind on my own and left them. Back at camp, still no Rusty. Nor next morning. I went around the sheep on horseback in deep mud. I did the same for the next four days and still there was no sign of him. I cursed every living being in New South Wales for taking my dog.

Droving friends George and Jean Kelly came by with a mob of bullocks from Midkin station, near Moree, which they had brought out of the flooded country. George's wagon was full of dogs, but Rusty wasn't among them. I told him the story. Then, with a silly grin that only George could produce, he said, 'I'll give you 300 quid for him!'

'Where is he?' I piped. He told me that six miles down the road at a dam on the left, there were 70 or so sheep, mostly with long tails, being looked after by a big brindle dog.

So that was it. The pet sheep we had in the mob had walked fearlessly past the peg dogs we tied up on the roadside. We hadn't seen their tracks because of the rain and it had been too wet to count the sheep in the mob and realise some were missing—and possibly work out that Rusty would be with them.

When we got to the dam, the lambs were on the dam bank. The water was a mile wide around it, so Rusty hadn't been able to get the pet sheep to return. I left the sheep there and Rusty reluctantly came back to camp with me feeling, I suppose, that he had let me down.

We went south to Moree and found that the Gwydir River was in flood. We camped on a sandhill in the bend of the river. Just on daybreak one morning, I got up to make a cuppa. It was still raining and water was everywhere over the black plains around us. The sheep were in a temporary yard made out of pig netting. I picked up the billy and, without thinking, threw out the cold tea and leaves. SPLASH!—onto the soggy ground they went, disturbing the deep quiet of the morning.

Every sheep hit its feet at once. They flattened the yard and rushed. Some went straight into the river, never to be seen again. Others went down the lane. The further they went, the faster they ran, taking fright at the ones following behind them. In all my lifetime around sheep I have never seen or even heard of sheep rushing like that.

But Rusty came to the rescue again. He went to the lead and held them until I could get a horse and catch up to them. Sheep were bogged for two miles along the track. We eventually got them back to the sandhill, but only after Rusty had brought them a few at a time to the road where I could collect and hold them. It was a long day's work mopping up after inadvertently frightening them that morning.

Droving dogs work hard and need their sleep, but even night-time can bring unexpected dangers. Rusty never got tied up so he always slept near the campfire. At the same Moree camp one night, I was cooking a four-gallon drum of meat for the dogs. A log that was supporting the drum had slowly burnt away and the next thing we knew, there was an almighty yelp. The drum had tipped over and boiling water sloshed under Rusty while he slept.

He levitated and rushed straight for the flooded river and out of sight. The night was very dark, the bank was steep and slippery and there was little I could do to help him get out of the river. I could hear him paddling, yelping every now and again when he hit some debris or some-thing. Two days later a poor scalded Rusty came back to camp. One complete side of him had no hair. I sprinkled talcum powder and borax on him and kept him warm and dry for a week with plenty of warm food. He healed up wonderfully.

We went northwards from there to North Star and then southeast to Wallangra. The sheep were shorn there, at a farm we had just purchased called Hidden Valley. From there we went south to Warialda where we were going to truck them to Inverell so they could be sold to raise money for the farm. On the way there, the grass was four foot high and we had no hope of driving sheep through it. All we could do was rush them down the bitumen at daybreak for five or six miles, then make camp. We would always meet a truck coming one way or the other, so Rusty would run over the sheep's backs, drop down in front and come back through the mob to part them and let the truck through.

One evening when we were camped behind the Warialda golf course, I whistled to the dogs to fetch the sheep into the yard. There was no response, so I went around the mob thinking a bitch must have been in season or something like that. Instead I found all my dogs lying dead— except for Rusty, who was in a pretty bad way. He was having fits but I saved him with some of the salt that I always carried in my saddlebag for that very purpose. He took months to recover from the poisoning, so we bought another dog to help load the sheep and truck them down the Gwydir Highway into Inverell.

When Rusty got better he worked at Hidden Valley and we found he also loved working cattle and rounding up wild pigs for me to catch or shoot. He continued helping with the mustering and yard work until he was fifteen. Then, on 9 March 1967, we dipped 3,000 sheep on Ena station, which was about twelve miles from Hidden Valley and which I managed.

Next morning Rusty was asleep on his bag at the back steps where I put on my boots every morning. He sat up and put his head on my lap. I patted him and went off to milk the two cows. When I came back he was dead. I buried him beside the patch of cacti out from the cottage on Ena station, near Wallangra, on the day of my 33rd birthday.

GLOSSARY

ag bike   agricultural motorbike, a tough machine especially designed for farm use

AI   Artificial Insemination or artificially inseminated

back   (verb) describes what a dog does when it runs over the backs of sheep to push them forward in a race, pen or yard

backer   a dog that runs over the backs of sheep to help force or bunch sheep up in a race or yard

backing   the act of running over sheep's backs

bark out   to flush out stock from inaccessible areas such as thick scrub or mountainous terrain with a dog that barks continuously on command

bindies   bindi-eye, a native grass with unpleasant prickles—usually *Calotis hispidula*

black sallee tree   *Eucalyptus stellulata*—a spreading many-branched tree growing in frosty, snowy areas

blue   (noun) a blue heeler

cane grass   tall, bamboo-like reeds growing in swampy areas in the Northern Territory

cast   the wide arc a dog will make in a paddock to move in around a mob of sheep or cattle

chain   a distance of 22 yards or 66 feet, a common distance between fenceposts

chain gave a wrap   what happens to a slack chain on an old motorbike when it misses a few sprockets before taking hold

cleanskin   an animal without an earmark or a brand

cloud   dog's coat of reddish colour flecked with white

coachers   a mob of quiet cattle used to lure wild cattle

coasty sheep   sheep with a cobalt deficiency, resulting in ill thrift

cock-horn   cow with one horn pointing up and the other down

cockies   grain growers and cockatoos

coolie   a working dog, usually with a flecked coat and wall eyes believed to be bred from a German strain

cover   sheep dog trial term for 'control'

dags   locks of wool on the breach of a sheep heavily coated with dung

dinkum   real, genuine

draw   the bringing of the sheep by the dog towards the handler in a three-sheep trial

eye, to have   to be able to control livestock by the force of an almost mesmerising gaze

gilgie   a small freshwater crayfish, like a yabby, found in Western Australia

Gold Coaster   a term for a dog allowed to roam free and lead a relaxing lifestyle around the farm

growers   producers of anything off the land, e.g. wool, meat, grain

hand gallop   faster than a canter, but not a gallop at full stretch

hanging one on him   punching someone

header   a grain harvesting machine

headlands   sections of paddocks that initially miss being ploughed when machinery negotiates corners. These are ploughed diagonally when the rest of the paddock has been completed

heeler   a dog which nips livestock on the back of the hind legs to make them move forward

hoggett   a sheep aged between one and two years

horse-tailer   the person responsible for ensuring the team of horses used in a droving or stock camp is looked after and rounded up for each day's work

jam tree   a small, wattle-like tree with hard, sweet-smelling wood, found in various parts of Western Australia's wheat belt

jumbuck   a sheep

keep-eggs   eggs rubbed with a greasy proprietary compound which preserves them without refrigeration

killers   sheep kept for household meat supplies

knocking them up   wearing livestock out by moving them too fast

merino rig   a male sheep that has been improperly castrated, thereby having the characteristics of a ram

merle   a dog's coat that is blue or red and intermingled with white flecks

mickey bull   a wild, cleanskin bull, often poorly bred

mules   to cut strips of skin from the breach area of lambs to prevent fly-strike. Named after JHW Mules who pioneered the procedure

night horse   a horse used to patrol livestock in a droving camp overnight, usually steady and unflappable

party line   a telephone line shared by two or more subscribers

peg dog   a dog tied to block a gateway, road, gap in fence, etc

pickled   (as in wheat) treated with fungicide and pesticide

poddy   a hand-reared calf or lamb, usually due to the death of its mother

quid   a pound. Currency before 1966, then worth $2

race   a narrow, fenced passage for drafting sheep or cattle

red cloud   a strain of working dog originating from the WA dog Red Cloud, bred by King and McLeod, or from King and McLeod bred parentage. Red Cloud was a big, all-red dog of outstanding ability. His name has been used to describe his descendants as in the case of the original Kelpie

ringer   a stationhand. Also, the fastest shearer in the team

run-out brumbies   inbred wild horses

sandy blight   an inflammation producing sandlike grains in the eye

shave off a break   prevent an animal breaking away from the mob

stag   a male sheep that has been castrated after reaching maturity

stool out   to throw out shoots from the roots

tail   the back of a mustered mob of animals

'the more you ate, the better you were payed'   Drovers' pay includes keep, so it stands to reason that they are being paid more if they eat more

tonguing   panting with the tongue hanging out

windlight   wind-driven power generator, usually 32 volts

windrow   hay, etc., raking into lines to allow it to be dried by the wind

wing   either side of a mustered mob of livestock

A BIBLIOGRAPHY OF AUSTRALIAN WORKING DOGS

*Helen Hewson-Fruend, Gunning, New South Wales and
Stephen Bilson, Orange, New South Wales*

Many of the books below are available through Noonbarra Dog Products, PO Box 1374, Orange, New South Wales 2800.

DOG STORIES

Baker, I, *Monday Sheepdog*, Angus & Robertson, Sydney, 1987. The story of the sheepdog, Charcoal, with his master in a range of farming adventures set in the imaginary district of Coonara.

Davison, F D, *Dusty: The Story of a Sheepdog*, Eye & Spottiswoode, London, 1947. The story set in Queensland of a kelpie–dingo cross.

Finger, C J, *A Dog at His Heel: The Story of Jock, an Australian Sheepdog*, John C Winston Co, Chicago, 1936. The story of an outstanding sheepdog, a crossbred Airedale terrier, Jock, set in the late 1880s in Western Australia and South America.

Goode, A and Hayes, M, *Great Working Dog Stories*, ABC Enterprises, Sydney, 1990. A collection of previously unpublished stories about predominantly South Australian working dogs.

Goode, A, *More Great Working Dog Stories*, ABC Enterprises, Sydney, 1992. A collection of 145 stories from all round Australia.

Jones, C and Collins, B, *Way of Life*, Farming Press, Suffolk, UK, 1988.

Lamond, H G, *Towser the Sheep Dog*, Faber & Faber, London, 1955. The story of a sheepdog, probably kelpie, set in western Queensland.

McCaig, Donald, *Eminent Dogs, Dangerous Men*, HarperCollins, New York, 1991.

McCaig, Donald, *Nop's Trials*, Lyons & Burford, New York, 1984.

McGuire, F M, *Three and Ma Kelpie*, Longmans, Green & Co, Croydon, 1964. A story based on fact set on a sheep station near Broken Hill. Ma Kelpie had three pups, but their owner and one of the pups were lost in the bush.

Patchett, M E, *Ajax the Warrior*, Penguin, Harmondsworth, 1953. Ajax was a wild dog rescued from a flood and raised on a cattle station on the Queensland–New South Wales border. Ajax was the canine protagonist in other Patchett stories: *Ajax: Golden Dog of the Australian Bush*; *The Call of the Bush*; *The Golden Wolf*; *Ajax and the Haunted Mountain*; and *Ajax and the Drovers*. All have been translated into several languages.

Pollard, J (ed.), *Wild Dogs, Working Dogs, Pedigrees and Pets*, Lansdowne Press, Melbourne, 1968. Reprinted in 1977 as *Great Dog Stories of Australia and New Zealand*, Rigby, Adelaide. A collection of previously published stories and poems about dogs from the previous 100 years. It includes several Henry Lawson dog stories and poems.

Webb, Z V, *The Shared Dog*, Georgian House, Melbourne, 1945. Originally published in the *Bulletin*. The story of Spot, a mongrel belonging to two swagmen probably during the 1930s Depression.

Willey, K, *Joe Brown's Dog Bluey*, Rigby, Adelaide, 1978. A story of a blue heeler cattle dog set in desert country in central Australia.

Wrightson, P, *Moondark*, Hutchinson, Melbourne, 1987. The story of an Australian cattle dog, set probably in Queensland.

TECHNICAL BOOKS

General

Brown, J G (compiler), *Dogs of Australia*, KCC of Victoria, 1973, 1984.

Hamilton-Wilkes, M, *Kelpie and Cattle Dog*, Angus & Robertson, Sydney, 1967, 1980, 1982.

Holmes, John, *The Farmer's Dog*, Popular Dogs, London, UK, 1989.

Kaleski, R, *Australian Barkers and Biters*, New South Wales Bookstall Co, Sydney, 1914, 1933. Facsimile edition, Endeavour Press, Sydney, 1987.

Sanderson, A, *The Complete Book of Australian Dogs*, Currawong, Milson's Point, 1981, 1987, 1988.

Cattle Dogs

Redhead, C, *The Good Looking Australian*, Readhead, Adelaide, 1979.

Robinson, N, *Australian Cattle Dogs*, TFH, Neptune City, 1990.

Shaffer, Mari, *Heeler Power*, Countryside Publications, Wisconsin, USA, 1984.

Sheepdogs

Border Collie

Bray, J, *The Border Checkpoint*, Bray, Mittagong, 1989.

Carpenter, E B, *The Blue Riband of the Heather*, Ipswich, UK, 1989.

Collier, Margaret, *Border Collies*, FH, USA, 1991.

Combe, Iris, *Border Collies*, Faber & Faber, London, 1978.

Larson, Janet, *The Versatile Border Collie*, Alpine Publications, Colorado, USA, 1987.

Moore, J, *The Canine King*, Standard Newspapers, Cheltenham, 1929.

Quarton, M, *All About the Working Border Collie*, Pelham, UK.

Swann, Barbara, *The Versatile Border Collie*, Nimrod Press, Hants, UK, 1988.

Vidler, P, *The Border Collie in Australasia*, Gotrah, Kellyville, 1983.

Kelpie

Austin, T and Zaadstra, P, *Our Australian Kelpie*, High Thunder, Mt Gambier, 1991.

Brody, J, *The Australian Kelpie*, Brody, Holbrook, 1980.

Donelan, M, *The Australian Kelpie*, Donelan, Wagga Wagga, 1982.

MacLeod, N, *The Australian Kelpie Handbook*, MacLeod, Altona, 1984.

Parsons, A, *The Working Kelpie*, Nelson, Melbourne, 1986.

Sloane, S, *Australian Kelpies*, TFH, Neptune City, 1990.

Other

Breckwoldt, Roland, *The Dingo: A Very Elegant Animal*, Angus & Robertson, Sydney, 1988.

Sims, David and Dawydiak, O, *Livestock Protection Dogs*, OTR Publications, Alaska, USA, 1990.

TRAINING, BREEDING AND CARE

Austin, T, *Breeding and Training Sheepdogs*, Austin, Coleraine, 1978.

Cavanagh, R, *Australian Sheepdogs*, Cavanagh, Whittlesea, 1990.

Dookie Agricultural College, *Dog Handling Workshop*, Victorian Department of Agriculture, Melbourne, 1981.

Glenormiston Agricultural College, *Working Sheep with Dogs*, Victorian Department of Agriculture, Melbourne, 1981.

Greenwood, G (ed.), *Farm Dogs*, Australian Government Publishing Service, Canberra, 1979.

Kelley, R B, *Animal Breeding and the Maintenance and Training of Sheepdogs*, Angus & Robertson, Sydney, 1942. Reprinted as *Sheepdogs, Their Breeding, Maintenance and Training*, 1949, 1958, 1970.

Lithgow, S, *Training and Working Dogs*, University of Queensland Press, Brisbane, 1987, 1988, 1989, 1991.

Means, Ben, *The Perfect Stock Dog*, self-published, Missouri, USA, 1970.

Parsons, A, *Training the Working Kelpie*, Viking O'Neil, Melbourne, 1990.

Russell, D W, *Managing the Sheep Dog*, South Australian Department of Agriculture, Adelaide, 1975.

Taggart, M, *Sheepdog Training An All Breed Approach*, Alpine Publications, USA, 1986.

Victorian Department of Agriculture, *The Working Dog*, Victorian Department of Agriculture, Melbourne, 1977.